Coquelle Thompson,
Athabaskan Witness

Coquelle Thompson (ca. 1848–1946). From a picture postcard. Photo courtesy Sina Thompson Bell and Dodie Bell.

Coquelle Thompson, Athabaskan Witness
A Cultural Biography

Lionel Youst
William R. Seaburg

University of Oklahoma Press : Norman

Also by Lionel Youst
She's Tricky Like Coyote: Annie Miner Peterson, an Oregon Coast Indian Woman (Norman, 1997)

Also by William R. Seaburg
(ed., with Pamela T. Amoss) *Badger and Coyote Were Neighbors: Melville Jacobs on Northwest Indian Myths and Tales* (Corvallis, 2000)

Library of Congress Cataloging-in-Publication Data

Youst, Lionel, 1934–
    Coquelle Thompson, Athabaskan witness : a cultural biography / Lionel Youst, William R. Seaburg.
      p. cm. — (The civilization of the American Indian series ; v. 243)
    Includes bibliographical references and index.

    1. Thompson, Coquelle, 1848–1946. 2. Coquille Indians—Biography. 3. Ethnographic informants—Biography. 4. Coquille Indians—History. 5. Siletz Indians—History. I. Seaburg, William R. II. Series.

    ISBN 978-0-8061-3448-2 (hardcover)
    ISBN 978-0-8061-6866-1 (paper)

E99.C8742 T469 2002
978'.04972—dc21
[B]

2002018960

The paper in this book meets the guidelines for permanence and durability of the Committee on Production Guidelines for Book Longevity of the Council on Library Resources. ∞

Copyright © 2002 by the University of Oklahoma Press, Norman, Publishing Division of the University. All rights reserved. Paperback published 2021. Manufactured in the U.S.A.

"That's just how people are," Ida'd say,
"They just got to talk.
You can't stop people from talking.
They talk and pretty soon you got a story,
and what's a human being without a story?"
                                        Tom Spanbauer

The saw-miller is neighbor and successor to the Indian.
                        Henry David Thoreau, Journal,
                                        January 29, 1856

Contents

List of Illustrations	ix
Acknowledgments	xi
Introduction	xv
List of Abbreviations	xxv

Chapter
1. Contact: The Coquille River Valley — 3
2. Conflict: End of a Way of Life — 20
3. Exodus: Removal to the North — 43
4. Survival: During and after the Civil War — 65
5. Revival: The Thompson Warm House Dance — 89
6. Maturity: Tribal Police, Anthropologists, and Fatherhood — 125
7. Severalty: Ties of Family, Culture, and Real Estate — 150
8. Assimilation: End of the Trust Period — 175
9. Remembering: Salvage of a Legacy — 205
10. The Last Decade: Jacobs, Marr, and Harrington — 228

Afterword — 254

Appendix
 1. Upper Coquille Athabaskan Culture 261
 2. Upper Coquille Athabaskan Villages 268
 3. A Guide to the Normalized Spelling of Indian Words 278

Notes 281

Bibliography 301

Index 313

Illustrations

Photographs

Coquelle Thompson   *frontispiece*

Following page 107
The steamship *Columbia*
Coquelle, Agnes, Coquelle Jr., and family, ca. 1910
Coquelle's house on his allotment near Thompson Creek, Siletz
    Reservation
Coquelle on the Siletz Reservation "swinging bridge"
Dr. Frank M. Carter
Doctor (Alsea) Johnson, ca. 1910
Feather Dance at Bayfront, Newport, Oregon
Agnes Newberry and family
Augusta Smith and George Thompson
Blanche Thompson and Coquelle Thompson, Jr., ca. 1908
The Rodman Wanamaker Expedition to the American Indian, Siletz
    Reservation, 1913
Coquelle's house on the Robert Metcalf allotment, ca. 1925
Coquelle Thompson, Siletz Reservation, ca. 1939

Agnes Thompson, Siletz Reservation, 1939
View of Siletz village from Government Hill, ca. 1925
Coquelle and Agnes Thompson, Siletz Reservation, 1939
Agnes Thompson and Coquelle Thompson, Jr.
Coquelle Thompson, Sr., Coquelle Thompson, Jr., and Coquelle Thompson III
Sina Thompson, Elveden Hall, England
Sina Thompson Bell and Dodie Bell, Fort Belknap Reservation, Montana, 1999
George Thompson, Siletz, Oregon, 2000
Portable electric phonograph recorder and its developers, 1934
Elizabeth D. Jacobs, ca. 1932
John Peabody Harrington

Maps

1. Western Oregon	xxix
2. Siletz River and North Lincoln County, Oregon	xxx
3. Coquille River	269

Acknowledgments

A work of this kind is not done in a vacuum. We had the assistance of many individuals, and we want to acknowledge our thanks and appreciation for their help. First, we need to mention the encouragement and support we obtained from descendants of Coquelle Thompson, Sr., particularly his daughter Sina Bell, his granddaughter Dodie Bell, and his grandson George Thompson and his family. They provided their remembrances and their photographs in addition to their enthusiastic support. Coquelle's step-grandchildren, including Frank Simmons, Lavera (Babe) Simmons, June Austin, and Dolly Fisher, were also supportive and gave us rare insights into Coquelle's last years.

Robert H. Kentta, Cultural Resources director of the Confederated Tribes of Siletz Indians, was exceptionally helpful, and our understanding of the Dawes Act allotments at Siletz would never have been clear without the maps and listings that he shared with us. He read the manuscript and provided a large number of useful suggestions. Sharon Parrish, a member of the Cultural Resources Committee of the Coquille Indian Tribe, gave her enthusiastic support in providing documents and suggestions.

Nathan Douthit, history professor emeritus at Southwestern Oregon Community College, read the entire manuscript, chapter by chapter, as it was written. Our frank discussions, and his sometimes pointed criticisms, inspired the authors to continually rethink the direction the project was taking. There is no doubt that the finished product is much improved owing to his contributions.

Several individuals read particular chapters or parts of chapters where the material entered their areas of expertise. Reg Pullen, former archaeologist for the Coos Bay District of the Bureau of Land Management, read very early drafts of the first two chapters. His unparalleled knowledge of the prehistory of the Coquille River valley added immeasurably to our understanding of that subject. Ann Goddard of Lincoln County had worked on the genealogy of many of the families of the Confederated Tribes of Siletz, and she graciously shared her knowledge with us, correcting us on several specifics. She read a draft of chapter 8, giving many thoughtful suggestions, and she shared with us her unique understanding of the background of the Siletz Feather Dance. Bob Mahaffy, of Mahaffy Tree Farms, shared his knowledge of historical trends in timber stumpage prices and the economics of forestland. He read and commented on sections of the manuscript that bore on that subject. Susanne J. Young and Laurel Sercombe also read parts of several drafts and provided valuable feedback.

All researchers are indebted to the support of knowledgeable librarians and archivists, and we are no exception. In Washington, Joyce Justice of the National Archives and Records Administration, Pacific Alaska Region, Seattle, was an invaluable guide to their Siletz Reservation archival materials. Bill Seaburg has been graciously assisted since 1975 by Karyl Winn, Gary Lundell, and Janet Ness of the Manuscripts, Special Collections, University Archives Division of the University of Washington Libraries. In Oregon we relied heavily on the staff of the Coos Bay Public Library and the magic of interlibrary loans, coupled with the miracle of the Internet, which made it quite practical to conduct much of our research from a comparatively isolated community. The Knight Library at the University of Oregon in Eugene holds the microfilm files of the *Lincoln County Leader*; the City Library of Toledo holds those and other newspaper files; the County Clerks Office for Lincoln County in Newport, and for Benton County in Corvallis, provided certain land and marriage records; the Oregon State archives in Salem hold the federal census microfilm and the original copies of death certificates in Oregon from 1903; the Oregon Historical Society archives in Portland hold certain manuscript files of the Siletz Indian Reservation and personal manuscript files of General Joel Palmer. To the staffs of all of those entities, we are most grateful.

Finally, we must acknowledge the help of close family members and friends, without whom the project would not have been done. Dave Lyons, of Fortuna, California, frequently acted as a computer consultant; Mike Vaughn, landscape designer, did the lettering for the maps. Lionel Youst's wife, Hilda, was constant in her support and encouragement, and accompanied him on several trips from Coos Bay to Siletz, and to Eugene, Salem, and Portland. His son, Oliver, was always ready with advice on computer problems (of which there were many). His daughters, Alice and Julia, were always and immediately available as sounding boards on any subject. Jeff Defty gave insights into the complexities of Coquelle Thompson's Ghost Dance songs and made his recording studio available for that purpose.

Bill Seaburg's family, friends, and colleagues at the University of Washington, Bothell, have been a constant source of encouragement and support. The Jacobs Research Fund at the Whatcom Museum of History and Art, Bellingham, Washington, provided grants that supported early stages (1975–78) of the research. More than any other individual, Bess Jacobs, from 1975 until her death in 1983, made this project possible through friendship and personal and financial support.

Introduction

During a few cold December evenings in Seattle at the end of 1939, Melville Jacobs (1902–71), professor of anthropology at the University of Washington, his wife, Elizabeth (1903–83), and John Peabody Harrington (1884–1961), ethnologist at the Smithsonian Institution, visited and talked shop. Of the two men, Jacobs was the younger. He was thirty-seven and had made his reputation as an anthropologist by seeking out and interviewing the last surviving speakers of the fast-disappearing native languages of Oregon. Nineteen thirty-nine would be his last year of fieldwork. Harrington was eighteen years older than Jacobs and had spent his life seeking the last surviving speakers from among all of the major language groups of North America. No one could match his knowledge and experience. As was his custom, Harrington took notes of the conversations.

Among the varied questions that interested the three of them, one was how the small, isolated bands of Athabaskan Indians had found their way into the Coast Range of Washington, Oregon, and California. Several groups of them were living there when the early whites arrived, and some were still living there in 1939. Harrington and Jacobs speculated as to the relationship of those tribes to one another and to other Athabaskans such as the Navajo, the Apache, and peoples of the interior of Canada and Alaska.[1] It seemed fairly obvious to both Harrington and Jacobs that the Pacific Coast Athabaskans had arrived after most of the rest of the country had been settled. Other groups had long been living on the tidal bays at the mouths of the rivers. That's where the richest food supplies were. Some had been there for hundreds, or even thousands, of years before the Athabaskan-speaking people ever appeared on the upper reaches of the Willapa, the Clatskanie, the Umpqua, and the Coquille Rivers.

Melville Jacobs pointed out that those migrations had to have occurred little by little, a family at a time, through the mountain passes of the Cascade Range. He said that there could have been no mass migration such as might have occurred on the Great Plains. For example, he remembered having talked to elderly Indians who claimed that it was their uncle who first crossed the Cascades through a pass south of Mount Adams. Gathering acorns, berries, and the other food and fiber that sustained them, they advanced the language a few miles each year. In a few hundred years they had covered immense distances, and isolated groups of Athabaskan-speaking peoples were found thousands of miles from their ancestral homes.[2]

Elizabeth D. (Bess) Jacobs had spent several months during 1935 interviewing an elderly descendant of one of those isolated groups of Athabaskan peoples who had settled on the upper reaches of the Coquille River of southwestern Oregon. He was known to the whites as Coquelle Thompson, the spelling of his first name reflecting the preferred pronunciation (ko-kwél). He was born about 1849, give or take a year, and had been the principal source of information on the Upper Coquille River Athabaskans to a succession of anthropologists.

Coquelle had been interviewed earlier, but during the 1930s there was a great flurry of effort to salvage whatever information still existed in the heads of the few remaining elderly speakers of the languages of western Oregon. Coquelle was thus interviewed in 1934 by two anthropologists from the University of California, Berkeley: Cora Du Bois (1903–91), who was researching the Ghost Dance of 1870, and Philip Drucker (1911–82), who was conducting an ethnographic survey of Athabaskan and non-Athabaskan cultures in western Oregon. The following year Elizabeth Jacobs interviewed Coquelle over a period of two or three months, collecting over eight hundred pages of carefully recorded notes filled with a wealth of ethnographic, folkloric, and historical detail. Possibly as a result of Harrington's conversations with Elizabeth in Seattle during December 1939, he had his assistant, John P. (Jack) Marr (b. 1921), make phonograph records of many of Coquelle's stories and songs in 1941. In 1942 Harrington conducted his own interviews with Coquelle, the last anthropologist known to have done so.

Introduction

Certainly the most extensive and ultimately most interesting of the material given by Coquelle was that obtained by Elizabeth Jacobs. She was not a professional anthropologist, but she had been instructed by her husband, Melville, a Boasian-trained anthropologist. Her interests were more textual and psychological than ethnographic. As a result, she tended to let Coquelle talk about whatever interested him most and copied it down quite rapidly and legibly in her notebooks. Those notebooks form the basis for much of what follows.

It had become apparent to Elizabeth that Coquelle was a master storyteller, and that he tended to answer specific questions with an extended example. Previous interviewers, interested only in specifics, had thus missed the most significant contribution that Coquelle had to offer: the content and style of his stories. He was a stylist, and he was an intellectual. Elizabeth Jacobs and the others who had interviewed him over the years seemed quite aware that his life had been of some significance.

Coquelle Thompson, Sr., was born around 1849 in an Upper Coquille Athabaskan village in the Coquille River valley of southwestern Oregon. As a result of the 1855–56 Rogue River War, his people, along with many of the other southwestern Oregon coastal Indian peoples, were removed from their homelands and resettled some one hundred miles north on what was to become the Siletz Reservation. Many did not survive the emotional and physical hardships and illnesses of the early days of the reservation, but Coquelle was a survivor, and he lived there most of his nearly one hundred years.

Coquelle led a very full and eventful life at Siletz. He was either a participant in, a witness to, or an oral memorialist of all the major events at Siletz from 1856 to 1946. For example, he was an active and enthusiastic participant in an offshoot of the 1870 Ghost Dance, known at Siletz as the Warm House Dance. He was an accomplished singer and dancer of both native and nativistic songs and dances. He knew virtually everyone on the reservation—and their kinship ties— as official heirship testimonies demonstrate again and again. Although he never learned to read or write English, he spoke it fluently as well as the local lingua franca, Chinook Jargon, and his native Upper Coquille Athabaskan, a language that only a few still spoke at the time of his passing in 1946.*

Coquelle was married three times and had eleven children, only two of whom survived beyond young adulthood. He is described by

---

* Archie Johnson, Nellie Orton, and perhaps others who were said to know the language outlived Coquelle.

those who knew him as a loving father. His third wife, Agnes, was well known as an accomplished midwife and practical nurse at Siletz and frequently assisted the local medical doctor.

Coquelle worked at various times as a farmer, a hunting and fishing guide for whites, a teamster, a tribal policeman, and an expert witness for six different anthropologists over a period of nearly sixty years, from 1884 to 1942. Most of what we know about the Upper Coquille Athabaskan language and culture comes from the memory of this incredibly able and willing consultant. Coquelle was a perceptive, intelligent observer, and he had a phenomenal memory—for language, oral history, and genealogy. He was also a master raconteur, and both Elizabeth Jacobs and Harrington recorded hundreds of notebook pages of his myth, tale, and historical event narratives. Very little of this incredible heritage has ever been published before.

Although Coquelle's work with visiting anthropologists focused on "salvaging" memories of the past, he did not live in the past. He was an active agent in the shaping of his own and his children's lives. He competently managed his long, busy life, including the many hundreds of acres of land he had accumulated, primarily through inheritance from the many people he was related to at Siletz. He also firmly supported modern education for his children, four of whom obtained their secondary education at the Chemawa Indian Boarding School.

He had been with the first of the Indians of southern Oregon who entered their new, one million-acre Coast Reservation in 1856, and he lived to see that reservation reduced to a mere four sections of tribal timber and seventy-seven individual allotments held in trust. He didn't quite live to see the termination of the reservation in 1954, but he did live to see his only surviving son graduate with a degree from Oregon State College in 1932. Later, he saw his youngest daughter join the Army Air Corps (WAC) and serve as a communications specialist at Third Bomber Group Headquarters in England during World War II.

The authors have long felt that the anthropologists' Indian consultants, individuals such as Coquelle Thompson, Annie Miner Peterson (Coos), Victoria Howard (Clackamas Chinook), Hoxie Simmons (Galice Creek Athabaskan), Clara Pearson (Nehalem Tillamook), and John Hudson (Santiam Kalapuya), have seldom received their due as culture brokers, as intellectuals in their own right. These people spent long hours working with visiting anthropologists: dictating stories, supplying linguistic paradigms, and remembering ethnographic details of a long-past way of life. Too often consultants have been seen as cultural representatives rather than as unique individuals, which is why we chose the biographical genre for our study of Coquelle.

A biography allows us to better see native peoples as agents, as active participants in the shaping of their lives, as individuals who made decisions, who strategized, who were not merely "tragic" and passive pawns of structural forces beyond their control. With this biography, only the second of any western Oregon Indian, we want to acknowledge and honor Coquelle's voice, not only as an informed consultant but also as a human being. Rather than treating him as a timeless, "representative" culture-bearer, we will demonstrate that Coquelle incorporated "a diverse and sometimes contradictory range of practices, attitudes and relationships that were dynamic, historically situated, and ethnically hybrid."[3]

Our knowledge of who Coquelle Thompson was and what his life was like is somewhat limited. We don't have any of the usual life documents, such as autobiographies, biographies, letters, diaries, or oral histories, which form the basis of most Western biographies.[4] In place of such documentation we have utilized a wide variety of sources, including newspaper news and feature articles, "News about Town" columns, and obituaries; federal documents, such as the Indian census rolls, extant Siletz Agency employment records, agency superintendents' annual reports, allotment files, and other official records; anthropologists' field notes, correspondence, and publications; and interviews with descendants and others. Each of these genres tantalizes the would-be biographer with different information about and understandings of Coquelle.

The writing of biography in the social sciences has undergone the same ethical and epistemological crises as the writing of ethnography.[5] The epistemological problem as we see it is this. Lives-as-lived are not narratives or texts; they may only be reflectively crafted as such, retrospectively as a life story or projectively as an imagined future. When a person's "life" is textualized as a story or narrative, it becomes subject to the constraints of discourse structure and the expectations of genre. It "takes on a life of its own," one might say.

It has been suggested by others that the biographical genre is a Western cultural construct. Its literary conventions reflect certain ideas about the "natural" progression of life, including the "assumption of a unified life."[6] The sociologist Norman Denzin describes this literary convention using the "whole cloth" metaphor: "A life, it is assumed, is cut out of whole cloth, and its many pieces, with careful scrutiny, can be fitted into proper place."[7]

A related assumption is that life as a whole makes sense, and the task of the biographer is to make sense of it. But "making sense" is not just an idiomatic phrase. Linguists Robert Hodge and Gunther Kress argue that the "characteristic structures of narrative themselves carry important meanings. Narrative links events into sequential and causal chains, and gives them a beginning and an end. These features are transparent signifiers of coherence, order, and closure."[8] In other words, biographers are making or constructing sense of another's life at least as much as they are finding it. As the writer Mark Doty reminds us, "storytelling is an act of framing and forging connections. The fact that both 'frame' and 'forge' have connotations of falsehood is no accident, because stories are made; they are artifices that pluck shape out of the stream of things."[9]

A third basic narrative convention of biography is selection: texts cannot reproduce lives-as-lived. Some details and events and people in a subject's life are judged to be more important than others. The biographer, usually having access to more information about his subject than he can use, "selects items which he feels are most representative, most vivid, and most able to communicate the sense of his subject to his readers." This selection process implies "that some details and episodes in a man's life more than others reveal the true nature of the man."[10] Other biographical textual conventions include the chronicling of family beginnings, noting "objective" life markers, and relating turning-point experiences. We have chosen to follow these Western biographical conventions in telling our chronologically organized story of Coquelle Thompson's life.

There is no *single* story of a person's life because the storyteller is implicated in the story—implicated by each of the manipulations or craftings of narrative construction, the selection, arrangement, foregrounding, interpretation, and so on. Thus Coquelle Thompson's "life," as pieced together here, is really our story. No doubt there are other ways it could be constructed and narrated, but as architects of the overarching text, we have utilized two dominant strategies. We have attempted to let Coquelle Thompson "speak for himself" by presenting his stories as he gave them to the several anthropologists and journalists who interviewed him over the years, and, where possible, we placed his stories within their cultural or historical context. For the reasons outlined above, we have tried to avoid essentializing Coquelle's life, that is, to characterize or sum it up as a totality.

As biographical *bricoleurs*,* we have used whatever source materials we could find, cobbling the various pieces together, irrespective of genre, with no pretense of or desire for a seamless whole. Some of Coquelle's narratives we felt needed interpretive commentary; others we have left alone. In all cases our hope is that Coquelle's voice will "speak to the reader over the biographer's head," whispering "Listen to me, not to [him]. I am authentic. I speak with authority."[11]

We have greatly benefited from previous historical scholarship on the Rogue River War and the Siletz Reservation, works such as Stephen Dow Beckham's *Requiem for a People: The Rogue Indians and the Frontiersmen;* E.A. Schwartz's *The Rogue River Indian War and Its Aftermath, 1850–1980;* and Nathan Douthit's articles published in the *Oregon Historical Quarterly*. These studies primarily rely on more traditional historical sources, such as government documents, Indian agents' reports and correspondence, newspaper accounts, and pioneer memoirs. Our biographical study of Coquelle Thompson and his historical context differs from—and we hope complements—this earlier research by drawing heavily on largely unpublished and underutilized anthropological field notes from work with Coquelle and other western Oregon Indian consultants. We believe we have created a thicker, richer narrative by the inclusion of such social and cultural information.

Our study also differs from previous historical scholarship by including, sometimes in excerpts and paraphrase and sometimes in their entirety, stories that Coquelle told, as well as stories from our own research interviews. Coquelle's preferred mode of talking about or explaining his culture and his life was in the form of stories—personal experience narratives, historical narratives, ethnographic narratives, myths and tales. Thus, in shaping our own narrative, we are building on the narrative strengths of much of the data collected from Coquelle by anthropologists, especially the material collected by Jacobs, Du Bois, and Harrington.

In the spring of 1999 we met with the Cultural Resources Committee of both the Confederated Tribes of Siletz and the Coquille Indian Tribe. Both of the cultural resource committees, and Coquelle's family, thought the project a worthy one, encouraging and assisting us with our research. We have utilized data from our fieldwork with family members and others who remembered Coquelle.

---

* *Bricoleur:* From the French, a kind of professional do-it-yourselfer or jack-of-all-trades, who uses a set of whatever tools and materials are at hand to construct his projects. The term was popularized by the French anthropologist Claude Lévi-Strauss.

Seaburg interviewed Elizabeth Jacobs during the summer of 1975. He also interviewed Coquelle's last surviving child, his daughter Sina Thompson Bell, at the Fort Belknap Indian Reservation, near Harlem, Montana, in August of 1999. Youst interviewed Coquelle's grandson, George Thompson, George's mother, Elma, and Coquelle's step-grandchildren Frank Simmons, Dolly Fisher, and June Austin. Both of us interviewed long-term Siletz resident Maude Lane. George Thompson and Sina Thompson Bell generously provided some of the photographs for this book.

Seaburg first became interested in Coquelle Thompson in the spring of 1975, when he received a small grant from the Melville and Elizabeth Jacobs Research Fund (now the Jacobs Research Fund) through the Whatcom Museum of History and Art in Bellingham, Washington. This small grant allowed him to travel to Seattle to interview Elizabeth Jacobs regarding her southwestern Oregon Athabaskan linguistic field notes. Although he was disappointed to learn that Jacobs's Upper Coquille Athabaskan texts were recorded in English rather than in the native language, he soon became fascinated by the content and style of the scores of narratives Jacobs had recorded from Coquelle Thompson. Seaburg and Jacobs spent many hours that summer discussing the cultural and folkloristic aspects of Coquelle's stories. Little did Seaburg know how important a part Coquelle eventually would play in his research life over the next twenty-five years.

In 1994 Seaburg finished a dissertation that focused on the intellectual collaboration between Coquelle Thompson and the half-dozen anthropologists who worked with him between 1884 and 1942.[12] Although one chapter of that work was a biographical sketch of Coquelle's life, Seaburg felt that Coquelle deserved the kind of extended biography that Lionel Youst had produced for another important anthropological consultant from western Oregon, Annie Miner Peterson.[13] In the spring of 1999 Seaburg approached Youst with a proposal that they collaborate on such a venture, and Youst agreed.

Youst probably first heard of Coquelle Thompson in 1977, in Stephen Dow Beckham's *The Indians of Western Oregon*. In 1990, he saw Coquelle's name again. This time it was in Beckham's essay in *Northwest Coast*, volume 7 of *Handbook of North American Indians*, and in Miller and Seaburg's article in the same volume. Later, during research for his biography of Annie Miner Peterson, he discovered that she had been acquainted with Coquelle, and had in fact talked about him during Cora Du Bois's Ghost Dance research in western Oregon in 1934. Youst became aware of Elizabeth Jacobs's extensive unpublished Coquelle Thompson field notes during his work on the Peterson biography, but it did not appear that the notes would help with those researches, and so he did not look at them at that time.

Both authors felt that a study of Coquelle Thompson's life would round out the story of the transitional generation of Indians in southwestern Oregon begun with the life of Annie Miner Peterson. Her ancestry was Coos (a Penutian-speaking people); Coquelle's was Upper Coquille (an Athabaskan-speaking people). Annie had lived most of her life *off* the reservation; Coquelle had lived most of his life *on* the reservation. Annie was a woman; Coquelle was a man. It would appear that the two biographies would complement each other in many ways. It was agreed that Youst would draft the chapters and provide the historical context, while Seaburg would provide the direction and most of the primary documents. It has been a very fruitful collaboration.

This study of Coquelle Thompson's life provides a unique view of both pre-reservation and reservation people and events and adds to our knowledge of the social and cultural history of the Siletz Indian community, as well as to our knowledge of the practice of "salvage" anthropology in western Oregon. We hope readers will enjoy reading about this man, his times, and his work with anthropologists as much as the authors have enjoyed researching and writing about him.

Editorial Note

As explained more fully in Appendix 3, we have "normalized" the spellings of certain Indian words wherever we had enough linguistic information to do so. Such normalized spellings are indicated by italics. All other Indian words have been reproduced exactly as they appear in the original source.

Abbreviations

CDB Cora Du Bois [1934]. Tututni (Rogue River) field notes. University Archives, Bancroft Library, University of California, Berkeley.
CIT Coquille Indian Tribe, Cultural Committee, miscellaneous files and documents.
CTS Confederated Tribes of Siletz, Cultural Resources Center, miscellaneous files and documents.
EDJ/MJC Elizabeth Derr Jacobs [1935]. Upper Coquille Athabaskan linguistic and ethnographic notes, folklore texts (in English) from fieldwork with Coquelle Thompson, Sr., Siletz, Oregon. In Melville Jacobs Collection, University of Washington Libraries, Seattle.
EDJ/WRS Elizabeth Derr Jacobs [ca. 1936; 1971]. Slightly edited longhand copy of Upper Coquille Athabaskan ethnographic notes and edited typescript versions of myths and tales from field notebooks in Melville Jacobs Collection, University of Washington Libraries, Seattle. (In possession of William R. Seaburg.)
JOD J. Owen Dorsey [1884]. Dorsey Papers. Manuscript No. 4800 in National Anthropological Archives, Smithsonian Institution, Washington, D.C.

JPH John Peabody Harrington, 1981, *The Papers of John Peabody Harrington in the Smithsonian Institution, 1907–1957.* National Anthropological Archives, Department of Anthropology, National Museum of Natural History, Washington, D.C. Microfilm edition, Part 1: Native American History, Language, and Culture of Alaska/Northwest Coast.

JPH/1943 John Peabody Harrington [1943]. Report and map showing tribal distribution of Oregon Coast. Manuscript No. 4360 in National Anthropological Archives, Smithsonian Institution, Washington, D.C.

JPH/JM John Peabody Harrington–Jack Marr correspondence. In John Peabody Harrington, 1991, *The Papers of John Peabody Harrington in the Smithsonian Institution, 1907–1957.* National Anthropological Archives, Department of Anthropology, National Museum of Natural History, Washington, D.C. Microfilm edition, Part 9: Native American Ethnography through Correspondence.

LCL *Lincoln County Leader* (weekly newspaper, Toledo, Oregon), March 9, 1893, to January 17, 1987 (microfilm) files at University of Oregon Library.

MJC Melville Jacobs Collection, University of Washington Libraries.

NADP Native American Documents Project, under supervision of E. A. Schwartz, assistant professor of history, California State University, San Marcos. The NADP Web site contains 112 documents relating to the Rogue River Wars and the Siletz Reservation. Citations include NADP document number and NA (National Archives) citation.

NA/PNW National Archives and Records Administration, Pacific Alaska Region, Seattle.

NA/ACF National Archives, record group 75, allotment case files, National Archives and Records Administration, Pacific Alaska Region, Seattle.

NA/DC National Archives and Records Administration, Washington, D.C. Reports from Lieutenant Colonel Silas Casey dated October 24 and November 24, 1851: reports C-14-1851 and C-17-1851 located in entry 3584 (letters received by the Department of the Pacific) of record group 393 (Records of U.S. Army Continental Commands).

Abbreviations

OSA Oregon State Archives, death records from 1903; decennial census records.
OHQ *Oregon Historical Quarterly*, the journal of the Oregon Historical Society.
OHS Oregon Historical Society manuscripts: MSS 114, pocket diary of Joel Palmer for the years 1854, 1856, and 1873 (typescript); MSS 114-2, uncataloged Joel Palmer documents; MSS 442, Siletz Indian Reservation documents.
PD   Philip Drucker [1933–1954]. Philip Drucker Papers. Manuscript No. 4516 in National Anthropological Archives, Smithsonian Institution, Washington, D.C.
YP   *Yaquina Post* (weekly newspaper, Toledo, Oregon).

Map 1, "Western Oregon," shows the major rivers west of the Cascade Mountains in Oregon, and selected towns and other sites. Many of the river names are the same as the names of the Indian groups (or languages) that originally lived there. Rather than presenting a generalized map showing the very complex interrelation of tribal and linguistic territories, the following explanation of map 1 should aid the reader in placing the approximate location of most of the peoples discussed in this book.

Beginning at the southwest corner of the map, Smith River (California) was home to the Tolowa, a Pacific Coast Athabaskan people. Twelve miles north is the mouth of the Chetco River (Oregon), home of the Chetco, a people closely related to the Tolowa. North of the Chetco as far as the Coquille River were a number of Pacific Coast Athabaskan bands collectively known as Tututni. Closely related to them were the people on the Upper Coquille and Upper Umpqua Rivers, as well as those on Galice Creek and the Applegate River of the Upper Rogue River.

Along the central Oregon coast, from the mouth of the Coquille River to the Yaquina River, languages classified as the Oregon Coast Penutian were spoken. Miluk Coos was spoken at the mouths of the Coquille and Coos Rivers. Hanis Coos was spoken in the upper Coos Bay and its tributaries. Siuslaw and Lower Umpqua were the designations given the languages spoken on the Siuslaw and Lower Umpqua Rivers. On the Yachats and the Alsea Rivers the Alsea language was spoken, and on the Yaquina River the closely related Yaquina language was spoken.

A Salish group of languages was spoken on the Siletz, Tillamook, and Nehalem Rivers.

Along both shores of the Columbia River, as far upstream as The Dalles, various Chinookan languages were spoken, and along the Willamette River and its tributaries were various dialects of the Kalapuyan. Both the Chinookan and Kalapuyan are classified among the Oregon Penutian language families.

OSA Oregon State Archives, death records from 1903; decennial census records.
OHQ *Oregon Historical Quarterly*, the journal of the Oregon Historical Society.
OHS Oregon Historical Society manuscripts: MSS 114, pocket diary of Joel Palmer for the years 1854, 1856, and 1873 (typescript); MSS 114-2, uncataloged Joel Palmer documents; MSS 442, Siletz Indian Reservation documents.
PD Philip Drucker [1933–1954]. Philip Drucker Papers. Manuscript No. 4516 in National Anthropological Archives, Smithsonian Institution, Washington, D.C.
YP *Yaquina Post* (weekly newspaper, Toledo, Oregon).

Map 1, "Western Oregon," shows the major rivers west of the Cascade Mountains in Oregon, and selected towns and other sites. Many of the river names are the same as the names of the Indian groups (or languages) that originally lived there. Rather than presenting a generalized map showing the very complex interrelation of tribal and linguistic territories, the following explanation of map 1 should aid the reader in placing the approximate location of most of the peoples discussed in this book.

Beginning at the southwest corner of the map, Smith River (California) was home to the Tolowa, a Pacific Coast Athabaskan people. Twelve miles north is the mouth of the Chetco River (Oregon), home of the Chetco, a people closely related to the Tolowa. North of the Chetco as far as the Coquille River were a number of Pacific Coast Athabaskan bands collectively known as Tututni. Closely related to them were the people on the Upper Coquille and Upper Umpqua Rivers, as well as those on Galice Creek and the Applegate River of the Upper Rogue River.

Along the central Oregon coast, from the mouth of the Coquille River to the Yaquina River, languages classified as the Oregon Coast Penutian were spoken. Miluk Coos was spoken at the mouths of the Coquille and Coos Rivers. Hanis Coos was spoken in the upper Coos Bay and its tributaries. Siuslaw and Lower Umpqua were the designations given the languages spoken on the Siuslaw and Lower Umpqua Rivers. On the Yachats and the Alsea Rivers the Alsea language was spoken, and on the Yaquina River the closely related Yaquina language was spoken.

A Salish group of languages was spoken on the Siletz, Tillamook, and Nehalem Rivers.

Along both shores of the Columbia River, as far upstream as The Dalles, various Chinookan languages were spoken, and along the Willamette River and its tributaries were various dialects of the Kalapuyan. Both the Chinookan and Kalapuyan are classified among the Oregon Penutian language families.

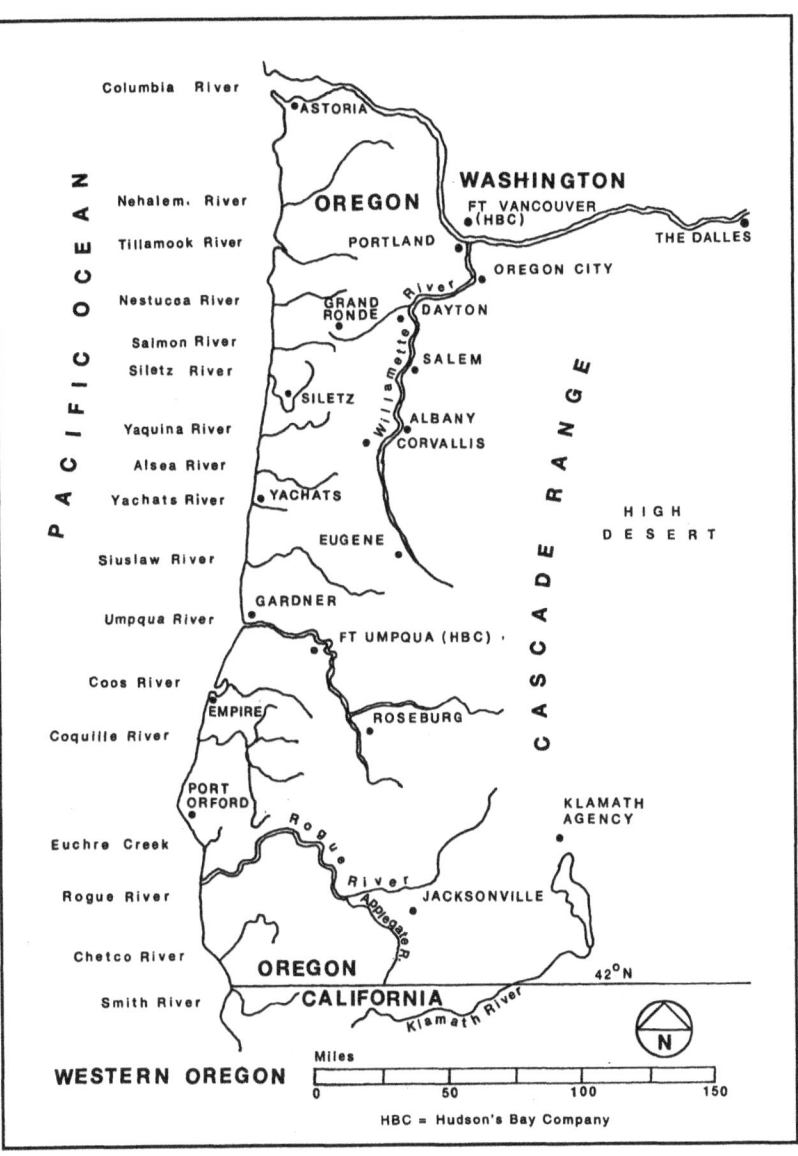

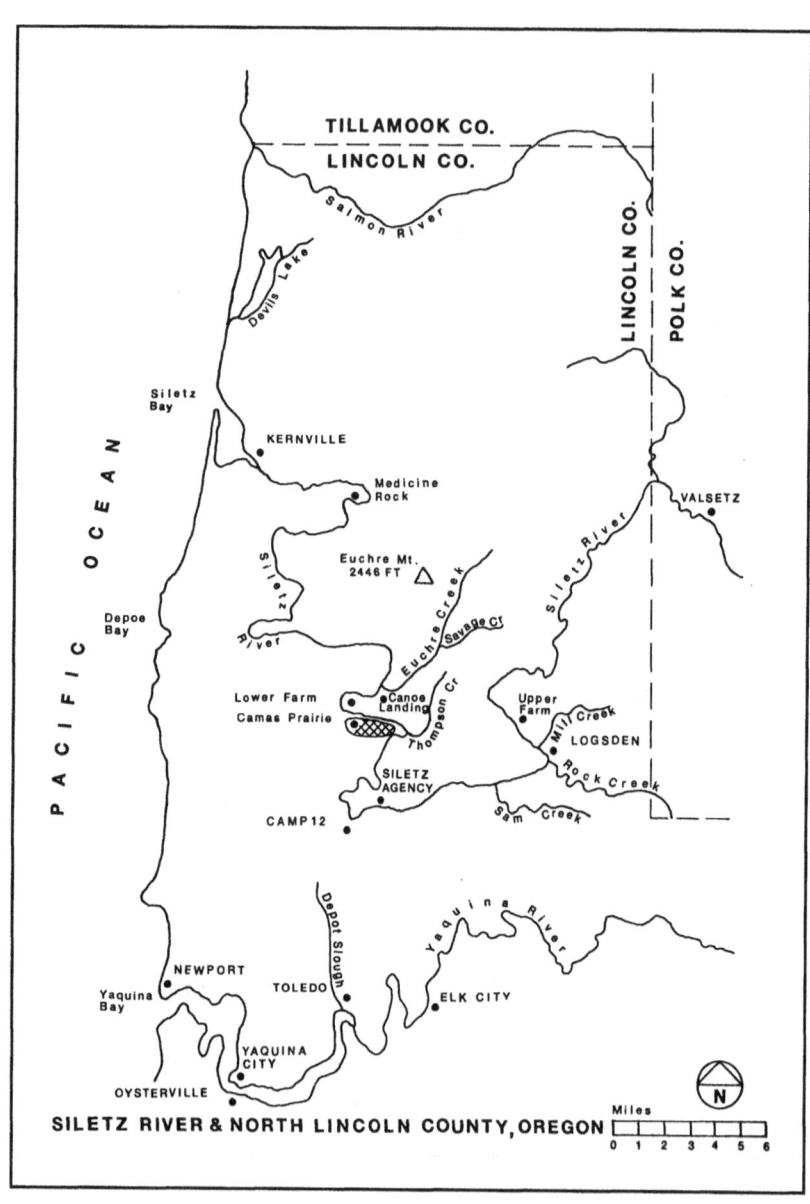

Coquelle Thompson,
Athabaskan Witness

Contact
The Coquille River Valley

Coquelle told Elizabeth Jacobs that his grandfather was an Upper Umpqua chief who, along with four brothers and their wives, crossed the Coast Range from the Upper Umpqua to settle on the Upper Coquille. "There was only one mountain to cross. They came along the ridge," he said.[1] They initially settled at *T'asan Ts'eghilh'adan*, which in English meant "Myrtle Point," the same name given it later by the whites. Coquelle said that about half the people at *T'asan Ts'eghilh'adan* "talked Umpqua," the remainder speaking the closely related language of Upper Coquille.* This was probably at about the turn of the eighteenth century.

The several branches of the Coquille River drain about two thousand square miles of the solidly forested Coast Range. At the time that Coquelle's grandfather arrived, that drainage was probably quite underpopulated, except for the settlements at the river's mouth. "People down river," Coquelle told Phillip Drucker in 1934, "different language."[2] According to archaeologist Reg Pullen, people had been living at many sites along the Coquille for at least 1,500 years, and at a few

---

* See appendix 3 for explanation of our normalized transcription of Athabaskan words.

of them for perhaps as long as 5,000 years.³ At one time or another, small groups had lived at least temporarily almost everywhere that two streams came together and there was an elevated, level spot for a shelter.

Exactly why the river was so sparsely settled at the time of first white contact—and presumably at the time that Coquelle's grandfather settled there—is unknown. There was probably not much over one person per twenty square miles, and archaeological evidence suggests that there had never been a time when the population reached the carrying capacity of the land.⁴

There has been speculation of depopulation by epidemic diseases, but there is no convincing evidence one way or the other on the Coquille River.⁵ It has also been speculated that the great tsunami known to have struck the Pacific Northwest coast in 1700 could have, given the right conditions, inundated the Coquille River to a depth of several feet for as far upstream as the limit of tidal influence. If so, it could have wiped out most or all of the villages along the way.⁶ Again, there is no convincing evidence one way or another. One thing is known, however: at the time of first white contact in the Coquille River in 1826, the valley was obviously underpopulated.

Coquelle gave Elizabeth Jacobs the narrative of a flood story, which could have originated in an actual event. "The big fat person said, 'The ocean is coming,'" Coquelle began. "When the flood came, all the people were in the house. Then they ran outside and heard someone holler, 'get your boats ready, hurry!' One had his boat already in the water; they already got in the canoe. Some had already started paddling towards the mountain. They hurried." As Coquelle told it, the story has the ring of actuality. He continued, "People were crying. Some tried to hang onto the boat but they let go and drowned. All were drowned." From that point the story became part of an origin myth, featuring the delivery of fire by Red Squirrel to the refugees on the mountain. To this day, the red squirrel is red on the back of the neck where he carried the fire.⁷ "Everyone knew that story," said Coquelle.

His grandfather and his grandfather's brothers stayed at *T'asan Ts'eghilh'adan* (Myrtle Point), only later returning to visit the Upper Umpqua. "After that," he said, "lots of Umpqua people came to get fish." Coquelle said that his grandfather and his brothers "bought *Hweshdan* women." *Hweshdan* was the furthest downstream of any of the Athabaskan-speaking settlements and was about five miles upstream from the ocean at the "great bend" of the Coquille River.* Coquelle said, "They talked same like us. Our language just the same only kind of slow sounding when we say it." They weren't relations, he told Drucker. The Upper Umpqua "went there to buy women."[8]

Below *Hweshdan*, nearer the mouth of the river, was a cluster of Miluk Coos (Kusan)-speaking settlements. Probably many residents were bilingual, and Philip Drucker believed that *Hweshdan* was "perhaps partly Kusan."[9] As one traveled upstream there may not have been any more year-round villages in the next fifteen swampy miles of river, between *Hweshdan* and the Athabaskan settlement of *Lhanhashdan*, which was about three miles downstream from the site of Coquille City.**

The principal settlement sites named by Coquelle were upstream from *Lhanhashdan*, on each of the several branches of the Coquille River. In addition to *T'asan Ts'eghilh'adan* (Myrtle Point), there were sites with names like *Ch'aghilidan* (perhaps at the confluence of the North Fork and the main river), *Chanchat'ahdan* (presumably Coquelle's home village, at the confluence of the South Fork and the Middle Fork), and *Nataghilidan* (maybe at a falls about eight miles up the South Fork). These were apparently year-round sites, but most of the others were seasonal. At times during the year all of the Upper Coquille peoples might be found at one site, and at other times they would be scattered.

Their map of their homeland was maintained mentally with the name of the site and the image of its location.[10] Their folktales, historical narratives, and personal experiences were often related to specific sites, the place names of which gave additional meaning to the stories. The names and locations that come down to us are the ones given by Coquelle, his uncle "Solomon," and Nellie Lane, who was from the far upriver site of *Nataghilidan*.

Place-names are a part of many of Coquelle's narratives set in his ancestral homeland. Those places are so clearly described that one would expect to be able to locate them on a modern map. However, since the Coquille River has a south, middle, north, and east fork, each

---

* JPH, 26:184, has it "2 or 3 mi from Coq. City." EDJ and Drucker agree it is farthest down river.
** JPH, EDJ, Dorsey, and Drucker all agree on the relative location of *Lhanhashdan*.

with numerous branches and tributaries, it is often impossible to know for sure which branch or fork of the river Coquelle is referring to.

John P. Harrington developed a special interest in the place-names and tribal boundaries of the Oregon coastal peoples. Concerning the Upper Coquille, he found that Coquelle Thompson "is the best informant on this region." Harrington interviewed scores of elderly coastal Indians during the 1930s and 1940s. In a report submitted to the Bureau of American Ethnology in 1943, he said, "After working with a Coast Indian even for a few days no one could fail to be convinced of the genuineness of the ancestral names and ownership of places transmitted by him."[11] The place-names and descriptions given by Coquelle to J. Owen Dorsey in 1884, to Philip Drucker in 1934, to Elizabeth Jacobs in 1935, and to Harrington in 1942 are quite consistent. They are also quite consistent with the place-names and descriptions given by his uncle Solomon to Dorsey and by Nellie Lane to Drucker, with only a very few exceptions. It should not be surprising that there are some inconsistencies; what is surprising is how few there are. It is clear that Coquelle had learned the map of his ancestral homeland quite accurately despite his removal to Siletz at an early age.*

Coquelle said there were five brothers (including his grandfather) who had migrated over the Coast Range from Upper Umpqua territory, and he also said that his grandfather had five wives. The number five occurs so frequently in Coquelle's narratives that it cannot always be taken literally. It is a cultural pattern number common throughout the Pacific Northwest, and it is sometimes used as an indefinite numeral, similar to the English word "several." It is often impossible to know whether or not the narrator literally means the number five.

There were some remarkable differences between this new home on the west side of the Coast Range and the old home to the east of it. For one thing, it rained about three times as much in the new home, and as a result there was a different kind of plant life here. In the Upper Umpqua territory, they could expect about thirty inches of rain per year; in the hills above their new home on the Coquille they could expect eighty to a hundred inches.

---

* See Basso (1996) for a study of a similar cultural trait among another Athabaskan group, the Western Apache of Arizona.

Contact: The Coquille River Valley

The oak trees with their acorns didn't grow in the lower forty miles of the Coquille River Valley. It was too wet. Instead, there were hundreds of acres of Oregon myrtle *(Umbellularia californica)* in the immense bottomland that stretched all the way to the ocean.* In some places, where branches from opposite banks touched each other, they made a canopy over the river.

Beneath those immense myrtle groves there was no direct sunlight and very little vegetation. Even ferns and moss had a hard time growing. But the myrtle trees of the Coquille River valley produced tons of myrtle nuts each year, there for the gathering. The botanist David Douglas, who was the first to describe them, said the nuts had "an insipid kernel, which appears to be the favorite food of squirrels."[12] They could, however, be hulled, dried, and baked in ashes and eaten later with other food.[13] In the Coquille River valley there was an inexhaustible supply.

Coquelle told Harrington about a man walking under those huge myrtle trees one night when "lots of nuts fell to the ground." The man didn't look up, "then tree shook again." The next morning the man told the children to "go up there and pick up myrtle nuts that fell on the ground last night." Coquelle claimed that dead people shake the myrtle trees like that.[14] The natural explanation, that a bear in the tree, or raccoons or other small animals might have done it, was never considered. In any case, it made for an easy harvest of a useful crop, a harvest often carried out by children.

There were other differences between the Coquille River and the Upper Umpqua River. The Coquille probably had much better runs of fish over a much more reliable succession of seasons throughout the year. There was, for example, a small run of chinook salmon in the spring, then a major run through July and August, peaking in September. By October there was a run of coho salmon, continuing until December. Steelhead ran from mid-November until March when the lamprey eels began. The eels ran through June when the cycle began again.[15] During any given year one or more of those runs could fail, but overall there was a much more reliable supply of protein on the Coquille.

---

* The range of *Umbellularia californica* extends through a large area of northwest California where it is known by the common names of "California-laurel" and "pepperwood."

The supply of vegetable foods was probably greater on the Umpqua. Oak trees with their acorn crops were more numerous on the Upper Umpqua. "Indian oats," the tarweed, grew in abundance on the Umpqua but not on the Coquille. The same was true of sugar pine seeds. The only vegetable crop that was as plentiful on the Coquille as on the Umpqua was camas, that vegetable staple of the Indians of the Pacific Northwest states.[16]

Coquelle Thompson's Athabaskan ancestors evidently adopted much of the culture of their neighbors in western Oregon. In fact, there seems to have been few cultural patterns distinguishing the Athabaskans of the Upper Coquille River from the people at the mouth of the river who spoke Miluk Coos, a Penutian language completely unlike Athabaskan. They ate most of the same foods and prepared it in much the same ways; they told similar myths and folktales and used the same stylistic devices in telling them; there were few major differences among their respective social customs; they shared a similar worldview and spiritual life; and they all were exogamous. All of the daughters married out, and all of the wives came from other settlements, often from far away and speaking different languages. As Coquelle told Philip Drucker in 1934, "Man from that town had to marry outside of town—they're all his kin in it."[17]

Even as Coquelle Thompson's grandfather was settling his and his brothers' families in the Coquille River valley and marrying women from the downriver settlement of _Hweshdan_, a new and unheard of people from halfway around the world were getting their first close look at the southern Oregon coast. On the afternoon of April 24, 1792, Captain George Vancouver, an officer of the British Royal Navy, anchored his ships *Discovery* and *Chatham* a little south of Cape Blanco. Three canoes from the Tututni settlements nearby visited the ships during the course of the afternoon and traded trifles with Vancouver's crew, hoping to obtain iron and beads. Vancouver was impressed by their "pleasing and courteous deportment" and by their honesty. Sixty years later the town of Port Orford got its name because Vancouver had left the name "Cape Orford," after his "much respected friend the noble Earl (George) of that title."[18]

No doubt Coquelle Thompson's ancestors, living at the forks of the Coquille River some sixty miles distant, heard about that visit without much delay. We can only speculate what impact the news had on those comparatively isolated people. What they could not have

Contact: The Coquille River Valley

known is that George Vancouver, with his short and uneventful visit, represented the vanguard of world forces that would within two short generations cause the end of traditional life on the Oregon coast.

Other things were happening in 1792, the year of Vancouver's visit. That year Thomas Jefferson suggested to the American Philosophical Society that they raise money to finance a competent explorer to find a land route across North America to the Pacific. This idea would stay with Jefferson, and in 1805 his Lewis and Clark expedition would actually arrive at the mouth of the Columbia River. Alexander Mackenzie of the Northwest Fur Company had already discovered the river named for him and had followed it to the Arctic Ocean. The following year, in 1793, he would follow the Bella Coola River to the Pacific and thus be the first person of record ever to cross the North American continent north of Mexico.

It was during the next generation, the generation of Coquelle's father, that the people of the Upper Coquille River finally received their first visitors from among those new, "moving people."* Hudson's Bay Company chief trader Alexander Roderick McLeod had left Fort Vancouver on September 15, 1826, with "fourteen Men and four Indians... to hunt and explore the Country South of the Umpqua."[19] The total expedition evidently grew to thirty men plus McLeod, including five Hawaiians, three Iroquois, one Klikitat, two Scots, and one Irish. The remainder were not listed as to origin, although they all had French names and probably most of them were Métis, that is, of mixed Indian and French parentage.[20] Accompanying them were an unspecified number of women and children and the botanist David Douglas, who was interested in the peculiar flora of southwestern Oregon.

On October 26, 1826, McLeod and a detachment of his brigade showed up at the mouth of the Coquille River during a heavy rainstorm. They had been exploring, trading, and trapping twenty miles north, at Coos Bay, where at least part of the balance of the brigade had remained. McLeod and the detachment had come down the beach to scout out the prospects for beaver on the Coquille. During the next four days they explored the lower parts of the river, looking for "beaver vestiges."

---

* The first whites, who were fur traders, were called "Moving People" by local Indians. For instances of usage in Hanis and Miluk Coos, see Jacobs 1939, 27ff.

The fur of the beaver made an exceptionally fine felt for fashionable hats that the newly rich of Europe and America could use to mark their status. Coquelle's own people had similar customs. He told Philip Drucker: "People come to count on a rich man. When he went someplace wore sea-otter blanket, buckskin cap with dentalia sewn on, wore money on neck, so people knew he was somebody."[21] The use of status symbols is universal.

McLeod and his group were on the Coquille for only four days during that reconnaissance. They were courteously received by the Indians, and obtained seventy-two beaver hides and three sea otter and three common otter hides from them. The evening before they left to return to Coos Bay, "some Indians cast up with the meat of an Elk, they found drowned in the river," McLeod reported in his journal entry for October 29. Coquelle told Elizabeth Jacobs that sometimes when the water was high, two or three men would wait in a boat for an elk to cross the river. "When he got in the middle they shot out into the stream in the boat, grabbed the elk by the ears—held him down in the water and drowned him."[22] McLeod was evidently put off by the prospect of eating a drowned elk, "yet my men relished the meat tolerably well, and made their supper of it," he wrote in his journal.

After returning to Coos Bay they trapped and traded throughout that area for the next three weeks. In his journal McLeod makes clear why nobody ever knew quite how many Indians there were, either on the Coquille or the Coos. "They are so much dispersed at this season of the year, that an Idea of their number must be erroneous, to a person passing amongst them: for my part I dare not hazard an opinion certain not to come near the thing."[23] He never offered an estimate of the population but only recorded the contacts he had.

On November 25, during some rare fine weather, McLeod reentered the Coquille, this time with the full brigade. They traveled up Isthmus Slough of Coos Bay, made the short, one-mile portage over to Beaver Slough where they had "trouble from the marshy ground, frequently above knee deep in mire and water."[24] For the next two weeks they trapped and traded from a base camp near where the slough entered the Coquille.

The village nearest the mouth of Beaver Slough was *Lhanhashdan*, which according to Coquelle had been founded originally by one of his grandfather's brothers. Coquelle had told Philip Drucker, "there was nobody lived at *Lh<u>an</u>hashd<u>an</u>* then—they founded the town."²⁵ McLeod heard that some of the local Indians were dissatisfied because he was not paying a "tribute" for trapping on the river, but nothing seems to have come of it.* He also discovered that "canoes are not easily got here, as the Indians have resorted to the upper part of the river where fish is more abundant."²⁶ While they were at that base camp McLeod sent a detachment upstream to the Forks, where they camped and traded with what were probably Coquelle Thompson's father's people.

McLeod's journal is concerned almost exclusively with beaver. Still, other than the interviews that anthropologists conducted with Coquelle Thompson between 1934 and 1942, this journal gives us the only firsthand information there is on the inhabitants of the Upper Coquille River prior to contact with the whites. As he traveled on up the river, from the mouth of Beaver Slough to the site of the present city of Coquille, McLeod noted "many Indian habitations, indifferently erected." He added: "Their owners poorly off[,] gave them a share of our stores." On December 10, McLeod, Xavier Seguin Laderoute, two Hawaiians, and three Umpqua Indians proceeded south another eleven miles to the confluence of the Middle and South Forks, which in those days was near the head of tide and the limit of canoe travel, some forty miles upstream from the ocean. McLeod wrote in his journal that there was "a small village, containing half dozen of men and families."²⁷ This was the village of *Ch<u>an</u>chat'ahd<u>an</u>*, one of the sites at which Coquelle said that his father was later the chief.²⁸

The two thousand square miles of the Coquille River drainage was settled sparsely enough to permit almost every family to have its own creek or other fishing site, claimed through use. Coquelle said, "All the people owned these places—outsiders had to ask permission to use." Trespass was apparently not much of a problem. Coquelle said, "They all got plenty good places to fish."²⁹

The Indians of the Coquille River used the beaver very little, if at all. McLeod noted that they "seemingly never molest those animals." He was perhaps a bit surprised at the natives, "who never trouble themselves about furs, and have little or no intercourse with strangers."³⁰ McLeod's party did fairly well, and on December 14 began to carry

---

* See Douthit 1995 for a fuller treatment.

their first load of furs out to the Umpqua via the Middle Fork of the Coquille, returning by the 26th to continue their trapping.

Trapping, however, was most difficult in the frequently inundated Coquille River valley. "The excessive rise and fall of the water baffle the skill of our trappers," McLeod wrote on December 9.[31] Six weeks later he was still complaining about it: "the rise and fall of water is so frequent and generally on either extreme which renders trapping a very precarious business at this season."[32] On December 31 he wrote, "Although beaver so common hereabouts, the ebb and flow of the Ocean is much against trapping." The tides at that time extended for forty-one miles upriver from the ocean, and there was the additional problem of rise and fall of the water due to freshets after the heavy rains.

Much of those bottomlands themselves were an impenetrable swamp. Where large myrtle trees had uprooted, new trees would grow from the roots and the trunk of the downed tree itself. No one who has not tried to negotiate such a tangle can appreciate how dense and difficult it is. McLeod described it well when he wrote, "The men can neither proceed afoot nor with a craft, brush, wood and fallen trees obstruct the various channels."[33] Reg Pullen has characterized the Coquille River valley of that time as "a little Amazon," meaning that it was a swamp and a jungle.

A party from the base camp went to Coos Bay for the purpose of trade but found the Coos Indians had raised the price at which they were willing to exchange furs. The Hudson's Bay Company men had no authority to pay more than the price stipulated by the Fort Vancouver Indian Tariff, and so there was no more commerce with the Coos at that time. Finally, on January 22, McLeod ordered all the traps to be taken up and to begin preparations for departure. He noted, "Women employed in scraping skins."[34] These were women who were married to the French Canadian trappers and were a part of the fur brigade.

McLeod with the rest of the party headed up the Coquille with intentions of taking their furs out this time by way of the North Fork, hoping it might prove a better route than the Middle Fork. It stormed so heavily, however, that they made only about nine miles and had to lay over the next day in the rain, possibly about the site of present-day Gravelford. He had certainly passed *Ch'aghilidan*, the village of Coquelle's father at the confluence of the North Fork and the main river. He noted in his journal for that day (January 27): "Three Indians stopped with us, on their way down stream, with a cargo of camas, their chief subsistence at present, fish having long ago almost entirely failed in this river which made the majority of the Indians to resort to other places."[35]

In 1934, Coquelle Thompson told Philip Drucker, "Nobody lived on North Fork of Coquille,"[36] but the following year he gave Elizabeth Jacobs the names and locations of several sites on that stream. In his journal McLeod notes having passed a few Indian habitations along the way in January 1827.[37] Coquelle's memories of the locations of the village sites, while fairly consistent, sometimes contain contradictions.

Coquelle Thompson's father came to manhood during those years. His names suggest his personality. One of his names was *Ch'adúghilh*. Coquelle told Elizabeth Jacobs that it meant "a mean man, no one can stop him when he's mad."[38] Later, he told Harrington that it meant "Mean; a maker of threatening gestures." But he also told Harrington that those were merely the names known to outsiders. His real name, known only to insiders, was *Hashe-gali*. That meant "Chief coming," and it was used as if describing the tide coming in.[39] He was, in other words, unstoppable. Coquelle added that his father became the chief "because his grandfather and great-grandfather had been chiefs."[40]

His parents no doubt arranged for his first wife, paying handsomely for her as custom dictated.* She was from the downriver Athabaskan village of *Hweshdan*. A string of large dentalium was reckoned nominally at $100, and Coquelle told Philip Drucker that a Coos Bay woman was bought "one time for 200 strings, sea otter skins, etc."[41] Drucker expressed disbelief at that exorbitantly high price, but if the wife was a really good one of an important lineage, the $20,000 price may not be too out of line. In any case, Coquelle's father soon

---

* To be respected, a woman had to be purchased for marriage. Children were illegitimate if the mother was not paid for (Miller and Seaburg 1990, 585). The process of "buying a wife" (as it was phrased in the Indian English of Coquelle Thompson's time) was in part a negotiation between the families as to an appropriate bride price, which was paid to the bride's family to compensate for the loss of her productive labor. But marriage was more than a purely economic transaction; it was also an arrangement between families that enhanced their prestige and provided legitimate claims to offspring.

obtained a Coos Bay wife. Her name was Se-ma-chus-cha, which meant "beads in her hair."[42] She was a first cousin to the future Hanis Coos chief Daloose Jackson,[43] and she would become Coquelle's mother.

From the forks of the Coquille to the Hanis villages at Empire on Coos Bay was about forty-five miles, all but one or two of which could be traveled with the tide by canoe. One wonders what thoughts the young bride Se-ma-chus-cha entertained on this long trip up an unfamiliar river to a strange village where the people spoke an incomprehensible Athabaskan language. It was a matter of no consequence to the husband because wives from that distance brought extra prestige, and the future chief of the Upper Coquilles would have use for the extra prestige.

The term "chief" deserves some comment. It is, of course, an English word meaning "one who is highest in rank or authority." The Upper Coquille Athabaskan word that Coquelle translated as "chief" was *hashe*, which also meant "a rich man."[44] But Coquelle pointed out to Elizabeth Jacobs that to be a chief *(hashe)* in reality one had to be the son of a chief and also be elected by the people. "Some time they might choose a nephew or first cousin of the chief," he said. "They always appointed a big strong man who could stand lots of trouble."[45]

Even in the smallest settlements one man was considered *hashe* (chief). His authority did not extend beyond his own settlement, which usually was only his own extended family, and for that reason the term "headman" is probably more appropriate than "chief." In the treaties and census that came later, the signatories were termed "Chiefs, Headmen, and delegates." That certainly would include everyone whom the people themselves would have considered a *hashe*.

During the years that Coquelle Thompson's father was coming of age and starting a family, the Hudson's Bay Company established a post on the Umpqua near its confluence with Elk Creek (present-day Elkton). Called Fort Umpqua, it was the southernmost of the Hudson's Bay Company posts, and it operated from June 1836 until it burned in November 1851. The Upper Coquille Indians apparently traded beaver hides there from time to time.

Coquelle Thompson described to Elizabeth Jacobs how one of his relatives, a man later named "Old Hunter," obtained his beaver. It was winter when the furs were good, and Old Hunter took off his clothes and dove in with a rope tied to one hand. He dove down through about ten feet of water, and "in just a little way it was dry and nice. He went a long way. He went forty or fifty feet. Then he found a bed. Oh! Lots (of beaver) lay down there." He continued, "That was all he'd do, tie beavers by the leg and they would pull them out. They got ten good hides."[46]

After Old Hunter had perfected the technique, he might have had others go in after the beaver, because later Coquelle told John Peabody Harrington, "Old Hunter used to have a boy go into beaver houses and slip a cord on beaver." He also told of Old Hunter running between two elk "shooting the elk right and then left of him, with a flint ignition gun."[47] The first permanent white settlers in the county reported that indeed, there were a few guns among the Indians, but they were "of an old English pattern."[48] The price for a trade flintlock was no doubt low enough that Old Hunter's beaver-catching method would have given him the wherewithal to buy one.

Old Hunter was related by marriage to Coquelle Thompson. His wife, Polly, was a sister of Coquelle's father.[49] He once told Coquelle about the great forest fire that had come through the Upper Coquille country in about 1850 or a little before. He said that they were out hunting, probably during an extremely dry, late September. He said, "We heard a noise just like the ocean coming, except that it was from the east." They didn't sleep that night, and in the morning they ran back home. "It was getting closer every day, and the noise was getting louder, more and more like the ocean." They saw droves of elk, deer, and bear. "Every kind of animal came into the river, running away from fire." The people got into their canoes. "All along the center of the river were canoes, there were many people."

"Now," he said, "there was fire all around us. It shot like rain across the river, but it did not drop on our boats. We could hear elk squealing just like cattle. The water became hot. Thus we were all saved, no fire dropped on us, it merely shot across the river like rain. It did not burn the houses, it jumped over them to the mountains." What Old Hunter was describing to Coquelle was a crown fire. For people living or working in the forest, it is the most terrifying and destructive of all the forces of nature, creating its own wind and traveling at up to 100 miles per hour; it can jump a mile or more. The fire from the crowns of the trees drops to the ground and burns the underbrush and the trees themselves, and so the fire can persist for days in a given area.

Old Hunter told Coquelle that after the fire passed "the smoke was so thick that people could not see for a whole month. It was pitch dark, the only way they knew when it was daylight was from the cry of some small bird. Then they would say, 'It must be daylight. We have to get up.'" A rainstorm finally came probably in early October and put out the fires.

Several of the young men went to the mouth of the Coquille River to see how those people had fared. The dialogue continues in Coquelle's inimitable style: "They arrived down there, they asked, 'How have you folks gotten along?' 'Oh, we have managed all right. You merely come to visit us?' 'Yes, the chief wanted to learn if you had got along all right.' 'Well, you go on down to the mouth of the river, where the ocean is, and you will see something there!' They ran down there, they saw ashes, about seven feet deep where the tide had come in. They had never seen anything like that before. Nothing but ashes, just fine ashes that had floated down river. They poked in those ashes. There were no tiny sticks even, merely ashes."[50] Probably not coincidentally, the native oyster of the Coos Bay estuary became extinct at about that time. The Coos Indians explained to the first settlers that the ashes had "colored" the tributary streams to the bay. The settlers assumed that the lye had destroyed the oysters, probably a good supposition.[51]

Within any given stand of Douglas fir forest, a fire such as the one described by Old Hunter might come through once each hundred to five hundred years. The fires were almost always in late summer or early fall after an exceptionally dry season. They were sometimes started by lightning, but probably as often as not they were started by the Indians themselves, who customarily burned selected sites during August and September, the two driest months.[52] During exceptionally dry years, with all conditions favorable for it, those fires could spread and become catastrophic. Throughout the Coast Range during the period 1845 to 1855, catastrophic forest fires were more frequent than during any known period before or since.* The incursion of whites into a part of the Coast Range might account for some of the fires, but not all, and almost certainly not for the one that Old Hunter had described.

---

* A recent review of historic forest fires on the Coquille River can be found in Bureau of Land Management, Coos Bay District, "East Fork Coquille Watershed Analysis, Appendix E, Fire History: 1534 to Present," 23 June 1999.

Contact: The Coquille River Valley

According to archaeologists Reg Pullen and Jeff LaLande, who have made a study of it, the Indians of southwestern Oregon used fire to a greater extent than was previously thought.[53] Coquelle Thompson described using fire to drive deer and to create a better hunting environment. He told in great detail how it was used in the harvest of Indian oats (tarweed) and to enhance blackberry production. It had other uses as well, including in the cultivation of tobacco, the only agricultural crop that the people of the Coquille River cultivated from seed. "They planted tobacco long before the whites came," Coquelle said.[54]

Tobacco played a significant role in the social and spiritual world of the men. They did all the cultivation of it, and they are the ones who smoked it. Coquelle described it to Elizabeth Jacobs: "They build a big fire—burn over the whole place. Now when the fire is all gone they cleaned the ground off, dug at it with a digging stick and then planted Indian tobacco seeds. They look like turnip seeds." He said that no women ever went around the tobacco field—"just old men." They would put up a fence of brush to keep the dogs out of the planted area, and after the plants went to seed they would take the leaves to smoke. He said that when the first white leaves came on, they were picked and thrown away. "The new growth that follows is fine tobacco," he said. "Later on they picked the seeds and put them in a little sack to keep until the following spring."

Coquelle enjoyed tobacco, used most moderately, all of his long life. He seems to have known that although tobacco can be quite pleasurable, the less it is used, the better. He said that a full sack the size of a fist "lasts a long time. You fill the pipe once and you smoke three or four times from that one pipe full. You fill the pipe, take a few puffs and put it away." He said that the men smoked every night and that when there were many people in the sweathouse "they had to light two pipes. Chief furnishes the tobacco." He said, "The chief doesn't say anything. He just lights his pipe and passes it. Each one when he smokes thinks, 'I wish I'll be alive a long time. I wish I will get something easy. I wish money come to me.' Then he blows out the smoke. All old men always do that."[55]

Following the McLeod expedition's visit to the Upper Coquille during the fall and winter of 1826–27, there were no more recorded outside visitors to that area during the next twenty-four years. And there is nothing in the oral histories given by Coquelle Thompson to indicate that any non-Indian outsiders visited the area during that time. But during those twenty-four years much was happening elsewhere that would finally lead to the abrupt end of native society on the river in 1856.

The most disastrous outside event during the period was the pandemic of "fever and ague" (since identified as malaria) during the early 1830s. This pandemic devastated the Indian population of the Willamette Valley during the summers of 1830 to 1833, the estimated loss running as high as 92 percent.[56] There is no evidence that this, or any other epidemic, hit the Coquille River with anywhere near this intensity, although Subagent Josiah Parrish in his census of 1854 noted that there was evidence of smallpox from thirty years earlier and of measles from eighteen years earlier.[57] There is no convincing evidence of the extent of any population change on the Coquille River after first contact with the whites.[58] The depopulation of the Willamette Valley, however, had profound historic implications that indirectly affected the Coquille Valley because it facilitated the large-scale settlement of whites in Oregon unopposed by a resident population.

In 1827 England and the United States renewed their 1818 treaty agreeing to joint occupation of the Oregon Country. American interest in the area was stimulated and given tangible support when, in 1834, the Reverend Jason Lee and other Methodist missionaries were escorted to Fort Vancouver by none other than Alexander McLeod.[59] Partly to counter what was perceived as an incursion of Protestants, the first Catholic missionaries came in from Canada in 1839. Their first purpose was to serve the employees of the Hudson's Bay Company and their families, nearly all of whom were Catholic.

By 1840 there were still only about two hundred people of European descent in the Oregon Country, exclusive of Hudson's Bay Company employees and retirees.[60] The following year 111 Americans arrived in Oregon, and in 1842 the great Applegate train of covered wagons brought in 875 more.[61] A provisional government was established in 1843, and the next year there were 800 more emigrants from the states. The migration peaked in 1845 with 480 wagons bearing 3,000 people.[62] The captain of a company of thirty wagons during that 1845 migration was a young Quaker from Indiana named Joel Palmer.[63] Ten years later he would hold in his hands the destiny of the people of the Coquille River, and the destiny of most of the Indians of Oregon.

Contact: The Coquille River Valley 19

The year following that great migration, England signed a treaty with the United States that established the boundary between them in the Pacific Northwest at the 49th parallel.[64] Oregon was no longer a fiefdom of the Hudson's Bay Company. It was now a territory of the United States. Yet it would be another five years before an American from the United States would ever see the Coquille River.

Contact with white culture had made very little change in the life of the people of the Upper Coquille River. Then, on the morning of January 23, 1848, at a sawmill four hundred miles south of the Coquille, the millwright of Sutter's Mill was digging mud from the tailrace when he saw, reflected by the early morning sun, the color of gold. He got a pan to test his suspicions, and what he confirmed altered history. Within two years over 100,000 people, mostly young, single men, had come to California to get rich. By 1853 the northern limit of that great, mad gold rush was reached. That northern limit was near the mouth of the Coquille River, and by that time Coquelle Thompson was already four or five years old.

2

Conflict

End of a Way of Life

It is unclear how many wives his father had at the time Coquelle was born. He said that there was one or maybe two from <u>Hweshd<u>an</u></u>, the Athabaskan settlement far down the river. His own mother, Beads-in-Her-Hair, was Hanis Coos. "Her mother and grandmother were all Coos," Coquelle told Elizabeth Jacobs.

His memory of their house was of "two wives and two fires, each wife in the two opposite ends of the house."[1] One of the two wives was, of course, Coquelle's mother, whom he called *shgága*. Her co-wife he called *shák'e*. His mother called him *sh<u>ashé</u>*, and her co-wife called him *sháshe*. He said, "Half brothers and sisters were called the same as my own brothers and sisters."[2] Coquelle had one older half-brother and two half-sisters. "There were no white names at that time," he said. His half-brother's name meant "black mark on wrist," and it seemed to Coquelle that he had another name, which might have been "feather feet." His younger half-sister's name meant "smelling all around," or "nose lifted up." "She did that," he said.[3] About three years after Coquelle was born, his mother had one more son, Latenosa, a name that Coquelle evidently didn't know the meaning of. Coquelle and Latenosa were his mother's only birth children.[4]

Just outside the door of the house were two spotted, black-and-white elk dogs. "Those dogs were just like people," Coquelle said, "knew their names and would sit down." When the people were eating, they would throw bones to the dogs, "who were expert at catching them in their mouths." One time little Coquelle was sitting in the door—which was about two feet high—offering meat to the dogs when one of them snapped at the meat and bit off the tip of his left forefinger. There was some talk of killing the dog, but it was agreed that "the dog did not hurt the boy." After all, a young, trained elk dog was valuable. "They never barked," Coquelle said, "except when they reached an elk." At night, while the men were sleeping in the sweathouse, the dogs stood guard over the house where the women and babies were sleeping.[5]

His mother, being Coos, would have nursed her new baby for about three years, as was the practice in most of the coastal tribes. Coquelle said, "I remember, oh that milk was sweet. I don't want to give it up."[6] When Melville Jacobs interviewed a Coos woman, Annie Miner Peterson, in 1933 and 1934, she told of the nursing practices of the Coos. She said that while nursing, there was no sexual intercourse. "That is why they did nothing with their wives, sometimes for five years." The habit of using the cultural pattern number five was strong; she corrected herself and said, "maybe for three years, then they began to do it to their wives."[7]

Coquelle told Elizabeth Jacobs that an infant was given a "pet" name at five days old. Only later, when they began to develop personality, did they get other names. As a child, Coquelle would listen to the bird sounds and evidently became quite good at imitating them. His parents thus called him "*Chash yadílyi*," which meant "make noise like a bird."

While Coquelle was still a nursing infant, the Upper Coquille River received its first visitors of European descent in twenty-four years—the first since Alexander McLeod's fur brigade left in February 1827. On a warm summer day in early September 1851, ten lost and starving men under the demonstrably inept leadership of William T'Vault stumbled down the lower part of the Middle Fork thinking they were on the Umpqua. They had left Port Orford three weeks earlier looking for a practical route from there to the gold mines at Jacksonville and the Shastas. T'Vault was a proprietor at Port Orford and had hoped to get rich by finding a route from there to the mines. The route did not exist, and he and his men were hopelessly lost.

Eventually they came upon the tidewater of the North Fork, just a few yards from the main river. They knew now that they were either on the Coos or the Coquille River, and the presence of the tide told them that they couldn't be too far from the ocean. In a short time "three canoe loads of Indians came up," according to L. L. Williams, a member of the T'Vault party. This was very near the village of *Ch'aghilidan* and the center of the authority of Coquelle's father. After some consultation they decided to hire the Indians to take them downriver to the coast, paying them with the few items of clothing they could spare. They headed downstream and that evening, when they were within earshot of the breakers on the beach, they stopped to camp.

In the morning they continued on, but hunger drove them to stop at "a large rancherie" on the north bank about two miles from the ocean. This was probably the Miluk village of Ni-Lae-Tun where a large number of people were gathered to catch salmon from the extensive fish weirs there. Coquelle referred to the Miluk people near the mouth of the Coquille as the "Saltchuck Indians," "saltchuck" being Chinook Jargon for "the ocean." "The saltchuck Indians were mean," he said, adding that they "were never good friends of the inland Indians."[8]

Whatever happened next, the upshot was that five of the ten men in T'Vault's party were killed. In at least one version of the story, they had been warned by the Athabaskan Indian accompanying them not to stop there, and it was due to him that T'Vault and Gilbert Brush were saved. He rescued them both and deposited them on the south shore from which they made their escape back to Port Orford.[9]

In October the army chartered the new side-wheel steamship *Columbia* to transport troops from San Francisco, arriving at Port Orford on the 22nd.[10] The objective was to "chastise" the Indians of the Coquille River for the reported assault on T'Vault's men. The expedition commander was Lieutenant Colonel Silas Casey, later to become a general during the Civil War. In his first report upon arriving at Port Orford he said that he found the "Cape Blanco Indians about 15 miles from here apparently friendly, but not to be trusted far."* He was referring to the Tututni band at the mouth of the Sixes River. He added, "The Coquilles are the only hostile Indians on the coast."[11] He had no interpreter, but engaged Gilbert Brush, who had

---

* We are grateful to Reg Pullen for bringing the report of Lieutenant Colonel Silas Casey to our attention.

Conflict: End of a Way of Life 23

escaped with T'Vault, to accompany the expedition to the Coquille River. They were evidently unaware of the difference between the Lower Coquille Miluk and the Upper Coquille Athabaskan Indians, and their respective roles in the T'Vault affair.

Although the incident with the T'Vault party had occurred at a Miluk village on the *north* bank of the river, Colonel Casey and his troops arrived at the mouth of the Coquille with fifty-five men and five officers and shelled the Miluk village on the *south* bank. The inhabitants fled, but "owing to the dense nature of the undergrowth and other reasons," Casey waited for the arrival by land from Port Orford of two surf-boats before ascending the river in pursuit. After rendering the boats watertight "by means of pitch obtained from pine trees," they left the mouth of the river before daylight on the morning of the November 17, with nine days' provisions. They destroyed the hastily abandoned lodges they encountered along the way, and "after passing upon the river about 25 miles," they arrived at what may have been Chief Jackson's village of *Lhanhashdan*.* There were two lodges that "contained large quantities of the different articles used by the indians, fishing nets, etc, together with three or four tons of dried salmon." The inhabitants barely got out in time. In one of the lodges "salmon was cooking," according to Casey, who ordered everything burned except the canoes, which he took for use by the army.[12] The awful irony is that Upper Coquille Athabaskan people whose property was destroyed were the very ones who had helped the T'Vault party to descend the river to its mouth, and had warned them of possible hostility of the Lower Coquille Miluk.

On the morning of the 20th, Casey's expedition was at the confluence of the North Fork and the main river, which was probably the site of *Ch'aghilidan* (called Choc-re-le-a-tan in the 1854 census and the 1855 treaty). Coquelle's father, Chief Washington, was credited as being chief there, and it may have been the site of Coquelle's birth. In any case, when the army arrived, the people were gone. Casey ordered destroyed "a number of lodges, and large quantities of their food and implements," then sent Lieutenant Wright with a scouting party in

---

* The miles given in Casey's report are not easily reconciled with the "river miles" shown on the current Geological Survey maps. Part of the difference may be attributed to the many meanders that were later removed due to diking, which considerably straightened the flow of the river.

one of the boats to search the North Fork. Coquelle's father's people may have been twenty miles upstream at the confluence of Middle Creek and the North Fork, where they had seasonal settlements. Lieutenant Wright went only about ten miles, and found no one.

Lieutenant George Stoneman (later governor of California), with a second scouting party, was ordered to "ascend the South Fork."[13] At the confluence of the South Fork and the Middle Fork, the site of *Chanchat'ahdan*, he "came upon a number of indians, one of whom commenced talking in a loud voice and motioned him away." The shouting escalated into an exchange of gunfire and "a shower of arrows." This site was evidently also within Coquelle's father's sphere of influence, but it appears that the people encountered there by Lieutenant Stoneman were actually refugees of the Lower Coquille Miluk, the people the expedition were out to "chastise." Lieutenant Stoneman returned to camp, where plans were made to attack the Indians the next day, November 22.

Colonel Casey and most of the troops followed a trail along the east side of the river, while the remainder of the command, under Lieutenant Gilman, ascended the river in the surf-boats. About a mile from the confluence of the Middle Fork and the South Fork, Colonel Casey sent Lieutenant Stoneman with twenty men across the river where they followed a trail that met the South Fork about a mile above the forks. Colonel Casey, along with Lieutenant Wright and his men, continued along the east bank of the river until they were within sight and range of the Indians. Unfortunately for the success of the operation, the boats came into range of the Indian's fire long before the main land force under Lieutenant Stoneman arrived. "To save the boats," Colonel Casey "directed the firing to commence." There were about twenty Indians involved, but due to the "war-whoops," which continued during the fifteen minutes that the skirmish lasted, Casey "perceived that we were in proximity of about 200 indians." Colonel Casey reported that although "a number of our men were struck by the missiles of the enemy, both balls and arrows, they were all grazing shots, which merely tore their clothing. Not one man was wounded."

The actual body count of the Indian dead was five, although Colonel Casey reported that "I have reason to believe that about 15 were killed." One "old U.S. musket and several balls" were recovered, "which were recognized as having been taken from the men who were murdered last summer." One wounded man was "seen to throw a rifle into the river" before he fled the scene. If true, possession of the musket makes it quite possible that the engagement might actually have been with the Lower Coquelle Miluk who had killed the five men of the T'Vault party. However, it was the innocent Upper Coquille Athabaskans who sustained devastating property loss. Casey reported that "during the operation on the river, we took and destroyed 20 large lodges, with quantities of implements attached to them. We destroyed about 2000 feet of boards, which had been split out from logs, some of them 3 feet in width. We took 15 canoes and destroyed about thirteen tons of dried salmon."[14]

The "chastisement" of the Upper Coquille Athabaskans, a people who were entirely innocent of the actions against T'Vault on the lower river, was one of those many tragic and inexcusable encounters that make the history of the "winning of the West" so depressing. Colonel Casey said, "I lament every day that I have no interpreter, and feel confident that the indians would now be glad to make peace. At any rate, before any further steps are taken against them, humanity demands that peace should be offered."[15]

Was it merely a breakdown in communications? Gilbert Brush was with Casey. One would think that he, of all people, would have been aware that there were two peoples living in the Coquille River valley, not one. In fact, Casey stated in his report that he did not pursue the Indians any further because "friendly tribes would be involved. Mr. Brush, who is with me, and was one of the survivors of the massacre, states that he found the indians a little further in from the forks friendly, and evidently on bad terms with the Coquille tribe."[16] With an interpreter, Colonel Casey could perhaps have known that those "friendly" Indians actually extended down the river to within a few miles of its mouth. He might have saved himself the trouble of destroying the sustenance of people against whom there should have been no quarrel. Fortunately, the expedition of Colonel Casey in November 1851 was the only time the Regular Army was ordered into the Coquille River valley.

Coquelle did not mention this incident in any of his narratives. Although his father was chief at *Chanchat'ahdan* (among other sites), this documented incident was apparently not among the "historical" tales that were passed on. After Colonel Casey and his troops left the valley, the approximately one hundred Upper Coquille Athabaskan people—almost none of whom had been seen by the army—returned to their villages from the hills and the headwaters of the streams. The hardships they endured as they rebuilt their homes and their canoes without their tools, and without the food they had so carefully and prudently preserved and stored, are not on record. We have only the dry, factual report of Colonel Silas Casey, mission accomplished.

The cycle of traditional life on the Upper Coquille went on. Coquelle might have been as old as three years at the time the army was there, about the right age to be weaned. As Elizabeth Jacobs was told by her Nehalem Tillamook informant, when they were "big enough to come in from outdoors and ask for it," it was time for weaning. The method was simple and direct. The sleeping quarters for the women, the girls, and the nursing infants was the house itself. The sleeping quarters for the men and boys was the sweathouse. To wean a boy, he was merely moved into the sweathouse with the men. When he was eighty-five years old, Coquelle told Elizabeth Jacobs, "When I suck, oh, it taste good, sweet. I can't forget it. (Then) my father take me (to the) sweathouse all (the) time, make me give it up."[17]

Coquelle said that his mother never spanked him, and that girls were never spanked, but that his father sometimes did spank him. "He's mean," Coquelle said. "He'd send me on the darkest night to get water. I'd have to go. When I'd bring the water back he'd say, 'you'll be all right when you get old—you'll live long.'" As an aside, Coquelle quipped, "He didn't say 'you will have money' or anything like that!"[18]

Those formative years during which Coquelle slept with the men in the sweathouse had an indelible effect. It was there that he first heard the myths and folktales of his people with their placenames and locations, and it was there that he picked up the narrative style that in later years so defined him. It was also there that he first picked up the values and worldview that he carried with him through his long life. It was in the sweathouse that he, and the generations of men before him, learned who they were.

Coquelle told Harrington, "The teller of these stories was always seated in the middle of the sweathouse and told long stories in the dark." Some of them might have been too long for young Coquelle's attention span. He said, "I would fall asleep, to awake in the morning sweating, since the fire had been built up."[19] Earlier, in 1935, he had elaborated on this to Elizabeth Jacobs. He explained that when the adult men built up the fire so that they could sweat, they put the smaller boys outside. He said, "(We would) sit up on top, they would sweat, make it warm. We sit up there half asleep." This would be "about 3 a.m. when it was getting cool."[20] He told Harrington that he would seat himself "above the sweathouse door, where warmth came up," and added, "It was nice in the sweathouse but cold outside with nothing on you."[21] After the men had sweated and went to swim, the boys would "duck back in, fix our beds, go to sleep again."[22]

The security that Coquelle felt in the sweathouse belied the dangers of living in a small settlement in the woods. As an example, there is the story he told Elizabeth Jacobs of the time that his grandmother was mauled by a bear, an exceptionally accurate description of such an encounter. He said she had gone to dig camas roots and suddenly met a grizzly. She stood still, which is to this day the recommended action, but the bear came to her, "put a finger on her nose, played with it, then got rough, threw her to the ground. She just laid on her belly like (she was) dead." That, again, was the right thing to do, but the bear "turned her over, put a hand on her heart, held it there quite a while, then began throwing her around again. He tore her basket, threw it away. Then he hit her on the back of the neck, turned her over, hit her in the chest, slung her all around." He then left her, stopped, looked back, returned, "picked her up, looked at her face and eyes for a long time. Then he slung her down, walked off again." This time he stopped, looked at her one more time and "then he went off."

Coquelle said, "She crawled a little ways, carefully, then ran. When she got close to the village she hollered." Here Coquelle uses the kind of dialogue that so distinguishes his storytelling style. "'What's the matter?' 'Why, grizzly bear played with me nearly all morning, almost killed me. You see I ain't got no basket.'" He said that she told them where it happened, but they didn't get him. "They were afraid to follow," he said. "Oh he's smart, awful smart."[23] "This happened at *Chanchat'a*," Coquelle said, fixing a place-name upon his narrative, as he often did.[24]

Chanchat'ahdan, the village at the confluence of the South Fork and the Middle Fork, holds a clear view to the north, across the main stem of the river, to a long, high hogback called Sugarloaf Mountain. One day in May 1853, when Coquelle was about four years old, the people from up and down the river had come to this site to catch and dry eels, which were spawning at that time. There were perhaps one hundred people of all ages busily at work with the various tasks involved when a formidable and terrifying sight appeared, coming down the trail off that mountain.

Forty mounted men with an additional forty pack animals carrying supplies were coming straight toward them. Understandably, everyone ran for their lives and hid. Barely eighteen months earlier this same village was the site of the engagement with Colonel Silas Casey and the U.S. Army Regulars. But this time it was not the army that was coming. It was a company of adventurers from the gold diggings at Jacksonville coming to claim land for speculation or settlement in the Coos Bay region. They had come up the comparatively well established trail from Jacksonville to the Umpqua River, but there they met with the same obstacles that Alexander McLeod had met twenty-seven years before.[25] The trail on to the Coquille was impassable for horses.

They were able to hire a guide from among the Upper Umpqua Indians, and sent six ax men ahead with him to open the Indian trail from the Umpqua to Camas Valley and then down the various ridges to the main stem of the Coquille River. They probably used the same route that Coquelle's grandfather had used when he came from the Umpqua to settle in the Coquille Valley two generations earlier. These would be the first horses ever to come into the upper Coquille River. After six days that the participants in later years remembered with pleasure, they arrived at the forks of the Coquille where Coquelle's father and his people were catching and drying eels.

Twenty-one of the adventurers, disappointed that they had found no promising mineral prospects along the way, gave up and went back to Jacksonville. Nineteen of the men remained and formed what they called the Coos Bay Commercial Company.[26] It was formed right there at Coquelle's village of *Chanchat'ahdan*. They were the first white settlers of what would later become Coos County.

William Harris, one of the members of the company, said that the hundred or so Indians camped there were catching and drying eels, and that the river "was almost filled with that delicious fish, and the Indians dried large quantities for winter use."[27] The Umpqua guide had some difficulty convincing the residents that these foreign visitors were here on friendly terms, but eventually he was able to communicate with a woman who was from the Umpqua. Through her, he set up a kind of conference with the various chiefs who were there from their respective villages. Gifts were exchanged and, as Harris said, "they became very friendly."²⁸

Present were three principal chiefs. Their names, to the English-speaking Americans, were unpronounceable and so each was given a new, familiar name. The chief from <u>H</u>wesh<u>da</u>n was given the name "King David." Chief Yáks<u>a</u>n, from twenty miles downriver at L<u>han</u>hash<u>da</u>n, was named General Jackson. Coquelle's father, whose name to outsiders was Ch'<u>a</u>dúghilh—the maker of threatening gestures—was given the new name of George Washington.²⁹ Those names stuck, and with minor variations they appear on census records and other legal documents throughout the life of their bearers. The little informal ceremony evidently pleased the chiefs, because the adventurers were able to hire "six leaders with their canoes to paddle them down to the river's mouth."*

Their guides took them on a leisurely trip down the Coquille, visiting the major villages along the way. Harris said that there were "Indians camped all along the river." They went only a few miles each day, camping first near T'as<u>a</u>n Ts'eghilh'ad<u>a</u>n (Myrtle Point), next at Arago—the seasonal fishing village of D<u>a</u>lw<u>a</u>tme'd<u>a</u>n, named "Fish-trap" by the whites."³⁰ They remained one night and half the next day there, "communicating with the shy and stoical redmen who were peaceable and friendly, though they looked upon the whites with astonishment as they were a different type of humanity than they had any knowledge of."³¹ In all, they spent a quiet and interesting six days traveling from the forks of the Coquille to the ocean, whence they went up over the Seven Devils to Coos Bay, where they established claims under the Oregon Donation Claim Act.

During those years most of the whites living on the West Coast were either thinking about gold, actually searching for it, or making money off those who were doing the searching. Many stories and myths developed out of experiences during the gold rush. It was all about wealth and getting rich, or trying to. The concept of wealth, however, is not limited to European-derived cultures. It was pervasive among the Indians of the Northwest long before the whites ever arrived, and the people of the Upper Coquille River were no exception.

Wealth was important enough in the Coquille culture that one major type of spirit encounter was with what Melville Jacobs called a

---

* See Douthit 1994, 481–82, for a discussion of "name-giving."

"wealth-encounter power."[32] For whatever reason, a being would sometimes take pity on a poor, suffering individual and reveal itself to that person, sometimes conferring wealth upon him. Coquelle told of a young man about fifteen years old who had encountered wealth. This was probably the hope of most young men, especially one such as this one, who was poor and lazy. He "mashed oats (tarweed seeds) and ate all the time," Coquelle said. Sometimes he ran errands for the other young men, and during one of those errands "a big snake went by and he got a little thing off its tail. He saw it hanging on the tail. It was Indian money." He hid it in the hollow of a tree and each day as he returned, there would be a duplicate of the original large dentalium shell, plus "about a basketful" of smaller ones. Coquelle said, "For five days money like that lay eggs." He would replace the original piece of money and the next day there would be more. This continued for nine days. On the tenth it stopped, but by then he had ten large dentalium shells and basketfuls of smaller ones. He told his oldest brother, "Go get the chief. Tell him to bring a little basket." "Oh, that chief was surprised" at the amount of money the boy gave him. "You're a poor boy (but) you'll get a wife," he said. The chief sent his youngest wife, whom he had never touched, to live with the boy. Coquelle said, "The chief had lots of money now. He could buy new women if he wanted to." As a moral to the story, Coquelle said, "That's the only way one ever gets wealth. Poor people get helped only that way."[33]

As Coquelle was becoming dimly aware of his surroundings during his nursing years, so the outside world was becoming more aware of this corner of southwestern Oregon. When news of the gold discoveries in California reached the French Canadian settlements at French Prairie, the entire population—including the priests—headed for the diggings.* Several of the French Canadian Métis began prospecting on the southern Oregon coast, including a man named Enos Thomas and two brothers named Groslouis.[34] During the early spring of 1853, the two Groslouis brothers discovered gold at an ancient mouth of the Coquille River about six miles north of the present mouth.

The Groslouis brothers, along with their four other brothers and sisters, had been with their Pend d'Oreille Indian mother and French

---

* See O'Hara 1911, "Oregon."

Canadian father during the unfortunate John Work expedition to the Sacramento Valley in 1832–33. The family, along with three-quarters of the brigade, had been stricken with malaria. Their father, Charles Groslouis (Sr.), died of it on September 17, 1833, at the mouth of the Mcloud River, named for Alexander McLeod.[35] The boys grew up and were educated along with their siblings at St. Paul's Catholic mission on French Prairie, near present-day Salem, Oregon.

The Groslouis brothers shared a mixed Native American and Euro-American heritage. Working their claim at Whiskey Run, they had the luck and they did encounter wealth. It is said that two Irishmen who had done fairly well with the beach mining further south, "Little Mac" McVey and "Big Mac" MacNamarra, became acquainted with the Groslouis brothers and offered $20,000 for their claim. They sold out and later, at the time of the Rogue River War, were with a small group of French Canadian Métis in Curry County.[36]

Immediately after McNammara and McVey bought the claim of the Groslouis brothers, word began to leak out about it. The nineteen men of the Coos Bay Company were barely settled at Empire on Coos Bay, having been there for only three months, when this new gold rush began. By the end of the summer of 1853, several hundred men were on the beach at Whiskey Run, scrambling for gold, buying and selling claims, and trying to enrich themselves off each other.* The men of the Coos Bay Company temporarily forgot their interest in peaceful settlement of the country and headed to Whiskey Run to get rich with the others in a new boomtown called Randolph. Like the poor boy in Coquelle Thompson's story, they were looking for a "wealth encounter."

At first, relations between the miners and the Indians in southern Oregon were peaceable, but across the border in California the Indians had been victims of vicious atrocities. By January 1854, some of the perpetrators of those atrocities—or at least some of their sympathizers—were among the men who were camped north of the mouth of the Coquille River. On the night of January 27 those men drew up a short list of petty grievances against the Indians, to be sent to the Indian agent in Port Orford and to a newspaper. Then, just before dawn on the 29th, forty of the miners surrounded the settlement of

---

* From the *Alta California*, 15 July 1853. Also, the Daniel Giles manuscript, reprinted in Wooldridge, 274.

Nasomah, on the south shore of the river, setting fire to the houses and shooting the men as they came out their doors. According to the annual report of the commissioner of Indian Affairs for 1854, fifteen of the Indian men were killed. The report also listed one woman killed and two others wounded.

The Indian perspective of the Nasomah massacre appears in only a few short narratives recorded by Melville Jacobs and John P. Harrington. During 1933 and 1934 Jacobs recorded a few biographical sketches from Annie Miner Peterson, whose maternal relatives were from the village of Nasomah. She told of Dji·xwánt'ɛ, both of whose parents were killed during that raid. She said, "They killed women and all. Others they did not kill. The boy babies the white people killed, the boy babies they killed."[37] Lottie Evanoff, daughter of the Coos chief Daloose Jackson, told Harrington that a father and his son hid in one of the houses, "but when the Whites burned the Indian houses that night, that man and his son burned to death." She said that "several of the people came running across to South Slough and hid there. The whites couldn't tell them from the South Slough people, since they talked the same language."[38] Miluk was the language spoken at the South Slough of Coos Bay, the nearby ocean beaches, and at the mouth of the Coquille River.

The massacre at Nasomah no doubt sent shock waves up the Coquille River, even to the Forks, where Coquelle was now five or six years old. He told Elizabeth Jacobs and, later, Harrington of certain events that occurred at and near his village around the time of the Rogue River War. Through those narratives we can see that war through his eyes as a child.

It begins with the story of three white men who stayed with his family during a big snow, probably during February of 1854. The snow on the ground was over people's knees. "Nobody hunt; can't get out in the wood." They saw the white men "coming down that Umpqua trail." That would be the trail down the ridge of Sugarloaf Mountain, just across the river from the village. He said that they "did not know what kind of people those white men were—whether white or Indians."[39] He said that they looked terrible and had long whiskers. They "all pack big blankets—no grub."[40] They were starving and asked for the chief, Coquelle's father.

Coquelle said that there were two young men in the village who wanted to kill the white men. His father "get after those two young men." "You keep quiet," he said. "Maybe they're good people. What did you talk about—going to kill anybody—kill innocent people!" He invited the white men into the house by the fire, had them take off their shoes, and motioned for them to eat. His father's wives "cut dry elk meat, made soup, put Indian salt on, gave them a pan. They ate. They eat. They nearly emptied that bucket."

Coquelle said that his father had "lots of fish. He had lots of help. His people hunt all time." The men unpacked their gear, mostly blankets and clothes, and gave his father a heavy wool shirt, which he put on. When the snow was gone, the men prepared to leave. They paid Coquelle's father two blankets and three $20 gold pieces. His father said, "'What I do with that?'" Gold! 'No, keep it.' He handed it back." But the men explained through gestures what he could buy with it, tied it in a handkerchief for him, and showed him how to put it in the pocket of his new wool shirt. The chief gave them three young men as guides and the use of a "good boat" to take them to the mouth of the river.

In the version of the story he told to Harrington in 1942, Coquelle said that his father told his men to "take the whites down quick and not to talk to any Indians on the way." He was afraid that "Coquille villagers" might kill them. He said that they should not be seen by the people at K'*ámashdani*, the Miluk village on the north side of the river. "They are sort of mean, might kill white men," Coquelle said. His father told them to go to the south side of the river and to go immediately to Port Orford.[41]

When comparing oral narratives with documented history, and even more so when comparing one oral narrative with another, it is not always possible to make full sense of it. Such is the case with Coquelle's narratives of incidents relating to the Rogue River War. But there appears in the pioneer reminiscences of the Coquille River valley an event that seems to be clearly related to the events described above by Coquelle. That was the discovery in early March 1854 of two dead white men identified only as "Venable and Burton" at Deadman's Slough (later renamed Iowa Slough), about fifteen miles upstream from the mouth of the river.

In the pioneer reminiscences it is said that the two white men were coming downstream in a canoe by themselves when they were approached by some Indians in canoes. One of the Indian canoes paddled up close "in a friendly way," and tipped Burton and Venable's canoe over. While the men were in the water, they were knocked in the head with clubs, then weighted and sunk in the river at the mouth of the slough. This was done, it was said, in revenge over the massacre of January 29.[42]

In Coquelle's narrative of the incident there are three white men, coinciding with his story of the three white men who had stayed with his father. He said, "One of the white men swam just like a fish." He escaped, but "the other two were drowned, killed." One of Coquelle's storytelling techniques was to add a detail to make the event more vivid: "The men tried to grab on to the edge of the boat but were hit on the head." When word of the killings got to the whites, "Oh, they were mad! They raised the dickens, 'Who did it?'"[43] "At last," Coquelle said, they put "the rope around an old man, they said to him, 'Do you know who killed those men?' He said in Jargon, 'Coquille sal djik sawa' (mouth-of-the-Coquille River people)."

Meanwhile, two Indians who were thought to have been among those responsible for the murders were apprehended and brought to Randolph for quick, vigilante justice. Coquelle told about it: "Those two Indian men had to be hanged right there at the mouth of the river. They saw the men hanged. Someone interpreted when the soldier's chief talked. He stood up on a big barrel. The chief or lieutenant spoke a little while. He said, 'You people know now. That's the way it goes, our law when white people kill each other, we hang them. You people didn't know; you killed innocent people. Now you know.' This was the first time the Indians ever see anyone hang. That's white man's law."[44] Of course, in the Indian narratives no distinction is made between the vigilante mobs and the military: they are all called "soldiers."

It was a vigilante mob that executed the two men, but Coquelle probably understood the justice of it in terms of blood payment. The Indians of the Coquille River valley would have had no trouble understanding the concept of blood payment. They used it themselves; it was only the method, the execution by hanging, that was novel to them. Coquelle's people would more likely have carried out a sneak raid on the offending village in the very early morning hours before daylight. In contrast, in the case of an individual shaman who had failed to cure a sick person and was suspected of poisoning the patient, the method would have been to cut her throat. "That's a special way to kill a doctor because she made no noise, no struggle for

Conflict: End of a Way of Life

children or family to hear. That's the way to kill a doctor," Coquelle explained to Elizabeth Jacobs in a narrative about a woman shaman who was killed for "poisoning."[45]

The same year as the hanging, in 1854, Abraham Hoffman and his wife Jemima built a cabin next to the village of *Chanchat'ahdan*.[46] They took out an Oregon Donation Claim on the property, and were the first white settlers in the area—if we exclude the transient miners further up the South Fork. It is altogether possible that the people of *Chanchat'ahdan* moved to *Ch'aghilidan*, five miles downriver at the confluence of the North Fork, in order to put a little space between themselves and their new neighbors. In any case, that is where they were found in July when Indian Agent J. L. Parrish arrived to take a census.

Parrish visited all of the villages between the Coquille River and the California border, attempting an accurate census of the population. At the confluence of the North Fork and the main river, at the village of *Ch'aghilidan*, he found assembled what were evidently all of the Upper Coquille Athabaskans—including the people of *Chanchat'ahdan*. He counted 105 individuals: 30 men, 40 women, and 35 children. He listed the band as the "Choc-re-le-a-ton," the closest he could get to a spelling of its pronunciation. The name was also used for the Upper Coquille Athabaskans in the Treaty of 1855. Parrish gave the chief's name as "Washington." Washington, of course, was Coquelle's father, using the name given by the Coos Bay Company when they had come through the previous year.[47] The name possibly indicated that Washington was "first among equals" in his status with the other chiefs or headmen. If the census was complete, Coquelle was certainly one of the eighteen male children enumerated.

At the end of the same month in which the census was taken, Congress passed the Indian Appropriations Act of July 31, 1854. Among other things, it authorized the superintendent of Indian Affairs for Oregon Territory to negotiate treaties with the coastal tribes. Joel Palmer had been appointed to that position in spring 1853, and had successfully negotiated several treaties with tribes from east of the Coast Range. All of those treaties were ratified by the Senate and signed by President Franklin Pierce.

In August 1855, Joel Palmer began the negotiations for treaties with the "chiefs, headmen and delegates" from among all of the peoples of the Oregon coast: all of the Indians living west of the crest of the Coast Range between the Columbia River and the California line. It was a very sparsely settled area of several million acres. Palmer was absolutely convinced that a one-million-acre reservation along the central portion of it could be set aside in which the Indians would be safe from the depredations of the whites and could continue life more or less in their traditional manner. He had reason to believe that he was acting in good faith, and he certainly believed that the treaty would be ratified by Congress and signed by the president, as had been the case with other treaties he had entered into with Oregon tribes. In this he would be mistaken.

Beginning with the northernmost bands, on August 11 Palmer obtained the "x" mark of forty-one of the "chiefs, headmen and delegates" from the various bands of what are now Clatsop, Tillamook, and Lincoln Counties. Working with surprising speed, a week later, on the 17th, he obtained the "x" mark of eighty-four such dignitaries of the Siuslaw, Lower Umpqua, and Coos peoples. In less than a week following that, he obtained the "x" of forty-two men from among the Lower Coquille Miluk peoples (called the Nasomah in the treaty). Exactly one week later, on August 30, he obtained fifty-four more "x's," this time from all of the various bands along what is now the Curry County coast from below the mouth of the Coquille to the California line. Finally, on September 8, he was with Chief Washington's people at *Ch'aghilidan* (called Choc-re-le-a-ton in the treaty) on the Upper Coquille River. This was the last group that Palmer had to deal with. Coquelle Thompson gives us his version of how the negotiations went.

Thompson told Elizabeth Jacobs that the Indians questioned Joel Palmer.[48] "'You say you take us Willamette. What kind of place?' 'Well,' Julian Palmer say, 'just like here, only more open place. The Willamette is a big river.' Question again from chief, 'I want to know, any deer in there?' 'Deer? Of course there's deer in there. Lots of deer in there!' 'Any fish in there?' 'Oh yes! Lots of spring fish. All kinds of fish, just like you got here.' 'Any eels?' 'Oh yes! Lots of eels, Oregon City. Big falls there! Lots of eels, hang that way!'"

Coquelle continued: "Oh everybody glad now. Indians ready to give up now, ready to go. 'Any elk there?' 'Oh yes, elk there! Everything you see here, everything there! Bear!' 'Any berries there?' 'Oh yes, everything you have here: strawberries, blackberries, salmonberries, everything you got here, just same there.' That's all they want to know, you see. All leaders stand up before treaty people. They say,

Conflict: End of a Way of Life

'We'll go now, we give up now.' Oh Jerry Palmer clap his hands. He was a middle-aged man. After that they made him agent here (at Siletz) for four years."*

The last entry in the treaty was signed on the Upper Coquille River by the six principal headmen, and first among them was Coquelle's father, Chief Washington, now called Washington Tom. "Tom" continued as part of his name throughout his life at Siletz, and it may be assumed that the name "Thompson" derives from it. He is called "Washington Tom" in the preamble to the treaty, but the secretary who copied the treaty placed an "x" on both the name "Washington" and the name "Tom" on the signature page, as though it were two people. In fact, only six, not seven, of the "chiefs, headmen, and delegates" of the Upper Coquille Athabaskans placed their "x" on the treaty.**

The signature page read:

We the chiefs, headmen and delegates of the Cah-toch-say, Chin-chin-ten-tah-ta, Whis-ton, and Klen-hos-tun bands of Coquille Tribe of Indians, after having had fully explained to us the above treaty, do hereby accede to its provisions, and affix our signatures, or marks this 8th day of September 1855.
Signed in presence of
    Chris Taylor, Secy.
    August V. Kautz, 2nd Lieut. 4th Infantry
    R. Dunbar
    John Flett, Interpreter
    Henry Hill Woodward

Washington Tom	His x mark Ls.
Che a le tin Tie	His x mark Ls.
Ni ich lo sis	His x mark Ls.
Lu si nah	His x mark Ls.
Jackson	His x mark Ls.
David	His x mark Ls.

---

* Palmer was agent at Siletz during 1871 and 1872, after his unsuccessful bid for the governorship of Oregon.
** A facsimile of the treaty is contained in Siletz Restoration Act, 270–81.

Joel Palmer's own signature, as "Superintendent of Indian Affairs, Oregon Territory," appeared before the signature pages and immediately following the articles of the treaty. The good faith of the negotiators and the signatories of the treaty, however, did little to stem the tide of violence that would soon be upon southwestern Oregon. More and more miners and prospectors were becoming increasingly desperate as the gold panned out.

The reminiscence of Major Ebenezar Burgess Ball gives some of the flavor of this.[49] Major Ball arrived at the diggings at Whiskey Run and the boomtown of Randolph with a pack train of merchandise and supplies for sale and did nicely until February 1854. Then "a heavy storm set in, and filled the beach up with gray sand, which stopped the miners from working." Later in the year, while they were waiting for another storm to wash the unwanted sand away, word of a strike at Johnson Creek, on the South Fork, emptied the settlement overnight, with Major Ball and his merchandise following the miners upriver, past Coquelle's village of *Ch'aghilidan*. At Johnson Creek he found few customers, and those who were there were having no luck. Meanwhile, another strike was rumored on Sixes River, and part of the customers headed over the ridge to the west to try their luck there. Major Ball followed them again. At Sixes, they heard that the beach at Port Orford was a richer find, and they headed there, and from there to the mouth of the Rogue River. Major Ball finally gave up on the coastal area and went to Jacksonville, the actual center of the gold rush in Oregon. Very few of the prospectors found anything of value, and the old idea of starting a war and drawing pay as militia soldiers seems to have been revived among some of them.

The Rogue River War was one of the several Northwest Indian Wars of 1855 and 1856. It may be said to have started as an outgrowth of the California Gold Rush and was, according to historian E. A. Schwartz, "the war to make money."[50] It began, so it was said, after a church meeting at Jacksonville on Sunday, October 7, 1855, almost exactly one month after the Upper Coquille Athabaskans had signed the treaty with Joel Palmer's men. Because of the outbreak of the war, the treaty was never to be ratified by the Senate.

The "church meeting" was led by the newly elected representative to the territorial legislature from Jackson County, one James Lupton. After the meeting, Lupton led an attack on a band of Indians at Little Butte Creek, near the Table Rock Reservation, which

Conflict: End of a Way of Life   39

had been recently established as a result of Joel Palmer's first treaty negotiations two years earlier. Reportedly, the predawn attack resulted in the killing of forty Indians (the actual body count was twenty-eight, half of them women and children). Lupton died as a result of an arrow wound, and ten other whites were wounded. The inevitable escalation of killings on both sides following Lupton's attack gave plenty of excuses to "tap the federal treasury," according to Schwartz.[51]

The Indians of the Rogue River Valley split into two factions. One group of 303 Takelma Indians remained at the Table Rock Reservation, which was inside their traditional territory. They remained loyal to the treaty they had made with Palmer in 1853 and were holding out hope that the army and the Indian agent would protect them. The other group consisted of 523 potentially hostile non-reservation Indians, from the several non-Takelma bands of the Upper Rogue River.[52] Eventually, many of them retreated down the Rogue River, bringing war to the southern Oregon coast.* Ultimately, the village at the Forks of the Coquille, where Coquelle was now about seven years old, would become involved in at least one incident related to that war.

When the war started on the Upper Rogue River in October 1855, the few whites then living in the Coquille River valley fled to Coos Bay and to Port Orford. Coquelle said that they were "afraid the Coquilles might fight too." With the few white residents gone and their houses empty, Coquelle said that "the Indian people got in, to get what they needed. There was lots of bacon. The Indians knew how to make coffee, how to bake bread."

He remembered that "one day a whole lot of soldiers passed by. They knew the Coquilles weren't fighting so they left us alone." What Coquelle had seen were not soldiers, however. They were the vigilante group that called itself "The Coquille Guards." After they left, "we burned the store," Coquelle said.[53] According to Dodge's *Pioneer History of Coos and Curry Counties*, Indians belonging to Chief Washington's band "commenced hostilities by burning Mr. Hoffman's house, robbing the house of J. J. Hill of four hundred dollars worth of provisions, robbing the house of H. H. Woodward, burning the residence of Harry

---

* See Schwartz (1997), Beckham (1971), and Douthit (1992, 1994, 1999b, and 2002) for good summaries of the war.

Baldwin, cutting adrift the ferryboat at the crossing of the Coquille with other similar acts of enmity."⁵⁴

Sixteen men from Coos Bay joined the nineteen men of the so-called Coquille Guards on November 22, and on the 23rd they "went to the forks of the Coquille for the purpose of persuading Chief Washington to go upon the reservation." They found that he had "erected a barricade on the front between the two branches of the river where he could only be approached by much difficulty. As the party came in view he stationed himself, gun in hand behind a myrtle tree, and twice raised it to fire, but seeing several rifles pointed in his direction refrained from discharging his rifle."⁵⁵ Chief Washington was probably wielding the only gun that his village had.

The "reservation" referred to above was a barn at the mouth of Catching Creek, just across the Coquille River from the village of Myrtle Point. Coquelle himself wasn't held there, nor was his father. "They couldn't find him," Coquelle said. It was, according to Coquelle, Chief Jackson (or *Yáksan*) and his men who were held prisoner there. They all escaped, according to Coquelle, except four men and one young man who was killed.⁵⁶

Finally, the Coquille Guards were disbanded by Indian Agent Benjamin Wright of Port Orford, but not before they had killed four men and hanged another.⁵⁷ Coquelle said that "at Coquille City they fixed it up for that boy who was killed. The white men said, 'We made a mistake.' They issued white blanket, red blanket, white blanket—they satisfied the Coquille Tribe so they had to forget this trouble. Of course they didn't want to fight but the white people were afraid they might, so they issued blankets. The chief said, 'No more trouble.'"⁵⁸

There was "no more trouble" on the Upper Coquille River, but the trouble was just coming to a head for the Indians and whites in Curry County. Chief John of the Applegates had led the war down the Rogue River with a vengeance. His faction joined Enos (or Ignace), one of the French Canadian Métis who were prospecting with the Groslouis brothers. Enos had established himself as the leader of the Indians of Curry County. His strategy was to perform a coordinated, surprise offensive to run the whites out of the southern Oregon coast once and for all. It happened on the night of George Washington's birthday, February 22, 1856, and it was eminently successful, in the short run. On that night twenty-three whites were killed and nearly every building south of Port Orford was burned.[59] Of course, it brought the inevitable backlash, and within weeks Regular Army troops were in Curry County in force. Three months later the war was over, and all of the Indians between the Coquille River and the California line were destined for removal to the Siletz River, 155 miles to the north.

The total population of the Upper Coquille Athabaskans, probably a little over a hundred, were obliged to leave their homes, their baskets, their canoes, and all of their belongings and go to the makeshift reservation at Port Orford. Coquelle told Elizabeth Jacobs, "They don't want to move, but at last, pretty near July, they gave up. Chief say, 'we stay here, maybe white people will bother us, and we kill white people. There will be nothing but trouble. We have to go where they tell us. Their gov't will take care of us.'" He added, "I was about six or seven. I can remember a little—about our traveling." Coquelle said that they had to leave almost all of their possessions. "My father had to leave two good canoes from Tillamook. Some canoes from California were redwood. Some people buried their Indian money. They couldn't carry it."[60]

Unfortunately, Coquelle did not describe for us that last sad parting of his people from the Coquille River valley. We can only imagine the emotions of the women who had to choose from among their prized baskets which one they would keep, filled with whatever food they could pack into it. They were told to just leave the fish that was drying on the racks. We can only imagine what they felt upon leaving the rest of their baskets and other possessions in their abandoned homes, to be burned later by the whites, and upon leaving their familiar places of gathering roots, shoots, seeds, berries, acorns, and nuts.

We can only imagine the emotions of the men as they left their fishing and hunting gear and their well-known fishing and hunting places and their tobacco plots and the places of their spirit quests and the river they had grown up on. We can only imagine the last loading of the canoes as they started down river with the tide, leaving their black-and-white elk dogs that would "sit like people" and only bark when they found an elk. And what did they think as they left their canoes on the shore near the mouth of the Coquille River, canoes that took as long as two years to build? What did they think as they started walking south along the beach, the women carrying the smaller children and all of their meager belongings, the men walking ahead. We'll never know. What we do know is that there had been an "ethnic cleansing" of the Coquille River valley.

By mid-June there were over 1,200 Indians concentrated in the makeshift reservation at Port Orford. Some of them had been there for several months hoping to avoid the violence. There were people from probably all of the Tututni bands of Curry County, and there were some from among the Tolowa and the Chetco. From the Upper Rogue River there were refugees of the Takelma, the Applegate, the Shasta, the Cow Creek, and the Galice. And now there were the peoples of the Coquille River—fifty or sixty Lower Coquille Miluk and about one hundred Upper Coquille Athabaskans. All were concentrated on the bluff above the harbor at Port Orford, waiting to be transported to a future they could not imagine.

One among them was a bright-eyed boy of six or seven who could make sounds like a bird. He would carry with him a boy's knowledge of the language and the culture they were leaving, and he would carry that knowledge well into the next century. His childhood name of *Chash yadílyi* would be forgotten, and he would carry into the future the name of Coquelle, the name by which his people would be remembered.

3

Exodus
Removal to the North

Shortly after midnight, the ship came in.[1] On the 20th of June it gets dark at Port Orford about 8:30, but two hours later on that particular night the moon was up almost full, and when the ship came in there were no doubt many people concentrated on the bluff above the harbor who were awake and saw it.* Those who had been there a month or more had seen the steamship *Columbia* come in several times, and Coquelle and his parents may have been there for that long.** For many of the rest of the people, it was probably the first time they had ever seen a steamship. And it was awesome: 193 feet long, it had two masts with sails. Although it anchored several hundred yards offshore, it filled the little harbor in the moonlight. Most impressively, its two huge wheels, one on each side, were twenty-two feet in diameter, and with them it walked on the water with smoke belching from its stack.[2]

---

* U.S. Naval Observatory, Astronomical Applications Department (Web site). "Sun and Moon Data for One Day." Friday, 20 June 1856, for Port Orford, Curry County, Oregon.
** Palmer to Harris, 23 May 1856, stated, "The Coquill Indians (unless it be fragments of families) are now all upon the Military Reservation at this place [Port Orford]." OHS MSS 114-2. It may therefore be assumed that Coquelle and his family had been there for about a month.

It had lights, and it made odd, mechanical sounds that represented a power probably beyond anything known to the native people of the Oregon coast.

Joel Palmer went to each of the groups of Indians and had them get ready to board the ship. He had spent the previous day (June 19) "counciling" with them, "in which many of them agreed to go by steamer." By nine o'clock the next morning they were loaded.[3] There was no berth for a ship at Port Orford. Ships anchored out about six hundred feet, protected from the prevalent northwest wind by Port Orford Heads and Cape Blanco. They couldn't come in at all during much of the winter, when the wind was from the southwest; there was no protection from that direction. But during most of the summer Port Orford was quite a snug, though inconvenient, harbor.

To load or offload passengers and freight meant using lighters, small boats that were rowed through the surf to the waiting ship. Captain William Dall had chartered the *Columbia* to the government to transport the Indians from Port Orford to Portland for ten dollars apiece. He could haul about seven hundred people at a time if he crowded enough of them on deck, but even so he would have to make two trips.

The success or failure of the operation hung on the shoulders of Joel Palmer. In his diary he stated that most of the people on the first trip had not taken part in the war and had, for the most part, been friendly to the whites. "Many were sick," he said.[4] The loading had to be done in an orderly fashion, mothers and children had to be kept together, the wishes of individuals and of chiefs had to be considered, and it had to be done without delay. Coquelle told Elizabeth Jacobs, "One man, his name Jerry Lann, . . . he could talk the Indian language. He interpreted. He explained what the Indians wanted and how they did things."[5]

Anyone who has embarked on a journey with a large number of people has perhaps experienced a degree of confusion. No one who has not been a part of a large, involuntary relocation—well known in the late twentieth century as "ethnic cleansing"—can appreciate what went through the hearts and minds of those people on board the *Columbia* at Port Orford that day. There had been rumors that after the Indians were on board ship and offshore, the whites were going to throw them overboard into the ocean. Based upon their recent experience with some whites, the scenario held a certain credibility in the minds of some of the Indians. Coquelle said, "Some people say, 'maybe they going take us on this steamer way out beyond on the ocean and put us in the water.' Julian (Joel) Palmer tell us not to be 'fraid, they won't do that."*

Almost everyone knew Palmer; he had visited all of their villages during the previous summer and had convinced their "chiefs, headmen and delegates" to put their "x" on the treaty and to give up their homelands for a new reservation further up the coast. In spite of all that had happened since, the Indians had to retain a certain faith in him. And Palmer would be on board ship with them during the trip.

When it came time for Coquelle's family to embark on the lighter to go through the surf to the waiting ship, only he, his younger brother, his mother, and his father's sister boarded.[6] "Women and children, old folks, all go on boat," Coquelle said. There wasn't enough room for everybody on the *Columbia*, even with two trips. Some would have to go by land, and those would be the able-bodied younger men and women unencumbered with small children, and especially those who were unwilling to go on the ship in the first place.** We don't know exactly why Chief Washington and his other two wives went by land, but it may have been his choice.

Coquelle told Elizabeth Jacobs that as they boarded the ship, "I remember soldier hold my hand." "They put us up front, little place like where the captain stay," he said. "They give us good place because my father was chief." There were staterooms on each side of the seventy-foot-long dining room, and it is very possible that Joel Palmer had allocated them to the families of the headmen. Coquelle, his six-year-old brother, Latenosa, his mother, Beads-in-Her-Hair, and his paternal aunt apparently endured the trip in comparative comfort.

Coquelle remembered that "they take all day to get in the boat." Joel Palmer's diary indicates that they were ready to leave by 11:00 A.M., but they had probably started loading well before daylight. A convoy of troops went with them, which caused some delay. There

---

* This and subsequent direct quotations of Coquelle within this chapter are adapted from Seaburg 1994a unless otherwise noted.
** A similar removal was accomplished the following year when about 1,300 members of seventeen bands of Ottawa Indians were removed sixty miles north from Grand River to Pentwater, Michigan, by the steamers *Ottawa* and *Charles Mears*, "The young men riding their ponies along the beach." Hartwick and Tuller, 28.

were 543 Indians on board when they finally stopped loading: "199 men, 226 women, 127 boys and 118 girls."[7] All of the staterooms, all cabins below deck, and the entire forward deck were filled. Captain Dall was probably a bit impatient to get under way because he would want to cross the bar of the Columbia River while it was still daylight the next day.

When the steam finally entered the pistons of the auxiliary engines and the capstan began to turn, slowly bringing up the anchors from the sandy bottom of Port Orford harbor, it was like an electric shock to the passengers. The entire ship vibrated like a living thing. After a few minutes the main engines started and the huge side-wheels began to churn the surface of the water as the *Columbia* began walking out of the harbor on her own power. The power was provided by two huge "side-lever" steam engines with a cylinder bore of fifty-seven inches and a five-foot stroke, built by Novelty Iron Works of New York.[8] In less than five minutes they were outside the protection of Port Orford Heads and in the open ocean where they hit the long swells of the Pacific. The ship began gently to pitch and roll, and those who were crowded onto the forward deck were invigorated by the brisk northwest wind on this beautiful, clear day, the first day of summer, 1856.

Coquelle remembered, "It go fast, go smooth. This was summer, you know." In about an hour they had rounded Cape Blanco, the westernmost point in Oregon and were heading almost due north steadily at some ten knots. It was certainly still daylight when they passed Cape Arago and a little beyond it the entrance to Coos Bay. Coquelle's mother, who was Coos, might not have known that her people were also being removed to the north and that two steam sawmills were being built on the ancient site of her people's villages.

On this, the longest day of the year and probably the longest day in the life of any of the passengers, the sun finally set but the ship continued throbbing steadily north through the darkness. Some slept. Some couldn't sleep for anticipation of what might be ahead. Others were succumbing to the lethargy of seasickness and could not, for the moment, care whether they lived or died. Coquelle seems not to have been affected by the motion of the sea. In the security of a cabin with his mother, his aunt, and his younger brother, he was drinking in the novelty of it all.

It was no novelty for Captain Dall and the crew of the *Columbia*. For them it was routine. The *Columbia* was built in New York in 1850 and rushed immediately to the Pacific Northwest to serve the needs of the gold rush. It was the first ship ever to be placed in regular service on the route between San Francisco and Portland, and was exceptionally well constructed for the rough and stormy North Pacific. The hull and decks were both double planked, and the hull was braced with diagonal iron strapping.[9] From 1850 until it was sold in 1862 the ship made more or less trimonthly trips, stopping irregularly at Trinidad, Crescent City, and Port Orford. It had already made more than one hundred round trips and had become a fixture and a legend on the coast. And the ship was big business. According to *Lewis and Dryden's Marine History of the Pacific Northwest*, during its first five years of service the *Columbia* had already carried "80,000 tons of freight and 10,000 passengers. It had burned 16,000 tons of coal at an expense of $480,000, and its payroll during that period amounted to $500,000"—and those were the dollars of the 1850s. Captain Dall was doing well for the owners of the *Columbia*.[10]

The sun rose at 4:39 A.M., revealing a clear blue sky and a blue but choppy ocean.* Coquelle remembered that because of the "good day," the boat stayed close to shore. It had, however, been an uncomfortable night for the people crowded onto the forward deck and chilled by the ocean breeze, and of course it was miserable for those susceptible to seasickness, no matter where they were. The people on deck did have the advantage of being outside in the fresh air, the best precaution available against seasickness. Coquelle remembered that "the Indians had vomited much."[11]

"They brought us bread and butter," Coquelle said. Joel Palmer regretted that the ship didn't have better covering and provisions for the passengers, but for those with queasy stomachs a little bread and butter was probably about right. After daybreak some of the Indians began worrying that the ship wouldn't go into the Columbia River at all, but might take them someplace else. Coquelle told Elizabeth Jacobs that there was one man on board who had been to the Columbia River before and he was appointed to watch. "They ask if he knew where *malhúsh* (Columbia River) was. He said, 'Yes, I've been there, I know that river.' They told him stand right there in front." Coquelle added, "If the boat pass the mouth of Columbia River there

---

* U.S. Naval Observatory, op. cit. Sunday, 22 June 1856, for Astoria, Clatsop County, Oregon.

was going to be war right there on the boat.... They ask him, 'How far?' 'Oh not far, we pass Nehalem,' he says. The boat go close to land because good day."

The man who had been to the Columbia River before was named "Chimley." Coquelle told John Peabody Harrington, "At about 3 o'clock the 2nd day out Chimley came down, he was white-haired, and said: 'right there.' The boat swung way round and then headed in."[12] He told Elizabeth Jacobs essentially the same thing. Chimley had said, "'Right here, everybody look, right here, *malhúsh*.' Now boat turn, turn, go in *malhúsh* water. Now everybody glad. They had been scared they take somewhere else."

According to Joel Palmer, it was about 6:00 P.M. when they finally crossed the bar and entered the placid waters of the Columbia River. He noted in his diary, "The passage has been rather rough."[13] It was an exceptionally routine crossing for Captain Dall, not at all like one the previous November during a ferocious tropical storm. Dall and the *Columbia* had been chartered by the army to proceed from San Francisco to Vancouver Barracks, as part of the logistics for the Indian war in Washington Territory. As they were crossing the bar of the Columbia River a huge wave nearly capsized them and put out the fire of one of the boilers. Steam ran down, and the ship was nearly lost, but they somehow got across and brought the ship and passengers safely to Vancouver. On the return trip they met with another storm, and this time the second mate was swept overboard and both engines were disabled. The ship continued under sail to San Francisco, arriving after twenty-seven days with her owners unaware that there had been a problem.[14]

But this trip up the Columbia River was slow and quiet. Palmer said that they arrived at Portland about eleven o'clock the following morning, which would mean that they had taken about seventeen hours to go upriver from the bar. It is 110 miles, and so they evidently traveled at about five knots. There was plenty of time during this quiet leg of the journey for those who had succumbed to seasickness on the ocean to get over it. The *Columbia* had already carried more than 10,000 paying passengers between San Francisco and Portland, and on every trip there would have been a certain percentage that suffered from the *mal de mer* and survived. This trip was no exception.

Palmer immediately wrote a letter to George Manypenny, commissioner of Indian Affairs. "I have the honor to inform you that I have this day arrived here from Port Orford in the steamship Colum-

Exodus: Removal to the North

bia," he began. He projected that "additional means are and will be required to carry out the objects in view to the extent, probably, of thirty-five to forty thousand dollars within the ensuing sixty days." A considerable portion of the moneys "will be requisite to the erection of a saw mill and a flouring mill."[15] Among the very first things needed on the new reservation would be a sawmill to manufacture the lumber for the houses, barns, and outbuildings that would hopefully be built by the end of summer.

Portland at that time had a population of a little over one thousand. It was the undisputed metropolis of the Pacific Northwest, but the Indians didn't get into the town. They disembarked at a temporary bivouac where, Coquelle said, "they already put up a tent for us to stay over night. Just open place, no house, just that open place; big lake below Portland."[16] He told John Peabody Harrington that they ate there and stayed overnight, but that "water came into the camp about 2 ft. deep."[17] Coquelle offered no explanation about the water. Whether it was from a sudden rise in the Willamette due to a spring freshet, from the incoming tide, or local runoff from a quick summer rain, it does indicate an error in selection of the campsite.

Coquelle said, "Soon as we all get out they clean that boat, put water in, clean it up, go right back." He told Harrington that four men were selected to return to Port Orford with the *Columbia* to assure the Indians waiting there that "the trip was o.k." The men who went back were, according to Coquelle, "Chetco Charlie, Depot Charlie, Bill Strong and Coquel Charlie." Coquelle Charlie was Coquelle's uncle.[18] On the second trip from Port Orford there were "about 700."[19] The remainder, including Coquelle's father and his other wives, were coming by land, up the beach.

Coquelle said that Joel Palmer "get out there; he had to go home. His home was Dayton, Oregon." After staying overnight, "Next day another big boat came. They say, 'You folks get in the boat here.' They take half. Don't take long, boat come back; they take the rest of us. We go as far as Oregon City. I remember big falls there. Big camp there; big tents." They had boarded the *Jeanne Clark*. Only two years old, it was the first sternwheeler in the Northwest.[20] It was about a fifteen-mile run up to the falls of the Willamette, and Coquelle, with his mother, brother, and aunt, evidently were on the second trip.

Coquelle's narrative continues after their portage to the top of the falls: "Now a little tiny boat made several trips, take to Dayton, they fix a big camp." This time the Indians were riding in a barge towed by the *Hoosier*, a small side-wheeler.[21] It was the first steamer to operate above the Willamette Falls, and indeed it was a "little tiny boat." It was originally a ship's longboat, which had been lengthened and fitted with a pile-driver engine.[22] It ran for many years between Oregon City and Dayton, which was situated at the head of navigation on the Yamhill River about five miles from its confluence with the Willamette.

Joel Palmer's home was at Dayton, and it was there on his farm that he established the camp to assemble the Indians arriving by boat and by foot. Coquelle said they were told, "'Don't cook!' Pretty soon they bring big boards and make a table. They bring lots of bread, all kinds of meat, coffee, we eat." It was probably about a week after Coquelle got there that some seven hundred more people from Port Orford began arriving, having come up on the second trip of the *Columbia*. Coquelle said, "Now the boat come back with more. They had brought another load to Portland from Port Orford. Every day a whole lot more people come, come. That little boat make over a dozen trips to Oregon City."

Coquelle remembered that it must have been on the "2nd, 3rd of July all settled down there. Oh they kill lots of meat—I 'member that. Two or three white men cook, make bread. Oh lots of Indian people, lots! Big camp. Lots come on land." The Indians from the Willamette, the Upper Umpqua, and the Upper Rogue River valleys had come by land to Dayton, and their experience was much less pleasant than that of the people who had come by ship from Port Orford.* But now they were together at the temporary camp at Dayton.

Coquelle said, "Next night all were tired, slept good. When it was almost daylight boom! boom! Everybody raise. 'War!' they say, 'War!' Everybody run, get knives. . . . Everybody wild for while. We thought, 'going to kill us now.'" But soon there was an explanation: "Some men run in who talk Jargon. 'Skookum Sunday, July.'" Firing the cannon was merely the beginning of the Fourth of July celebration. "About ten o'clock that day we start the big July dinner," said Coquelle.

The forced removal from their homes to the Coast Reservation was the major turning point in the history of the people involved,

---

* For accounts of the removal by land up the central valleys of Oregon, see e.g., Curtis, 93–95; O'Donnell, 251–52; Beckham 1977, 139–40; Metcalfe to Palmer, 16 January 1856, Applegate 1988, 282–83.

and for Coquelle it became a fairly well rehearsed story. Several versions of his remembrance of it exist, and for him the story became the equivalent of an origin text. It documented the point of departure between an irretrievably lost way of life and a new, ominous beginning.[23]

"I don't know how long we stay at Dayton," Coquelle said. "One day a team of oxen come, white men roll up our blankets, take grub, take us to Grand Ronde." In Joel Palmer's words, "The old infirm and helpless" along with all property belonging to the Indians and rations of flour for twelve days were loaded onto wagons drawn by ox teams and taken the thirty miles up the Yamhill River from Dayton to Grand Ronde. Palmer had appointed a missionary/trapper named Courtney Walker as "conductor and Local Agent" to remove the coast bands encamped at Dayton to the Salmon River, and he appointed William Church as "assistant conductor." He believed that "sixteen ox teams, two yoked to each team" would be sufficient, but Church was later quoted as saying that they went to the Salmon River "on thirty-five wagons hauling the old and crippled, and their general merchandise, arriving at their destination on July 23, 1856."[24]

Coquelle told Elizabeth Jacobs that when they got to Grand Ronde "already people camped there and soldiers were there." In fact, by the time Coquelle arrived at Grand Ronde there were well over fifteen hundred Indians there from among the Willamette, the Upper Umpqua, and the Rogue River peoples.[25] He said, "Our people already there and Clackamas and Oregon City people—Molalle people. They had been moved first and there were soldiers watching them." Some of them had been there since April amid much disorganization, confusion, and suffering. By the time Coquelle's people arrived, however, many of the logistical problems had been worked out. He noted that "everything was ready. Just unroll your blanket and you all right—and we got all kind of blanket."

Because of the overcrowding at Grand Ronde, the coastal peoples were moved without much delay on over the Coast Range and down the Salmon River to its mouth. It was Palmer's hope that they would quickly get used to that area and want to stay. Coquelle had evidently ridden in one of the wagons. He said, "I wake up at Salmon River. Soldiers already there." He mentioned the mussels "they wanted," and said, "We stay there maybe a month." It was a "big camp."

Coquelle's father and his two other wives came in by foot with another 215 people from Port Orford at about that time.[26] Coquelle said, "My father come on land because he's chief." By way of explanation he added, "Lots of people didn't want to go on the boat." He told Harrington, "Many Indians were brought along the beach, bringing ten heads of cattle, they swam the cattle across all the rivers—no bridges at that time, and they killed one bossie every day to feed the Indians."[27] He had told Elizabeth Jacobs, "Every time they camp they kill one beef. That made enough so each person get one piece." If, on the average, the beef dressed out at 250 pounds, that would be about one pound of beef per person per day.

On the route up the beach there were supplements to the diet, especially mussels from the rocks. One teenage girl from the Euchre Creek band was with them. As an old woman she told Lottie Evanoff of stopping for a time at Yachats to collect mussels. She told about finding the tree burial of an Alsea Indian, but there were no living Alsea there. They had, according to Lottie, all died of the smallpox a few years earlier.[28]

While Coquelle and his people were at Salmon River, Joel Palmer received a letter from Washington, D.C. He had been fired from his job as superintendent of Indian Affairs in Oregon Territory. The position was a political appointment, as were all government jobs in those days, and Palmer had generated enemies from within all political factions. He had been very critical of the war, the army, and General Wool; he was thought to be too "easy" on the Indians; and he tended to appoint men to jobs irrespective of their political affiliations.[29]

Palmer had set for himself the almost impossible task of saving the Indian people of western Oregon from the violence of their white neighbors by extinguishing their title to the land and removing them to this 1.4-million-acre Coast Reservation. His objective was to do it as humanely as possible and to begin the job of teaching the younger generation the skills they would need to survive in the modern world. The Rogue River War, which he opposed, had actually provided the impetus that made a quick removal possible, and imperative.

The Democratic caucus recommended a loyal party man, an affable steamboat captain named Absalom Hedges, to replace Palmer as the new superintendent of Indian Affairs. Upon his appointment, Hedges had the good sense to contract almost immediately with the only person who had the integrity, ability, and interest in turning the uninhabited land of the Siletz Valley into a productive reservation—that is, Joel Palmer.

The contract with Joel Palmer and his brother Ephraim called for them "to plow and put in three hundred (300) acres of winter wheat, at twelve ($12) dollars per acre. . . . To make rails and fences for same with six-rail fences, staked and double ridered, for five ($5) dollars per one hundred rails and stakes." They were also to build the house for the agent: "To erect one log or Splitboard Dwelling house, with requisite Doors, Windows, Chimneys, &c, Sixteen by thirty (16 × 30) feet, two rooms for five hundred ($500) dollars." And they were "to erect one Blacksmith Shop, build Forge, put in Anvil block, Vise Bench and Doors for two hundred ($200) Dollars." They were to transport the blacksmith tools, set them up, and make five hundred bushels of charcoal at twenty (20c) per bushel. All this was to be completed in a workmanlike manner by February 6, 1857.[30] Those improvements were the beginnings of the Siletz Agency, which would remain in existence for the next sixty-five years.

Coquelle said that while they were at Salmon River the soldiers caught the fugitive Enos, the leader of the Washington birthday massacre of whites on the Rogue River. Enos is referred to as a "Canadian halfbreed" in pioneer accounts of the Rogue River War, but Thompson characterized him as "a French man who lived with an Indian woman and help Indians fight white people." "Half-breeds" were usually considered as "whites" by the Indians (and as Indians by the whites). Coquelle had heard the Tututni women talk about Enos, and added, "He kill lots of white people. He got lots of gold. Indians knew that. They know he wanted gold."[31]

Michael Riley was the first sheriff of Curry County in 1857. In his reminiscences he said that he went to Fort Vancouver by steamer (no doubt the *Columbia*) to bring Enos back to Port Orford for trial. Enos, he said, "was chained hand and foot," and after more than a month he was finally delivered to the makeshift county jail at Port Orford. Riley said that Mrs. Christina Geisel, who with her two daughters had been held hostage by Enos and other Indians, was the only witness against him, but she could not be found at the time of the trial. According to Riley's son, "the justice ordered Sheriff Riley to turn the prisoner loose. It was necessary to take him to the blacksmith shop to have the chains on his legs cut off." As Enos left the blacksmith shop, he was, according to Riley, "seized and taken away."

Riley said that the "next morning he was hanged on historical Battle Rock."[32]

Coquelle elaborated. He said, "now they got him, take him back to Port Orford. They hang him there. When they put the rope on, one Indian was there. When they put rope on, those men ask him, 'Do you want to say something?' 'No, what would I want to talk about?' 'You want to tell where you put the gold, you kill lots of white people?' 'Yes, I got lots of gold, but I won't tell you. That gold can stay right where I bury it.' That's the way he answered them and they hang him."[33]

Concerning their stay at the mouth of Salmon River, Coquelle said, "We stay there maybe a month. Now all wanted to get to Siletz." Joel Palmer had specified "to have the Coquills placed south of the Seletz River," and it was during some time in September that they made the move. Coquelle said, "That fall we come to Siletz, I walk over there close to river. I remember Chinook salmon spawn there, must be fall time."[34]

The contract that Joel Palmer and his brother Ephraim had entered into with the Office of Indian Affairs was dated September 20, 1856. That was probably very close to the time that Coquelle and his family were moving into the Siletz Valley and settling at Camas Prairie, the large meadow "south of the Siletz River" that Palmer had designated for the Coquille people. Coquelle would spend much of the next ninety years of his life within a few miles of that meadow.

They had moved into an almost uninhabited valley. Coquelle said, "People who belonged here were very few, one or two families only, scattered along Siletz River. They couldn't talk." Of course the native Siletz Indians couldn't speak any language that the people from southern Oregon could speak. Coquelle said that there was one man "named Siletzic John, he must belong here." "They said used to be lots of them here, all along the beach to Newport." Very few of the original Siletz people had survived the successive epidemic diseases that had ravished almost all of the peoples between Yachats and the Columbia River since even before their first contact with the whites. Presumably they had been infected by other Indians who contracted the diseases through earlier white contacts. Coquelle concluded, "Smallpox had killed them all."[35]

It has become axiomatic to condemn the selection of the Siletz River as the relocation site for the Indians of southern Oregon, but when Absalom Hedges, the newly appointed replacement for Joel Palmer, arrived from Oregon City to see it for himself he was pleasantly surprised. In his letter to the commissioner of November 7, 1856, he said, "The Siletz Valley exceeds my warmest expectations—The land is very rich, grass abundant, prairies beautiful—... It is fine country, admirably suited to the Indians, more secluded from the white settlements than the Grand Round [sic] Reservation and more easily reached with supplies." More easily reached with supplies, that is, "if the entrances of the Yaquonah and Siletz are found to be safe for vessels."[36] One of the major problems that first winter was the discovery that Siletz Bay was not safe for vessels.

Hedges said that he contemplated that the Indians from west of the Cascade Mountains, except the Willamette Valley tribes, would be placed "upon the Coast Reservations, principally in the Siletz Valley and around Yaquohah Bay." That, of course, had been Joel Palmer's plan from the beginning; Hedges had merely inherited the final implementation of it. Palmer, and Hedges after him, assumed that the Indians would maintain their social structures and live in settlements not unlike their traditional homes. That was in fact the pattern that emerged at Siletz. Coquelle said, "Soon as we get here—Lower Farm—they build sweathouse right away. Every group built a sweathouse."[37]

The "groups," as Coquelle termed them, tended to find the places most like those they had been used to in their old homes. The Lower Coquille peoples, for example, settled first along the tide flats of Yaquina Bay—a bay even richer in food than their former home at the mouth of the Coquille River. The Upper Coquille peoples settled mostly at Lower Farm, two or three miles above the head of tide on the Siletz. Building the sweathouse was their first action aimed at maintaining their old way of life in this new land.

There were about one hundred people of the Upper Coquille Athabaskans settling in at Lower Farm. "The whole tribe," Coquelle said. Most of the other peoples from between the California line and the Coquille River were also settling in. Coquelle summed it up, saying, "Everybody was there."[38] In later years he admitted that he didn't know the names of many of his people. "People all died before I learned many names," he said.[39]

However, he did come to know a few of the old-timers who had come to Siletz from the Upper Coquille, and over the ensuing years they would exert an immense influence on his character. Among them were, of course, his father, Chief Washington; his father's half-brother Coquelle Charlie, and his father's cousin Chief Jackson. There was Coquelle's maternal uncle Old Hunter, for whom he appears to have had the utmost respect and who died many years later at Coquelle's house; there was the group's only Indian doctor, Dr. Alec, another relative; there was Jim David, who sang for the Indian dances and most of whose songs Coquelle learned; and there was an old man named *Wéste*, who told most of the stories Coquelle learned in the sweathouse and whose style Coquelle very likely adopted. There were certainly others, but those are the ones that he mentioned frequently. We can assume that it was from them he picked up the essential elements of the Upper Coquille Athabaskan culture and so himself became a cultured man in the Siletz Valley.

The Siletz River valley actually has many good features, among them the ones that Hedges describes. It heads near the crest of the Coast Range, and on the central Oregon coast that range is not nearly as rugged and inaccessible as it is further south at the heads of the Coos and Coquille Rivers. The river itself was characterized by John Peabody Harrington as "the crookedest river in the world, exceeding in its meandering that of the famed Meander of Asia Minor."[40] He found that the Tillamook name of the Siletz River meant "I coil it," as one would coil a rope.[41]

The Siletz Valley is in the shape of a big U, with about 5,000 acres of meadowland more or less evenly distributed in three areas. Near the bottom of the U is a large meadow at which the agency headquarters and the home of the resident agent were established. This area came to be known as "Agency Farm" and is the site of the present town of Siletz. About six miles northeast of Agency Farm on the upstream, or right-hand leg of the U, is another large meadow that came to be known as "Upper Farm." On the downstream, or left-hand leg of the U, about four miles due north of Agency Farm, is Camas Prairie and a series of meadows that became known as Lower Farm. Chief Washington and his people were settled near there.[42]

The contract with Palmer would help satisfy some of the long-term problems of establishing two thousand people on a new land. With winter coming on, however, there were more immediate concerns. Food and shelter were prime among them. The two thousand people had been transported to the vacant Siletz with no material possessions beyond what they had managed to carry with them. They had left behind their houses, their baskets, their hunting and fishing gear, their valuable canoes, and even the fish drying on the racks. The U.S. government had created for itself a community of two thousand people who were almost totally dependent. The embarrassment of failure, and the judgment of history upon them if they failed, weighed heavily on those most immediately responsible, and for the moment the responsibility rested with the new superintendent of Indian Affairs, Absalom Hedges, and upon the newly appointed agent for the Coast Reservation, Robert Metcalfe.

At the same time that Hedges entered into the contract with Palmer, he entered into one with Berryman Jennings to transport a cargo of flour to Yaquina Bay. It was delivered on October 28 in good shape. The little schooner *Calumet*, which Jennings had purchased for $5,000 specifically for this contract, had run into the first tropical storm of the season, and the crew had to jettison a part of the cargo, including ten kegs of badly needed nails, but they did get in with the flour.

In a letter dated November 7, 1856, Hedges said, "I think the mouth of the Siletz can also be entered—if so, another great advantage will be gained, as the Indians can transport provisions up the Siletz River in canoes."[43] He and Metcalfe were both confident that Siletz Bay would work as a port, and they encouraged Captain Jennings to deliver the second load of flour there. When Agent Metcalfe arrived at the mouth of the Siletz to meet the *Calumet*, she was, he said, "lying on the beach." In his letter to Hedges of December 12, 1856, he said that her cargo had been taken off and stacked above high tide "where they supposed it would be safe." He continued, "I put four men to work immediately to erect a log cabin for the cargo, but before they were ready to remove the flour, there came a heavy blow from the west and destroyed almost the entire cargo. . . . The schooner was blown over the bar into the bay carrying away her masts—all of her canvass was lost with the flour and nothing but the hull of the schooner remains."[44]

The small amount of flour that did arrive at Siletz was quickly distributed to the chiefs and headmen. Even with the culture as acquisitive as it tended to be, there was a strong sense of noblesse oblige. Coquelle said that everybody was treated the same, "except for poor people. You had to help them, notice them: what they are doing and what they need." His father had gone on horseback to the agency and received one 100-pound sack of flour. "He opened it and issued it around to every house." Coquelle added that it was done "long time ago in the same way."[45]

More flour was not forthcoming. To compound the problems, Captain William Tichenor of Port Orford delivered eighty-five more Indians by ship from Port Orford to Oregon City on about November 11. Hedges said, "It is found impossible to retain them in Port Orford neighborhood and avoid constant trouble."[46] In later years the story of the removal by ship from Port Orford includes the description of a long voyage through stormy seas.* As that was demonstrably not the case with the first two shiploads during the summer, that portion of the story could possibly have originated with passengers who were on the trip in November.

The pressures were too great on Hedges. He submitted his resignation as commissioner of Indian Affairs for the Oregon Territory, claiming illness as his reason. The prospects for the survival of the Indians at Siletz through this first winter were bleak enough to make anyone ill.

Although Hedges resigned under the immense pressure and impossible conditions of that first winter of the Coast Reservation, Robert Metcalfe stuck with it. He moved into the newly constructed agent's residence, "purchased" a young Coquille woman as a wife, and began the business of enriching himself on bribes and kickbacks from government contracts. Coquelle said, "Agent took Indian women, soldiers (too). Were no white women in here at all."[47] He told Harrington that "Metcalf married a Coquel girl," but that he didn't know her name.[48] He added to Elizabeth Jacobs that the "agent treat her good. Give his wife's folks lots government blankets and government grub." Metcalfe was, in effect, paying the culturally appropriate bride price, but at government expense.

The moral example given by the whites to the Indians at the reservation was the subject of concern and discussion at the Oregon

---

* See accounts in Beckham 1977 and Schwartz 1997. These accounts appear to have derived from a widely reprinted story that was originally written in the sixth grade by George Louis Thompson, grandson of Coquelle Thompson, Sr., from information dictated to him by his father, Coquelle Thompson, Jr. The Siletz school superintendent, Tom Caughey, was so impressed with the story that he gave a revised copy to the *Lincoln County Leader*, which printed it on March 2, 1950. It was subsequently reprinted in the other Lincoln County newspapers, and in Hays 1976, 34–35.

and Washington Territorial Conference of the Methodist Episcopal Church, held the summer of 1857 in Corvallis. Although the activities of Robert Metcalfe might have been on the mind of the conferees, his name wasn't mentioned in a letter written on their behalf to the commissioner of Indian Affairs. In it the secretary, William Roberts, said that the conference "respectfully suggest that too Careful regard cannot be had to the moral and religious characters of the persons Selected to carry out the noble purposes of the general government in regard to the Indians." The conference was afraid that the Indians would turn away "in Complete disgust from the proffered benefits of Civilization and Christianity." The problem, as seen by the conference, was that the Indians "are permitted to see infidelity, profanity, prostitution, intemperance, Sabbath breaking, fraud & abuse, without check or disapproval."[49] All of which was probably true.

Meanwhile, Chief Washington and his people were settling on Camas Prairie, not far from the mouth of Euchre Creek. Chief Washington didn't have his elk dogs here, or his gun, and measles or smallpox is said to have come during that first winter with devastating effect. The wonder is that any of them survived to see the first spring on the Siletz.

Coquelle said of the sickness, "They were afraid to call it by name. They spoke of 'That kind of sickness.' One little spot and a person would die." His imagery of the epidemic is reminiscent of imagery from the Black Death of the Middle Ages: "It was just like cutting brush," he said. "Men, woman, children—all go. A few got better, lived through it. I've seen old people with little marks all over their face, from small pox. No one could cure for that kind of sickness. They were afraid, you know. Terribly." The best hope of prevention, according to Coquelle, was "if you drank nicotine from pipe stem, mixed with water, small pox will pass you by, just like a person would." He said, "People fixed crow's blood or nicotine water for themselves. No magic—just drunk. They tried everything." But some did not get sick. "Only my father never got it," Coquelle said. "He had to go between and help take care of people."[50]

When spring arrived, it brought another serious disappointment. There was no spring run of salmon on the Siletz as there had been on the Coquille. Later in the summer there was a good run of eels, but getting by until then challenged the abilities of the chiefs and headmen, and fortunate were those groups blessed with good leadership.

It appears that the Coquilles, with Chief Washington, Jackson, and a few others, had that good fortune. Their energy that summer of 1857 went into preparation for permanent survival in this valley, and as deprived as they were they went into it with a surprising degree of optimism.

Coquelle said that it was during that second year that the agent moved in. "And soldiers up on (the) hill—they built big log house. They drill them right there. They look nice when they drill."[51] It is possible that Coquelle, like many another boy his age, was impressed by the uniforms and precision drill of the soldiers. And like many another boy, those impressions may have influenced him in subtle ways throughout his life. He spent fifty years as a tribal policeman and, in his later years at least, "wore 'Army clothes' most of the time."[52]

The Siletz blockhouse quickly became a focus of government power and government largesse. Coquelle said, "My sister go there (to) get bread." This may be the sister who died at Lower Farm during those first years, when so many died. But there was also some material progress. Coquelle said, "Pretty soon, next year, come oxen, five or six teams for plowing (a) nice open place. White people do that, tell Indians, 'You got to work.'"[53]

Coquelle was ten or eleven years old when, on November 6, 1858, C. H. Mott, an inspector with the Department of the Interior, held a council with the "chief men of the Coast tribes, with a view to ascertain their wishes and expectations concerning the treaty." Ah-ches-see of the Euchre Creek band stated his expectations quite clearly. He said that he had been to Kings Valley and seen how rich the whites were. "I know that by working we can have everything like they do," he said. But he knew that it wouldn't be possible without capital investment. "When we get mills," he said, "we will be white people."

Ty-gon-ee-shee, the Port Orford chief, was more pessimistic. He told Mott, "General Palmer promised that if we would sell our lands, and come here we should have houses and live like white people. We come and have been very poor ever since. I am not the chief I was, but more like an old woman." Ty-gon-ee-shee probably reflected the feeling of many of the former chiefs and headmen, as it became clear that they would from now on be dependent upon someone other than themselves for much of their sustenance. Those men, who before had

Exodus: Removal to the North

made the decisions upon which the survival of their people depended, felt that they had been emasculated.

Some of the groups, however, retained strong leadership and seem to have been more able to adapt to the new conditions. Chief Jackson of the Coquilles said, "Palmer asked us to sell our land, and we did so. I am willing to give it up, but I am tired waiting for the pay he promised." After complaining about the fact that the Indians with ratified treaties got more clothing than the Coquilles, he concluded by saying, "The land is good here and I am satisfied with it. I am a Chief and don't work myself, but will make my people work, and will soon be like the whites. Tell the President we will always be friendly towards the whites, and we hope he will make Palmer's talk good, by building us a mill, and giving us houses to live in. My talk is ended."

Mott concluded his report by noting that Agent Metcalfe has had "much trouble in the management of the Indians upon this Reservation." The cause, Mott said, was "that some receive annuities and others do not. If these Indians are to be kept together," he said, "the treaty with the Coast Tribes should be ratified and they put upon an equal footing with the Rogue Rivers."[54]

The plight of the "nontreaty" Indians, such as the Coquilles, who did not receive clothing (as the "treaty" Indians, such as the Rogue Rivers, did) is made quite personal by Coquelle's remembrance. Elizabeth Jacobs said that he "remembers going in knee deep snow for wood when he was about ten. He was barefoot. There was no money to buy shoes."[55] And people continued to die. Coquelle's younger brother, Latenosa, died when he was about ten years old, probably around 1860, and it was perhaps two years later when his mother, Beads-in-Her-Hair, passed on.[56] Those who remained did the best they could.

A few whites showed up from time to time, casually scouting out the resources of the Coast Reservation. An article in the *Oregon Weekly*, May 21, 1859, announced that a Captain Munson and C. B. Hand of Corvallis had just returned after about five weeks at the coast. "They found game, quite plenty, and succeeded in killing several deer, one bear, one elk." They represented the Alsea Valley as being "beautiful and fertile," and "they say the Indians treated them very friendly, assisting them in the transportation of their provisions and ammunition up and down the Alsea and Acquina [Yaquina] Bays." The whites were hunting for pleasure. For the Indians on the reservation it was a matter of survival.

Coquelle told of a hunting trip during those first years. He said, "My father was hungry and Jackson was hungry: 'I'm tired of that wheat,' they said. They went to see Old Hunter." Old Hunter (Coquelle's uncle by marriage) might have been the only one of their people who had a gun and knew how to use it expertly at that time. It was very probably a single-shot, muzzle-loading .45 caliber obsolete army rifle. Coquelle, in his narrative, has Old Hunter say, "What can I do for you folks." "Oh, you have to take us hunting, we're hungry." Old Hunter laughed and said, "Well, if you folks want to go hunting, we'll go tomorrow." Later he asked jokingly, "Why don't you old fellows eat wheat?" "Oh we don't care for that. We're *hungry*."

Three men went with Old Hunter, whose muzzle-loading flintlock was the only gun. Chief Washington, Chief Jackson, and Jackson's twenty-year-old unmarried son (probably Dick) made up the party. "They took a bit of wheat and went," Coquelle said. At home the wheat berries could be pounded and rubbed in a mortar by hand, or they could be boiled. On the trail they could be chewed and eaten, and after they swelled in the stomach, they provided a sense of satiety. They are not, however, the stuff of steady diet. These people needed meat.

Coquelle said, "They went toward *Yú·gi* Mountain." *Yú·gi* was the self-designation of the people from Euchre Creek in Curry County. The whites evidently first pronounced it "Ukah Creek," which soon became "Euchre" (probably from the popular card game of the time). The *Yú·gi* people settled initially on Lower Farm at Siletz, and the creek that came in from the east, across the river from the place where Chief Washington and his people had settled, became known as *Yú·gi* (or Euchre) Creek. One of the tributaries of the Euchre Creek at Siletz is called Savage Creek. According to McArthur's *Oregon Geographic Names*, Savage Creek was the original name given by the whites to the Euchre Creek of Curry County. This is just one interesting and convoluted example of the extent to which southern Oregon was moved north with the Indians.

About four miles up into the woods to the west of Euchre Creek is Euchre Mountain, 2,446 feet high. That was the general direction that Old Hunter took when he found elk tracks "going to Cedar Creek." Cedar Creek heads on Euchre Mountain, and Old Hunter knew then where the elk were. He went back to where the rest of the party was preparing camp, saying, "Now you old folks listen! Elk always whistle early in the morning, about three o'clock." Coquelle, with his penchant for detail, said, "He didn't smoke from the old people, but used his own pipe. He cleaned his gun and studied how he was going to get the elk."

Old Hunter didn't sleep, but, according to Coquelle, "sat up and smoked, waiting for daylight." As soon as he could see, "He started up the hill. Halfway up he looked around. He had come into about a ten-acre open place right on top of *Yú·gi* (Euchre) Mountain. There was no brush—just fine grass." There he came upon a herd of elk quite unconcerned with humans on this knoll some 2,400 feet above the Siletz River. Coquelle continues, "He saw a cow elk get up. He shot it. Another got up; he shot it. Another and another. How quickly he shot, loaded and shot. He shot four times—four elks. He was looking for that man elk. Another cow got up—he shot it. That made five cow elks. At last that man elk got up over in the corner. He shot him."

It would have been a poor story if the pattern number five had not been allowed to appear, and Coquelle used it to good effect in this case. It is also very possible that Old Hunter himself was so imbued with that cultural pattern number that he subconsciously needed to kill five cow elk before he could get the "big man elk." There was a certain symmetry involved, which oral tradition seemed to require.

Back up on the top of Euchre Mountain the four men began to take care of the elk. Coquelle said that as soon as they'd get to an elk, "they slit his throat and caught the blood. Hands full of blood gushed out—they drank it." Remembering from his own hunting experiences, Coquelle added, "It was kind of greasy." They would drink a handful or two and "that was enough for them," he said.[57] Then, they "cut open the bellies so the meat wouldn't spoil. Those old men couldn't cut all the meat by themselves. They worked all day." They put up a drying rack and sent Jackson's son back down to the river "to tell people to come. He took two or three hearts." Then the people came, "women and children—lots of people came." Coquelle summarized by saying simply, "He knew how to hunt, that old man."[58]

From Coquelle's remembrances and other sources it appears that quite a few of the Indians had guns. Guns, however, were used for more than subsistence hunting. The thrusting together in close proximity of so many tribal groups could not help but bring with it friction and a continuing low level of violence. Coquelle told Elizabeth Jacobs that the agent said nothing about that kind of violence. "He furnished bullets and powder and let the Indians kill each other." He later told John Peabody Harrington that during Metcalfe's time as agent, the Indians at Siletz "were fighting each other, and he issued powder and bullets to the Sixes, Joshua and Yugi peoples here." He added, "This was when I was a boy at Camas Prairie."[59]

Robert Metcalfe tendered his resignation on September 30, 1859, after four years as the agent at Siletz. According to Francis Fuller Victor's account in her influential *Early Indian Wars of Oregon*, Metcalfe had accumulated $40,000 by that time.[60] It is said that he took it with him a few months later upon the outbreak of the Civil War when he was offered a commission in the Confederate army.

4

Survival

During and after the Civil War

On Valentine's Day 1859, the Oregon Territory was admitted to the Union as a free state. The federal elections the following year divided the country into North and South over the issue of slavery, and the resulting Civil War brought administrative changes to the Coast Reservation. The Indians struggled to survive and continued, insofar as they could, to live according to their traditional values and practices.

At Siletz, agent Robert Metcalfe was not the only Indian Service employee who was a Southern sympathizer. The newly appointed subagent for the Alsea Subagency located at Yachats, Joshua B. Sykes, was another. In November 1860, Sykes had completed moving the Coos and Lower Umpqua Indians from the mouth of the Umpqua River to Yachats, but upon secession of the Southern states over the next few months, he was given a commission "as Commissary in a certain regiment of the rebel Army." After he left, irregularities were found in his accounts for 1860, and the "balance due" was to be "placed in the hands of the District Attorney for collection."[1] Sykes's boss was the new agent at Siletz, David Newcomb, and he too was a Southerner. It was alleged that he sold "20 U.S. muskets & 20 U.S. Colt revolvers" to the Indians. It was evidently feared by some that the secessionists were arming the Indians to rise against the Union and to fight for the Confederacy.[2]

Despite the Civil War tensions, the army and the Indian Service worked together to keep the Indians in line and on the reservation. There was usually a detachment of twenty-two men from Fort Hoskins stationed at the Siletz blockhouse for that purpose. Corporal Royal A. Bensell was detailed to Siletz from duty at Grand Ronde in February 1864. His diary entries give a glimpse of Siletz at that time through the eyes of an intelligent and observant soldier.

The day he arrived, February 12, he said, "Living here is good, duty light. The scenery in the vicinity is indeed grand." He noted that there were "any amount of Squaws, young & old," and that he could not deny the existence of "Soldiers concubines."[3] The following Sunday, he sat on the top of the blockhouse and watched a large number of Indians playing a game of "Coho," a rough form of shinny.

Coquelle didn't talk much about shinny, and it may be that the Upper Coquille didn't take the game as seriously as did some of the other tribes. It would be surprising, however, if an athletic young man like Coquelle had not played. Corporal Bensell watched the games almost every Sunday, and on the 28th he saw a big game played between the "Toot-tootneys versus the Salt Chucks." Sundays were also distinguished from other days by "horse racing, foot racing, shooting, wrestling, fighting, gambling and dancing," according to a correspondent to the *Oregonian* who evidently disapproved of such uses of the Sabbath.[4]

Gambling is a recreation that Coquelle seems to have had knowledge of because he described it in some detail. The gambling was done in a house about three miles upstream from the agency. The house would be ready when the gamblers arrived. "No food," Coquelle said. "They put money at each end. They might play all night and nobody win the game. They'll promise to play two nights. The next day a big crowd comes in to watch and help sing. Maybe 40 or 50 people at a big game." A player takes a bundle of sticks, one marked, and holds them behind his back while shuffling them. The other player has to guess which hand the marked stick is in. "If I don't win I have to give up, let somebody else play," Coquelle said. "Big sing—one man drums on a basket drum."[5]

Boys were taught to gamble from about the age of thirteen. "Since a boy has never touched a woman, he will be lucky finding the stick," Coquelle said. "As soon as a boy has pubic hair, he's considered a man. They figured they couldn't use him any more. He's spoiled now because he might have a woman." Married men had to train to gamble. "We all go to the sweathouse together every night," Coquelle said. When they swam afterward while training, "They never talk; it would spoil their game."[6] Like gamblers everywhere, these men adhered to certain ritualized behavior to enhance their luck.

A sawmill owner named Benjamin Simpson was the agent during those Civil War years and afterward. He obtained a reputation from his detractors for flogging and incarceration, sometimes for trivial offenses.[7] Corporal Bensell was at the Siletz blockhouse from February 12 until October 5, 1864 (except for twenty-one days while he was gone to Coos Bay), and made daily detailed entries in his diary. The only flogging that he noted during that time was on August 19. Two Indians named Frank and Little Charley had taken off from confinement but returned the next day. Bensell's diary entry reads, "Kaiser, the Guard who let them escape, gave each 15 on the Bare Back. Hard sight."[8] A hard sight indeed, but probably not as frequent as other writers would make it seem.

The Indians during those years were held on the reservation almost as prisoners of war, even though the war in which some of them had been involved had been over for eight years. They were usually punished when caught after leaving the reservation, as Bensell's March 2, 1864, diary entry reveals: "Miller came in with the Indians, 3 of whom go in the Guard House. Most of these Indians have money, having worked 'outside.'" Agent Simpson, he said, "has taken some $80 in cash from the Indians. Depend upon, this will be the last the 'poor savage' sees of his 'chickamum [money].'"[9]

There was one thing that Agent Benjamin Simpson was able to do perhaps better than any of his successors. He was a sawmill man, and he kept a close eye on the operation and maintenance of the mill. Unfortunately, the stream used to power the sawmill at Siletz was so small that it almost completely dried up during the late summers. "The water in the mill race has been insufficient to enable us to do anything with the sawmill," Simpson said in his second annual report, September 12, 1864. "It has also become so dry as to require some repairs before it can be put into operation." By contrast, the sawmill at Grand Ronde, where Simpson was also agent during most of 1864, was in good repair and quite productive. During the time that he was in charge, the Grand Ronde sawmill "sawed out fifty-nine thousand one hundred and twenty-two feet of lumber," according to his report.[10] He shut it down during the dry season to build a better dam. This was an enterprise that Simpson understood.

There is some irony in the fact that even while the Civil War was being fought with such intensity over the issue of Negro slavery, there were Indians at the Coast Reservation and elsewhere for whom a quite different kind of slavery was a normal thing. Coquelle talked about it from time to time. He said, "A chief could enslave a person who didn't behave. He might sell him off as slave. A chief could sell a young man for three or four hundred dollars." He said that some "might sell his own younger brother."

His father, he said, bought two or three slaves: one from Siletz, one from Yakima. "Women were bought as slaves too," he said. "They dug roots, worked, helped the women in the household." He told Elizabeth Jacobs about the two women slaves that his father had bought. "He didn't fight anywhere, he bought them," Coquelle said. Three or four months later he sold them to the Umpqua chief, who in turn "took them to Old Fred, Corvallis Kalapuya chief." Eventually, after being bought and sold several more times, "they went to Topenish, then the Klickitat people bought them—they married there." It was, according to Coquelle, possible to marry a slave. "A slave-wife was treated like any other wife," he said, then continued: "The last we heard was when those two women wanted to know if my father were living yet. My father treated them well. He didn't hurt them or abuse them at all."[11]

Coquelle was acquainted with a younger boy named Abraham (Abram) Lincoln whose mother, originally from the Rogue River, had been purchased by "Coquille people who sold her to some Yakima people."[12] The Thirteenth Amendment to the Constitution (December 18, 1865) had the surprising effect of freeing an unknown number of Indians being held as slaves by other Indians in the Pacific Northwest. This boy, son of a slave woman, had evidently been named Abraham Lincoln in honor of the Great Emancipator. The boy was present at the Siletz school in the spring of 1866 when it was visited by Mr. Richard Williams, who later wrote an article about it for the *Corvallis Gazette* (July 28, 1866). At that time, the school had only "twelve or thirteen orphan Indian boys and girls," according to Williams. "All orphans, picked up from the various tribes, the Indian parents refusing to let their own children attend the school." Williams was impressed that young Abraham Lincoln "wrote his name down in good plain English."

In addition to the social institutions such as slavery that the Indians brought with them to the reservation, certain economic realities came with them as well. Among the unwanted economic realities during the first ten years or so was the reality of "hungry time," which comes in early spring after the winter food supply has run out and before the spring and summer foods are ready. Government rations should have ameliorated conditions, but hungry time on the Coast Reservation was probably more severe than it had been back home on the Coquille. Royal A. Bensell remarked in his diary for March 26, 1864, "Some Indians steel a few potatoes from the Agency roothouses last night. Poor Devils are Starving." Two days later he noted that the soldiers had killed a beef for their own use and the Indian women had salvaged all of the offal for food.[13]

One thing the Indians would have liked very much was more guns. As Sixes George told Superintendent of Indian Affairs William H. Rector, "If I was allowed a gun again I could kill some elk." At the same meeting the chief from Euchre Creek, Ah-ches-see, echoed the sentiment: "I want a gun. If I had a gun I could kill some elk." He then added, "I want something done with the mills. I have never received any good from them. My people want camp kettles, and other things to cook in. We want to live like white people and we look to you for help. I hope that you will let me have a gun."[14]

Another thing they wanted was carts and horses. The men, of course, would not pack anything—that was women's work. William, chief of the Chetco, said, "We should have one wagon and two yoke of cattle for each tribe. Our women are packed like mules. They haul all the potatoes and pack all the wood. They packed most of the things the ship brought from the Depot to the agency and get one cup of flour for a days work." Ah-ches-see agreed. "We want carts to haul our potatoes and wood in. Our women pack everything now." There was a distinct division of labor based on gender: men hunted; women packed the provisions. When the garrison at Fort Hoskins was preparing for a ball in February 1864, it requisitioned "3 mule loads of oysters" for the occasion. Corporal Bensell wrote in his diary, "2 little squaws come in, packed with Oysters. I weighed a bag, contained 91 lbs. They carry this weight 8 miles for 'ick dolla [one dollar].'"[15] The oysters came from Oysterville, a settlement on the upper part of Yaquina Bay where the native oysters grew prolifically. They had not gone extinct from the effect of catastrophic forest fires, as had occurred at Coos Bay some twenty years earlier. The Yaquina Bay oysters would, however, be extinct within a few years from overharvesting for the market in San Francisco, thus depriving the Indians on the reservation of another source of food. Some of the Indian women worked in the commercial oyster harvest, earning up to $1.25 per day "culling" oysters, while they lasted.[16]

If the reservation was ever to become self-sufficient it would have to raise cereal grain. It was by now apparent that wheat was not a crop that would do well in the coastal climate of the Siletz Valley. Oats, however, sometimes produced remarkably good crops. George Megginson, the government farmer at Lower Farm, was doing quite well with them. Ah-ches-see said, "I hope Mr. Megensin will not leave us. We could not live without him." But oats were not an attractive food to most of the older Indians.

In Samuel Johnson's *Dictionary* of 1755 there is a much quoted definition of oats: "A grain, which in England is generally given to horses, but in Scotland supports the people." Oats went a long way toward supporting the people at Siletz, amid many complaints. Sixes George said, "Palmer told me that I would be a white man in two years. I have been here five years and am not a white man yet. I don't know but I will soon be a horse as I am eating oats." He later admitted, "I can eat oats, but don't like them."[17]

Coquelle Thompson was coming into his teens during those years, and he ate many oats as he was growing up. One might suppose that he would learn to dislike them, but in an interview his daughter Sina was asked what was his favorite food. Without hesitation she replied, "Oatmeal mush. With sugar." Coquelle's taste for oats, a despised food among the older generation at Siletz, is only one of the many ways in which his character defied the stereotype. He was his own man.

Coquelle was growing up to be a handsome, athletic, and intelligent youth. He was by then an excellent swimmer, and he swam in the Siletz River during summers, well into his seventies. By now he knew all the stories and the songs of the older men, and he could tell them and he could sing them. He had already learned the skills of hunting and fishing, skills he enjoyed and kept throughout his life. He could dance and sing and "make sounds like a bird." He could even make the sounds of the animals in the myths and the folk tales.[18]

He also probably was developing an eye for the girls. He said, "If I know I like a woman, when I see her, I sing. Every time I see her

I sing, in my *heart*—not out loud." Coquelle had learned from the Rogue River people that if he had a dog, that dog might go a long way to visit a female dog. "If a person could learn that dog's song and sing it when he sees a girl, she will like him." He said that if the girl sits in the house, he could try to get her out by singing, "I wish the fleas would bite you, so you cannot sleep and you'll come out of doors." He said that he would sing that in his heart, "and pretty soon the fleas bite her and she goes outside." Coquelle then could tell her, "I made you come out."[19]

When he was sixteen or seventeen, Coquelle went to an Indian round dance with the Upper Rogue River girl who had taught him that song about the fleas.[20] He told Elizabeth Jacobs, "We get stuck on each other. I take her to my father's home. He didn't say nothing."[21] We know from Coquelle's statements that if his father "didn't say yes; he didn't say no, that meant 'go ahead.'" The result in this case was a turning point in Coquelle's life: his first marriage.

Her name was Annetti, or Annet, or Nettie, and she was one of the Athabaskan Applegate Indians, born at the village of *La'kho·ve'* near the mouth of Applegate Creek, on the Upper Rogue River.[22]* Her father's name was Nindanano, which in the Jargon was translated as "Illahee Muck-a-muck," Dirt Eater.[23] He was given that name, according to Annetti, because "he was mean, like a grizzly bear."[24] He fought during the Rogue River War and was killed along with two-thirds of the men of the tribe as they held out to the last, retreating down the Rogue River through the wilderness toward the coast. Many of their women and children died; among them was Annetti's mother. Their leader, Chief John, would not give up, and the Applegate people were the last to turn themselves in to the U.S. Army.

Annetti was "a good sized girl" at that time, and was probably one of the ninety children who came into Port Orford on July 2, 1856, along with Chief John and his surviving thirty-five men and ninety women, all that was left of the Applegate people.[25] There was no room for them on the second trip of the steamship *Columbia*, and so on July 9 Major Reynolds of the Third Artillery was detailed to escort them the 125 miles up the coast to the reservation.[26]

---

* The neighboring Galice Creek Indians' name for the Applegate Creek Indians was "*da'koh* or *dá'kohbe' dade*" (Miller and Seaburg 1990, 587). Location of the site is near the present city of Grants Pass.

Annetti came of age at Upper Farm, where most of the Upper Rogue River peoples were settled. She had the three vertical tattoo marks on her chin, traditional among the Athabaskan peoples of southern Oregon. Coquelle always considered those tattoo marks to be attractive, and they were so considered by the Athabaskan people. "If you aren't tatooed you don't look good," was the explanation that Lucy Metcalf, who was about Annetti's age, gave to the anthropologist Cora Du Bois.[27] Annetti, in any case, was a strong, assertive, and intelligent young woman, and she and Coquelle were now "stuck on each other."

The authority of the chiefs was breaking down. Coquelle had broken with tradition in choosing as his wife a girl he had gotten "stuck on," rather than accepting a wife chosen by his parents. He said, "My father did not pick out my wife because we have white law by then." He said that his father didn't ask, "Did you buy this woman." If he *had* asked, "I was going to tell him, '*You* have to buy her.' But he didn't open his mouth."

A traditional marriage included a bride price, but Chief Washington may not have approved of this marriage. Annetti was evidently a little older than Coquelle, and she had been married to a man named Evans Bill and had a baby, which died.* For whatever reason, Chief Washington decided to stay out of his son's current love affair; others in the family still felt the weight of tradition. Coquelle's uncle, Coquelle Charlie, stepped forward and paid the bride price in full. "My uncle, pay one horse, one gun," said Coquelle. Uncle Charlie was a half-brother of Coquelle's father.

Coquelle also chose a co-wife for Annetti, or perhaps Annetti chose her. The co-wife was Annetti's first cousin and friend. "They get along good together," Coquelle said. "White people try to make us have only one wife but couldn't make it stick. People in every tribe had two or three wives." He said that he had "two Applegate wives. Not sisters—not one father, just first cousins. I was 16, 17, 18—something like that. I marry young, can't behave."[28] One time he told Elizabeth Jacobs that co-wives never quarreled, were never jealous, "all

---

* See NA/ACF, allotment S-30, testimony of Spencer Scott, and of David John, 5 December 1933. There is conflicting testimony as to the children of Annetti, but it appears that there were two: the girl, Sina, daughter of Coquelle and Annetti, and a boy who died young, by Evans Bill.

loved each other." But at another time he told her, "If two wives fought, the husband had to separate them. He wouldn't punish either, but would tell them, 'go ahead and cook, keep busy. I'm right here.'"[29]

There is no indication from Coquelle's narratives how long the relationship with the second wife lasted, or what her name was, but the relationship with Annetti probably lasted about fifteen years. They had one daughter, Sina, born in 1872. A girl named Eva Thompson, evidently born in 1874, is listed as "daughter" in the Coquelle Thompson family on the Siletz census for 1888 and for 1889. It is tempting to suppose that she was a daughter from the Applegate co-wife, but there is no evidence to support it. Who she was and what happened to her remains a mystery.

Coquelle never said whether or not he continued to sleep in the sweathouse after he and Annetti were married. It is very likely that he did, at least for a while. From the time he was ten or twelve years old he had been hunting with the adults, and it was at about the same age that the boys began listening with particular interest to the stories that were told in the sweathouse at night. According to Coquelle, the men lay with their feet toward the fire and their heads toward the walls, the storyteller also lying down. When someone began a story, someone else would repeat the words. Anyone could answer, but if no one did, "he has to shut up," Coquelle said. The boys lay next to their fathers, and a boy "might tell, if he remembers the story." They would "tell in the wintertime," he said, "to make winter go fast. Sometimes one story would last ten nights."

Coquelle said that when it got dark everybody went to bed. "Somebody brings in firewood," preferably dry vine maple, and if everybody is asleep, he goes to bed. But usually "somebody begins to tell yarns." "Talk, talk," Coquelle said. "One old man was named *Wéste*, he told most of the stories. He was smart. He could tell anything. That's the way I felt when he talked. He was a good speaker." Some people, Coquelle pointed out, "just naturally were better speakers." In what is no doubt an understatement he added, "Not every one could tell even as much as I have told from long ago."[30]

Within some of the stories were contained the worldview of the older generation, a worldview that Coquelle appears to have retained all through his life. There had been a worldmaker, separate from and predating Coyote. Coquelle translated it as "God," and explained that it was "home where fish come from." In the beginning, "He threw sand in the ocean, made the land come up to walk on. Water closed in behind them." There were actually five of these worlds, and the people were on the last, the fifth one.[31] It was Coyote who transformed that last world to make it useful for the people.

The Coyote stories, in all of their adolescent, ribald variety, were favorites. Parts of some of them were occasionally told to the whites, who seem not to have understood that Coyote was a "person." To help them out, Coquelle said, "They started calling 'Coyote Jim' ever since white people came because they didn't understand Coyote was a *person*.... Before that he was called 'Coyote.'"[32]

There was always a certain amount of white interest in the Coast Reservation. There were powerful commercial interests in the Willamette Valley that had their eye on Yaquina Bay as a deepwater port, and a railroad through the reservation from Corvallis would connect the Willamette Valley with that port. This would supposedly make some white people very wealthy and, according to the project's advocates, would bring general prosperity to the area. The first thing that was needed was to close the central and most productive part of the reservation and open it for white settlement.

That is what happened by executive order signed by President Andrew Johnson on December 21, 1865. A wide strip of land, which included Yaquina Bay and the Yaquina River, was opened for white settlement. The "Saltchuck Indians" who had been permanently established there very rapidly found themselves in conflict with whites who came in almost immediately to settle. The Indians involved included some of the Alsea and native Yaquinas, who had up to this time never been moved, and some of the Chetco and the Lower Coquille Miluk who had been removed to the Coast Reservation in 1856.[33]

Trouble began almost immediately. "Whites are seizing farms & houses of Indians on Relieved Part of Coast reservation. What shall be done?" read a telegram dated January 16, 1866, from J. W. Perit Huntington, superintendent of Indian Affairs for Oregon to D. H. Cooley, commissioner of Indian Affairs in Washington D.C.

Letters to the editors reveal a lot about the feelings of at least some of the whites toward the reservation. The letter writers had definite ideas of what should be done. A correspondent signed "Rialto" wrote to the *Corvallis Gazette* from Yaquina Bay, November 1, 1867, saying, "While the Indians are undoubtedly doing very well, the white man could do much better." He recommended that the entire reservation "should be thrown open for settlement to the highest bidder (in parcels to suit) then people could go to bed without fear of being scalped before sunrise."*

One almost immediate effect of opening the central portion of the reservation to white settlement was improved transportation. A road was opened from Corvallis to the coast in 1866, and by August 1867 there was a triweekly stage running from Corvallis to Yaquina. "Good teams, comfortable stages, and careful driving. Fare only four dollars," according to an advertisement in the *Corvallis Gazette* of August 3, 1867. The stage terminated at Elk City, the head of navigation on the Yaquina River. Passengers embarked from there on a steam riverboat for the remainder of the trip, which ran past Depot Slough, about six miles south of the Siletz Agency. This had the unwanted effect of making the people on the reservation more accessible to the influence of undesirable whites, especially those who came to sell whiskey or buy women.

Many of the soldiers from Company D, Fourth Infantry Regiment, remained in the area after the demobilization following the Civil War. Corporal Royal A. Bensell, Private Josiah Copeland, and George Megginson, chief farmer in charge at Lower Farm, filed the first land claims on Yaquina Bay as soon as that area was opened for white settlement. In 1868 Bensell and Megginson set up a steam sawmill on their claims at Depot Slough. The sawmill at the Siletz Agency was an old-fashioned reciprocating water-powered mill, and so Bensell and Megginson had the first steam sawmill on the lands within the original boundaries of the Coast or Siletz Reservation.[34]

Most of the annuity supplies and other freight going into the Siletz Agency came by schooner into Yaquina Bay and on to the mouth of Depot Slough at the site of the present city of Toledo. The cargo was then transferred onto flatboats and taken, during high tide,

---

* Prejudice against Indians at that time is somewhat shocking to the modern sensibility. An example of where Indians fit into the hierarchy of the peoples of Oregon during that time is indicated by a page 1 article on the "small-pox patients" in the *Corvallis Gazette*, February 6, 1869. It gives the names of the recent smallpox cases that had resulted in death, listing the whites first, as follows: "John Walker, Joseph Martin, John Martin, James Hubbard, Bertha Breitbarth, Mrs. Brewer, Sophia Love, Isaac Cowan (colored), and three squaws."

four miles up the slough to Depot Mills. Prior to Simpson's time as agent, Indian women were employed to pack the cargo the six miles from the depot to the agency, sometimes paid as little as a can of flour for the day's work. Coquelle said, "A big stout woman would pack over 100 lbs, barefooted over the ridge to Siletz, never resting. Everybody packed his own grub; few had horses then."[35]

A stable of horses and oxen was gradually built up at the agency during Simpson's time, and from then on Indian men took over the freighting. Coquelle Thompson was soon working as a teamster driving the four-horse teams hauling freight over that muddy road. About a hundred tons of freight was transported in that manner each year. Joel Palmer said that when he arrived as agent in 1871 it was "a constant source of trouble in caring for and subsisting teams while in use by Indians and the constant change of teamsters many of whom appear to have but little or no knowledge of the management of teams."[36] Coquelle seems to have learned the "management of teams," because he continued as a teamster off and on his entire life. In the census of 1910, for example, when he was over sixty years old, his occupation was still shown as "teamster." In an interview, his daughter Sina remembered "he took care of the Agency horses," evidently until the last agent departed in 1925.[37]

For those teamsters with their own horses and wagons, the pay was 1/2 cent per pound (50 cents per hundred). Spencer Scott, a friend of Coquelle's (and later husband of Coquelle's first wife, Annetti), told John Peabody Harrington of hauling freight. He said that his was a two-horse team, only loaded with 1,200 pounds. The four-horse teams hauled 2,400 pounds. Spencer said, "There were Indian teams all along the road that had balked or something wrong." He said that he passed two four-horse teams that had gone into the ditch. "Some of the loads took three days to get to Siletz," he said. "Bacon, flour, beans, rice, sugar, coffee."[38] The job of teamster was a job that could give self-respect to a man, and self-respect was a commodity much needed on the reservation. Within a few years, Indian teamsters were doing all of the freighting amid general appreciation for their skill.[39]

About forty miles northeast of Siletz was the much smaller but more agricultural Grand Ronde Reservation. Coquelle occasionally went to Grand Ronde, and at least once he stayed there with an aunt for an extended period. "It had many French-halfbreeds," he said, "but there was no fish at Grand Ronde. It was hard to get fish, everybody was kicking about it."[40] The many "French-halfbreeds" Coquelle mentioned were the Métis descendants of Hudson's Bay Company employees and retirees. Many of them had sold their property at French Prairie to American immigrants and had moved to Grand Ronde when the reservation opened. Some of them had education and farming experience, and as a result the Grand Ronde Reservation was quite unlike Siletz. Coquelle no doubt found it quite foreign.

Coquelle told of seeing a transvestite doctor at Grand Ronde, the only one he had heard of. "I know 'her,'" Coquelle said. "I was there." He had gone to Grand Ronde, arriving late in the evening to see an uncle who was sick. The uncle told Coquelle that he had hired a "1/2 man, 1/2 woman," who was "a good doctor." All the people were assembled when "that doctor came in, dressed like an old woman. That fellow danced, then he said, 'I can't see your sickness; I can't help you.'" Coquelle suggested sarcastically to Elizabeth Jacobs that "maybe he was just like a Boston doctor," implying that the white doctors weren't much help either. Coquelle described him as having "a big voice, was a big man." He would, according to Coquelle, go berry picking with married women and make out with them. "That's the only one I ever heard of. None in my own people," Coquelle declared. And he had "never heard of a woman who wanted to do man's work and dress like a man."[41]

The Métis who lived at Grand Ronde were Catholic. In 1860 a missionary priest from Belgium had arrived to minister to their spiritual needs. Father Adrian Croquet was to remain headquartered at Grand Ronde until 1898, when he retired and returned to Belgium after almost forty years with the Indians of western Oregon. In 1864 a Catholic church was built at Siletz, and as the only priest in the area he held Mass there from time to time. Two of Coquelle's later wives were Catholic, and Father Croquet baptized at least two of his children. Coquelle himself was never attracted to any of the Christian religions.

Protestant Christian churches and missionaries, however, were quite interested in Indian reservations at that time. They lobbied to get the administration of President Ulysses S. Grant to change the long-standing policy of political appointment of Indian agents, and instead to let churches recommend the appointment of agents with the objective of "Christianizing" the tribes. It was naively thought by some that this approach would reduce the corruption that had so permeated the Indian Service. Under the new "Indian Peace Policy" of December 5, 1870, "such religious denominations as had heretofore established missionaries among the Indians" took control of the agencies. At that time there were thirty-eight Indian agencies in the United States in which Catholic missionaries were first to establish themselves, Siletz and Grand Ronde among them. Only eight of those agencies were subsequently turned over to the Catholic Church, Grand Ronde among them.[42] The Siletz Agency was one of those turned over to Protestant denominations, and after 1870 the agent at Siletz would be recommended by the Oregon Conference of the Methodist Episcopal Church. The first agent appointed to Siletz under this new policy was none other than General Joel Palmer, who was quite familiar to the older Indians.

Joel Palmer had not done well during the fifteen years since he had been politically removed from office in 1856 as the superintendent of Indian Affairs for the Oregon Territory. He had lost most of his money, and his wife's, in investments in railroads, flour mills, and other enterprises. He had failed to get himself reappointed to any significant office, and most recently he had lost in the election for governor of Oregon—by only 631 votes.[43]

Palmer had never been a Methodist; he was a Quaker, but there was no Quaker community in Oregon. He had never joined any church, but acquaintances within the Methodist Conference persuaded him to join theirs, and they in turn recommended him as their first agent of the Siletz Reservation.[44] He was probably happy enough to get the appointment, but his tenure as agent at Siletz turned out to be another disappointment for him.

When Palmer arrived at Siletz on April 30, 1871, he found the reservation to be in appalling condition. There were eleven horses, five mules, and forty-two work oxen belonging to the government. Palmer said in his first report that many of them were so "unfit for service that they had to be turned out to graze." There was no grain to feed the horses and mules except for about forty bushels of oats at Lower Farm. Some of the oxen were so old, Palmer said, "they could not masticate dry hay." The fences had rotted down and would only partially keep out hogs and other stock. The road to Depot Slough was impassable, "having been washed out by winter rains and obstructed by land slides & falling timber." During his first month "considerable sickness prevailed among the Indians," and six deaths occurred. In his report for May and June Palmer noted that "many Indians belonging to this Agency were about without leave, . . . and their supply of provision being exhausted I was necessarily careful to give passes to a large number as I had no means to subsist these upon the reservation."[45]

An article in the *Portland Oregonian,* July 17, 1871, reported: "Of the seven hundred Indians (estimated) on and connected with the Siletz Agency (over half of them are now absent leading a roving life among the whites), three or four can read in the primer and write their names; none have been discovered who have Christian principles or belief." The sixty-year-old Palmer found there was too little he could do to help. "I would rather have taken these people precisely in the condition they were when I sent them here nearly sixteen years ago, than now," he wrote in August.[46]

Palmer's frustration is clearly expressed in his diary entries for February 20 through 22, 1872. He rode out on the morning of February 20, heading to Salem where he hoped to get funds "to purchase teams, seed wheat, garden tools, and materials for agency use." He said the roads were bad and the water was high. On the 21st it "rained nearly all day." At 2:00 P.M. on the 22nd he reached Salem and had a meeting with Alfred B. Meacham, superintendent of Indian Affairs for Oregon. Palmer was informed that there were "no funds to be obtained not even to pay traveling expenses." According to his diary, he had already spent $3.25 getting to Salem and it would certainly cost him that much more to get back. He added, "The whole Indian Department very much demoralized." The absence of funds was attributed to mismanagement on the part of Palmer's predecessor, Benjamin Simpson. There had been a "sad application of funds through Simpson in purchasing goods for Siletz agency. Paid too high prices and for many articles not wanted."[47] As he was powerless to effect any material improvement in the condition of the Indians at Siletz, Palmer's promises of eighteen years earlier could only be held up in mockery against him.

He had hoped to be able to break the hold that the Indian doctors had on the minds of the people, but in this he also failed. "Their medicine men and women, as they are called exert a powerful influence over the minds of these people and sometimes actually cause the death of persons by their persisting efforts to drive the bad spirits,"

Palmer wrote in a letter to Meacham. By Palmer's second year, when the Methodists discovered that he had done nothing to win over the Indians to the Christian faith, he was replaced by an agent with more aggressive missionary zeal.[48] This ended Palmer's involvement in matters concerning the Indians and his dream of a better life for them.

There seemed, however, to be very little that even the Methodists could do to change the beliefs and practices of the older generation. Coquelle's account of his brother's Make-Doctor Dance, and of various healing sessions, clearly illustrates what a powerful influence the doctors held over the people. This was evidently Coquelle's older half-brother, whose name was Black-Mark-on-Wrist. Coquelle said, "He was about 30 when he had his dream." Coquelle wasn't sure when he had started dreaming, but he had dreamed for quite awhile. "I was there when his wife told him, 'you have to go to that place to your make-doctor dance. They've already cleaned it all up to make you a doctor.' . . . 'Well, I suppose everybody has got ready there,' he said. Then he went." The Make-Doctor Dance was held at Camas Prairie, and "it was just some other people's house," Coquelle said. "A big house—so they took it. Dr. Alec [who had been the only Coquille doctor for many years] was the one who sat in the middle. He was the one who made all the arrangements."[49] Coquelle's brother's doctor dream was about all kinds of birds, hawks, and so on. "Each bird gave a different kind of pain and different kind of power and different kind of song," Coquelle said. "He would dress and paint the same way. Doctor always wore paint in day time so people would know."[50]

Coquelle described a number of doctoring sessions. One was for a Coquille man at Upper Farm who had been near death for three days. His relatives brought two horses and two guns to hire Evans Tom, a Rogue River doctor who lived nearby. Tom was "already a doctor when he came to Siletz, 40 or 50 years old," Coquelle told Philip Drucker.[51] He told the story in detail to Elizabeth Jacobs. The doctor said, "I'll try. I won't say I'll make him better, but I'll try." They then sent for all the people—fifteen or twenty came to the house to help, including the doctor's two wives.[52] Children were told to stay outdoors during doctoring. There was no danger to them, according to Coquelle, "but they don't want their noise."[53]

The doctor took his time getting ready. "He blackened his face and the backs of his arms from the elbows down. He took off his shirt, stood only in pants." Coquelle then described a coyote skin that he draped over his shoulders and tied under his arms to look like a live coyote. He then took off his shoes and was ready to begin doctoring. The house was now full of Coquille and Rogue River people, and they all sang, the doctor included. Finally the doctor announced, "Well, I didn't find it yet." He pointed to his coyote skin as he continued, "but this fellow here says he is looking for it. I'm going to get it."

The doctor had one young man go outside and "holler three times," then began to dance, and when he finished he said, "All right now, I know who did it. It is no long ways away; it is right in this house here." The doctor said that it was Jim Buchanan's poor old mother who had done it. She was Coquelle's aunt, and a doctor herself, and she was right there in the room. "Everybody was surprised," Coquelle said. But the doctor told them, "Let her alone; we'll go ahead with the sick man."

"Now he danced," Coquelle said of the doctor. "He danced about twenty minutes, people sang, the speaker shouting, the doctor sweating, everything lively." Then the doctor told his assistants, "The minute I get that pain, you fellows cover him up quick!" Then he began to dance again. "He danced over here, he danced over there. There was lots of noise; he shook. He jumped, he clasped the pain in his hand and the men pulled on his belt. He was holding the breast of that sick man—now he put his hands in the water. It was just like putting a hot rock into water! His hands just sizzled! My! I never knew anything like that before."

Coquelle said that the sick man was becoming "kind of alive now," his wife sprinkling water onto his chest. Then the doctor sang "maybe two more songs," but he didn't dance any more. After he had cooled his hands in the water, he had his assistants place a wide, old-fashioned knife in front of him. "The doctor blew; blew on the pain in the palm of his hand, finally picked it out, put it on that knife. You could hardly see it—it was just like ice. . . . Every so often that worm wriggled a little. It was just a little bit alive. Then the sick man looked out from under the blanket and said, 'I'm hungry.' 'Take him down to the river and let him swim,' the doctor said. He went to swim; he wasn't sick any more." The doctor said that it was grizzly bear pain, one of the strongest kinds.

They then asked Jim Buchanan's mother how she made that man so sick. She said, "I never did that; I never *knew* I did it." It seems that she had meant to use that pain to get after a jealous woman, but she said, "I dreamed that pain. It's pretty bad. You can't keep control over it. I can't handle it. I want this doctor to help me, cure me." The people agreed, saying that the pain had to be sent back to Grizzly Bear. The doctor said, "I'll fix it." Then he started to sing, and everybody sang, "he danced and danced and the speaker talked." He picked up the pain from the knife, "rolled it in his hands, blew, nothing was left on his hands." Then the doctor said that his coyote skin told him that the pain hadn't gone back to Grizzly Bear because Grizzly "wasn't looking this way." The doctor danced more, then he grabbed Jim Buchanan's mother by the hair and whipped her with his belt. "He made her run around the fire every so often and then whipped her some more with that belt. Sweat came like rain on that woman's face." He then made her sing the Grizzly Bear song, "It's the last time you'll sing it," he said. He made her dance while he was still whipping her and at last the doctor said, "That Grizzly Bear song is all gone. It has gone back to that fellow. This skin says he looked this way and everything is all gone."

Coquelle's father gave the doctor, Evans Tom, one more gun. The man who had been sick said, "I'll give you my sister. You take her along." Coquelle said that the sister, a middle-aged woman, was sitting right there. She was glad to go, he said, "because her brother had been saved. She would do anything." Coquelle said that they laughed at that doctor after he left. "He's got *three* wives!" they said.

Not all medical problems were treated by shamans. There were "home remedies" sometimes used without the help of the Indian doctor. When Coquelle's father, Chief Washington, was beginning to feel some of the symptoms of age, he suffered badly from rheumatism in his knee. Coquelle described his treatment for it. He said his father took cedar bark and chewed it very fine, then dried it. "He lay down and they put that cedar bark in the joint of his knee, then lit it." He said that it would take two or three hours for it to burn down. It burned through the skin until the bone was exposed, at which time the bark was removed. Coquelle said, "It leaves a big sore, but he walked right around. They did it to hurt that pain."[54]

In a narrative of the death of Coquille shaman Dr. Alec, Coquelle expresses his faith in the traditional belief system. The narrative also illustrates the shaman's power and tribal relations at Siletz. Dr. Alec was, according to Coquelle, the Coquille's only doctor from the time they arrived at Siletz in 1856 until Coquelle's brother was made a doctor in perhaps about 1875. "He was young when he became a doctor," Coquelle said. He was from *Nataghilidạn* on the Upper Coquille, and "they were good people. If you went to their house they would treat you good. They were spoken of as being good people," he insisted.[55]

Dr. Alec had several sisters who married Rogue River people, and he had a brother who never married. The brother "was no leader," according to Coquelle. "He just looked out for Alec." Coquelle explained, "Alec had to be looked after because people were always trying to kill him. But you mustn't let a doctor be killed until something was proved against him. So he was taken care of." Coquelle elaborated: "He made lots of money. Sometimes he was paid two horses, many blankets, Indian money and white man's money. He took in lots of money. He was well off." And there were pecuniary arrangements between the doctor and Coquelle's father, Chief Washington. "My father and Tyee Jackson were behind him," Coquelle said. "When people accused Alec of poisoning, my father and Jackson had to pay, to keep things quiet. Then what he made, he give my father one horse and Indian money and that's why they depended on him."[56]

One of Dr. Alec's sisters was Nellie Lane, who had married a namesake of General Joseph Lane.[57] She had a chin tattoo that Coquelle thought was quite attractive, but her husband took her to a white doctor and had it removed. Coquelle said, "It left an ugly scar." In 1935 Nellie was interviewed by Philip Drucker, and among her remembrances were accounts of her own doctoring power and several anecdotes relating to her brother, Doctor Alec.

Nellie said that Alec had begun dreaming when he was a small boy, sleeping in the sweathouse. "He didn't want to get up, didn't want to eat." They would wake him with a little fire of medicine-root. Their grandfather asked Alec (whose Indian name was Skandatu) what he dreamed about, but Alec "refused to tell." He said that he wanted to get five powers, "so he be doctor. He trained, swam, kept pure, clean. Have to, to get doctor power," Nellie said. "He dreamed each power, shot pain into his body; he fell 'dead.' This meant he had that kind of power."[58]

When Nellie was a child, her brother Alec took her to one of his doctoring sessions. She watched while "he sang, trembled, foamed at mouth." Nellie became frightened "but was reassured by her aunt." Alec jumped toward the sick man five times, then said, "Take off the blanket." The sick man lay, according to Nellie, gasping for breath, but Alec "sucked out the pain." Her mother sang, urging him on. Nellie said that her mother had some power and was "good to help."[59] Alec's five powers were, according to Nellie, the eagle, grizzly bear, crow, coyote, and black bear.[60] "Alec met a big grizzly in the mountains one time," Nellie said. "The bear growled and was about to attack but Alec talked to him, told him who he was, petted him and they departed good friends."[61]

But people were always trying to kill Alec, and so there was, from a non-Indian perspective, a degree of paranoia. From the native point of view, Alec was warned by his dreams. For example, one morning he got up and said, "I think somebody is going to come after me. Don't give me anything to eat." Nellie said that a man came telling of a young girl who was about to die while having a baby. Alec was afraid to go to help her, thinking it was a trick to kill him. He said he didn't know anything about it; he couldn't help her. "She died," Nellie said.[62]

Coquelle Thompson told Elizabeth Jacobs the story of the demise of Dr. Alec. Alec was treating Tyee Jackson's son Dick Jackson, who was gravely ill. In spite of the doctor's efforts, Dick's condition continued to worsen. Suspicion was directed toward the doctor, but he was clever enough to convince the family that the real cause of the illness was a Sixes doctor who at the time was living near the mouth of the Siletz River. Coquelle told the story to Elizabeth Jacobs in his characteristically dramatic style. "Who's to kill that [mouth of] Siletz doctor?" he asked rhetorically. "The chief pointed to Coquille Johnson and two young men."

Johnson and his two companions went by canoe down the Siletz River that night, arriving at the Sixes people's camp at the mouth of the river in the morning. After some formalities Johnson asked the whereabouts of the doctor: "Do you know where he is?" "He's around somewhere." Johnson asked the Sixes doctor to go with him to Salmon River—"Some people up there owe me," Johnson said. He then told his two companions to wait. "As soon as I kill him, I'll hurry back here."

Coquelle continued the narrative to Elizabeth Jacobs, using his penchant for detail to fine effect: "They went quite a long ways.

Every so often the doctor would turn around and look at Johnson. Maybe he kind of *noticed* something." They passed some people who were fishing; then "they went across to a little sandy place, about a quarter of a mile. Johnson shot the doctor from behind with his rifle and then cut his throat."

As in most murders, a mistake was made. Coquelle said, "Now when you kill a doctor you have to turn him around so he's facing the opposite way. Otherwise he'll follow you. Johnson was in a hurry and didn't stop to turn that doctor around. He was in too big a hurry, too scared and he didn't do that." There were some Coquille people camping and fishing at the mouth of the Siletz, evidently near the Sixes people's camp. The body was soon discovered and the chief of the Sixes people, Sixes George, told the Coquille people, "We have to be paid, that's all. They killed our doctor. We have to get ready. In two or three days we'll go (to Lower Farm) and get paid."

Dr. Alec was camping at the time on Drift Creek, "right above the mouth of the river," Coquelle said. He helped the three men cross the Siletz to make their escape. The route took them back up the river to Lower Farm, through the many miles of a dark "timber belt" of 350-year-old Douglas fir and Sitka spruce that stood between them and home, one of the thickest stands of merchantable timber known on earth.[63] Coquelle said, "Now they went on the trail, traveling at night. Someone was following behind—they heard steps, and when they'd sit down it would pass them. They go on for an hour, it would come behind them again, they'd all have to sit down quick. They'd hear it, z-z-z-z-zt—just like wind it passed." It was, of course, the ghost of the murdered Sixes doctor that they heard.

When they arrived at Lower Farm they found that the sick man, Dick Jackson, was worse and in fact was near death. "That's how they knew it was the wrong doctor they had killed," Coquelle said. "If he had really done it, the sick fellow would be better right away with the doctor's death. But the sick one was sinking lower." They knew now that they would have to pay the Sixes people "lots of money." Coquelle said, "Oh, they all feel bad."

There was fear that the Sixes people would attack them, and so no one at Lower Farm slept that first night. The next day they picked four or five Tututni men who were good talkers to act as intermediaries with the Sixes—"men-in-the-middle," Coquelle called them. He said they were "to be in the middle and tell both sides to be still."

Coquelle continued: "Now about forty Sixes men returned home with their chief. One time they come and go back. Our people start in to pay now. One of the men-in-the-middle said to the Sixes, 'They put up that much money. They do not want to fight. They made a mistake and killed your doctor. An innocent man they killed. They will pay so much.' Then those Sixes were satisfied. 'We'll pay tomorrow,' the talker said."

Chief Jackson's son Dick had already died, and that very night Chief Jackson himself died. They asked the Sixes people "to wait two or three days for payment while they buried Jackson." When they paid, it was Dr. Alec who put up a large portion of the money. Coquelle said, "Finally they caught on that he himself was the one who had done it."

Sixes Annie confirmed for them that Alec was indeed the guilty party. She was "a young good looking woman" that Dr. Alec sometimes stayed with even though "he's a married man with two wives." Jim Jackson, another of Chief Jackson's sons, had got the information from her. Jim said that Alec had told her, "I'm doing pretty good. I killed off all those best men."

Jim then went to Chief Washington and said, "Uncle, that's your folks, but I have to kill him." Coquelle told Elizabeth Jacobs, "Now my father won't say anything. He won't say, 'Yes,' he won't say, 'No.' That means 'Go ahead.'" According to Coquelle, Jim thought it would be best to kill Alec in front of everybody. Here is Coquelle's description of the killing: "He had to go across a little creek where Alec was. There was a door in our house to the creek. His [Alec's] horse was tied right outside. That fellow Jim, he was left handed. He heard Alec coming to his horse and he cocked his gun. He called out, 'Alec, you there?' 'Yes.' 'Come up for a while.' As soon as Alec stepped in the door, Jim shot him dead. The Coquille people put him in a blanket, put him on his horse and took him back where he lived."[64]

Coquelle never commented on the rightness or wrongness of the killing of Dr. Alec. He may have been saddened by it, however. "He saved lots of people," Coquelle said simply. "He insulted no one. A good fellow."

It was probably not too long after the death of Dr. Alec that Coquelle's father, Chief Washington Tom, died. Coquelle "was about 18 years old," according to his own testimony, and he was the last of the immediate family still living.⁶⁵ His Uncles Coquelle Charlie and Old Hunter were still alive and active, as was Old Solomon and the singer Jim David and certainly other elders from the Upper Coquille. But his father had been an important influence in Coquelle's life, and when such a father dies, it gives pause.*

"When a person died," Coquelle said, "a non-relative washed the face." It had to be somebody who knew how to wash the dead, "always a woman who tends a dead woman, and a man tends men. No charge. No pay for that." They burn fir boughs around the house and burn the bedding of the deceased. "When they bury him they put everything they can in the grave with him," Coquelle said. "People come. His friends put things—Indian money—on the grave. Some speaker, some man who knows how to speak, says before the body is put in the ground, 'You people understand this: we all have to go one way. That's the law. The law has been made that we all have to go. You people all understand that. So don't fight, make mischief, do wrong wherever you go. Eat food good and it goes good in your body. But when you have done wrong somewhere, you just think what you've done. And when you eat that food it will be no good to you. It just feeds the wrong-doing in you. Don't talk about a person that's dead; he's done now. Just speak to others about how to live long.'"⁶⁶

Coquelle Charlie, as the brother of the deceased, would have been responsible for dividing the remaining property equally among any surviving sons, but in this case there was only Coquelle. Any money, along with other small, personal items, would have been buried with Chief Washington, but valuable property such as houses, horses, and canoes were not destroyed. Charlie, who had paid the bride price for Coquelle's marriage to Annetti, succeeded as chief. Coquelle said, "If the people didn't like him, just tough."⁶⁷

Coquelle told John Peabody Harrington that after his father died he would go to a favorite place on the Yaquina River where he could hunt and fish in solitude. It was about three miles above Elk City, and Coquelle would stay with an old Upper Coquille man named *Lháyu·shi* who lived there. That part of the reservation had been

---

* The earliest marked grave at the cemetery on Government Hill is from 1879. There are no marked graves at Siletz dating from the time that Chief Washington died, and so we don't know where he was buried.

opened for white settlement in 1865, but it was still very sparsely settled and old *Lháyu·shi* had not moved. Coquelle said, "It was a fine place."⁶⁸ There he could reflect upon how, from now on, he would have to make all judgments on his own without looking to his father for support. And he could reflect upon the fact that he would himself soon be taking on the responsibilities of chief of the Upper Coquilles, for which he had been preparing all his life.

Most unsettling to reflect upon was the manner in which the government agent had taken on much of the authority of the chiefs, even to the point of being called "chief" by the Indians. Among some of the tribes, including the Coquilles, the shamans had taken advantage of the social instability, upsetting the traditional balance of power between them and the chiefs.* Coquelle's uncle Coquelle Charlie took on what was now an almost symbolic and bureaucratic role. Coquelle would have reflected upon his own responsibilities, because he was next.

As elders died off, the culture at Siletz increasingly broke down. The old chiefs were gone and the new chiefs had no authority over younger men, many of whom could no longer act as the protectors and providers of their families. Younger women frequently chose white men as mates, infant and child mortality rates were alarmingly high, and a large percentage of the population suffered from venereal diseases, both primary and congenital. Coquelle and Annetti tried to raise their daughter Sina in this new environment, but it was never certain what the future would hold. The community was ripe for revival.

---

* See Spier 1927, 44, for the same phenomenon on the Klamath Reservation.

5

Revival
The Thompson Warm House Dance

The opening of reservations to white settlement made life for the Indians on reservations increasingly insecure and opened the way for charismatic leaders of renewal movements. In 1869, the same year that the first transcontinental railroad was completed, Wodziwob, a man of the Northern Paiute from Fish Lake Valley, Nevada, dreamed that a train was coming from the east, and he announced at a dance that the dead Indians would return in four years.[1] Within a year that very appealing idea was introduced to the Klamath Reservation in southern Oregon by Northern Paiute who had relatives there.[2] Facilitated by tribal connections through marriage, it quickly diffused through northern California, and simultaneously, as early as 1871, a version of this "Ghost Dance" had been done at the Alsea Subagency and Siletz. Coquelle did not attend any of those first dances, but many Indians did.*

---

* The resurrection of the dead and visions of their imminent return were ideas quite familiar to both Indians and whites in the Great Basin. The idea was superficially similar to certain doctrinal features of the predominant white religion in that area, the Church of Jesus Christ of Latter-day Saints, the Mormons. In fact, the Mormons were later able to get Indian converts on the basis of the similarity of beliefs (Jorgensen, 661–62).

Frank Drew told Cora Du Bois how Isaac Martin (Coos), and Cyrus Tichenor (Tututni), went south to visit among the Tolowa at Smith River, California, and "brought the news that the people to the south were working hard to bring the dead people back."[3] As a twelve-year-old girl, Annie Miner Peterson (Coos) attended a Ghost Dance gathering at Yachats and found it to be great entertainment but knew of no religious significance attached to it.[4]

At about the same time another version of the dance and the idea of a resurrection came directly to Siletz from central California. Coquelle told Cora Du Bois that Sixes George, a Tututni at Lower Farm, had caught onto it and "started them dreaming and getting excited. . . . The whites were to be driven back across the ocean where they came from and no one but Indians would be here." Coquelle seems to have understood some of the psychological and emotional stresses that might bring someone like Sixes George to believe in the new doctrine. He said of Sixes George, "He had lost his wife and his son. He felt badly. He wanted to die and go where his relatives were. That is why he started to dream and dance."[5]

Coquelle said that Depot Charlie, another Tututni, then "started to dream like Sixes George" and took his dance to the Tolowa in northern California. Coquelle noted that "the dream dance they used was old, but it started up strong when this new message came. Everywhere there were Indians dancing."[6] As Louis Fuller, a Tillamook, said, "They used the old-time Dream dance but with this new idea in it."[7] Some of the Shasta Indians from Siletz then went to central California, and when they got back "they told all they remembered— the songs and how they danced in California. They thought the dead would come back." They then built a dance house at Klamath Grade, about three miles from the agency, and it was used by the Shasta Indians living there.

Some of the whites who lived around the Siletz area were evidently alarmed, fearing that these enthusiastic outpourings were "war dances." Several letters to the editor, as well as straight news reports, reflected that fear. Joel Palmer was still the agent at Siletz when the first Ghost dances appeared there, but he had no such concern about them. On February 8, 1873, he wrote his own letter to the editor, pointing out that there was no part of it that involved expelling the whites. He said the dances were "for the spirits of their departed relatives, with a hope that they may be restored to them on this earth. . . . "

He opined that the dances were "less harmful than gambling" and concluded, "I presume two-thirds who have engaged in these dances did so for mere amusement."*

Coquelle first attended a version of the Ghost Dance at Corvallis during the summer of 1873. He and many others from Siletz had a pass to work the harvest in the Willamette Valley when Bogus Tom, a man named Peter, and a woman named Mollie, Shastas from California, came on horseback. They came to introduce a version that in California was called the Earth Lodge Dance but in Oregon became known as the Warm House Dance. According to Coquelle, they "stopped to dance at every town. I guess they must have stopped at Jacksonville, Medford, Eugene, and Corvallis." At Corvallis, Coquelle said, "They put up a round canvas tent ca. 20 feet in diameter. You paid about one dollar to get in. They stayed at Corvallis for about one week and made quite a lot of money."[8] Later in the year, Bogus Tom and his entourage introduced the new "Warm House Dance" at Siletz, setting up among their relatives, the Rogue River people at Upper Farm.

By this time, Coquelle was a man of some authority, having been appointed captain of the newly formed and experimental tribal police at Siletz. With the decline of traditional tribal authority, the federal government encouraged Indian agents to institute tribal courts and tribal police forces. Immediately after he had abolished the whipping post used by his predecessor, Joel Palmer experimented with having certain offenses heard by a court consisting of himself and two Indian judges. He was encouraged by the interest the Indians had shown and thought it was a good thing for them to learn the essentials of laws and courts. The next step was to appoint the tribal police.

At Siletz there were seventeen different tribal groupings. The agent initially asked each of the twelve largest to choose one member as their policeman. A captain and a sergeant were selected from among the twelve, and they were under the general guidance of an agency employee. Coquelle was chosen as the policeman for his people, a position he held off and on for almost fifty years.

One of the first "police" assignments Coquelle received from the agent was to investigate this new revival dance that had been brought to the reservation. Would he go and "get the dope on it?" As

---

* Palmer's letter to the *Corvallis Gazette*, February 8, 1873, is quoted in Du Bois (1939) 26.

he rode his horse from the agency, and up the Siletz River to Upper Farm, he did not know what a turning point it would be in his life.

When Coquelle arrived to "get the dope on the dance" at Upper Farm, he found "lots of people camped there." Bogus Tom had supervised the building of the dance house, which Coquelle thought was of the type used by the Shasta of California. It was a pit some twenty feet square and five or six feet deep, covered with a roof supported from a pole in the center of the pit. It would hold about a hundred people and had taken them about two weeks to build. This was the dance house of the California Earth Lodge Cult, a version of the Ghost Dance of 1870.[9]

Coquelle knew everybody. Some were his own in-laws because Annetti, being Applegate, was from among those Upper Rogue River peoples. He was greeted by the *chimá·t'u'*, "the man who keeps the dance going, who keeps the fire going, at an inside-dance." Coquelle thought the term was from the Applegate, his wife's people, but according to Du Bois it was from the Patwin of California.[10] In any case, the *chimá·t'u'* told him, "all right, come in." He took Coquelle by the arm and led him around the circle five times counterclockwise, five times clockwise, then had him sit on a box. There was a dressing room in the corner, screened off with a canvas, and "everybody stood up" when the five male dancers came out.[11]

The dancers were shirtless and painted with red and black stripes across their chests and on their cheeks.[12] There were several novel features of the dance, which were of great interest to Coquelle and others at Siletz. The music, which was faster and more syncopated than the music they were accustomed to, tended to galvanize their attention. No drum was used, but a new percussion instrument was introduced: elderberry limbs that had been split and that when struck on the hand made a nice clapping sound.[13] These *k'amá* clappers, as they were called, had always been used at Siletz as cooking tongs, but in California they were also used to help with the music.

The songs were in a foreign language, perhaps Northern Paiute, and were sung as vocables, with no sense of the meaning of the words. Coquelle liked them and told Cora Du Bois, "Some big man in California had dreamed this and made good songs."[14] The message of the Ghost Dance was preached at intervals following the singing of two or three songs. Bogus Tom would preach: "You dance this. It is a good word, a good dance, like church. Don't do wrong, don't try anything bad. Be good." He admonished the Indians not to believe in white ways. He said of the whites, "They put things down in books, anything they want. We Indians see what is right [for us]."[15] Coquelle said, "People had to pay to learn how to dance." He said the people gave "horses, guns, money to the California people. The *chimá·t'u'* came around [and] took up the collection."

Coquelle got the impression that Bogus Tom sincerely believed that the dead would come back, "but he never said when and didn't talk much about it." He told Elizabeth Jacobs that before Bogus Tom came, "they only danced once a year—the old fashioned way like I told you. When they said the dead people would come back, I said, 'Oh no. I'll dance, but I don't believe that.'"[16]

Women were very much a part of the dance, and had specific parts in the singing. One enthusiastic participant was Coquelle's wife, Annetti, who the previous year, in 1872, had given birth to their first child, a daughter. Coquelle and Annetti gave her the unusual name of Sina (pronounced Sye-na). Evidently fond of this firstborn child, he was to give his last daughter, born in 1920, the same name.

But there was more going on at Siletz than revival dances. At a council held with the chiefs of the Confederated Tribes on December 15, 1873, Coquelle's Uncle Charlie was listed as "Chief of the Coquilles," and speaking in Jargon he expressed his frustration with the bureaucracy. "Agents write to Washington (D.C.) for things and I ask them when will the answer come? They say soon, soon. My opinion is that letters are lost, and the Washington chief does not know about us." Next, he pointed out the plight of his people: "Do you see all these people? Are they like whites? Do whites live in cellars; in smokehouses; are they starved? Our agent says these Indians are becoming good. That is my opinion, too. I want you to tell the chief about us, and write the answer." The fear they all had was the fear that they would lose the lands that had been given them and upon which they had lived for the past fifteen years: "Bad white men want our lands. I don't want to give it up. The President gave it to us, and we want it."

He then came to the point of the meeting, which was the issue of giving individual families their own farms with help and supervision from the government. "I want the land divided into farms like the whites so that we can learn to live like them. I want my agent to look close after us. I want him to come up and see us." And as a final, parting shot, he exposed the kind of rivalry between tribal groups that had from the beginning characterized the Coast Reservation: "I want the farmer at Upper Farm discontinued, so that more tools can be issued us." In other words, if there were no government farmer and equipment at Upper Farm, it would mean more at Lower Farm.

Charlie expressed his desire to have "the land divided into farms like the whites." This was the latest idea on how to improve the condition of the Indians on the reservations: divide the arable land among them, and let them manage it "in severalty," which is to say in separate, family-sized farms rather than communally as one large unit. The Bureau of Indian Affairs was seriously contemplating such a change in policy. When Joel Palmer first arrived as agent in 1871, he "deemed it best" to make only temporary repairs to the fences because, he said, "the allotment of land in severalty to these Indians is now in contemplation."[17] Palmer actually had some of the subdivision surveys done during his tenure as agent.[18] Over the years the fences rotted down, the property corners were lost, and the land had to be resurveyed. This happened several times, over the years. By the time the Dawes Severalty Act (or General Allotment Act) finally became law in 1887, the idea of allotting the land was an old idea that had been implemented and well tried at Siletz.

In 1875 the government gave Indians reason to be concerned about their land. That year the Alsea Subagency was opened to settlement, as well as lands along the northern end of the Siletz Reservation, which reduced the total land area to 250,000 acres from the original 1856 area of about 1.1 million acres. The Coos and Lower Umpqua Indians living at the Alsea Subagency were given the choice of either moving to Siletz or moving out into the white world. They chose the latter. The 360 Coos and Lower Umpqua Indians who lived there ceased to be wards of the government as they drifted south, back toward their ancestral homelands, where they virtually disappeared from the records for the next hundred years.[19] The Alsea Indians, who were living within the Alsea Subagency and had never previously been moved, were, over the next ten years, pressured into moving to Lower Farm on the Siletz where they, too, almost disappeared.

A "Petition of the chiefs and Head men in Council at Siletz Agency Oregon, Feb 12, 1878" registered strong opposition to closing the agency. "All we ask is a good start and a good title to our lands," it stated. "Let us have our agent here until we have our lands allotted, our houses and barns built, and our children educated at which time we will be ready to become Citizens and you can close up our Agency as soon as you please." It was signed by twenty of the more politically active headmen from among the Alsea, Chasta Costa, Tututni, Rogue River, Klamath, and other peoples. Most of the more prominent leaders were present, including George Harney, John Adams, Chetco Charlie, Robert Metcalf, and Alsea Jackson.[20]

In the years leading to the breakup of the reservation, the Coquille Indians appear to have survived better than some of the other groups. The first detailed annual census of the reservation of which a copy is available was for the year 1877. Only a few of the old generation of Coquilles are on it. Chief Washington's name is of course absent. At the head of the list of Coquilles is "Charley." "Thompson" is further down, with a family of four: presumably Coquelle himself, Annetti, their five-year-old daughter, Sina, and another female over ten but under twenty years old. The population of the Coquilles at Siletz in 1877 was 84 persons, down only about 16 from the 100 that had been moved there twenty years earlier. This represents a much better survival and reproduction rate than for the reservation as a whole, the population of which had declined by more than 50 percent during that time.* It may be that the wisdom and good leadership of Chief Washington, Chief Jackson, Old Hunter, Dr. Alec, and the other elders who had so shaped Coquelle's life and character were at least partly responsible for the comparatively better survival rate of the Coquilles.

One elder, the singer Jim David, was Coquelle's greatest musical inspiration. It was mostly Jim David's songs that Coquelle remembered and sang for Elizabeth Jacobs in 1935, the words of which were strong, inspirational poetry. Coquelle told of Jim David's first song, "when he first started dreaming. He just said, 'Everybody look up and cry.' I don't know what people cry for—maybe to heaven people."[21]

Coquelle said, "He always sang plain and good, that old fellow. It must be that he dreamed of God, raising people up from sickness of this world." Coquelle translated the words of one of his dream dance songs that was concerned with sickness:

---

* Schwartz 1997, 182, 200: citing House Report 1870, 795. Schwartz reports a population of 2,300 in the Siletz portion of the reservation in 1869; citing House Report 1876, 636, 622, he reports a population of 1,100 for the 1877 census.

> Sickness
> Lots of sickness in this world.
> I'm God.
> Raise up from sickness.
> God.
> God I am.
> I raise (people) up
> From sickness,
> I raise them up.
> On this earth,
> I raise them up.

Coquelle said that Jim David had himself been sick and that in his dream a man had given him another song and told him he'd be better if he sang it. Songs of the sun, rain, and weather were evidently favorites of Jim David.

> Sunny
> Warm day
> Will make you better.
> On the ground
> You'll get better.

He had Sun Dream songs, Rain Dream songs, and Frost songs. His Sun Dream Song said,

> All over the world
> I make light.
> I'm sky people.

Of his Rain Dream Song Coquelle said, "There'll be a little shower, that song means."

> Gets little fine shower
> On the land.
> Falling
> A little fine rain.

The weather meant a lot to Jim David. Here, for example, is his Frost Song:

> That's how they come.
> With heavy fog
> I come.

All over the world, spreading,
I come.
With heavy fog
I come.

Most important in David's repertoire were songs that could be used in the Dream dances, and in the Ghost Dance, after it made its appearance at Siletz. Following is his song for the *m<u>a</u>lh nát'a* (Dream) dance:

On top of the ground
Come down and dance.
Down in this earth,
Dances.

Coquelle said that Jim David was "a fine actor, a good actor. He was Coquille. He dreamed Ghost Songs."

On top of the ground,
I'll run.
On land,
I'll run.
On the flowers
In the field
I dance.
On the white ground,
I dance.

The traditional ceremonial songs that Coquelle sang for Elizabeth Jacobs (including the Jim David songs) had a relaxed tempo and lacked a fast, steady, accompanying beat. They had a small melodic range and short, repetitive phrases. This was in marked contrast with the songs introduced with the Ghost Dance from California, which were quite lively, with an accompanying beat that was fast and steady. There were evidently no words in the Ghost Dance songs that were intelligible to the people at Siletz. The vocal lines consisted of vocables, and tended to have a descending melodic contour. They were often rhythmically complex.* There were no frame drums: time was

---

* We are grateful for personal communications from ethno-musicologist Dr. Laurel Sercombe (8–15 December 1999) for these insights into the differences between the traditional musical style of the Oregon coast and the style of the Ghost Dance music that had been brought in from north-central California.

kept by stomping on a plank on the floor, or tapping on a board suspended from the ceiling. The "song master" used the *k'amá* clappers made of the split elderberry limbs, and the dancers used whistles made from the bones of bird legs. For some of the dances, a chorus of men's and women's voices was carefully orchestrated by the leader.[22] Coquelle described one song in which "women helpers stopped singing when the leader raises his stick. Start again when stick comes down." He described another song in which three or four men came in with whistles and sang one melodic line while the "others all sing 'hí hí hí' throughout in time with drum beat."[23] When Coquelle started going to the Warm House Dance (as the Ghost Dance was called at Siletz), his musical sense must have been awakened and stimulated by the new rhythm and syncopation of this music from California.

With the words of the songs in vocables that had no meaning, the message of the Ghost Dance had to come through in the preaching, only a part of which would have resonated with Coquelle. The emphasis on "doing good" would no doubt have appealed to him, but if we are to take him at his word, he rejected out of hand the idea of an impending resurrection of the dead. The problem is that we cannot take him, or indeed any other participant of the Ghost Dance, at his word. Anthropologists who interviewed the elderly participants found that many of them tended to derogate the entire movement. Many "expressed failure to understand how interest could be evinced in anything so patently 'crazy.'"[24] Coquelle gave excellent and accurate accounts of the movement and the activities of other participants, but like many others, he consistently minimized his own role. There seems to have been a retrospective embarrassment about having been swept up in the revival.

A colloquial meaning of "crazy" is to be distracted with eager desire, excitement, and so on. That definition probably fits the sense in which the word is often used in eyewitness accounts of the Ghost Dance. However, the term was sometimes used in the sense of being "insane or demented." Actually, Coquelle believed that before the Ghost Dance, Indians "never got crazy." That, he said, was because unlike whites, Indians "don't study too much."[25] He did, however, recall the case of a man at Lower Farm who showed obvious symptoms of late onset schizophrenia. "I guess he's crazy all right," Coquelle admitted, ". . . they hear him holler out in the mountain.

Then down below he holler on another side, just holler all around. At daylight he came down to the boat sober as a judge." Anticipating the obvious, Coquelle assured Elizabeth Jacobs that there was no whiskey involved.

"After he came to his senses," Coquelle explained, "he said 'people tell me to come and go and I go with them.'" Coquelle asked, "Well, what kind of people?" "People just like you. . . . They come and holler. I have to answer. I have to go with them. Night and day, just the same." Coquelle asked him if the people gave him "some song and dance?" "No, they don't say nothing about dance." Coquelle said that one time the man was in a boat with the boys. "He started in hollering to answer people. He got up and danced all around the edge of the boat and hollered. Everyone kept still—didn't paddle. After that he quit. No more after that. He was about 40 or 50 years old." Coquelle said that the only way to understand what had happened was in terms of the man's spirit power. "It must be his power does that to him," Coquelle concluded.[26]

It was probably a healing session that finally converted Coquelle to a belief in the Warm House Dance. He was sick with fever, and his uncle, now Chief Coquelle Charlie, had him brought to the Warm House Dance. "My people agreed to carry me there," Coquelle told Cora Du Bois. He said they got there just before dark and the chief was at the door calling the people to come in. Coquelle was brought in last and made to walk around the fire a total of five times, then was set on a box. Evans Bill, a Takelma, announced that there was a sick man with them and that they had feathers that came from California, "and they believed in them." Old Jack, a Shasta, was there and "talked a long time with an interpreter." The men and women stood around Coquelle and sang, and Klamath Charlie "blew his whistle in my ears, nose, and mouth. He kept coming back all through the dance and blowing on me. I got awfully tired. I thought they would never stop." "Finally," Coquelle said, "Charlie took off his feather coat, brushed me with it and blew his whistle some more." Then they all took an hour's rest.

Coquelle went over to sit by his wife, Annetti. "I told her I was feeling better but not to say anything because I wanted them to go on working on me." After the break, the *chimá·t'u'* "built up the fire and they started again." For the next two or three hours, until "nearly daylight," they continued to dance and sing, "wiping me off with their feathers," Coquelle said. "They didn't touch me with their hands."

At the end, "Three men, each in a feather cape, danced around the fire and then stood one in back of me and one on either side. The chief told everyone to get up and help, to do good, if they did good, their names would be good." By then it was daylight and all the dancers "went down to the Siletz River to swim." After they came back they had Coquelle stand for about twenty minutes and brushed him off with their feathers. "Klamath Charlie said it would take two or three nights to help me right," Coquelle said. He asked Coquelle how he felt: "Yes, I feel better." Everyone clapped and "went out and had breakfast." Coquelle declared that "the Warm House Dance helped your sickness. . . . You needed to have it wiped off."[27]

In a sense, the Ghost Dance gave power to the people. It was a truly popular movement, and the traditional doctors weren't necessarily a part of it at all. The anthropologist Leslie Spier found at the Klamath Reservation that the secular Ghost Dance "dreamers" had gained influence that rivaled that of the traditional shamans, and that the shift of power was encouraged by the chiefs.[28] From the accounts of the Warm House Dance at Siletz, it would appear that a similar shift in power also occurred there. Curing was not an original feature of the Ghost Dance, but because the dances were so open to interpretation by anyone, they could take on curing functions or anything else.

Hoxie Simmons told Cora Du Bois, "After a time people went crazy and changed the rules of the Warm House Dance."[29] Frances Johnson (Takelma) told John Peabody Harrington that "a man came out of the sweathouse with no pants on, shirt on, and said that men went this way (and) . . . women were to go naked that way."[30] Annetti and Spencer Scott told Harrington that at one of the Warm House dances at Siletz "they took two old women and wrapped them all up in blankets and burned some spruce twigs and smoked them thoroughly in the white smoke, telling them to get alive again."[31]

Coquelle told of the time that "Grisco Jim's wife and another woman got together and went crazy. They burned everything in their house." After the incident was reported, the agent sent Coquelle, who was a policeman at the time, to "find out about it and bring them to him." Coquelle was reluctant to go because the women, he said, "were crazy." When he got to their house, they were "almost naked." "They ran up to me and asked if I believed their way, if I believed in God." They took Coquelle's hat off his head and looked inside the sweatband, asking "what the marks were." Coquelle told them that it was a number seven hat. They said "that was all right" and put the hat back on his head, but Coquelle said, "I was afraid they would get me down and rip off my clothes."

Coquelle left to find the husband, Jim. "They had singed all the hair off that poor old fellow, even his eyelashes and eyebrows." They had burned all of his blankets and clothes. Coquelle said, "We hitched up Jim's team and told the women to go and put on dresses. They were quiet by then and did it. Then we drove to the agency." At the agency the two women were quite subdued. Coquelle said that they were afraid of the agent, who merely asked them why they had burned up everything. "She said she had heard voices telling her to," Coquelle said of Jim Grisco's wife. The agent scolded her for treating her husband so badly. "Then he gave them clothes, blankets, and food, and sent them home. After that they were all right."[32]

Certainly not everyone who became involved with the Warm House Dance went "crazy" with it. There were some who were enthusiastic about the dance and saw commercial possibilities, using it as a branch of show business. Chetco Charlie, who lived at Lower Farm and was a good friend of Coquelle's, decided that he would like to take the dance down the Oregon coast and show it to the whites and the Indians along the way. Coquelle had obviously been interested in the movement and knew all the songs and the dances, and so Charlie invited him to go with him as a partner. Charlie made "four or five capes out of chicken feathers and gunny sacks," Coquelle remembered. He also made whistles out of bird bones for the dancers and "a split-stick clapper" for Coquelle as chief singer.[33]

Charging money for dances was nothing new. In this acquisitive, wealth-centered society almost everything had its price. Coquelle told of the earlier Dream dances whereby dancers would just show up at a village. "They paid them because they came so far to dance in your house. If people come to your house and dance all night you have to pay."[34] He told of dancers who came to Lower Farm and danced at his place. "I didn't call for them, but I have to pay for it," he said. "They have to take whatever you pay. You do the best you can." He concluded, "They just do that to get money, just like show people, I guess."[35] Speaking of the Ghost Dance, Abe Logan told Cora Du Bois, "All this cost money. The chiefs had to feed the dancers. A whole lot of people were ruined on account of this dance."[36]

It was in April 1877 that Coquelle Thompson and his wife, Annetti, along with Chetco Charlie and his Coos wife, left Siletz, taking the Warm House Dance on a tour of the Oregon coast. It turned out to be quite an adventure, and Coquelle didn't get back to Siletz for a year. The dance they introduced came to be known as the Thompson Warm House Dance.

Their first stop was at the mouth of the Alsea River, at the site of the present town of Waldport. Although that part of the reservation had been opened to white settlers for over two years, the Alsea Indians had not yet moved. Coquelle said, "We spread a blanket on the ground and some old people laid shirts and beads and things on it." The preaching was in Jargon, "so we could understand each other." Coquelle claimed that Chetco Charlie did all the preaching, although others who were present at Coquelle's dances reported that he did a great deal of preaching himself.

Coquelle thought that at Alsea "they liked it," but there was evidently only audience enough to justify one performance. A young Coos woman named Annie Peterson was married to an Alsea Indian named William Jackson, and they attended the dance.[37] She remembered that Coquelle "charged people to come in and see it. He said if they danced the dead would come back, but he never said when." He showed the people how to do the dance, which was held "in a white man's kind of house." She remembered that Coquelle used the *k'amá* split-stick clappers to keep time and that she had never seen anything like that before. Of the spiritual significance, Annie merely said, "Nobody had trances during his dance."[38]

After the one-night stand at Alsea, they moved the performance down to the Siuslaw River, near the present site of the town of Florence. Two of the Alsea men went along with them, William Smith and John Watson, the chief. Many of the 360 Coos and Lower Umpqua Indians who had left Yachats when the Alsea Subagency had been closed three years earlier were living there. The Siuslaw Indians themselves had never been moved because the Siuslaw River was, prior to 1875, within the boundaries of the reservation. Here was a large potential audience for the Warm House Dance.

It was a long day's ride from Alsea to Siuslaw, but when they arrived they were greeted as friends. Coquelle had cousins there, descendants of his uncle Old Solomon. One of those cousins was Frank Drew, who was later an important ethnographic informant for several anthropologists. An older nephew on his mother's side, Jim Buchanan, also lived there, and he, too, would later be an important linguistic informant regarding the Hanis Coos language.[39]

The chief, Umpqua Dick, knew Coquelle's father and invited them to eat. "He said he would like to hear our songs," Coquelle remembered. That evening Annetti taught some of the songs to the women, and Coquelle "taught seven or eight men." "The chief liked the songs," Coquelle said. "About midnight he made a speech asking us to stay."[40] The comparatively sophisticated rhythm and syncopation of those Ghost Dance songs proved to be an attraction wherever they were introduced.

They spent the next two weeks building a proper Warm House Dance house on the hill facing the North Fork of the Siuslaw, near its mouth. Frank Drew, who was there, estimated the size to be twenty by forty feet and six feet deep. It was of a different construction from the one that Bogus Tom had built at Upper Farm. Besides being larger, this one had a ridge pole and a pitched roof. Coquelle said that Chetco Charlie and the chief, Umpqua Dick, took charge of construction. The central vertical pole was a tree trunk two feet in diameter, painted white, and used as a symbol of "the Father." Lottie Evanoff, who was there, said that Coquelle appointed Umpqua Dick to blow smoke on it before the dances. Frank Drew said, "They had lovely songs and the young people learned them fast. It stirred up the Indians around here quite a lot."[41]

Frank Drew said that "Chetco Charlie and Thompson had to have presents for bringing this news. At the first meeting there were about one hundred people, and they all gave shirts, blankets, and beads." Coquelle told Cora Du Bois that he thought they danced there "for about a week." Frank Drew thought they danced about ten days. During their time at Siuslaw both Coquelle and Charlie reportedly engaged in amorous relations with some of the women.[42]

Coquelle was a handsome, powerful man very much in the prime of his life. When he entered the dance floor naked to the waist and began singing in his superb voice, it is very possible that he attracted the women's attention. Chetco Charlie, although he had his wife with him, married one of Coquelle's nieces who lived at Siuslaw.[43] She was a sister of Coquelle's nephew Jim Buchanan, who became a leader of the dance movement after Coquelle departed.*

---

* We hear no more on this tour of Coquelle's wife Annetti, nor of Chetco Charlie's original wife. The Alsea chief John Watson returned home from Siuslaw at that time and the two wives may have gone back with him.

In any case, at the end of the performances at Siuslaw, Coquelle and Charlie decided to take the dance on down to Gardiner and show it to the whites. Gardiner was a mill town on the north shore of the Umpqua River, a few miles from the old Fort Umpqua where the Coos and Lower Umpqua had been held from 1856 to 1860. It was the first white settlement they came to, but it was settled with a rough and tumble assortment of loggers, sawmill workers, longshoremen, and sailors, hardly the kind of audience that was likely to appreciate the finer points of an esoteric ethnic dance.

According to Frank Drew, "everyone went to Gardiner," a one day's ride down the beach. "Thompson rented a hall in Gardiner and charged fifty cents admission. Quite a crowd came." According to Frank, they weren't doing this for money: "they wanted to convince the whites," he said. Isaac and Jesse Martin, Coos Indians from Siuslaw, were the doormen and weren't supposed to let anyone in after the dance started. That was easier said than done, however, because the music had barely begun when a group of drunks tried to get in and start a fight. According to Frank Drew, one of them knocked Jesse Martin down, whose brother Isaac then jumped into the fray. Coquelle and Chetco Charlie joined in and evidently expelled the drunks, but, according to Frank Drew, "the meeting was broken up and the Indians went back to Florence."[44]

The Martin brothers had a first cousin named Alice. She was eighteen or nineteen years old and was evidently one of the women who had become infatuated with the thirty-year-old Coquelle. In any case, we find her with him at Coos Bay. By his own later statement to Siletz superintendent Knott C. Egbert, they lived together "married by Indian custom" until the following April, when they "divorced by Indian custom."[45]

Coquelle told Egbert that it was during the fall of 1877 that he arrived at Coos Bay. It took two days down the beach to get there from Siuslaw. The lower bay was about one mile wide, and after crossing it they landed at Empire, a sawmill town and the county seat of Coos County. It was located on the village site of Coquelle's mother's people, and many of the Coos Indians who had left the Alsea Subagency when it closed in 1875 were living there. There were also descendants of Indian women who had been married to white men and had not gone to the reservation at the time of the removal in 1856. Among the Indians living there were several of Coquelle's maternal relatives,

Revival: The Thompson Warm House Dance

and he stayed with them. Some of them worked in H. H. Luse's steam sawmill, which was cutting 15,000–20,000 board feet of lumber per day.

Coquelle quickly made arrangements for space to put up a canvas fence within which to hold the dances. Several hundred whites were living at Empire at that time, and Coquelle said, "The whites all liked it." The dances were performed three times per week and continued for about a month. Some of the whites evidently liked it well enough to return and bring friends to see it. Coquelle mentioned specifically a white bachelor named Bill Rose who liked it and "used to bring white girls to see the dance."[46]

Coquelle said, "When we were all through, Chetco Charlie and I divided the money. I took all the white man's money and Charlie took all the beads and clothing. I didn't have any use for Indian money. I wouldn't have known how to use it." Coquelle's part of the gate receipts was evidently enough to last him through the winter because he didn't return to Siletz until his liaison with Alice was ended the following April.

There were many things at Coos Bay that would have interested Coquelle while he was staying there. For one thing, he had any number of second cousins who had not been removed to Siletz in 1856. On his paternal side there were the children of his father's aunt Giscuae, whose daughter Susan had married Charles Hodgkiss, with whom she had a daughter, Laura. After Hodgkiss departed, Susan became the wife of his sawmill partner, George Wasson, in a process known in the fur trade as "turning off:" the white husband who was leaving would find another white man to take his wife (and family if there was one).[47] Generally that was considered a humanitarian and honorable action, and such it was in the case of Susan and her marriage to George Wasson. They had five boys and four girls and many descendants down to the present generation.[48]

There were also any number of second cousins from his mother's side. Among them was the Coos chief Daloose Jackson, who along with several other relatives had taken up residence at North Bend, the site of the second of the two steam sawmills on the bay. There were others that Coquelle was interested in seeing. One was a former chief of the Lower Coquille Miluk who had been removed to Siletz in 1856 but was now living at Empire. His name was Chief Lane, and Coquelle said that he would "sell fish and get whiskey for it."

Whiskey was pervasive at Empire. Coquelle said that Chief Lane had two wives, but "whiskey at last got the best of him."[49] It may have been while he was at Empire that Coquelle himself developed a taste for whiskey, a taste that he retained in moderation throughout his life. This trip to Coos Bay was Coquelle's only opportunity to visit the homeland of his mother. He never in his life visited the homeland of his birth in the Coquille River valley, only twenty miles further south.[50]

Sometime in April 1878, Coquelle decided that it was time to pack up and go home to Siletz. He headed north on horseback, up the beach route. The first night he stayed near the mouth of the Umpqua, twenty-five miles north. Coquelle said, "When I was at Umpqua I met an old man who asked me, 'did you know Umpqua language?'"[51] Of course the Upper Umpqua was mutually intelligible with the Upper Coquille, which he spoke, but he didn't know any of the Lower Umpqua. The Chinook Jargon was the common language with which the peoples of the Oregon coast still communicated, when they couldn't communicate in English.

Coquelle seems to have taken his time and stopped to visit with friends on his way north. One afternoon at about three o'clock he was a little north of Siuslaw when, as he told Elizabeth Jacobs, "coming home from Coos I arrived where people were camping. There were lots of seals there." He knew most of the people, and they asked him to stay. "They gave me a place to tie my horse where there was plenty of grass." After he had taken care of his horse, he walked down to the beach where, he said, the seals "were crawling around."

One of the seals had been butchered, and Coquelle described how they cooked it. "They cut the meat right off with the skin. They used it like bacon. They burned the fur off over the fire just as they did with bear." This was a novelty for an upriver person like Coquelle, who had never eaten seal meat. He didn't say that he relished it, but he did say that he tasted it. "It was fine food," he concluded.[52] After taking his leave of friends and relatives near the Siuslaw, Coquelle headed on north toward Siletz, which, if he didn't make any long stops, he would have reached in another three days. He had been gone a year, and had experienced many things.

Coos chief Daloose Jackson's daughter Lottie Evanoff told Cora Du Bois, "After Thompson's Warm House Dance they called it Dream dances because people dreamed of their dead relatives who gave them songs." Coquelle told Du Bois that there was nothing new at all about the Dream Dance. "The Dream dance has been going on ever since there have been people in this world," he said. "They used to have these Dream dances in the old days whenever they were lonesome and wanted some fun."[53]

The Dream dances that followed the Thompson Warm House Dance revival were popular on the Oregon coast well into the 1890s. At Coos Bay "they were held every six or seven days, like church," Lottie said. Frank Drew described one that he attended at North Bend, where Daloose Jackson was living at the time. "There were 40 or more dancing the spirit dance there," he said. "Old Taylor, a Coos Bay Indian fell dead indoors at that dance."[54] Fainting and trance were common, and sought after during those dances. It was customary to leave the person alone until he or she came out of it and reported the visions that had come. When Old Taylor "fell over," Frank Drew said, "they let him alone. That was the rule. He never got up again. He was dead." Frank explained, "He was a big fat man and something must have gone wrong with his heart."[55]

Ninety years after the revival called the Thompson Warm House Dance, Coquelle Thompson and Chetco Charlie were immortalized by the poet-monk Thomas Merton. In the last section of his book-length poem *The Geography of Lograire*, Merton combined the names, calling his character "Coquelle Charlie." In the preface Merton says that he used the experience of the Ghost Dance to "enact the common participation of the living and the dead in the work of constructing a world and a viable culture."* That is exactly what Coquelle Thompson had attempted.

---

* Thomas Merton, *The Geography of Lograire*, 1–2, 131–37, 152–53 n 131. We are indebted to Nathan Douthit for calling the Merton poem to our attention.

Steamship *Columbia*, in regular service Portland to San Francisco from 1850 to 1862. Frequently chartered by the U.S. Army for troop transport, it was charted in June 1856 to remove most of the Indians from the southern Oregon coast. Coquelle Thompson, as a child of six or seven years, was aboard and was later to give the only Indian eyewitness account of the removal. Woodcut from *Lewis & Dryden's Marine History*, 1895, 35.

Coquelle Thompson lived the rest of his life at the Siletz Indian Reservation raising families from three successive wives. This photo shows Thompson and his last wife, Agnes, with their extended family, about 1910. Left to right, Coquelle Thompson, Sr.; his wife, Agnes; their son, Coquelle Jr. (Tom), standing in front of Agnes. The others have not been positively identified. Photo Courtesy Oregon History Center, Newport, Oregon.

Soon after the turn of the century, Thompson and many other Indians at Siletz received cash from government sale of reservation timber land. With this cash, Thompson and others were able to improve their allotments, and many of them (including Thompson) built comfortable homes. This is the house on his allotment near Thompson Creek, Siletz Reservation. On the porch are (left) Coquelle Jr. (Tom) and (right) his sister, Blanche. Photo courtesy Sina Thompson Bell and Dodie Bell.

Among the first improvements in land transportation at the Siletz Reservation was construction of cable "swinging bridges" across the Siletz River at various locations. This one crosses the river near the Coquelle Thompson allotment. Coquelle Thompson, in suit and hat, is standing on the plank approach to the bridge. Photo courtesy George Thompson.

Dr. Frank M. Carter (1843–1937) was the physician at Siletz during almost all of his working life. He was well acquainted with everyone enrolled at the reservation. Coquelle's wife Agnes often worked as his practical nurse, including at the time of the great flu pandemic of 1918. On the left, an unidentified Indian woman with an open-weave pack basket and tumpline. Photo courtesy Oregon Coast History Center, Newport, Oregon.

Doctor (Alsea) Johnson, a Tillamook Indian native to the Siletz region, was a renowned hunter, despite a paralyzed right arm, the result of a severe burn when he was a young man. Photo from a postcard postmarked 31 May 1910, courtesy Oregon Coast History Center, Newport.

A traditional ceremony called the "Feather Dance" came into frequent use at Siletz during the 1890s, following the demise of the Warm House Dance. It was used as a religious ceremony by the Indians, and was often performed at public events for spectator entertainment. For at least twenty-five years it was performed at Fourth of July celebrations in Newport, at Siletz, and elsewhere throughout the county. This photo shows the ceremony being performed at Bayfront, Newport, Oregon, probably for a Fourth of July celebration. Photo courtesy Oregon Coast History Center, Newport, Oregon.

After Coquelle's "Tututni" wife, Emma, died in 1903, he married Agnes Newberry, thirty years his junior. She had been Emma's nurse during her last illness and was the abandoned mother of two children at the time. This photo shows her family, about 1895, after she completed high school at Sacred Heart Academy, Los Angeles, California. Standing rear, Agnes Newberry and her brother (or half-brother), John Newberry. Seated front, Mary Martin, their mother, and Albert Martin, Mary's husband at the time. Photo courtesy Oregon Coast History Center, Newport, Oregon.

Seated, Augusta Smith, Agnes Thompson's daughter from her marriage to Louis Smith. The boy is George Thompson, son of Coquelle and Agnes. Photo courtesy Sina Thompson Bell and Dodie Bell.

Coquelle and Agnes Thompson's daughter, Blanche, and their son, Coquelle Jr. (Tom), ca. 1908. An Alsea Indian photographer, Tom Jackson, had a studio in Siletz during that time, and the photo is probably one of his. Coquelle Thompson was quite pleased with this photo and had postcard copies of it made. Photo courtesy Sina Thompson Bell and Dodie Bell.

The Rodman Wanamaker Expedition to the American Indian at the Siletz Reservation, August 20, 1913. Signing the Declaration of Allegiance to the U.S. government: Coquelle Thompson, facing camera with white mustache, suit, and Dakota hat; James McLaughlin helping an unidentified Indian make his thumbprint on the declaration; Joseph K. Dixon, expedition leader, looking on (in Army clothes, pen in hand). A Feather Dance was performed as part of the ceremony, and two of the Indians in the photo are dressed for the dance. Photo courtesy William Hammond Mathers Museum, Indiana University.

In 1917, Thompson and his family leased out their allotment at Thompson Creek and moved to the Robert Metcalf allotment, three miles nearer to Agnes's work at the Siletz boarding school. Agnes took in washing throughout her life with Coquelle: note the clothing on the line in front of the house. This photo taken about 1925. Courtesy National Archives and Records Administration, Pacific Alaska Region, Seattle.

Coquelle Thompson, Siletz Reservation, ca. 1939. Photo courtesy Sina Thompson Bell and Dodie Bell.

Agnes Thompson, Siletz Reservation, 1939. Photo courtesy Sina Thompson Bell and Dodie Bell.

View of Siletz village from Government Hill, ca. 1925. Courtesy National Archives and Records Administration, Pacific Alaska Region, Seattle.

Coquelle Thompson and his wife Agnes, Siletz Reservation, 1939. Photo courtesy Sina Thompson Bell and Dodie Bell.

Agnes Thompson with son, Coquelle (Tom) Thompson Jr. Tom was a star fullback for the Oregon State Beavers. He was the third Indian to graduate with a degree from Oregon State, in 1932, the first Indian to graduate there since 1888. Photo courtesy Sina Thompson Bell and Dodie Bell.

Three generations: Coquelle Thompson, Sr., his son Coquelle (Tom) Thompson, Jr., and (in sailor hat) Coquelle Thompson III. Photo courtesy George Thompson.

Coquelle's daughter, Private Sina Thompson (1920–2002), Communications Specialist, Third Bomber Group, Eighth Air Force, Elveden Hall, England, 1943–45. Photo courtesy Sina Thompson Bell and Dodie Bell.

Coquelle Thompson's daughter, Sina Thompson Bell (front), and his granddaughter, Dodie Bell (back), Fort Belknap Reservation, Montana. August 1999. Photo by William R. Seaburg.

Coquelle Thompson's grandson, George, at his home in Siletz, Oregon, 2000. Photo by Lionel Youst.

A portable electric phonograph recorder developed by Philip A. Jacobsen (left), University of Washington, Dept. of General Engineering, and his assistant, Orin Johnston (right). They are delivering it to Melville Jacobs at Charleston, Oregon, summer of 1934, to aid in his field research. Photo courtesy William R. Seaburg.

Elizabeth D. Jacobs (1903–83), wife of Melville Jacobs. She interviewed Coquelle Thompson during 1935, compiling over 800 pages of field notes from him. Photo, ca. 1932, courtesy William R. Seaburg.

John Peabody Harrington (1884–1961). An ethnologist with the Smithsonian Institution from 1915 until 1957, and a legend in his own time, he was the last anthropologist to interview Coquelle Thompson. Photo courtesy National Anthropological Archives, Smithsonian Institution.

6

Maturity
Tribal Police, Anthropologists, and Fatherhood

By 1875 the 1,440,000 acres of the original Coast Reservation had been reduced to 298,000 acres of what would now be called the Siletz Reservation. As the traditional "gentile system"* at the Siletz Reservation broke down and the tribal groupings merged into the larger reservation community of a confederated tribe, individuals became increasingly "several and distinct." The allotment of land "in severalty" was coming much nearer to a reality. Coquelle separated from his wife, Annetti. Their daughter, Sina, was about to leave them to attend one of the first classes of one of the first Indian boarding schools in the United States, at Chemawa. The elders, as elders do, continued to die. The first wave of scholars from the East came to study and record what was left of the old languages and traditions before they became extinct, as it was known they would. And old ideas and ways of life were in direct conflict with the new.

* "Gentile: of or pertaining to a tribe, clan, nation, etc." This term was used by anthropologists during the last half of the nineteenth century, as seen in the title of J. Owen Dorsey's 1890 paper, "The Gentile System of the Siletz Tribes." A "gens" implies a group of persons tracing common descent in the male line. Some tribal groups trace descent in the female line, and so the term was found to be misleading and fell into disuse.

In keeping with the old ideas, Coquelle told Elizabeth Jacobs, "A man is head of his family; he can do anything he likes." Evidently, male fidelity in marriage was neither expected nor encouraged. The exception, according to Coquelle, would be "unless the woman he went with was married." That meant, "getting in trouble." But Coquelle had not gotten "in trouble" on his twelve-month venture to the south. He had come back to his wife and daughter, and he fully expected that Annetti would acquiesce in his adventures. "Wives didn't care," Coquelle said, "Never got mad." From Coquelle's perspective they never got mad "as long as it wasn't doing wrong with a married woman."[1] Coquelle had been careful about that.

But he told of an instance in which a wife did care, with tragic consequences. Her husband's name was Bill Strong, and he "kept staying down at Lower Farm—wouldn't come home." Coquelle explained that Bill had been "running around to see other women all the time. Three or four women." When he finally did come home one morning his wife "insulted him," according to Coquelle. She said, "Did you get enough now, you finally come home? Did you get enough?" He was too tired, evidently, to respond right away and lay down to rest "for a few hours." When he got up he was angry, and asked her crossly, "Say it over, what you said to me this morning." She answered, "I asked you, did you have enough to *eat*, that you just come home now." He let that go for a few minutes, then growled, "You'd better tell me again what you said to me this morning." She growled back, "I said you got enough to *eat* so you come back. That's what I said." Her mother was in the adjoining room and heard the quarrel. "Then Bill went out to the sweathouse," Coquelle said.

Coquelle continued the story with the telling details that were his hallmark. "The wife went out doors, untied the wood basket rope, hid it under her clothes. She went down to the river and went across. She spotted an old alder. She tied the rope there—fixed it. When nearly everyone had gone to bed, she put her neck in that rope and jumped. Her feet didn't quite touch the ground. She made a noise, choking. The old lady heard her and ran outside: 'Hurry! My daughter went out. I don't know which way, but I hear a noise across the river.' They took a light and went. They saw her hanging there. She was already dead. They raised up the body, cut the rope, put her in the boat and brought her home."

Coquelle said that they made Bill Strong pay for that. "It was his fault. He killed her himself," he said. "The Old Lady heard them growl." Coquelle noted that "very seldom a thing like that happened a long time ago. Very few Indians do that."[2] But in another context he said that suicide was fairly common for women, but that "a man never killed himself."[3]

From time to time a wife left her husband. Dan Jerdon's wife, the mother of his many children, left him. This was a bitter pill for old Dan, and he went for revenge. He told Coquelle that he sneaked into her house and got a lock of her hair and put it in the graveyard. Coquelle declared, "That woman died in less than two years. I asked him, 'What did you do that for?' He said, 'I just didn't like it that she got another man; that's why I did it.'"[4]

Coquelle and Annetti had no such animosities toward each other, but by this time they were probably drifting apart emotionally. They had been together since they were in their teens, and no doubt the one thing still holding them together was their only child, Sina. Sina had been attending the Siletz school, where the old ways were being replaced by the new. She was learning to read and write.

During those years a Methodist minister was teaching the Siletz school. That had been a bone of contention with Joel Palmer while he was agent at Siletz, and it was still a problem for some. Palmer complained that he was obliged to keep a Methodist minister on the payroll, drawing the same pay as the government farmer. To get some work out of him, Palmer had him assigned to teach school, but when one or two cases of rumored smallpox showed up, the teacher abruptly left teaching and became a blacksmith. Palmer indicated that he would be amenable to the services of "divines and missionaries," provided they would "labor for the good of the cause, and not solely for the dollar."[5]

The parts of the reservation at the mouths of the Siletz and Salmon Rivers were remote enough to be seldom visited by either the agent or the Methodist minister. They were, however, frequently visited by Father Adrian Croquet, the Catholic missionary priest at Grand Ronde. He was well acquainted with all of the Indians living there and introduced to them his friend Richard W. Summers, the Episcopal priest at McMinnville. In August 1878, Summers visited all of the houses looking for "antiques." His journal entry for that trip poignantly reveals the tenuous hold those people had on their past.

At Siletz Bay, he found a plain wooden spoon, a basket hat, a burden strap, a half-dozen miscellaneous baskets, a rattle, and a fish-gig. "There was absolutely no other antique among them. We were rejoiced to obtain these, the last remnants of their own civilization," Father Summers wrote in his journal. He was not unmindful of implications. Earlier in his journal he described an aged chief, "Lip-ma-shell, of the Santiams," who had agreed to allow Summers "to see some *ictas* (relics), which he said he had and would sell to me." There was only a carved spoon and a basket, "which had once been his when he was a great Chief over a powerful tribe. . . . I almost wept as I looked at his aged figure and thought once more, Poor old man! Victim of my race!" Summers was perhaps the first of the serious "curio hunters" in the Siletz area and left his collection to the British Museum.[6]

The earliest Christian instruction for Indians at Siletz was from Father Croquet. From time to time he would come to Siletz to hear confessions, hold Mass, perform marriages, baptize babies and the elderly, and generally attend to his flock. This had been going on for over twenty years when, in 1883, he arrived and according to Archbishop Charles J. Seghers, was "treated rudely by the present Agent at Siletz, who made use of his police to interfere with the religious freedom of his Indians." The archbishop complained bitterly to the secretary of the interior over this "intolerable piece of petty tyranny."[7]

Coquelle Thompson was on the Indian police force, and although he never mentioned it, he may very well have been detailed to take part in that disgraceful incident. Father Croquet was in no way an intruder, but removing actual intruders was probably the most important duty that fell to the Indian police. Coquelle told John Peabody Harrington that he was frequently detailed to take white intruders to Toledo or Newport.[8] In an interview, his daughter Sina (II) remembered that Coquelle had enjoyed that part of his job. The intruder would have to ride bareback, behind Coquelle's saddle. Coquelle would say, "They had to ride my behind!"[9] Budget constraints were so severe that the police were seldom reimbursed for travel expenses. On August 19, 1884, for example, the commissioner of Indian Affairs in Washington, D.C., authorized $21.75 travel pay for the police, but declared that "future expenses will not be allowed."

The pay of the policemen was so low that the incentive to serve likely came from the small degree of prestige and authority that went with the job. Agent Edmund A. Swan stated in his report of August 28, 1882, that "the force of twelve men was continued though the year, rendering good service for the remuneration received. The amount is so small as not to prove an incentive to efficiency, or lead them to exercise a feeling of pride in their official calling." The pay was eight dollars per month for the captain and five dollars per month for the sergeant and the privates.

As a further example of the type of work the police were engaged in, Swan reported for 1882 that "some few whites have been driven off for minor offenses." He noted that he had removed "Joseph Howard, a quarter breed, and his wife, an Indian woman" because of Howard's "persistency in gambling and drinking when outside." He said that "Howard left the reserve when ordered; his wife refusing to go was taken off by the police." The problem seemed to be chronic. In his 1884 report, Agent Wadsworth complained, "I have trouble with the low tramps about whiskey, and they tamper with my police as well as others."

The Indian police were also commonly called to respond to domestic disputes. Agent Wadsworth stated in his report of August 13, 1883, "The greater portion of complaints brought are for wife-whipping." It is not clear from the report whether there was a lot of "wife-whipping" at the time, or just relatively few other offenses being committed.

Studies on the causes of domestic violence usually indicate that where such violence exists, alcohol can increase its level and intensity.[10] Alcohol was a major concern of the agent, and one in which he might hope the police could help. The sale and consumption of whiskey was illegal on the reservation, but one of Coquelle's nearly lifelong habits, which he may have picked up during his stay at Empire, was the moderate use of whiskey. This led to what was probably his only run-in with the authorities.

It was no doubt an excruciatingly humiliating incident for Coquelle. He had been appointed captain of the police force several times in the past, and reappointed and confirmed by the commissioner of Indian Affairs as of July 1, 1883. Two and a half weeks later, on July 17, he was caught giving whiskey to another Indian. He was "removed from the force and also punished by confinement and hard labor," according to Agent Wadsworth's report to the commissioner dated August 13, 1883. Although he was later rehired many times as a private and sometimes again served as captain, this incident probably constituted the nadir of his career.

One of the more delicate problems with which the Indian police had to contend concerned relationships of white men and Indian women on the reservation. Following the Civil War most of the states passed laws that prohibited marriages between whites and blacks. The Oregon legislature in 1866 passed one of those laws, which specified that whites could not marry anyone with "one-fourth or more Negro, Chinese or Kanaka (Hawaiian) blood, or any person having more than one-half Indian blood." It passed the lower house with almost no debate, 47 to 8. The state senate passed it into law with a vote of 15 to 4.* The penalty was up to one year in jail, and the minister conducting the ceremony could, in addition, be subjected to a $1,000 fine. Joel Palmer was a member of the state senate at that time and was one of the fifteen senators who voted in favor of the law.

Joel Palmer may have been shocked when he later discovered the results of a law he had voted to pass. He first described the unfortunate situation in his December 26, 1871, letter to Alfred B. Meacham, superintendent of Indian Affairs. He said, "Wilst on my recent trip south I found quite a number of white men living with Indian women to whom they have not been married. Several of them have children. There are also a number around Yaquina. Numbers of such expressed a willingness to marry such women if permitted by law to do so." During the years prior to passage of the antimiscegenation laws, white men who wanted to legally marry their Indian wives could do so, and many did. But now there was a serious social problem created by those ill-conceived laws. Palmer pointed out, "The Coose Bay and Rogue River districts have become notorious for this class of cases, and where there are no binding obligations the women and children are often thrown onto the cold charities of a prejudiced people without any redress."[11]

Palmer had sought authority for a solution to the problem, and was seeking legal advice. He asked, "Have we by virtue of our office as Indian Agent residing upon a reservation exclusively under the jurisdiction of the United States Government and laws, though within the boundaries of a state whose laws prohibit such marriages, the right to issue licenses for solemnizing such marriages within the limits of such reservation!" The answer turned out to be "no," he had no such authority.

---

* *Acts and Resolutions of the Legislative Assembly of the State of Oregon*, 1866, p. 10. 1866 *Senate Journal*, p. 236, pertaining to the evening session of the Senate on October 17, 1866, indicates that Palmer voted yes on that act. The final vote tally was 15 yes, 4 no, 3 absent. This act remained law in Oregon until it was repealed in 1951.

The problem did not go away. In a letter written a year later, on November 23, 1872, Palmer pointed up another aspect of the problem: "Quite a number of the women properly belonging here are living with white men in the Rogue River and Coose Bay settlements, and along the sea coast between Yaquina and Crescent City, a portion of whom are legally married, but a large number are united in accordance with Indian custom, to be cast off at the will of their pardners without redress tho many such are raising families. Many of the relations of such seek to abandon the reservation to be near them." Palmer wanted either to be authorized to issue marriage licenses or, as he said, to "prosecute such as entice these women from the reservation."[12]

That was a major problem. Several years later it was still plaguing the reservation, as in an incident described in a letter to the *Corvallis Gazette*, written by the agency physician, Dr. John Boswell. Pointing out the advantage of having a tribal police force he said, "It has had a good effect, so far, in checking crime on the reservation, and we recently had a fine illustration of its beneficial effects on a certain class of white men." It seems that a white man had recently come onto the reservation and without checking in at the agency, stopped at a house nearby. The Indian head of household, who was at home, tried to get the man to check in at the agency, but he refused. That night the Indian police arrested the intruder, who was placed in the guardhouse. In the morning he was "sent under escort of an Indian policeman, off the reservation."

The police escort could very well have been Coquelle Thompson, because that was exactly the kind of assignment that he often had. Dr. Boswell said that while on the way off the reservation the intruder told his police escort "that his object was to get a squaw for his wife, and live among the Indians; that he had had one squaw wife and wanted another." The good doctor told the readers of the *Gazette* that any of "this class of persons . . . that find their way here" can expect the same kind of treatment. He concluded with his own personal opinion: "Whether the Indians here are making advancement in other respects, or not, they do not propose to furnish any more wives to men that call themselves white, and yet are too low down to get wives among their own people."[13]

Indians were certainly making advancement in their self-reliance. In Agent Edmund A. Swan's fourth annual report (1882) is a section concerning the sawmill. A steam sawmill had replaced the obsolete water-powered mill several years earlier, and Swan reported that "the labor in the mills is all performed by Indians with a single exception. I am pleased to say that a number of Indians, so far as I know for the first time, cut their timber, drew their logs, and sawed their own lumber without the aid of government, thus proving themselves on the road to self-support and independence, a thing of which they feel a pride."[14] The need for lumber was always great, and the Alsea Indians who had been dislocated from their homes on the Yaquina and Alsea Rivers were trying to establish themselves at Lower Farm. They needed houses, as did others. But there was seldom money in the budget to pay the sawyer and the engineer, who were white.

Swan's successor, F. M. Wadsworth, expressed the opinion in his first annual report (1883) that it had been a great mistake "in making these mills steam power instead of water power. If they had been provided with water power the Indians could have used them without assistance. As it is, the saw-mill cannot be run without an engineer and head sawyer, and we must ask the Department for funds to work with."[15] Of course, there was no reason at all why Indian men could not have served apprenticeships in those positions, and it is almost certain that by 1883 there were Indian men who could run a steam engine and saw logs with no problem. The custom of having white men do those two specialized jobs was ingrained, however.

At least by 1884, when he was about thirty-five years old, Coquelle became the titular chief of the Coquille Indians at Siletz. Coquelle Charlie, about whom we hear no more, had evidently died some time before. Coquelle held the title of chief from 1884 until his death more than sixty years later.

In late August of 1884, Coquelle and most of the other residents of the reservation were preparing to go to the Willamette Valley to pick hops when a sickly looking white man arrived and wanted to interview the chief. The man was J. Owen Dorsey (1848–95), an Episcopal deacon who as a missionary on the Great Plains had become an authority on the Siouan languages and was now employed as a linguist and ethnologist with the Bureau of American Ethnology (BAE). The BAE, later incorporated into the Smithsonian Institution, was embarking on an intense campaign to salvage as much information as possible about the many native cultures of North America before they disappeared. The intellectual framework for the effort came from

Lewis Henry Morgan's influential book *Ancient Society*, published in 1877. In the preface, Morgan succinctly described the problem: "The ethnic life of the Indian tribes is declining under the influence of American civilization, their arts and languages are disappearing, and their institutions are dissolving. After a few more years, facts that may now be gathered with ease will become impossible of discovery."[16]

Dorsey had been sent from Washington, D.C., to Siletz "for the purpose of procuring linguistic material to assist in completing a classification of the Indians of the United States." The previous year Dr. Willis E. Everette had been at Siletz, possibly the first of many anthropologists to follow. Everette had collected "words, phrases, and sentences in the language of the Tu-tu-te-ne and nine confederated tribes of Siletz River, Oregon," but he evidently did not record anything in the Upper Coquille Athabaskan.* Dorsey, in a letter to his boss, John Wesley Powell, said that "the Indians here dislike Dr. W. Everette, who paid them nothing for the information which they gave him last year."[17]

Dorsey was ordered to "be on the alert to discover languages new to linguistic science."[18] The data was to be incorporated into Powell's *Indian Linguistic Families of America North of Mexico*, which became immensely influential after its publication by the BAE in 1891. There was probably no one in the United States at that time who was better qualified than Dorsey to do the fieldwork.

There were twenty languages and dialects spoken at Siletz, according to Dorsey's count. He had been given four months to collect enough information to classify them all, but he was not in good health and he could not adjust to the wet climate. In a letter to Powell on September 6, he indicated that he was afraid of catching pneumonia. "I find my blood almost too thin to stand the dampness (in the morning) which no clothing seems able to exclude, even on fair days, to say nothing of rainy ones." "Rainy ones" would come with increasing frequency at Siletz during the coming months, and so Dorsey felt the need to finish the job and get back home as soon as possible. He was, according to J. N. B. Hewitt, "methodical, rapid, and untiring, accomplishing in a given time an amount of labor that was astounding in its extent and accuracy."[19] Even so he was concerned that he would not have time to get all he wanted because so

---

* From James C. Pilling's *Bibliography of the Athapascan Languages* (1892), 30.

many of the Indians who could act as linguistic informants would be off the reservation, working the harvest.[20]

After arriving at Siletz on August 20, Dorsey launched immediately into his work. Within two days of his arrival he was interviewing Coquelle Thompson, collecting Upper Coquille Athabaskan words. Probably a few days after that the bulk of the inhabitants of the reservation left for the Willamette Valley to pick hops. Dorsey busied himself interviewing those few who remained and was soon to discover that the 150 words he had received from Coquelle Thompson appeared to be in a "modern dialect, influenced by Tutu [Tututni], Sixes, etc." Dorsey said in his report dated October 1, "It will be necessary to get the services of an old man who speaks the pure Coquelle."[21] Coquelle Thompson had, of course, grown up at Lower Farm among the several closely related southern Oregon Athabaskan peoples, and the language, as he spoke it, probably had many words that had not been spoken by his father's generation on the Upper Coquille River.

The "old man" that Dorsey employed was Coquelle Solomon, about fifty years old and married to one of Coquelle's paternal aunts. They lived at Upper Farm where they had two sons, Billy and Frank.[22] Dorsey interviewed Solomon on October 1.[23] A few days later the hop-pickers began returning from the valley, and on October 18 Dorsey interviewed Coquelle Thompson again.

Old Solomon may have been present during the Coquelle Thompson interview of the 18th, but the evidence suggests that Coquelle was the primary consultant.[24] Occasionally Dorsey would place the initial (S) or (T) indicating whether it was Solomon or Thompson who gave a particular word, but more often he did not. Dorsey probably checked one against the other and merely noted by initial the cases where they differed. On one page he wrote, "All entries below were given by Coquille Thompson," but there is ambiguity as to whether or not the information on subsequent pages was also given by Thompson.

Dorsey had been given a list of vocabulary items, which was being used by investigators throughout North America. In effect, Dorsey would say, "Here is an English word—what is the Indian equivalent?" Using the phonetic alphabet recommended by Powell, he would then write a transcription of the word given by his informant.

He recorded 745 entries for the Upper Coquille, elicited from his two informants, Coquelle Thompson and Old Solomon. What he compiled was basically a word list, a lexicon, which overwhelmingly consisted of nouns. There were, in addition, a few possessive pronoun paradigms, some demonstrative and adjectival forms, and a few verbs and verbal paradigms, but there were no syntactic constructions or texts.[25] Once the close relationship of the Upper Coquille to the Tututni had become clear from the word list, Dorsey concentrated on the Tututni. He elicited 3,962 entries from his twelve Tututni informants.

Dorsey gained a favorable impression of the Indians living at Siletz. He was surprised, and pleased, to find that they "all wore clothing of civilized people, and dwelt on their farms in comfortable houses," as he indicated in a letter to Powell. He concluded, "The politeness of these Indians was remarkable, the writer having seen but one man who did not greet him with a smile, and say, 'Good morning' or 'good evening,' if able to speak a little English."[26] The pleasant demeanor of the people, however, hardly compensated for Dorsey's inability to cope with the damp climate. He had to get out of there.

The railroad had not yet come to the Yaquina River from the Willamette Valley. After the first rains, the stages could not get through to Corvallis. Dorsey hoped to be able to go to Newport and from there to San Francisco by ship, but that turned out to be impossible. There was no regular shipping into Yaquina Bay. Agent Wadsworth was leaving Siletz for Portland on October 30, and Dorsey decided to accompany him. "It will be my best chance (for some time) for securing a conveyance, there being no stages running between Elk city and Corvallis on account of the roads," Dorsey wrote to the BAE director.[27]

By the time he finally left Siletz on October 30, Dorsey had filled 749 pages of field notes with vocabularies of twenty different languages. They formed the basis for classifying most of the languages of western Oregon, including a dozen from the Athabaskan; the Alsea and Yaquina; the Siuslaw and the Lower Umpqua; the Miluk Coos; Takelma; Shasta; and Klikitat Sahaptan. Some of those languages were, in the words of the orders that had sent him to Siletz, "new to linguistic science."

Using Dorsey's data along with data from other field researchers throughout North America, John Wesley Powell and his staff at the BAE proposed fifty-eight distinct "linguistic families" and assigned each language a place within a particular family.[28] Although the term "linguistic family" has been adjusted and redefined several times over the years, Powell's placement of the individual languages within the scheme has remained almost unchanged to the present.[29]

Dorsey had consulted with forty-six different speakers of the languages at Siletz, paying them from a dollar to a dollar fifty cents per day for their help.[30] That was presumably about the same daily rate as they received for picking hops in the valley. Coquelle received perhaps three or four dollars for his three days of interviews, which provided vocabulary for the Upper Coquille Athabaskan. He evidently enjoyed what he did, although it would be fifty years before he would have another chance to work as a consultant to a field researcher.

Coquelle was sought out by Dorsey (and by later researchers) because he was thought to have knowledge of the language and traditions of the precontact peoples of the Upper Coquille River. His knowledge of the Upper Coquille was quite remarkable for someone who left that area when he was only six or eight years old, but much of that knowledge was not firsthand. It came from his elders after they had moved to the Siletz. He had, in fact, become familiar with much of the million-plus acres of the original reservation, and insofar as he was aware of them, he was respectful of the sacred places. He did what he could to keep such traditions going.

There were very few surviving Indians who were native to the Siletz River and who thus knew of those traditional places, but one of them, a man who lived in comparative isolation at the mouth of the Salmon River, was a close acquaintance of Coquelle and his wife. His name was "Doctor Johnson." Whether his name implied that he was a shaman is unknown. Mrs. Thompson told John Peabody Harrington that Johnson's father was Tillamook and that his mother was one of the few natives of the Siletz River who had lived into the reservation period.[31] He was sometimes listed in official documents as Doctor (Alsea) Johnson.

Coquelle had become acquainted with Doctor Johnson because from time to time the Indians from the mouth of the Siletz and Salmon Rivers would show up at the agency to receive their entitlements of flour and other staples. Coquelle, who was an employee at the agency, said that he "used to give [Doctor Johnson] a dispensation of grub."[32] The first trip that Coquelle made by canoe the thirty miles down the Siletz River to its mouth was with Johnson, and it was from him that Coquelle learned about Medicine Rock.

Medicine Rock is twenty miles downstream of the agency. They arrived there about noon. Coquelle wanted to be sure to get to the mouth of the Siletz by sunset, but Doctor Johnson insisted that they stop. He told the story of a man and his wife who had been there and had evidently been turned into that rock. In any case, you were supposed to leave an offering of some kind, "You have to feed them," Johnson said. Coquelle told Elizabeth Jacobs, "All kinds of things were hanging there. I gave a handkerchief." Johnson told Coquelle, "Never stop without giving them something or you'll have bad luck." "Now I understood," Coquelle said. "So every time I went, I gave it bread or something."

Doctor Johnson was a great hunter and as such was highly admired by Coquelle. His right arm had been paralyzed as a result of a severe burn when he was a young man, but in spite of the handicap, Coquelle said that Johnson "hunted all over, as old Indians did." He made good money, "especially when he caught beaver or otter." One of his specialties was bear. "He got bears every spring," Coquelle said. The bear would come onto Camas Prairie (at Lower Farm) to get skunk cabbage, and that is where Johnson would set his steel traps. One time a bear had got into the trap and "pretty near had worked his paw off cutting it more than half way through." Johnson arrived and "clubbed the bear on the head; the bear got loose and attacked Doctor Johnson and tore his scalp bad." Johnson held his hands to his throat so that the bear couldn't bite it, and finally got into the creek. "The bear gave him up for dead and went away." The agency medical doctor attended Johnson, who survived and continued to hunt. According to Coquelle, "He never wore shoes."[33]

Coquelle was himself known as a hunter, a fisherman, and guide. While working as a guide, his contact with a variety of whites gave him a chance to observe them at close quarters. In the woods, on a two- or three-day hunting trip, Coquelle could accurately observe both what he had in common with his white clients and what was irreconcilably different about them. Although nothing in his narratives indicates that he held a prejudice against the whites, he always regarded them as something curious and apart and he sometimes slipped in comments that revealed his attitude.

All of Coquelle's hunting skills had been gained after arriving on the Siletz. Boys started hunting with the men when they were ten or twelve years old, and Coquelle had been at Siletz for about four years by the time he reached that age.[34] His principal mentor appears to have been his uncle Old Hunter. Coquelle probably could not have had a better teacher. "Old Hunter knew everything," Coquelle once said.

One time Coquelle and his cousin Ben Johnson were with Old Hunter. The three of them were guiding a "boss man" named Bill Beck and another white man on a hunt near the headwaters of the Siletz. They were following a creek to the westward when Bill Beck killed a deer. They weren't hungry, so "we just fixed the deer so bear couldn't get it. Then we went on towards the mountain." The expedition was getting off to a good start, and they were all alert and in good spirits. The two white men were in front when they came to an open place and "suddenly just thirty steps in front of us, an elk got up and stretched himself." They told Bill Beck, "You shoot." That, of course, was the job of a good guide: to place the client into a position to shoot a trophy. "He shot in the right place. The elk turned, ran a little ways and fell down. That big elk lay there, horns that wide," Coquelle told Elizabeth Jacobs, gesturing with his arms outspread, fingertip to fingertip.

They hunted on into the next day, and Old Hunter sent Ben Johnson back to get more people to help pack in the meat and the trophy. By then Bill Beck, satisfied with his hunt, was ready to return. Old Hunter told him how to get back. "Just take that first ridge," he said, but cautioned him not to get over to the other side of it. Coquelle commented that Bill Beck "didn't know much about the mountain," and so, as a precaution, Coquelle followed him. "I thought he ought to go down to the river, but he went a different way. I knew he was lost then, but I didn't say anything."

They came to the head of a little creek and Bill Beck said, "Oh, here's Palmer Creek." Palmer Creek is about two miles long and empties into the Siletz River from the north, near Upper Farm. Coquelle asked, "Yes? How far is it from Palmer Creek to the river?" Bill Beck said, "Oh, just a little ways." "It was near sundown now," Coquelle said, "So I told him, 'We're lost, we'll have to build a fire.' Oh he felt badly." At that point in the story Coquelle broke into laughter. "Ha Ha! We had come to the head of Jerden Creek, you know!" The head of Palmer Creek was a good half-day's walk away.

"The next morning," Coquelle continued, "he sent me up a tree to look. I saw the mountain at Upper Farm. `We'll have to go this way,' I told him. 'All right,' he said. Now *I* walked ahead." Bill Beck, the outsider boss, turned over the lead to Coquelle, who quickly exercised his new authority. "We went along," he said. "In one place we found a fine bird. He tried to hit it with a stick. 'Don't bother things like that on the mountain.' 'What's the matter?' he asked. I told him, 'Well, you got lost once, maybe you'll get lost again if you don't leave it alone.' 'Oh don't say that.' 'Well let it alone, then.'" Humbled, Bill Beck followed Coquelle "back onto that lost ridge," from whence they arrived at the head of Palmer Creek, "and we got home about noon."[35]

In March 1885, only a few months after Dorsey left Siletz for the East, the long-awaited steam railroad from Corvallis to Yaquina Bay made its first run.[36] The now easy rail transportation between the reservation and the Willamette Valley brought with it a new boom of real estate speculation and a new influx of intruders to the reservation. However, the railroad ran both ways, and so it also became easy and practical for the Indians to travel out. One consequence of this new, fast, and easy travel was enrollment at the federal Chemawa Indian Boarding School of a few Indian students from the Siletz Reservation. The boarding school opened near Salem about six months after the railroad had arrived at Yaquina.

The Chemawa Indian Boarding School (which is still in operation and is the oldest operating Indian boarding school in the United States) had been established at Forest Grove in 1880, but in October 1885 was moved and reopened on 171 acres of donated land a little north of Salem.[37] Among the first of the students sent to that boarding school from the Siletz Reservation was Sina Thompson, daughter of Coquelle and Annetti.[38]

Most of the Indian parents at Siletz were understandably reluctant to turn their children over to this new institution. The supervisor at Chemawa had previously complained that the Siletz Reservation had not furnished any students.[39] Coquelle, however, had spent his career working between the white and the Indian worlds. Sina had completed as much schooling as was available at Siletz, and Coquelle apparently saw advantages to her obtaining the training offered at Chemawa. She entered the boarding school on December 22, 1886, barely a year after it had opened at Salem. She was fourteen years old.

Agent Wadsworth was likely instrumental in preparing the application and making arrangements for Sina to enter Chemawa. We can imagine that sometime before Christmas 1886, Coquelle hitched up the wagon and drove Sina to the railroad station at Toledo, ten miles south of the agency. It is not known whether he went to Chemawa with her on the train, but it is altogether possible. The original superintendent of the school, Lieutenant Melville Wilkinson, encouraged parents to visit and even attempted to get the Indian Service to pay for such visits. He found that when the parents became acquainted with the school, most of their fears and misconceptions about it were alleviated. The visits actually turned out to be a good marketing tool, because parents sometimes returned to the reservation with "positive remarks about Chemawa."[40] Over the years, Coquelle sent all of his older children there, and so it is almost certain that he had become familiar with it.

At the time that Sina entered Chemawa, it was offering five years of high school vocational training for Indian students from the northwest states. Sina attended for four years, leaving on May 1, 1890, when she was eighteen. Academic classes were held in the morning and vocational classes in the afternoon. During the time that she was at Chemawa, her vocational training included working in the harvests in the Willamette Valley. During September of her first year, for example, the students "went out and picked hops earning about $1500," according to the report of Superintendent John Lee. Lee explained that "one half of these wages [was] paid to themselves in cash, the rest being applied as a payment on the tract of land, consisting of eighty-five acres, purchased last year."[41] The school was chronically underfunded, and the supervisor attempted to make it as economically self-sufficient as possible by using student labor to help obtain a land base large enough to produce the food for the student body, and by using student labor to work the farm. This labor was considered to be a valuable part of the vocational training of the school.

The objective of government policy at that time was to prepare Indian children for full assimilation into the general society. The boarding schools were used, in part, to further those ends. What is often not understood is the extent to which the schools reinforced a sense of Indian identity. Judging from interviews with alumni, it appears that the students at Chemawa were appreciative of the fact that they were in school exclusively with other Indian students, and they also tended to appreciate the educational and vocational skills they received there. As Sonciray Bonnell noted in a summary of her interviews with twenty-three alumni of Chemawa, they "were able

Maturity: Tribal Police, Anthropologists, and Fatherhood

to view Chemawa in a positive light because students molded their boarding school experiences to fit their needs. Students created their own families (friends), community (school), and resisted the institutional suppression of Indian boarding schools."[42] The net result was that the school tended to increase, not decrease, their feelings of Indian identity.

Many of the students found their mates at the school, married, and had children. After graduation some of them moved with their new spouses to other reservations and other parts of the country. Coquelle's two children who lived to marry and have children of their own both found their spouses at Chemawa: his son Coquelle Jr. met his wife there; a few years after graduation his youngest daughter, Sina II, married a former classmate. He was from the Belknap Reservation, Montana, where Sina lived for most of her life. It is almost certain that Coquelle recognized the benefits to his children of being educated at Chemawa, because his four children who lived long enough to finish the program at Chemawa, did so.

Coquelle apparently got along well with most of the agents who came and went over the years at Siletz. He and they seemed to have held each other in mutual respect. T. Jay Buford, who came in 1888 and remained for thirteen years, may have been typical of them. One time Buford hired Coquelle to guide him and his family and another family in two boats down the Siletz River on a camping trip to Devils Lake. When they got to Medicine Rock, Coquelle, true to what he had learned from Doctor Johnson, insisted that they give something. The whites all laughed.

"I said, 'It's all right if you don't want to believe it, but give something anyhow, give a piece of bread but give something." They all gave something, and Coquelle told them, "You'll get good luck." As they came into Siletz Bay that evening they killed a harbor seal and caught two of the seal pups, which the women and children of the party wanted to play with. Coquelle told them, "Don't bother them—don't feed them." As he told the story to Elizabeth Jacobs, he laughed as he added, "You know how white people are!" He said that the girls "hung onto them just like little pups. They're cute, you know."

A Euchre Creek Indian named Curly was at the beach. He told them that they shouldn't bother the seals, or there would be a big storm. They made camp, put one of the boats on top of drift logs so the tide wouldn't carry it away, and pitched tents. Coquelle said, "It's lots of work when you take white women. They played with those seals." The implication was clear that the white women, unlike Indian women, would do none of the work. About eleven o'clock that night a big storm woke them up. "Big thunder," Coquelle said. "The ocean raised the dickens and water came right in the door. Oh! I got scared. They all got up, holding on to those little seals. Big wind! I heard something bust. It was the boat tipping over and going to pieces. Rain, rain, rain!"

Curly came back and told them, "Put them [the seals] back in the water or there'll be something doing." So Coquelle made the girls put the seals back into the water. "I walked with them," he said. "Those seals swam around good. One went to the ocean. The next morning I heard one still swimming around. It cried like a sheep. By noon I didn't hear it any more. The next morning was a fine day."

Having lost one of the two boats, they hired two teams to haul the party up the beach to Devils Lake.[43] Along the shores of the lake was fine grazing and unoccupied pastureland,[44] and near its northeast corner is a creek that opens onto a few hundred acres of that grazing land. There was very little that escaped Coquelle's notice, and he filed this observation away in his memory. The information proved to be very useful later on, when an eighty-acre allotment was granted to each family member. At that time Coquelle selected the land along that creek for his then eight-year-old son, Jacob Walker Thompson. But we are getting ahead of the story.

Now that Sina, their only child, was at the boarding school at Chemawa, life changed for Coquelle and Annetti. Coquelle described it succinctly: "We were not married, so we parted."[45] They had been together about fifteen years.

Coquelle had been seeing a thirty-one-year-old Tututni woman. Her name was Emma, and she was born in 1856 in Curry County, during the Rogue River War. She had an older half-sister, Martha Johnson, from the same father but a different mother. The father, whose name was Glas-eh, had been killed during the war.[46] Emma's mother, Sa-tusk-ka, died some years later at Siletz. Coquelle had never met Emma's mother, but was well acquainted with the half-sister, Martha.

Emma was a strong woman who was orphaned young and grew up very fast. When she was still in her teens, she went from Siletz to northern California with a Tututni man named Dandy James. She had two children by him in California, but both the children and Dandy James died there. She returned to Siletz with a Tolowa man, this one called Smith River Johnny, but broke up with him about a month later.[47] It was then that she married Robert Felix, a Tututni man who may have been temperamentally unstable.[48] They were together about eight years when Felix moved in with another woman, Lavina, with whom he had several children. Emma and Felix had no children together, and it was following their breakup that she began seeing Coquelle.

Coquelle and Emma were seeing each other at least by September 1887. We know very little else about the affair, but we do know that Coquelle and Emma were married "by license" on January 17, 1888, by a minister named David Enes. The witnesses were M. G. Short and Annie Short. Four months after the wedding, on May 28, 1888, their first son, Paul, was born. The Catholic church records for Grand Ronde, Register II, page 42, have the following entry for the day after Paul's birth: "May 29, 1888, I the undersigned Rector of St. Michael's Church baptized at Siletz among the Indians Paul, born yesterday to Coquille Thompson and his wife Emma. (Signed) A. J. Croquet, Pr." Perhaps due to the weight of "white man's law," Coquelle took this marriage very seriously, and they remained married until Emma's death in 1903. Paul does not show up on the annual census for 1888, or on any subsequent census. It is fair to assume from this that he died in infancy. Of infant death, Coquelle said, "A little baby who dies goes to the same heaven. They say 'the baby goes back into its water.'"[49] Paul is not buried at the Coquelle Thompson family plot in the Siletz cemetery, and nothing more is known of him. Paul was presumably the first of many of Coquelle's children who died young.

According the Chemawa school records, Sina "went home sick May 1, 1890—Bronchitis." She was eighteen years old. There was an appalling number of tuberculosis cases among the students at the school, and one wonders if possibly the "bronchitis" might have been a misdiagnosed case of TB. Mckeehan quotes a complaint by the agent at the Klamath Agency, which gives some idea of the incidence of disease at the time that Sina was at the school. He said that of the nineteen students from Klamath Falls who attended in 1885, the year before Sina enrolled, five died that same year. There were 200 remaining on the reservation, of whom only two died during the same period.[50] In any case, Sina must have been very unsure of her future. Her parents had separated, and her father was remarried and starting a new family. Her mother, Annetti, was now working as a cook at the Siletz school, and she would remarry two more times over the ensuing years. Having been "sent home sick," what was she to do?

She evidently ended up at Oysterville, on the south shore of upper Yaquina Bay. Coquelle told John Peabody Harrington that his and Annetti's daughter died at "Oyster Bay," which is what he called Oysterville.[51] The date of Sina's death was May 1, 1893, exactly two years after she had been sent home from Chemawa "sick with bronchitis." The chance is very good that she died of tuberculosis, the most common cause of death at Siletz during those years. Her body was returned for burial in the cemetery at Siletz, and hers is the first marked grave in the Coquelle Thompson plot. She was twenty-one years old, filled with hope and potential. She was the second of Coquelle's children to die.

A few weeks after Sina had completed the program at Chemawa, the Siletz Agency received another scholar from the East. He was to stay for three weeks, from June 12 until July 2, 1890. He was Franz Boas, a German immigrant and at the time a professor at Clark University, Worcester, Massachusetts. He is often considered the father of American anthropology. This was Boas's fourth field trip to the Pacific Northwest. Although he was to make eight more (most of them focusing on research in British Columbia), this was his only visit to Siletz. He had come across the continent on the Northern Pacific Railroad, arriving in Tacoma, Washington, on June 9. He proceeded directly to Portland, and the next day he took the train to Albany, and thence to Toledo on the new Oregon Pacific Railroad. Boas said in his diary: "When I arrived in Toledo that night I found to my dismay that there was no means of going on right away. I spent the evening as well as I could and started to pester them the next morning at six o'clock to move on. But it was eight o'clock before the carriage was ready."[52]

Boas described the trip from Toledo to the Siletz Agency: "The trip to this place was very nice. The road goes along the Coast Range, through hilly country, and is very steep and winding. The first part traverses territory which burned twenty years ago; there is now a young and very lovely forest. Later on one rides through deep forest. At the end, the road leads deep down into the valley, apparently the ancient bottom of the ocean, about two English miles wide. Here lies the main part of the Siletz reservation, extending to the ocean with the Siletz River, a quite small, torrential mountain stream, running through the center. The road leads down to the valley and then fords the river. At about ten o'clock we arrived."[53]

Boas noted that there were "about six hundred Indians on the reservation." He also noted that there was a store, and that the agent lived in a rather nice home. The rest of the staff consisted of a secretary, two teachers (one a craft teacher), and a doctor. Boas made arrangements to stay at the "rough-looking little house" of the crafts teacher, "with all the windows nailed shut." He said, "I eat with the owner of the store and go into the school when I want to write my notes. If it rains I work with my Indians in the attic of the agency; when the sun shines we sit in the open." The number of languages, he said, "is really large." He noted that "most of the young people speak English."[54]

Boas was searching for Salish-speaking Tillamook persons, of whom there were only three on the entire reservation. He went immediately to work with Hyas John, who spoke Tillamook and "was quite good from the ethnological point of view," according to Boas. After ten days with Hyas John, he worked with one of the two last persons to speak the related Siletz language.[55] Over all, Boas was quite pleased with the ethnological and linguistic material he obtained.

His academic background was in geography and physics, but he almost invented modern American anthropology. He was prodigiously productive, perhaps the only anthropologist to contribute equally to American Indian ethnology, descriptive and theoretical linguistics, and statistical physical anthropology.[56] As part of his work in the latter, he made anthropometric measurements and physical observations of some ninety-eight persons while he was at Siletz. Coquelle Thompson was able to provide a very modest contribution to Boas's statistics. He was one of the ninety-eight persons that Boas measured.

The Boas anthropometric data was reviewed during the 1990s by Roberta Hall. She stated that from among the Coquille people at Siletz, Boas measured three adult women and five adult men, one of whom was Coquelle Thompson.[57] The men ranged in age from eighteen to seventy-five years; the women from twenty-two to eighty years. The men averaged "just under 5 feet 3 inches tall," and the women averaged "less than 5 feet 1 inch." The hair and eyes of the Coquille subjects were listed as "black or dark brown." Coquelle Thompson, it is revealed, was a comparatively big man. He measured four inches taller than the average of the Coquille men, being "about 5 feet 7 inches."* He had "straight black hair and dark brown eyes," according to the data sheet. Boas listed Coquelle's age as "about 40," which was very close. He would have been somewhere between 40 and 42 years old in 1890.

There was a lot of sickness during the mid-1890s at Siletz. Coquelle, who was almost never ill, came down with a case of pneumonia during that time. He later described the illness and the cure. "One time I nearly died," he began as he told the story to Elizabeth Jacobs.[58] "Old Dr. Carter said to the Indian Agent, 'I don't think he'll live till morning.'" Dr. Frank Carter had seen a lot of death on the reservation over the years. He was appointed physician at Siletz shortly after he completed a course in surgery at the Toland Medical Institute in San Francisco, in 1874. He remained off and on as physician at Siletz for almost fifty years, until he died at the age of ninety-four in 1937.[59]

Dr. Carter gave Coquelle some white-man's medicine, but it did no good. Coquelle said that he didn't remember anything, hadn't eaten for two weeks. "I am overpowered with fever, pneumonia—can't breath," he said. There was a Coquille woman Indian doctor in attendance, but she was stymied as well. "I wish I knew something," she said. She sang; she danced. Coquelle's wife, Emma, later told him what she did. "She got a wad of hair from the top of my head, she spit in a pan—just full of blood, black. She suck around my eyes, just black, black, like blood. The old men danced, danced, and she sucked and sucked. I didn't know it." Coquelle said that people stayed up all night singing. "When it was getting daylight," Coquelle said, the woman shaman announced, "He's on this world yet; he's not gone yet." The men said the same thing, according to Coquelle. Then, "they all rested a little."

When daylight came, they got "at the doctoring again." The house was full of people, and they began dancing. Coquelle was beginning to wake up, and he had a terrible pain in his temples. "I

---

* The agency records for 1886 showed his height as 5' 9", weight 170 lbs (Seaburg 1994a, 221).

finally feel someone sucking there. I wake up and have sense." He remembered seeing all of the people sitting around, and he thought, "I must be near dying." But, he said, "that old lady and the old men danced and danced. They hold me up sitting. They suck all around." Pneumonia, Coquelle explained, "is just like poison pain, you know." It was about ten o'clock that morning when he was fully awake. He asked, "Got any water to drink?" The old lady gave him a drink and, he said, "I was better that day." They left him alone after that, no more doctoring. "They know I'll be all right," he said. That night he slept well, and the next day he asked for something sour; he wanted crab apples! It was in the fall, and so they went out and picked a few. Coquelle ate "three or four ripe ones." He slept awhile and when he woke again "about noon" he wanted soup. "They fixed boiled wheat. I ate a saucer full," he said. The next day he put on his pants and shirt and "sat down." The old lady shaman told him to "take it slow. Don't try to go right away." "But," she said, "you're all right now." Coquelle said that after an illness "just whatever you asked for they would get it for you."

"In two or three weeks I was at the Agent's place on horse-back," he said. The agent told him, "Why, the doctor said you were dying two weeks ago." Coquelle answered, "Yes, I was dying, but the Indian doctors made me well. I don't believe in no medicine, but Indian doctors—some Indian doctors—are good doctors, maybe." The agent replied, "I won't say I don't believe it." Coquelle said, "I believe it all right. She made me better." As an aside, Coquelle noted that "It didn't cost me anything. She's my folks!"

A boy had been born to Coquelle and Emma in July 1891. They named him Jacob Walker, and when Father Croquet made his rounds to Siletz from Grand Ronde the following November, he was baptized. The Catholic church records have the following entry for the event: "November 29, 1891, I the undersigned Rector of St. Michael's Church, baptized at Siletz Jacob Walker, aged 4 months, son of Washington Thompson and his wife Emma. Godfather was Bernard Williams. A. J. Croquet, Pr."[60] It is interesting that Father Croquet used Coquelle's father's name, Washington. Two years later, in 1893, another boy was born to Coquelle and Emma. They named him Washington; so there was certainly a hope that the name of Coquelle's father, Chief Washington, would carry on. After the earlier deaths, there was renewed hope for descendants after all.

But that hope died with Coquelle's children. By the end of the 1890s all of his children were gone. The first boy, Paul, evidently died soon after he was born in May 1888. Then, on May 1, 1893, Sina died at the age of twenty-one, the same week that Washington Thompson was born. Three years later, on May 6, 1896, Washington Thompson died. Three years after that, on March 12, 1899, his last son, Jacob Walker, died. He was eight years old, about the same age his father Coquelle had been when he was removed to Siletz back in 1856. Three of the four children, Sina, Washington, and Jacob Walker, were buried side by side in what became the Coquelle Thompson plot in the Siletz Indian cemetery on Government Hill.

It may be that the death of his children brought on an "encounter with ghosts" that Coquelle described in some detail to Elizabeth Jacobs. The encounter demonstrates his continuing adherence to the worldview of his people. In about 1895 he was working for a white man named George Collins,[61] whose Indian wife had died leaving him with two small girls. Coquelle was staying in the barn, which he thought would be quieter than the house where the two children would keep him awake. He said it was a "nice clean place."

He had a little table and a light. It was in the fall of the year, and after supper he undressed, "taking my time." He couldn't get to sleep, and when he put out the light he looked up and "saw a light through a hole in the barn." He heard someone walking and thought that George Collins was coming. "Then it got noisier. I could feel all kinds of people walking in the barn. I thought, 'What's the matter?'" "Then pretty soon," he said, "I feel somebody coming by me. More people came by me—they stepped over me, I felt them—till pretty soon that room was full."

Coquelle continued: "Now I began to feel different. They touched my foot. I got up, reached all around, couldn't touch anything." He fixed his light and said, "You fellows come on. Come on, dead people, you don't scare me." But there was nothing there. Coquelle lay still until the candle burned down about halfway and then he got a large club and held it. "I'll knock the son-of-a-gun down," he said, and waited. He put out the candle, slept a little, then about midnight "they kick the door, kick the house around outside." Coquelle had his club ready as he hears them coming. "I just keep still. They came now, were stepping over me. I could feel them standing round, chuck full in the house." He swung his club around, but

"I didn't hit anything, he said. "So I lit the candle again. I put the chair there again. They had moved my chair, tried to take my blanket—that was when I fought." After awhile he sat on the chair for a long time, then decided to try go to sleep again, this time in the wagon. "So I put my bed in the wagon. Now it must have been three o'clock, two, anyhow."

"Pretty soon," Coquelle said, "they come to the wagon. They catch the wagon wheel and just shake, shake. I never moved. I thought, 'They can't get in here. There's no room for them.'" He put his blanket over his head, "but they come feel all around me. Then one put his finger right on top of my head." Coquelle explained at this point that it "paralyzes you if they touch you." "Oh," he said, "I was just dead two or three minutes, then came up fighting." They came back "about three times" after that, shaking the wagon. Coquelle didn't move. "I saw their heads all 'round. They went back in the barn. I could see people, but when I fight I don't touch nothing. That's what beat me," he concluded. "When the chicken crows, just like that it becomes all right. From there I sleep. They don't bother me no more. I never wake up till half past eight," he said. The girls from the house were already up and Coquelle heard them say, "Thompson, he moved in to the little house last night but he's in the wagon now."

When he told people about his experience with the ghosts, they would say, "Oh, maybe it was wood rats." He would challenge them, saying, "You go stay there sometime!" But his employer George Collins seems to have understood, saying, "I know." He had lost his wife and his baby, and these ghosts were a part of the aftermath of those losses. He explained, "I see my wife. She tells me she will come get my baby, so I lost my baby. I know. Thompson is right. My people follow me 'round. I don't mind. I know who it is. Since she took the baby I never see her or dream of her no more."[62]

The fear of contact with the ghosts of dead people is a worldwide cultural belief. In this case, George Collins and Coquelle Thompson appeared to be in perfect harmony with what happened and why. In Coquelle's culture, there was a benefit attached to a successful encounter with ghosts. It could bring good luck. As Coquelle stated it, "I got help from that, kind of get lucky—get little easy money."

7

Severalty

Ties of Family, Culture, and Real Estate

In 1894 Coquelle and his family received their allotments under the Dawes Act of 1887. Although agricultural land had been informally allotted to individual families on the Siletz Reservation since 1872, in 1894 the final, legal allotment of the land was completed. A total of 44,459 acres were allotted in eighty-acre parcels (more or less) to 551 individual Indians.[1] Coquelle, his wife Emma, and their son Walker each received their eighty acres, the government to retain the title, in trust, for twenty-five years.* Elsewhere in the United States (but mostly in Oregon, Washington, Nebraska, and Idaho), approximately 3,285,000 acres were allotted to 32,800 individual Indians during the 1890s. During the same time the tribes sold or ceded an additional 28,500,000 acres of "surplus" reservation land, which reduced the Indian holdings by about one-half.[2]

Coquelle and Emma each were allotted eighty adjoining acres three miles north of the agency, on "North River Road." At that time the road extended two miles beyond Coquelle's place, as far as Canoe Landing at the mouth of Euchre Creek. The Thompson allotments

---

* The Coquelle Thompson allotment S-456 contained 82.15 acres; Emma Thompson S-457 contained 80 acres; Walker Thompson S-458 contained 83.12 acres.

were directly across the Siletz River from the eastern end of Camas Prairie, the large bottomland that Joel Palmer had reserved for the Coquille tribe back in 1856, where Coquelle had grown up. A salmon-spawning stream runs through the allotments, and that stream is shown on the Geological Survey maps as Thompson Creek.

Seventeen miles north, on the northeast side of Devils Lake, lies the eighty acres allotted their one-year-old son, Walker Thompson. The creek that runs from the east through that land and empties into Devils Lake is also shown on the Geological Survey maps as Thompson Creek. Thus, Lincoln County has two Thompson Creeks, one named for Coquelle and one for his son.

Coquelle's allotment was probably the same property as his earlier, informal allotment prior to the Dawes Act, and he had probably been living on it for a number of years. It was "prairie," a term that, in Oregon, could mean any tract of ground that was comparatively flat and treeless. There was a small amount of commercial timber on it. Emma's adjoining allotment had not been cleared at all, and it, too, had some commercial timber. Walker's allotment, while on comparatively level ground, was probably grown over with noncommercial tree species.

Coquelle's allotment was called "Lower Prairie," but he always called it "Low Prairie." He told John Peabody Harrington that before it was plowed, it had been covered with low, black-huckleberry bushes about one foot high. Those low bushes were called prairie huckleberries and locally were considered a different variety from the larger bushes that grew in the surrounding hills, although they were of the same species *(Vaccinium ovatum)*. The berries, Coquelle said, were "dark blue, awfully good." The Indians, he said, "used to sit down to pick them."* The Indian name for Coquelle's place was *qw'ánnán'-tlh'û·mhe'*, which meant "Prairie-huckleberry Prairie."³

Allotments were not limited to tribal members who were resident at the reservation. As a result, a number of people from Coos

---

* JPH 20:093. Margaret Collson, a nonlinguistic informant for John Peabody Harrington called them "blueberries," which "are native and more delicious than the Euchre Mt. sp. of blueberries." The blueberry *(Vaccinium corymbosum)* is a non-native species that was introduced to the Pacific Northwest from the eastern United States. The native huckleberry *(Vaccinium ovatum)* is frequently misidentified as a type of blueberry.

Bay and elsewhere filed for allotments and moved to Siletz. Among them were a few who had gone south from the Alsea Subagency at Yachats after that agency was closed in 1875, or their descendants. Some were relatives of Coquelle, and others were very well acquainted with him from his time in Coos Bay during the period of the Warm House Dance. For some of those people, much of what they knew of their genealogies came from Coquelle, who had a phenomenal knowledge of the subject.

Among the Indians from Coos Bay who moved to Siletz to file for allotments was "Sailor" Mack McDonald. After Coquelle left Coos Bay in the spring of 1878, Mack had, by "Indian custom," married the same Alice that Coquelle lived with while he was there. Shortly thereafter, a daughter, Agnes, was born. In 1892 Mack lived at Siletz and claimed three children as his own: Ida (9), Frank (13), and Agnes (15). Unfortunately, Sailor Mack died at the mouth of the Siletz River before the allotments were final and he did not receive his. Agnes and Ida were living at Coos Bay with their mother, and so neither of them received allotments at Siletz. However, a Siletz allotment was granted to Mack's son, Frank, who died on January 8, 1897, while he was at Chemawa Indian Boarding School. He was eighteen. Presumptive heirs to his allotment were his mother, Alice, his sister, Ida, and his half-sister, Agnes. Because of the uncertain paternity of Agnes, decisions about inheritance dragged on for years. Coquelle was eventually named as the father of Agnes, and he made several depositions in the case.[4]

After the allotments had all been distributed, another 191,798 acres of unallotted land remained, which was declared "surplus" by the Department of the Interior.* As a part of the agreement with tribal members, the government retained five sections of timberland in trust for the tribe and paid them $142,600 for the remainder. Of the purchase price, $100,000 was placed in trust, with members of the tribe being paid around March 1 of each year from the interest.[5] The remaining $42,600 was to be paid in installments of $75 per person per year until it was depleted.

Coquelle, along with many others, maintained running accounts at Mrs. Clarinda Copeland's store at Siletz, to be paid from the trust fund. Mrs. Copeland (1852–1929) was the first (perhaps only) woman

---

* Siletz, 268; Zucker, 116. The area was originally estimated to be 178,840 acres. Later surveys established it as 191,798.8 acres.

Severalty: Ties of Family, Culture, and Real Estate

to have obtained a federal license as an Indian trader, and was in business with her first husband at Siletz from 1881. "The Indians do not even smoke in her store!" reported Agent F. M. Wadsworth in 1886. After her husband died, she remarried, then reopened the store in her own name in 1893, remaining until 1906.[6] Coquelle's original account sheets with Mrs. Copeland from December 1895 until June 1907 were placed in his allotment file and provide rare insight into his daily life during those years.[7] The first entry in his account, on December 17, 1895, was $14 for a new suit.* The following summer, Emma purchased a quantity of calico, gingham, sateen, lining, buttons, shoes, and hose, as well as making two purchases of thread. It appears that Emma made all of her own clothes. The total expenditures over the years for men's clothing and for material for making women's clothing was about equal.

Coquelle and Emma made purchases at the store at least once a week, and sometimes twice. They bought coffee and sugar virtually every time, and almost as frequently they bought a can of lard. Coquelle liked coffee, we know from his comments to Elizabeth Jacobs.[8] His daughter Sina said in an interview that he liked "lots of sugar" on his oatmeal, which was his favorite food. At least once a month they bought a box of rolled oats.

Since his youth when he slept in the sweathouse with the men, Coquelle enjoyed a little smoke in the evenings. About once a month there was a charge on the accounts for five or ten cents worth of tobacco. There are very few purchases of other luxury items: once or twice a year there would be five cents worth of candy or a sack of nuts; cookies a little more frequently, but still quite rare. Other indications of their taste in food are fairly frequent purchases of bacon, ham, beef, pork, salmon, and sardines. A few items were purchased only on one occasion: a packet of gum, some hardtack, pepper, and butter. Apart from salt, it doesn't appear that Emma and Coquelle used much seasoning on their food. Emma no doubt made her own butter from milk from their cow. Judging by the amount of sugar and lard that they bought, it appears that she did a lot of baking.

Regular purchases for the household included soap, matches, candles, and oil for the lamps. Twice they bought a new lamp, and

---

* The 1902 Sears, Roebuck catalog has custom men's suits ranging in price from $10 to $14. Coquelle's $14 suit was on the high end.

once they bought a lantern. Emma replaced her broom about every six months, and twice she needed a new washboard. Once every few years she bought a dishpan, a pitcher, a sugar bowl, or other items of tableware. By August 1899, Emma was in her forties and evidently becoming conscious of her figure, for she purchased a corset. The accounts show a lifestyle not much different from what might have been seen in a white family of similar economic status in that area at that time. They were very plainly living on the money economy, with only a part of their subsistence coming from the homestead.

We know that Coquelle had a team and wagon and that he bought fifteen cents worth of axle grease about every other month. Once he bought a curry comb; another time he bought a whip. On at least two occasions he needed a new axe handle, and from time to time he bought nails and other small hardware items. Mrs. Copeland evidently had gotten in a quantity of seeds in 1900, because three times during March and April Coquelle and Emma bought seeds. In June 1899, there was an ominous entry in his account: for the first time, he purchased a padlock. The presence of strangers coming in to settle the unallotted lands was beginning to be felt.

In January 1901, D. W. Manchester, special U.S. Indian agent, arrived to arrange for distribution of the $100,000 trust fund. The difficulties of determining exactly who had a right to share in the money kept Mr. Manchester busy through most of the year. Finally, during November, the fund was at last distributed to those who were present in 1894 when the treaty was ratified, and to the heirs of those who were deceased. The November 23, 1901, *Yaquina Post* noted, "Mrs. C. G. Copeland is in it, the Siletz Indians having paid their store bills in full, aggregating thousands of dollars."[9] Coquelle's balance at Mrs. Copeland's store up to that time was $517.84. Over the ten years that Coquelle maintained the account with Mrs. Copeland, his purchases totaled $1,365.68.[10]

The Dawes Act fundamentally changed the status of the Indians. By law, they were now citizens, at least for certain purposes. They could vote in Oregon, for example, as soon as they got their allotments. There was some concern at Toledo of the effect the Indian vote might have on elections, but Dr. Franklin Carter set the local minds at rest in a letter to the *Oregonian*, which was reprinted in the *Lincoln County Leader*, October 7, 1897. "The fact is," Dr. Carter declared, "the Indians are nearly all republicans and vote that ticket

Severalty: Ties of Family, Culture, and Real Estate

without being dictated to from any one." The staunchly Republican readership of the *Lincoln County Leader* should have been reassured by that information.*

The advocates of the Dawes Act hoped to solve the "Indian Problem" once and for all: to break up the tribal land base and to thereby force the new generation into full assimilation with the general population. Ancillary to the Dawes Act were other policies aimed at the same ends. In the 1892 "Rules for Indian Courts," for example, dances and the "practices of medicine men" were listed among the punishable offenses. Those practices were thought to prevent the Indians "from adopting and following civilized habits and pursuits."[11] The grave and deadly seriousness with which infractions could be viewed was known to everyone because the tragedy at Wounded Knee, South Dakota, on December 29, 1890, was a still-fresh wound on the nation's conscience. It had been the reaction of the army to what they thought was a "War Dance" but in fact was a Ghost Dance.

The version of the Ghost Dance at Wounded Knee, South Dakota, had its beginnings exactly one year earlier. During the total eclipse of the sun on January 1, 1889, a Northern Paiute man named Wovoka at the Walker River Reservation, Nevada, reportedly fell into a trance and experienced a "Great Revelation."[12] It was not unlike the revelation experienced twenty years earlier by Wodziwob, the Northern Paiute prophet who inspired the Ghost Dance of 1870, which spread west and north into California and Oregon (and inspired the Coquelle Thompson Warm House Dance, among other things). Wovoka's Ghost Dance of 1890 spread east, along the tracks of the Central Pacific Railroad, and was greeted with much excitement by the Indians of the Great Plains. It created alarm with Colonel James Forsyth of the U.S. Seventh Cavalry and ended with the tragic Battle of Wounded Knee, which left 153 Sioux Indians and 25 cavalrymen dead.

A possible legacy at Siletz of the Wounded Knee massacre was the emergence of the so-called Feather Dance, an alternative term for the old-time Dream Dance. Cora Du Bois said that the term

---

* Lincoln County was formed in 1893, encompassing that portion of Benton County that had been previously within the Coast Indian Reservation. The newspaper was founded the same year, with both the county and the paper taking the name of the first Republican president.

"Feather Dance" "seems to have become attached to it after the [Dream] dance was secularized and actual dreaming was no longer the chief impetus for a performance." She also suggested that the "Oregon Dance" of the Tolowa in Northern California may have been "an imported Dream or Feather dance."[13] Using the feathered regalia and songs of the Warm House Dance and the Dream dances, the older Indians were able to continue their tradition with the overt encouragement of the whites. It continued to be an important part of their spiritual life even while it was frequently done for spectator entertainment.*

Coquelle and the rest of the older men took considerable pride in their regalia and seemed always willing to do the Feather Dance for special occasions. Beginning in 1899 the dances were frequently reported in the *Lincoln County Leader*. An article in the July 7, 1899, issue described that year's Fourth of July celebration. "The feather dance from 4 to 6 p.m., one of the main features of the occasion, was held in the government barn, and headed by Citizen John, and was a great success." The writer of the article lauded the decorum of the event, having seen "no drunkenness or boisterous conduct." He said, "All honor is due to the Indians, who perfected all arrangements and had absolute control of all exercises."

During this 1899 Fourth of July celebration, the Methodist Episcopal minister, E. H. Bryant, delivered the patriotic oration, no doubt extolling the virtues and power of the nation in having so recently won the war with Spain. His speech was followed by "three cheers for the Oregon Boys," the Second Oregon Volunteer Infantry, now in the Philippines and soon to be engaged in the Philippine Insurrection, a protracted and miserable war over control of those distant islands. The *Lincoln County Leader* reported, "A deafening shout went up from every man, woman and child—everybody yelled." There is one veteran of the Spanish-American War buried at the Indian cemetery on Government Hill at Siletz.**

---

* A revival of the Feather Dance began at Siletz around the time of its tribal restoration in 1977, drawing much of its inspiration and impetus from the Nay-Dosh World Renewal Dance of the Tolowa at Smith River, California. Adherents of that revival explain its antecedents in different terms than those used by Cora Du Bois (Caldwell; Goddard; Kentta).

** Charles Larsen (1869–1934), Q.M. 2cl. U.S. Navy, Spanish-American War.

Severalty: Ties of Family, Culture, and Real Estate

The Fourth of July had been the favorite holiday of the Indians at Siletz ever since Coquelle heard the cannon go off that morning in 1856 while they were all camped at Dayton. For the 1899 Fourth of July he bought a flag and a $3.50 hat, the most he had ever paid for a single clothing item.* Coquelle may have needed the release of a good celebration at about that time because this last Fourth of July of the nineteenth century was coming at the end of a decade in which a very large number of Coquelle's children, his relatives, and his friends had been buried.

There was a high mortality during the 1890s on many Indian reservations throughout the west. At Siletz Reservation, the actual population at the end of fiscal year 1899 was 497, according the annual report of Agent T. J. Buford.[14] This was down from the 551 who had received allotments five years earlier. In his report Buford said, "Consumption continues to be the leading cause of death. Medicine men are not now permitted to practice their incantations openly, and give little trouble."

The federal census of 1900 indicated the Indian population nationally at the lowest ever, 237,196.[15] Increases were shown in the 1910 census, and all subsequent censuses. At Siletz a net increase was at last shown during fiscal year 1901, with twenty-two births and only fifteen deaths, a remarkable improvement over the experience of the previous decade.[16] The October 12 *Yaquina Post* stated, "The Doctor has received orders to revaccinate everybody on the Reservation, so as to make it immune to smallpox." The vigorous preventive measures that were taken after the turn of the century were too late for many, however.

Coquelle told about the sicknesses that visited Siletz during the 1890s: "Lots of people died of ague at that time," he said. Intermittent chills and fever, usually but not always associated with malaria, was called ague. The sickness Coquelle mentioned may have been a form of influenza, or grippe, as it was more commonly called. "It was against the law for the Indian doctor to dance," Coquelle said. "They wanted them to use Government medicine."[17] But in spite of the prohibition, Indian doctors continued to practice.

---

* The 1902 Sears, Roebuck catalog shows Stetson hats in the style worn by Coquelle (Dakota, Columbia, or Graeco) costing $3.50. These are among the most expensive men's hats in the catalog.

There was one kind of doctor, called *ch'ashéne*, who didn't dance, and was effective only on fever and ague. Elizabeth Jacobs paraphrased Coquelle's description: "He blows, talks unintelligibly, talks and blows on a person. He blows water—just like ice it feels." "One old *ch'ashéne* was pretty good," Coquelle began a story. "I saw him doctor a California man who was nearly dead. People went and got that old man." His name was Warner, and he sat down and spoke to the body of the sick man: "Well, you people sit down too much. Fever and cool sickness sit on man too much. I'll fix you fellows now." Coquelle said that he took a rag, waved it over the sick man, singing a little, rubbing him. "Too many ague sit on you, sitting on your eyes—all over. They're little people, about as big as that," he said, holding out his forefinger. Coquelle said that the sick man recovered. "The next morning I saw [the doctor] leading a cow home. They paid him one cow."[18]

The last surviving members of many families were wiped out, as had occurred during the sicknesses of the early years of the reservation. This resulted in a major redistribution of the ownership of allotments, and Coquelle and Emma became heirs to several of them. A distant maternal relative of Emma died in April 1895, a five-year-old boy named Abram Mack. Because he was living at the time of allotment the year before, he had his eighty acres. It would, in the course of the law, succeed to his next of kin. His mother, father, and siblings had all died before him, and his closest living relative was his grandmother, Mary Tyee, but she died two years later, in November 1897. Emma's maternal uncle John Tyee was next, and he inherited the Abram Mack allotment and two others. Emma was his next of kin. Allotments had been in effect at Siletz for only three years in 1897, but already there were 166 inheritance cases, amounting to over 9,000 acres of land.[19] The Dawes Act and high mortality had turned the agent into an administrator of real estate and inheritance.

Coquelle and Emma may not even have known who five-year-old Abram Mack was at the time he died, so distant was the relationship. They were, however, to attend the funerals of many much closer relatives. Between April 1895 and April 1896 all of the descendants of Coquelle's maternal great-aunt Louisa Pete died. First, her granddaughter Emma Williams died, then her grandson George Kiowinds, and finally her daughter Louisa Bob, all of whom had allotments. Louisa Pete, in her late seventies, moved in with Coquelle and

Emma, who took care of her for the next eight years. Coquelle was her next of kin.

On May 6, 1896, Coquelle and Emma's three-year-old son Washington Thompson died and was buried at the Coquelle Thompson plot in the Siletz Indian cemetery on Government Hill. He lies next to his half-sister Sina. They were not allotted.

Five months later Nina Jim died. She was the wife of Coquelle's first cousin, Coquelle Jim. Jim moved in with Coquelle and Emma and lived with them until he died seven years later, in 1903. According to the 1900 federal census, Coquelle Jim was full-blood Coquille born in 1848, and could not read, write, or speak English. Coquelle was his closest living relative.

Coquelle and Jim were evidently quite close friends, about the same age, and had participated together in the Dream dances of an earlier time. Coquelle said that Jim was "chief of the dance," and that he "dreamed a lot." "He slept upstairs," Coquelle said, "and when the first chicken crowed, I heard him singing." Coquelle once asked Jim, "What do you dream, that you sing all the time?" "I just see dead people," he answered. "I hear them talking about people dancing all over. Later on this dance will be all gone. It will be no more." Coquelle explained, "He meant the dance people would all die, I guess. The dance is all gone. For eight or ten years they danced. Every night. It didn't do any good." [20] Coquelle Jim is buried at the Coquelle Thompson plot in the Siletz Indian cemetery.

In February 1899, another of Coquelle's first cousins, James Thompson, died, leaving Coquelle as his apparent closest relative. After the tribes arrived at Siletz in 1856, the strict rules of exogamy and patrilineal descent began to break down. Descent now would sometimes be traced through the female line. James Thompson provides an example. James took the family name of Thompson from his mother, who was Coquelle's paternal aunt. For the funeral, Coquelle bought a coffin at Mrs. Copeland's store for $27.50, a new shirt and tie (probably for the deceased), and new gloves and hose for Emma.

James Thompson's wife, Anna, had predeceased him on December 23, 1894. They had adjoining eighty-acre allotments about a mile up Mill Creek from Upper Farm. The 160 acres were sold for $992 to Emil T. Raddant in 1902 under provisions of the "Dead Indian Act," which had been passed that same year so that inherited trust lands could be probated and sold in an orderly and legally acceptable manner. Coquelle was found to be the sole heir to the estate in 1904, by order of the court, but the case was later reopened because by then there were two other claimants. On May 4, 1908, Coquelle agreed to share any proceeds from the estate with Stewart Rooney and Jacob Johnson, Jr. It was now possible for Mr. Raddant to obtain clear title to the land he had purchased in good faith six years earlier.[21]

In March 1899, perhaps the saddest of all the deaths occurred when Coquelle and Emma lost their last remaining child, eight-year-old Jacob Walker. He was buried next to his brother Washington. Emma bought some velvet, sleeve buttons, gloves, and hose at Mrs. Copeland's store. Coquelle bought another new shirt, collar, and tie, and he paid $15 for a child's coffin. It had been a devastating decade, and sorting out the inheritances, with the inevitable conflicting claims of distant kin, would not be completed for another thirty years.

The *Lincoln County Leader* published its first issue on March 9, 1893. On May 4 appeared the first of many articles describing the resources of the Siletz Reservation. This interest in the reservation stemmed from anticipation that the government would open the unallotted land—the land ceded in 1892 by the Siletz people under the agreement for $142,600—for settlement by homesteaders. A description of the timberland gives an idea of what was at stake. On June 6, 1895, a reporter for the paper stated, "There are some of the finest bodies of spruce and fir contiguous to the Siletz and its tributaries that there are in the Coast range. The time is not far distant when there will be mills on the Siletz that will be sawing thousands of feet of fine spruce and fir lumber each day, which will be carried by the lumber schooners to all parts of the coast."

A legal notice in the May 30, 1895, issue of the paper informed its readers that the unallotted lands would be opened for entry by settlers "on and after Thursday, July 23, 1895, at 12 o'clock noon of said day."* It was not a great historic land rush such as had swept Oklahoma on three previous occasions, most recently on the May 3 opening of the Kickapoo lands. The July 27 edition of the *Oregonian*

---

* There were at least two men (Martin Hammer and John Mitchell) who had gone in sooner, in violation of the rules, but the courts later upheld their claims (LCL, 20 May 1897).

described the Siletz opening, saying "not over a half dozen people crossed the line when the conventional gun was fired."[22]

The lack of interest in making claims stemmed from the fact that even after the stringent provisions of the Homestead Act were met, the homesteader was still required to purchase the land from the government at $1.50 per acre. There was very little unallotted land that had been surveyed within the reservation that would justify such an outlay of time, work, and money. The act was changed in 1900, dispensing with the requirement to pay the $1.50 per acre.[23]

During those first few years following the turn of the century, there was a scramble on the part of timber companies and speculators for any timber that could be placed in private ownership in the Pacific Northwest. The virgin timber resources in most of the rest of the United States had been exhausted through the exploitative practice known colloquially among the loggers as "cut out and get out." Timber companies would typically purchase the virgin timberland, remove the timber, and leave the now logged-off and almost valueless land to revert to the counties for nonpayment of taxes. Many (but not all) of the firms that moved into the Northwest adhered to the same practice, and great fortunes were contemplated.[24]

Up until this time, the only sawmill cutting Siletz timber was the small, obsolete, and worn-out steam mill belonging to the agency. By 1897 it had stood for almost twenty-five years and was in need of a new boiler. "It is very dangerous," said the *Lincoln County Leader* on December 26, 1897. "Can get up only sixty pounds of steam to run the mill. Mr. Hollman (of the Albany Iron Works) is bidding on the new boiler which is to be two feet longer than the old one, and ten feet more of smoke stack. We hope they will get the new boiler in before next spring as we need the mill so bad." That sawmill could have cut lumber in the Siletz timber forever, and not have made a dent in the supply. The *Leader* summed it up three years later: "It will take many sawmills and an army of men years to manufacture this fine body of timber into lumber, and it is the tin-bucket men who put money into the country."[25]

Surveyors and timber cruisers had been in and out of the forested parts of the reservation almost continually ever since 1895, when the land was first opened to outside settlement. The July 13, 1900, *Lincoln County Leader* reported that there were two parties of government surveyors running survey lines at that time. They were "followed by settlers who locate as fast as the lines are run," it stated. It was later discovered that most of the locations at that time were filed on by "dummy entrymen," and not actual settlers. The result, by 1905, was that the Siletz timberland became part of a national scandal known as the "Oregon Land Frauds." Several high-ranking officials and politicians were indicted, and a few were convicted and served time.[26]

Many of the fraudulent entries had been made by elderly army veterans who had allowed themselves to be convinced by speculators that they would not actually have to reside on the land to "prove up" on it.* They were told that their military service would count in lieu of residence. With the scandals in the papers, many of the veterans feared that they, too, might suffer prosecution. They were quite anxious to relinquish their claims, and anyone who was willing to comply with the homestead laws could usually buy such a relinquishment for two or three hundred dollars. By 1905, the only available Siletz timberland was in the form of such relinquished claims.

A. W. (Jack) Morgan was one of the settler-speculators who bought a relinquishment for $250 in 1905. In his memoirs he described walking the twenty-five miles from Toledo to the east slope of Euchre Mountain to locate his claim, which was about five miles up Euchre Creek from its mouth. The claim had a couple acres of bottomland with alder and salmonberry on it, which would be easy to clear. The rest of the 160 acres was a heavy stand of "fine quality fir timber, with some spruce along the creek and some cedar and hemlock in the gulches," according to Morgan's own description.[27] This timber was twenty-five miles from the railroad at Toledo, and five miles from the Siletz River, which could only float logs during a freshet, and in any case there was no market for logs at the mouth of the Siletz. It took considerable vision and imagination to think that a profit could be made from the investment in time, labor, and money that would be needed to get clear title to the claim.

Morgan built his cabin, cleared the two acres for a garden and pasture for a cow and a horse, and lived there with his wife six months

---

* After the Homestead Act requirements of residency and improvements had been fulfilled, the homesteader was said to have "proved up" on his claim. He would then present "proof" to the local land office in the form of witnesses and testimony, after which he would be granted an original "fee simple" patent on the land.

of each year for three years to establish proof on his claim and obtain clear title to it. A wagon road, of sorts, ran north from the agency through Coquelle's place and thence another two miles to Canoe Landing, at the mouth of Euchre Creek. From Canoe Landing, Morgan could reach his claim on the east slope of Euchre Mountain by pack trail. Because he passed through Coquelle's place every time he went to town, the two became acquainted. In a letter to an old friend late in his life, Morgan remembered the Indian men he had known during his homesteading years. He said, "I got some inspiration from each of these little men, for they had someway learned patience, kindness and appreciation. I always admired Ned Evans, Coquill Thompson, and many others of these older men, and I liked Scott Lane and Hoxy Simmons, and Bob Tronson was a good old scout that I regarded highly."[28]

Morgan said of Bob Tronson, "He and I worked together in a logging camp on Coos Bay the summer of 1890. I hope he lives until every hair of his head turns to a candle to light him up to glory."[29] Logging was the one profession in western Oregon that was always open to capable Indian men, and the friendship and respect that loggers sometimes had toward each other transcended race. Over the years, the Siletz Indian men came to think of themselves as "the best loggers ever known," and some of them probably were.[30] Coquelle's son, grandson, and great-grandson became loggers, and the tradition carries on to the present day.*

Logging was the harvesting of a crop that in western Oregon was considered to run ideally in a 100-year cycle. This is in marked contrast to agricultural pursuits, almost all of which run in annual cycles. A comparatively small acreage can be justified economically if there is an expected annual return—such as from raising oats, raspberries, or dairy cows. If, as with timber, the harvest from a particular plot is only once in 50 or 100 years, then very large landholdings are needed in order to produce a steady income. The eighty-acre allotments of land with timber at Siltez would usually bring a cash return only once in the owner's lifetime, and after the timber was removed (or if there had never been timber on it), the land was nearly worthless. There

---

* One of the authors (Lionel Youst) worked during the early 1950s in several logging camps in western Oregon and Washington, and in northern California. In most of the camps one or more of the loggers were Indian and, as often as not, from Siletz.

were sound economic reasons for the efforts of the timber companies and speculators to consolidate the many small homesteads and allotments into large, manageable timber holdings.

Homesteader Jack Morgan gathered another twenty-two men, each of whom agreed to purchase relinquished homesteads and complete the residency and improvement requirements. Once they had all obtained title to their claims, Morgan would try to sell the combined holdings as one block, for a commission. He said, "When all the boys got settled in there, there was quite a colony of us." They took daily turns going to Siletz for mail, necessarily passing through Coquelle's place each time.[31] The sudden increase in population had a profound effect on wild game. The Siletz elk herd was already extinct, but, Morgan said, "we had lots of venison." He said that there was an open burn where deer congregated a mile north of his homestead, at the head of Cedar Creek. "It was good picking for hunters and Major Ludson [Alsea] and Tom Jackson [Alsea] used to go there hunting."[32] "Deer were plentiful when we went in there," he said, "but not so when we came out."[33]

Morgan found his buyers for the combined homesteads in two astute businessmen: Louis Werner, of St. Louis, Missouri, and William E. Boeing of Seattle, Washington. They shared similar views on the investment potential of the timber, but it turned out to be an exceptionally long-term investment for them. They paid taxes on the land and assumed the risk of insect and fire damage for forty years, and didn't begin logging until World War II. As late as 1950 at least four square miles of the timber at Euchre Mountain was still standing in its pristine and virgin state.[34]

During those years of timber-buying frenzy, speculators could always be found who were willing to invest. However, the supply of timber was so vast when compared to the demand for lumber that buyers of standing timber frequently waited decades to realize a profit. Asa Simpson, owner of the Simpson Lumber Company, was one of the most daring entrepreneurs in the business, but he counseled his son against buying timber for speculation. In his belief, stumpage prices would not be any higher twenty-five years from then, and his predictions were borne out exactly.* In 1906 standing timber in the Douglas fir region was about one dollar per thousand board

---

* "Simpson, Magic Name in Lumber," *Timberman*, June 1946, 60.

feet, and timber could be found for the same price as late as 1940. The return on speculative investment in timber during that period came from the growth of the trees. Investors hoped to profit from favorable markets, and failing that they assumed that the increase in volume over years would more than equal expected returns from other kinds of investments.

If owners of land with timber on it sometimes had to wait forty years for a return of profit, those who owned land with neither timber nor agricultural potential fared much worse. The problem was particularly vexing if it was inherited trust land under the Dawes Act. The allotment of Coquelle's deceased son Jacob Walker Thompson at Devils Lake is a case in point. Walker died March 12, 1899. By that time, the problem of inherited land was becoming acute, there being no orderly provision for determining heirs, or for the subdivision or sale of the inherited land. The Act of May 27, 1902, commonly called the "Dead Indian Act," was passed to alleviate those problems. It authorized the sale of inherited lands, with the proceeds to be distributed among the heirs. According to Janet A. McDonnell's study of the subject, "The 1902 law opened the floodgate for the wholesale dissipation of the Indian landed estate."[35] That law, as amended by the acts of May 8, 1906, and June 25, 1910, had immense impact on Coquelle and his family through the rest of his life and beyond.

On December 12, 1902, just two months after the BIA had established its "amended rules for conveyance of inherited Indian lands" under the Dead Indian Act, Coquelle placed his "x" on a petition for the government to sell the Devils Lake allotment of his deceased son Walker. Only one bid came in. On April 20, 1904, W. D. Hamilton of Roseburg bid $332.48 for the eighty-three acres, but the government rejected it. On February 27, 1905, Coquelle asked that the land be relisted. That time, there were apparently no bids at all.[36]

Coquelle petitioned at least once more for the government to sell the land, this time on August 26, 1907. Again, it did not sell. On July 1, 1909, he asked to have a fee-simple patent issued to him. He stated in his petition, "I have advertised this land a number of times but have not received an acceptable bid. I am able bodied and capable of managing my own affairs." With a fee-simple title to the land, he could sell it himself, or do with it as he pleased because it would no longer be held in trust by the government. Lincoln County, however, would be assessing its value and demanding that property taxes be paid on it. This would be new to Coquelle.

As Coquelle entered the middle period of his life, his prestige no doubt was enhanced accordingly. He carried a certain degree of moral authority by virtue of his hereditary status as chief of the Coquilles, and his position on the tribal police force placed him near the center of almost anything of interest that was happening on the reservation. The pay of the police had increased gradually over the years, until in 1890 he was receiving $15 per month. From July 1, 1891, until June 30, 1892, he was employed as a night watchman and disciplinarian at the Siletz Agency boarding school at a salary of $300 per year. During the terms of 1897 and 1898 (and possibly during other years as well), he sat as a judge on the tribal court.[37]

During the 1890s there were a few interesting crimes committed on the reservation, and Coquelle took part in some of the police work that was involved. He described one such case to John Peabody Harrington.[38] "Ben Johnson killed an old man and a boy at Pool Slough, where the trail came down from Waldport," he began. There was no doubt in Coquelle's mind as to the identity of the murderer, but the sheriff did not believe that Ben Johnson had done it. The murdered man's money had not been stolen, so the sheriff assumed that an Indian had committed the crime: "They claimed that an Indian who did not know the value of greenbacks must have done it," Coquelle explained.

Coquelle was subpoenaed as a witness, although he told the lawyer he knew nothing about it. Thompson and John Adams "had to escort Alsea Polly and her young baby to the trial." She was a key witness, having been near the man when he was murdered. "I had to swim my horse across the Siletz, Salmon, and Tillamook Rivers to get up there," Coquelle said. The trial was at Corvallis and lasted a week. Coquelle said, "They couldn't prove it onto Ben Johnson. They even exhibited the mud imprint of shoe soles in the court and had a shoemaker to swear he made the shoes." Ben Johnson was not convicted, and Coquelle explained the final outcome: "Three Indians were given three years at Vancouver in prison for that killing. One was killed there in trying to get away," he said. "John Adams and I helped to take Alsea Polly back to her home in Siletz town."

The most talked about crime of the period was the killing of U. S. Grant, a highly regarded Alsea Indian who was apparently a close acquaintance of Coquelle and Emma.* Abe Logan and Albert Martin were indicted for the murder. Grant had been the chief judge of the tribal court, the same court on which Coquelle served as an associate judge. A few months before he was killed, Grant had officiated at the wedding of John Albert and Eliza Fairchild. The best man and maid of honor at that wedding were Coquelle and Emma Thompson.[39]

Coquelle probably did not participate in the murder investigation because his wife, Emma, was sick during that time and died a week after the murder. She had been sick a long time and was being nursed by a young midwife named Agnes Smith, but as she worsened a Chasta Costa doctor named Old John tried his best for her. Old John was Emma's maternal uncle and was getting quite elderly. At first, Coquelle said, "He split a bundle of fine little fir wood pitch sticks." He put them on the fire, and "when he danced, it got hot." It made a high flame, and "he put the burning wood in his mouth, then throw it away." Coquelle said that he did that five times. The next morning Coquelle asked him if his mouth was sore. "No! He ate, drank hot coffee, just the same as ever." Old John had long whiskers and Coquelle was afraid that he would burn them, because "he was not any longer such a strong doctor as he was getting very old." But old John "helped my wife all the time," Coquelle said.

The last time he came, Emma was "pretty bad," according to Coquelle. He tried to doctor her but she told him, "It won't do any good. I'm gone already. It won't do any good. Don't bother yourself." Coquelle said that Old John felt awfully bad, and wept. The next day "my wife got him sugar, coffee, and food and sent him home. He was a bachelor." The day following that, someone from Lower Farm came and told Coquelle that Old John had died. "I didn't want to tell my wife, she was pretty low," he said. After the person left, Emma asked, "what did that fellow want?" Coquelle evaded the question. Emma's half-sister Martha, who was married to the singer Jim David at the time, was present. Coquelle told her, "Don't open your mouth!" After a while Emma said, "We have people to feed. You'd better go to town, hitch up the horses and go get some food." "So I went," Coquelle said.

In Siletz town Coquelle usually would eat dinner at the hotel, "where I got good coffee," he said. He was there, having coffee, when

---

* On October 20, 1903, Grant was found dead at the edge of the Siletz River near Siletz town, apparently having been hit in the head with a rock and drowned.

Pete Muggins, who worked for Coquelle, came in and said, "She just died." Coquelle lamented, "I never saw her; she died, you know. If she didn't ask me, I would not have gone, you know." She had been sick a long time, and, said Coquelle, "it cost me lots of money. At last I gave up. I had no more money and nothing helped her." As for the death of her uncle, Old John, "I just kept that quiet." Her half-sister Martha took everything in the house that belonged to Emma except the dishes, which Coquelle kept. He wanted "her trunk and clothes to go, and have everything cleaned up."[40]

Emma was forty-seven years old when she died on October 28, 1903. They had been married for fifteen years. Two days after she died the weekly *Lincoln County Leader* stated, "Mrs. Coquille Thompson's death is expected at any hour." She was buried alongside her children at the Coquelle Thompson family plot at the Indian cemetery on Government Hill. The requirement for death certificates in Oregon began in 1903, and Emma's is among the first. Almost none of her entries are filled in, there is no medical certification, and the only signature is of the store owner, Mrs. C. G. Copeland, who signed as undertaker.[41]

Almost exactly a month before Emma died, her uncle John Tyee died, leaving Emma four allotments: John's own allotment and the allotment of his deceased wife, Mary, and of Mary's deceased son Jacob Mack, and of his son Abram Mack. With Emma now gone, Coquelle stood as prospective heir to all four of those allotments, plus Emma's. In addition, Coquelle, along with the others on the reservation, received lump sum payments from the money held in trust from the 1894 sale of the unallotted land. The "Siletz Siftings" column of the *Lincoln County Leader* congratulated Coquelle and several others for "wisely using the money paid them by the government to build with and secure stock, machinery and etceteras for maintaining their homes in comfort."*

Coquelle did indeed have a comfortable home. It was a well-built farmhouse of the "American Four Square" style, with hipped roof and two brick chimneys. The two-story frame structure, about thirty feet square, had enough room for his extended family and one or more distant relatives who lived there most of the time.

---

* The individuals mentioned were "Tenas Charlie, Klamath Charlie, Spencer Scott, Charlie Depot, Coquille Thompson, David John, Bob Felix, Wolverton Orton, Brown Arden, John Adams and several others" (LCL, 16 January 1903).

By 1905, just ten years after allotment of the Siletz Reservation, 256 of the original 551 allottees had died.[42] Coquelle, as heir to several of the allotments, actually profited from some of them. The records at the office of the Lincoln County Clerk reflect that on August 14, 1908, for example, Coquelle received $2,400 for sale of eighty acres of particularly fine farmland at Logsden (Upper Farm), seven miles east of the agency. On June 11, 1910, he received $1,000 for sale of the adjoining eighty acres.[43] These were the allotments of Jacob Mack and Mary Tyee, which Coquelle had inherited through probate of Emma's estate.[44]

Coquelle said that before Emma died, she told Agnes, who was caring for her, "Take care of my old man."[45] Agnes was twenty-three years old, the mother of two small daughters who were in need of the security of a stable home. Coquelle was about fifty-four, but of the eligible men on the reservation at that time, he was probably among the most stable and reliable. On March 29, 1904, just five months after Emma had passed away, Coquelle and Agnes were married at the home of the store owner, Mrs. C. G. Copeland. Robert T. Bryant, the Methodist Episcopal minister, performed the ceremony. According to the wedding announcement in the local paper, the Siletz school where Agnes worked gave her as a wedding gift a set of silver teaspoons.[46]

Coquelle was fifty-four years old, and all of his children had died. Agnes was healthy and loving, and she brought her two young daughters into the marriage. Having children around again was probably like a tonic for Coquelle, who loved children, according to interviews with those who remember him.[47] Agnes was Coquelle's last hope of progeny, giving him what many middle-aged men dream of: a new life with a young woman. After losing Emma to a lingering illness, he was ready to start over, and the evidence shows that he had the capacity to enjoy himself.

Two months after the wedding, as the weather warmed, Coquelle was having fun in the river. "A delightful experience is to accompany Coquille Thompson in his canoe over the riffles from the Agency to his home three miles north," said the *Lincoln County Leader* on May 20, 1904. The following month the lamprey eels were running during the nights, and Coquelle enjoyed catching them at the riffle above the agency.* He often caught eels with Tom Jackson, who always seemed

---

* The sea lamprey, *Petromyzon marinus*, while not a true eel, is called an eel on the West Coast.

to have time to hunt or fish.[48] Watching the Indians catch eels at night, with lights, became a spectator sport for the newly arrived whites living at Siletz.[49] Few of the whites would eat them, however, thinking that eels resembled snakes.

Agnes was skillful at cleaning eels. She would cut off the head and then with one swipe of the knife (or a river mussel shell), make the ventral slit from the throat down, quickly removing the few guts. The trick was to remove the chord—a transparent membrane about the size of a pencil that the lamprey eel has in place of a backbone. A sharp stick (or sometimes a bent nail) was used to grasp the chord near the tail, so that it could be pulled out.[50] It took practice, and she could clean four or five eels for every one eel cleaned by the men who caught them. She taught all of her children and grandchildren how to do it.[51] She was evidently well known and well liked at Siletz, as indicated in a July 22, 1904, newspaper comment: "On your way to Canoe Landing or locality stop at Coquille Thompson's and ask Mrs. Thompson for a dish of those delicious raspberries."

Agnes was part white, three-quarters according to the 1900 census. Her mother, Mary, was born in 1860, daughter of a full-blood Umpqua mother and a white father. Mary had two boys who carried the family name of Newberry, but nothing is known of their father. Although Agnes used Newberry as her maiden name, she is not always listed as part of the family on the census and other records, and there is nothing to indicate that her biological father was necessarily named Newberry. She was born in Portland on June 15, 1878, two years older than the oldest of Mary's sons.*

Agnes told an interviewer in 1945 that after she was born, her mother moved to Siletz (or returned to Siletz). Agnes was "left in charge of an Irish woman in Los Angeles where she made her home until the woman died."[52] It is not known who that woman was, but she was perhaps a relative of Agnes's biological father. Agnes was then placed in an orphanage, and later attended Sacred Heart School, a Catholic boarding school in Los Angeles, for five years, presumably between 1890 and 1895.[53] There are no records to indicate how or why she attended that particular school, but it is known that at least a part of the student body was recruited from two nearby Catholic

---

* We are grateful to Ann Goddard for sharing with us some of her genealogical researches into families of the Confederated Tribes of Siletz.

orphanages operated by the Sisters of Charity.* In 1892, while Agnes was at school in California, her mother, Mary, and Albert Martin, a full-blood Joshua Tututni, were wed at Siletz.

After Agnes completed her schooling at Sacred Heart, she found her way to Siletz, searching for her birth mother. In August 1895 (at age seventeen), she married Louis Smith, a full-blood Lower Umpqua Indian, who was about five years her senior. He was a "hunter and trapper" living alone at Pikesville (now Kernville) on the lower tidewater section of the Siletz River. According to Agnes, "no one else lived on the river." One year later, when labor pains of her first pregnancy came upon her, she was gathering peppermint along the riverbank and could "hear the bears chomping the skunk cabbage." Hunters found her and took her to "Uncle Tom's Cabin," a trapper's cabin nearby where her son, Arthur, was born.

Two years later, in December 1898, Agnes was again ready to deliver. Rain was coming down in torrents, but her mother was with her this time and insisted that she be taken to Siletz for the birth. In a large dugout canoe three men paddled all day against the current bringing Agnes, her baby, and her mother to Canoe Landing. Of all her trips on the river, "this was the worst," she told the interviewer in 1945.[54] She couldn't travel any further, and so the men "broke into a smokehouse and carried hay in for her to lay on." There, at midnight on Christmas eve, her daughter, Marie, was born. Agnes and her family remained at Siletz, where she worked at the Siletz school.

On August 28, 1900, a second daughter, Augusta, was born. Agnes quit her job cooking at the Siletz school in May 1902, and in August the boy, Arthur, died. Shortly thereafter Agnes and Louis separated, and he immediately remarried. Agnes was again working as a cook at the Siletz school the following year, during Emma's final illness and death.[55] Somewhere along the line she had learned nursing skills, and became a trusted and much sought after midwife.

The 1900 federal decennial census indicated that Agnes was "not taxed," "not allotted," and "not a citizen." Categorization of that kind reflects the ambiguous status of mixed-blood people at that

---

* Sr. Julia Freitas, archivist for the Archdiocese of Los Angeles, telephone conversation, 29 January 2000. Sr. Freitas said that the records for the 1890s are incomplete and the fact that no one named Agnes appears on those that remain in no way implies that Agnes did not attend during those years.

time. She and her mother had different surnames, her father was evidently white, she was not enrolled as a member of the Confederated Tribes of Siletz, and in any case she was most probably in school in California at the time of allotment (1892–94). For purposes of classification, she was not white and she was not Indian, but she received all of the disadvantages and none of the advantages of both categories.

On November 23, 1903, her stepfather, Albert Martin, was found guilty in U.S. federal court in Portland of the murder of U. S. Grant. Martin's alleged accomplice, Abe Logan, was acquitted in a separate trial, after which federal judge Bellinger reprimanded the jury for bringing in the wrong verdict. He told Logan, "You are acquitted: but I think you are a bad man and that you killed Grant. . . . The blood of Grant is on your hands." The jury evidently arrived at the not guilty verdict based on sympathy for the defendant's wife and children rather than from the evidence presented to the court. The reporter who covered the trial for the *Oregonian* considered it a "strange verdict."[56] The reported behavior of Judge Bellinger appears no less strange.

With Abe Logan acquitted, Martin filed for a retrial. A week after the wedding of Agnes and Coquelle, on April 4, 1904, the new trial was allowed. On December 7 the case was dismissed and Albert Martin was set free. In the *Portland Morning Oregonian*'s coverage of the Logan trial there was emphasis on intertribal feuding as a factor in the murder. In its coverage of the Martin trial, there was emphasis on the role of whiskey.[57] In a letter, the Indian agent John J. McKoin gave what he thought was the cause: "The murder was caused by whiskey drinking. Logan and Martin were sent by Grant for a quart each, which was bought in Toledo." During the time of the trials there was a force reduction in the tribal police, and Coquelle was dismissed.* The reduction in force could have been part of the agent's reaction to the murder of U. S. Grant, and Coquelle's tolerant attitude toward whiskey may have been a factor.

Coquelle said that the bartenders at the saloons in Toledo wouldn't sell whiskey to full-blood Indians, but would sell to Indians they thought were "halfbreeds." Depot Charlie and Bob Metcalf, for exam-

---

* The records show several occasions in which Coquelle was "dismissed" from the police force, but over a period of forty-seven years he was never off the force for more than one month at a time.

ple, "could get whiskey at any bar," according to Coquelle. They were "fine looking men, black mustache both of them." Coquelle also wore a large, well-trimmed mustache, and he, too, could get whiskey at Toledo. Old Ned and his wife Susan, full-blood Miluk Coos Indians from the mouth of the Coquille River, once visited Coquelle for about a week. When they were ready to return to Coos County, Coquelle hitched up his team and wagon and drove them to Toledo. There he bought a bottle of whiskey and gave it to them, and Old Ned told Coquelle that he would "drink it little by little." Susan and Old Ned "walked all the way back to Coos Bay, sleeping on the ground," according to Coquelle, evidently with only the whiskey to keep them warm.[58]

Probably the happiest and proudest day of Coquelle's life was March 28, 1905. Agnes delivered to him a healthy boy, which they named Coquelle Jr. This would be the son who would carry on the title of "Chief of the Coquilles" in a direct line that ran back from long before Washington Tom. Agnes's two girls, Marie and Augusta, now had a baby brother, and Coquelle, at about fifty-six years old, had the makings of a new family.

Coquelle's household was frequently filled with more than his immediate family. He evidently felt the responsibility of caring for his last, elderly relatives, and several of them lived out their declining years with him. The only entertainment in his house was conversation; he never played cards or engaged in other recreational pursuits. His leisurely conversations with those extended family members confirmed and solidified his knowledge and understanding of the genealogy, mythology, ethnography, and history of his people.

Coquelle's great-aunt Louisa Pete lived with him for eight years, after all of her family died during 1895–96. Coquelle was her nearest relative, and they had been close ever since he was a small boy. During the eight years that Louisa Pete lived at Coquelle's house, there was ample opportunity to talk of relatives and relationships, and it is from her that he confirmed the relationships within his maternal, Coos relatives. "She knew all these things," Coquelle said.[59] After Coquelle's wife Emma died in October 1903, Emma's half-sister Martha Johnson, who lived at Upper Farm, took care of Louisa Pete until she died four months later, on February 17, 1904. Two years later, Coquelle and his new wife, Agnes, inherited Louisa Pete's allotment, which was located at the site of present-day Otis Junction, on the Salmon River. On December 1, 1906, they sold half of it (forty acres) to Alphonse Seguin.

From 1906 until he died in October 1909, Old Hunter, and his wife Polly, lived with Coquelle and Agnes. Coquelle's admiration for Old Hunter was without bounds, and this was an opportunity to learn as much as he could from him. Old Hunter talked of the great fire on the Coquille River back in the 1840s, and of catching beaver by going into their houses and tying a cord onto them. He told of a night of shooting stars, during the fall of one year. "There was a big wind," he said, "and a rain of stars fell, thick all over." He said that they were "like burned out shells, the size of your hand." [60] And he told of another extraordinary event. Once he and Old Johnson were returning on horseback from the Rogue River. He said they "camped at the mouth of the Coquille River and turned their horses out on the grass," then went to sleep. There was an earthquake that night while they were sleeping. Old Hunter told Coquelle that they "woke up 50 yards away."[61]

And they talked about hunting. Old Hunter was so uncannily skillful as a hunter that Coquelle was sure he had shamanistic power. Their relationship was close enough that they could discuss subjects that would otherwise have been taboo, and so Coquelle said to Old Hunter once or twice, "I think you dreamed." "No, I never dreamed," he answered. "Elk and deer are too easy for you. How do you do it?" "Well, you have to study. You don't have to sleep when you go hunting. You stay awake and study how to do it. That's all I do. I never dreamed." Coquelle was skeptical. He explained, "A man didn't tell if he had a dream. He kept it to himself *always*. If I tell my dream, that dream is no good. I can't get any luck. That's how it goes."[62]

The government sold Old Hunter's allotment while he was still living, having declared him incompetent to manage his own affairs. When he died, Coquelle went to Mrs. Copeland's store and bought the coffin and a suit of cloths for him to be buried in. Coquelle Hunter and his wife, Polly, are buried adjacent to the Coquelle Thompson plot in the Siletz cemetery on Government Hill. On January 11, 1913, the government paid Coquelle and Agnes $200 from Old Hunter's estate, the amount claimed for three years' room, board, and expenses.

8

Assimilation
End of the Trust Period

Coquelle may not have been the only person who interviewed Old Hunter. Dr. Roland B. Dixon of Harvard was at Siletz during parts of the summers of 1903 and 1904, and Archie Johnson, whose mother was Upper Coquille, said that Dixon interviewed Old Hunter at that time.* Archie, according to John Peabody Harrington, "wants one of the books."[1] There was no book, and a search of the literature does not reveal that Dixon published anything on the Athabaskan languages or ethnography. However, the fact that Archie Johnson, probably two generations younger than Old Hunter, wanted a book on the subject is revealing. There was an evident yearning for the knowledge of elders like Old Hunter, even if that knowledge came in the form of a book.

Another scholar was at Siletz during the summer of 1903. Harry Hull St. Clair II, having obtained his master's degree in linguistics under Franz Boas at Columbia University the previous year, was seeking folklore in the Hanis Coos language. Boas had insisted that in

---

* The "Siletz Friends" column of the *Lincoln County Leader,* July 1, 1904, confirms that Dixon had in fact been at Siletz. It states that "Professor Dixon of Harvard College, who made many friends here during his stay a year ago, is with us again."

studying languages that had no written literature, it was necessary to collect a body of texts from among traditional oral sources. St. Clair collected twelve myths in the Hanis Coos from Tom Hollis, one of the Coos Indians who had moved to Siletz in 1894 in order to get an allotment.[2] That was the first time that any Coos texts were preserved in the original language.

The funding came through a grant from Henry Villard, the German-born tycoon who controlled most of Oregon's railroads.[3] There was irony, and perhaps justice, in the fact that Villard was granting funds to preserve aspects of the fast-disappearing languages. His railroads had brought industrial and agricultural development to much of Oregon, thereby indirectly accelerating the destruction of the very cultures and languages that his grants were intended to salvage. In 1910 his widow gave an additional grant so that the Coos work, and work with the Alsea language, could be completed. The new Coos work would be with Coquelle's nephew, Jim Buchanan.

While scholars pursued their research, life at Siletz continued, punctuated by births, marriages, and deaths. Some of those rites of passage involved people close to Coquelle and not a few of them must have brought back ghosts of the past. On January 15, 1904, for example, the first love of his life, Annetti, now about fifty-five years old, married his longtime friend Spencer Scott. She had been working as a cook at the Siletz Indian Boarding School, where Coquelle's current wife, Agnes, also worked.

Agnes was delivered of a girl on September 2, 1907. They named her Blanche, but she lived only two years and is buried next to Emma. Agnes's daughter Marie, who was twelve years old on the 1910 census, does not appear on the 1911 or any subsequent census. She vanishes from the records, and so we assume that she died. On January 24, 1911, another girl was born. They named her Lulu, but she lived only ten months.

With all of the sadness that inevitably accompanied so much loss, the need for periodic relief must have been acute. The people of Siletz found pleasant relief, among other places, in the annual harvest of hops in the Willamette Valley. Coquelle had been going to the hop harvest regularly since the 1870s.[4] It was an annual outing for nearly all of the Indian families, and it seemed to have grown more important to them as the years went by. Schools were sometimes let out so that the children could go with their parents, and special cars were put on the railroad to get them over to the valley.

The hop harvest fit perfectly with the Indian tradition of seasonal migrations for harvests of various kinds. After eels in the late spring, "Oat harvest next, then hops, then salmon," was the order of things at Siletz.[5] But hops seemed to be the most important to the most people, and there was good economic incentive. Sometimes there were advertisements that the hop yards would pay "50 cents a box, with good pasture for horses."[6] But beyond economics, there was a strong social and cultural draw that caused many of the Indians at Siletz to drop everything they were doing and head for the hop fields as soon as the harvest began in September of each year.*

After the railroad came to Toledo it was easy to get to the hop fields, but Coquelle would hitch his team to the wagon, load up his family, and head to the valley the old-fashioned way. Coquelle, Agnes, Augusta, and Coquelle Jr. would start out on the road toward the summit of the Coast Range, plodding along in the wagon hour after hour, along with a convoy of wagons doing the same thing. Coquelle Jr., at six or seven years old, repeatedly asked his father, "How much further? How much further?" Coquelle would say, "Just a little ways." Eventually, it was dusk and they would stop to camp. It took two full days to drive to the hop fields from Siletz with a team and wagon.[7]

Once at the hop fields, there was the atmosphere of a huge, extended family outing. The days were hot, but the nights were warm and pleasant, much warmer and more pleasant than at Siletz. At the larger hop yards over two hundred pickers would be employed. At the James Seavy yards at Corvallis, most if not all of the pickers were Indians from the Siletz and Grand Ronde Reservations, and babies were sometimes born to them there. Agnes would perform the duties of midwife.[8]

The arrival of the Indians was newsworthy. "Indian dances will be a form of Amusement at the Seavy yards during the next month that will interest numerous Corvallis people," said a notice in the *Corvallis*

---

* Hops were used exclusively to flavor beer and ale at the rate of about a pound per barrel. The hop industry began in Oregon in the 1870s, and by 1905 there were 30,000 acres under cultivation in the Willamette Valley, making Oregon the largest hop-producing state in the nation.

Gazette Times.[9] There were dances, and the women could sell baskets, beads, and other craft items that had come into demand among white collectors and curio hunters.[10]

To the Indians, the collectors must have appeared strange. It was certain that many of them had no idea of the function and significance of the articles they collected. Coquelle told of seeing a collector one time, at Albany. "A steamboat came to the big wharf at Albany," he said. "Finally along came a white man wearing a woman's basket hat. I thought that he was a woman. I remember that. It looked so funny on him."[11]

In 1905, Portland, Oregon, held a world's fair in commemoration of the centennial of the Lewis and Clark expedition. The Indian exhibit was to be "a large and expensive one." Edwin L. Chalcraft, superintendent of the Chemawa Indian School and soon to be agent at Siletz, was put in charge. "The finest collection of Indian baskets ever displayed will be a feature of the exhibit," the *Lincoln County Leader* asserted.[12] The fair's special emphasis on the work of Indians of the Pacific Northwest spurred new interest in collecting local items. Almost a year before the centennial opened, the newspaper noted, "Curio hunters were visiting among Siltezites this week."[13]

The largest and finest collection of Siletz items was owned by Mrs. Clarinda Copeland. Aside from being the owner of the store at which Coquelle traded, she was federally licensed as an Indian trader. She was a knowledgeable and careful collector who obtained most of her items through barter, the preferred system of exchange among the Siletz women for baskets, beads, and other craft items.[14] The correspondent to the *Lincoln County Leader* viewed her collection and commented on it in the November 14, 1906 issue. "She has 250 strings of beads in full length, of various kinds; also baskets by each tribe. She will not part with them, she says."*

The women who knew the ancient art of basketry now had a trade with a reliable market, and "Siletz baskets" were sought after by tourists and serious collectors alike. Made of tightly twined spruce roots and often decorated with traditional geometric designs, some of

---

* Mrs. Copeland's Indian artifact collection was auctioned off at the Ross Theater in Toledo shortly after her death in 1929. The city of Newport obtained the collection and maintained it until it was acquired by the Lincoln County Historical Society during the 1960s. See Wyatt.

them grace important collections today.[15] Maude Lane told the authors that her mother-in-law Minnie Lane made baskets all year in a corner of the living room of their house. She would take them to Nye Beach at Newport on the Fourth of July and sell them all that same day, year after year.[16]

As the Dawes Act, the "Dead Indian Act," and other public laws were "severing" Indians from their land base, it was assumed that Indians, as Indians, would soon disappear and that the younger generation would "assimilate" into the general population. According to Agent Knott C. Egbert, by 1910 at least half the people living within ten miles of the Siletz Agency were white.[17] It was looking as though the Indians might indeed disappear. That belief on the part of the general public engendered a strong sense of nostalgia, the sense that something was being irretrievably lost, and that some of it must be preserved.

A motley assemblage of devotees worked single-mindedly to preserve bits of Indian culture. There were collectors (e.g., George Gustav Heye), photographers (e.g., Edward S. Curtis), showmen (e.g., Buffalo Bill Cody), artists (e.g., Frederic Remington), scholars (e.g., Franz Boas and his students), philanthropists (e.g., Rodman Wanamaker), and governmental entities (e.g., the Smithsonian Institution). They were all of one mind: salvage as much from those fast-disappearing cultures as possible, as quickly as possible, while something of them still remained. Those individuals and organizations often worked at cross-purposes, sometimes in fierce competition, but they perpetuated the romantic image of the American Indian that was held throughout the world during much of the twentieth century. Their influence on the Indians themselves was no less profound.

A turning point was 1913. Woodrow Wilson was sworn in as the twenty-eighth president of the United States on March 4. His administration was marked by a strong spirit of progressivism and individualism, and "freeing" the Indians from government control fit well into that spirit. The assimilation policy of the Dawes Act was pushed "to its extreme limits" by the completing of allotments on most reservations, and there was a strong push to give the allottees fee-simple title to their allotments before their twenty-five-year trust period was over.[18]

Assimilation was facilitated from other sources as well. On New Year's eve, 1913, "the Indians held a feather dance in Metcalf hall," according to the Siletz column of the *Lincoln County Leader*. The Feather Dance was about all that was left of the old order at Siletz. In that year Arthur Bensell came home with an automobile, the first resident of Siletz to do so. Later in the year, the first airplane ever to land in Lincoln County arrived from Coos Bay after having flown "as high as 5,000 feet, and 90 miles per hour." The white settlers who had bought the farmland from the Indians had joined together to build a cheese factory at Siletz, and most of the cropland was being turned into pasture for dairy cows. At Upper Farm they were joining their homes together with a local telephone system. A steel bridge was being built across the Siletz River on the main road from Toledo, and surveyors were laying out the future route of a logging railroad.* The *Lincoln County Leader* explained to its readers the advantages of a new road: "The building of the road will mean more sawmills, the sawmills more people, the more people will give a better market to the farmer for the products of his ranch at a cash price."[19] Siletz had finally arrived in the twentieth century, and there was no turning back.

Amid all this material progress at Siletz, there were even some indications of "high culture." In July, McCloy's Vaudeville Troop performed to a full house, the first troop of outside entertainers to appear at Siletz. That was not the first stage production, however. As early as March 24, 1911, the Siletz Dramatic Club had given its first performance, a one-act farce entitled *Beautiful Forever*. "It was presented by Missus Raddant and McDonald and Messrs. Walter Hall and L. J. Frachtenberg," according to a March 3 notice in the paper. The following month the Dramatic Club presented another "delightful comedy," this time with a much larger cast, which again included Miss McDonald and L. J. Frachtenberg.

The names of L. J. Frachtenberg and Miss McDonald frequently appeared together in newspaper notices. Leo J. Frachtenberg (1883–1930) had recently been granted his Ph.D. in anthropology under Franz Boas at Columbia University. He was at Siletz under the grant by Mrs. Villard to complete the Coos and Alsea linguistic and ethnographic work that was started in 1903. Miss Claudia McDonald was the government stenographer. Agnes Thompson said that she was "one half Indian, pretty, black hair and black eyes, from some eastern tribe." Agnes marveled on "how Frachtenberg and that girl

---

* These are all items from the *Lincoln County Leader* during 1913.

danced and played cards."[20] They were married May 22, 1913, the newspaper from then on addressing them always as Dr. and Mrs. Frachtenberg.

Although Coquelle did not work with Frachtenberg, he may have helped to find Alsea and Coos informants for him. Coquelle's nephew Jim Buchanan and Agnes's former husband, Louis Smith, each provided myth texts. Smith gave to Frachtenberg one significant Alsea myth, in English. Buchanan provided nineteen myths in the Hanis Coos language during the summer of 1909. He lived across the Siuslaw River from Acme (near Florence), Oregon, and was Frachtenberg's sole Coos informant. Of Jim Buchanan, Frachtenberg said, "He is at the present time the only member of the Coos tribe who still remembers and can relate coherently some of the myths and traditions of the by-gone generations."[21] In fact there were a few others, but Jim Buchanan was probably the best among them at the time. Most of what is known of the Hanis Coos language is from Frachtenberg's volume of texts, and his grammatical sketch derived from the material he obtained from Jim Buchanan.[22]

Agnes gave birth to another boy on April 22, 1913. They named him George Earl Thompson. Augusta was thirteen, and Coquelle Jr. was almost eight years old. With two older siblings to baby and look after him, George was, by all accounts, well taken care of. Coquelle was sixty-four years old, the age at which one would expect to be a grandparent, but here he was with three children, ranging in age from newborn to thirteen!

On August 20, 1913, an unusual ceremony was conducted in honor of the Indians at Siletz. According the newspaper, "Dr. Joseph K. Dixon, representing the Rodman Wanamaker Expedition of Citizenship to the American Indian, with assistants, was there."[23] Rodman Wanamaker was heir to a New York and Philadelphia department store fortune. He was among the many Americans, mostly from the East, who wanted to do something to improve the lot of the Indians. He had the money and the name to get attention of the press, the Congress, and even the president of the United States.

Dr. Dixon (the "Dr." was apparently honorific) was a photographer, lecturer, and promoter hired by Wanamaker to spearhead his projects aimed at reform of Indian policy and at education of the public on matters pertaining to Indians. He had first been a Baptist minister, and then a representative of the Eastman Kodak Company in Europe before being hired, at age fifty-two, by Wanamaker. He was said to be eccentric and pompous, but he was a good photographer and cinematographer in addition to being an effective publicist and promoter. In 1908 he made a pioneering attempt at a narrative ethnographic movie for popular consumption, filming Longfellow's *Song of Hiawatha* at the Crow Agency, Montana, using an all-Indian cast.* He had no prior experience in matters pertaining to Indians, but he nonetheless became quite influential in the Indian reform movement, which led ultimately to the citizenship and enfranchisement of all Indians in 1924, and rejection of the Dawes Act with the Indian Reorganization Act of 1934.[24]

Dixon's party arrived in Toledo on the evening train Tuesday, August 19, traveling in their private Pullman car. They were met at the station by a welcoming committee from Siletz headed by Dr. Leo J. Frachtenberg, and were escorted to the agency. The ceremonies were conducted the next morning with "more than a hundred Indians" present. "A message from President Wilson, delivered by phonograph," was given. The chiefs of the various tribal entities making up the Confederated Tribes of Siletz each signed a declaration of allegiance to the government, took an oath, and were presented with an American flag. "The chiefs signing the declaration and taking the oath were, John Adams, Ned Evans, Jim Poinsee, Jim Battisse, Wm. Smith, Spencer Scott, John Williams, Joshua Louie and others," according to the paper. Among the others may have been Coquelle, who was certainly a peer of those whose names were listed. Coquelle appears prominently in a photograph of the signing, resplendent in his white mustache and wearing a suit and a Dakota Stetson hat.** The newspaper account concluded, "A feather dance was given, in tribal costume, which as usual was a drawing feature of the exercises."

Dixon and his party left on the afternoon train. They were visiting eighty-nine Indian reservations, comprising 169 tribes, each of which was presented a silk flag. Their travel plans called for 18,189 miles by train, 2,298 miles by stage, and 315 miles by boat. It was a

---

* The first successful narrative ethnographic movie was *In the Land of the Headhunters* (1914) by Edward S. Curtis; the second was *Nanook of the North* (1922) by Robert Flaherty.
** The full collection of 8,000 Indian photographs taken by Dixon between 1908 and 1923 is at the William Hammond Mathers Museum at Indiana University.

Assimilation: End of the Trust Period

big project, with plans to erect a National Indian Memorial at Fort Wadsworth on Staten Island. When completed, it would stand opposite of and larger than the Statue of Liberty.[25] World War I turned the public's attention away from its romantic attachment to Indians and the project was never completed.

If Dixon had arrived two weeks later, he would have been disappointed in his ceremony and his photo opportunities. As usual, everyone left for the hop harvest in the Willamette Valley. The September 12 *Lincoln County Leader* observed, "The absence of the majority of the Indians from Siletz has turned this burg into a very quiet place." A month later, it became even quieter when Dr. and Mrs. Frachtenberg departed for New York. "Dr. Fractenberg has finished his work at Siletz," said the *Lincoln County Leader*, "and will leave with his young bride for New York City, where he expects to resume his duties at Columbia University. The Doctor will be back in Oregon next summer."[26]

Coquelle found himself concerned with more mundane affairs during much of this time. He had become an absentee landowner, and as such was "land poor." He was living on about $300 per year, while "owning" eight hundred acres of trust land scattered throughout northern Lincoln County. None of the land was providing income, and most of it was in estates that had not yet been settled.

In August 1913, he was confronted with an irritating minor incident that reflects the attitude of neighboring landowners. Coquelle had petitioned for and had obtained a title in fee simple for the allotment of his son Walker. The fee patent was issued April 15, 1910, taking the land out of trust and enabling Coquelle to sell it on his own, but the land was remote from settlement and far from a road. As a result, it had not sold.

An adjacent landowner, Mr. Cecil Casper of Devils Lake Farm, had cut a few small trees that may have been on that property. No doubt trying to be helpful to Coquelle, Superintendent (the new title for the agent) Knott C. Egbert wrote a demanding letter to Casper. The reply tells much of the time and the place. Casper admitted that his men, building a road, may have cut "two or three small trees" east of the lake on land that was presumably north of Coquelle's land. "It is barely possible that they were cut on his land but it was the intention to cut them on land adjoining his," Casper said. He pointed out that cutting the trees as part of building the road brought the county road one mile nearer Mr. Thompson's place. "I suppose that I am entitled to all the curses which may be heaped upon me by thankless nonresident land owners of both races," Casper said. He named the person who, he suspected, "made the helpful suggestion to Brother Thompson." He ended sarcastically, "Trusting that the matter can be settled before reaching the Supreme Court of the United States, I remain, Very Respectfully, Cecil Casper."[27]

It was not only his inherited lands and his own allotment that kept Coquelle preoccupied. He was frequently called to testify in other heirship cases. On February 3, 1912, he testified in one that may have come to him as a surprise: a hearing for the allotment of Frank McDonald, who had died fifteen years earlier. Alice Johnson, Coquelle's paramour during his time at Coos Bay in 1877–78, and Ida, Alice's daughter by Sailor Mack McDonald, had originally been declared as the only heirs. Now that the land had been sold there arose the question of Alice's other daughter, Agnes (Aggie), and whether or not she should share in the inheritance.

Superintendent Egbert stated in a letter to the commissioner of Indian Affairs that he had "never heard of Aggie Johnson until April 23, 1910." He presumed that Aggie had not been considered a lawful heir to Frank McDonald's allotment because "she was considered by the probate court and her relatives an illegitimate daughter," and would therefore not be entitled to inherit "under the laws of Oregon." The Dawes Act (as amended February 28, 1891) stated, however, "that for the purpose of determining the descent of land to the heirs of any deceased Indian . . . every Indian child, otherwise illegitimate, shall for such purpose be taken and deemed to be the legitimate issue of the father of such child."[28] Egbert needed instructions as to the rights of Aggie Johnson from the commissioner of Indian Affairs in Washington, D.C. As a precaution, and in fairness to both the purchaser and to Aggie, Egbert had asked her to sign the papers for sale of the land.

In Alice Johnson's own testimony in connection with another heirship case at Gardner, Oregon, on July 8, 1911, she was asked, "Is Aggie Johnson your daughter?" Answer: "Yes." Question: "Who is her father?" Answer: "Coquille Thompson." A marriage card indicating "first marriage" of Alice with Coquelle was filled out for the records and filed at the Roseburg office of the superintendent of Indian Affairs.

During the Siletz hearings on the Frank McDonald allotment, Alice and her daughter Agnes were both living at Coos Bay. Ironically, they requested that Coquelle be their "representative at the hearing" at Siletz. Coquelle knew almost everybody and their relationship to each other, but in this case he found himself being questioned about his own relationship with Alice Johnson. Coquelle's testimony, as recorded in paraphrase, explained the relationship: "In reference to my alleged relations with Alice Johnson will say that I went down there in the fall of 1877 and stayed with her by Indian custom till the following April when I returned to Siletz. This was just before the advent at Silitz of Agent Swan. Mack McDonald afterward told me he married her (Alice) by Indian custom the same year I left (1878). Mack McDonald had Agnes' name with that of Frank and Ida on a little book he showed to the Agent (Buford) in order to get allotments at Siletz for his children. He claimed all three of the children as his own."

Coquelle was not asked his opinion as to the actual paternity, but several other relatives and acquaintances were asked whether they had "any idea as to who the father of Aggie is?" The answer in every case was "I do not know."[29] The question was to come up several more times over the years.

During the spring of 1914, the county bridge across Thompson Creek at Coquelle's place collapsed, falling in of its own weight. No one was on it at the time; it had merely rotted out. According to the newspaper report, "It has been dangerous for some time."[30] A contract was quickly let to replace the bridge, and the next year contracts were let so that roads to Upper Farm and to Lower Farm could be planked.[31] The introduction of automobiles into the Siletz area brought the problem of building roads good enough for them to drive over, and with an "inexhaustible" supply of timber, plank roads were an obvious, though short-term, answer.

That summer the Siletz Agency got a new superintendent. Edwin L. Chalcraft, a lifetime veteran of the Indian Service arrived in July 1914. He would remain until November 1925 when the agency was closed and administration was moved to Chemawa. Chalcraft's office at Siletz was divided in half by a large desk. The outer part, next to the entrance door, was open for people who had business to transact with the superintendent or his clerk. The inner part, behind the desk, was occupied by file cabinets, Chalcraft, his clerk, "and any policeman that might be present." Chalcraft wrote in his memoirs that the third day he was on the job "an Indian came in and with a lordly air stated what he wanted, and when I asked him a question he said, 'you are paid to know that.' I did not reply, but turned to Coquelle Thompson, a policeman, and said, 'Put him out of the office.' Thompson did this and, after the Indian had gone a few rods I told Thompson to bring him back." Chalcraft again asked the man what he wanted and "he acted the gentleman this time and went away with the information he wanted."* Coquelle was a large man and commanded respect, qualities needed in a policeman.

During 1914 the Siletz Indian school farm was subdivided, and on November 27 it was sold at auction. There were 112 townsite lots and 24 acreage tracts, which brought $19,983, about $1,200 over appraisal.[32] The Siletz Agency would now become an actual town. Coquelle ended up with "lots 3 and 4 of block one, Townsite of Siletz," which he subsequently sold to John Albert (Alsea) for $200.[33]

Land continued to be a preoccupation (or perhaps only a distraction) for Coquelle, who was called to testify in heirship cases with increasing frequency. The Wilson administration was stepping up its national efforts to give fee patents to allottees at the same time that the twenty-five-year trust period was coming to an end at Siletz. Inheritance examiners were hard at work, ensuring that all the land titles would clear, with all claimants having been heard and judicious decisions made. A review of documents contained within the Allotment Case Files at the National Archives and Records Administration, Pacific Alaska Region, Seattle, reveals that the inheritance examiners performed their duty scrupulously.

In April 1914, Coquelle and several others gave a deposition in the case of Abram Lincoln, who died in January, at about ninety years old. Lincoln's mother was the Tututni woman discussed earlier who had once been a slave of the Coquille and Yakima Indians. Coquelle had no claim or other interest in the case; he was merely called to corroborate the testimony of others in establishing heirs. Lincoln's daughter Mary Dick was his only heir, but as his allotment had already been sold, there was no property.[34] The practice of the examiners was to gather testimony from the claimants and from among their relatives,

---

* From "Memory's Storehouse," a personal memoir of Edwin Chalcraft. Box 1, folder 7, p. 248, Edwin Chalcraft Papers, Washington State University Library, Pullman, Washington.

acquaintances, and neighbors, thus obtaining a consensus within the community of the relationships, whether or not there was any property involved.

The laws relating to inherited lands were changed several times, and as a result some of the inheritances were reexamined more than once over the years. In 1915 the inheritance examiners reexamined Emma's allotment, which Coquelle had inherited under previous laws soon after she died in 1903. In his testimony this time Coquelle gave interesting genealogical information concerning Emma's parents—their names and where they were from, and of her previous marriages. John Adams and Robert Metcalf gave corroborating testimony to the effect that Coquelle was the only heir. The file was then forwarded to the commissioner of Indian Affairs in Washington, D.C. It was returned approved on May 27, 1922, nineteen years after Emma died!

Allottees could apply to have fee patents issued on their allotments at any time, and during the Wilson administration the applications were usually granted. Coquelle made the mistake of obtaining a fee patent for the allotment of his deceased son, Walker, only to discover that he then had to pay taxes on it. Agnes Thompson alluded to the Walker Thompson allotment in a letter she wrote years later in Coquelle's name to the superintendent at Chemawa. "I kept up the taxes as long as I could," she said, "then had to give up."[35] "Giving up" on the taxes, in this case, produced complicated results. Through the good offices of Carl S. Davis, a real estate agent in Newport, the taxes were paid by Charles L. Litchfield in 1917. In return, Coquelle quitclaimed 30 acres of the land to Litchfield, who in turn quitclaimed 53.12 acres to Coquelle. Thus, through a cooperative arrangement with honorable citizens, Coquelle lost only a part of the allotment through the nonpayment of taxes.

In 1919, Coquelle finally found a buyer for the 53.12 acres. Mr. E. J. Abbey agreed to pay $600, but the title would not clear because Coquelle had failed to record his quitclaim deed from Charles Litchfield, and three years of unpaid taxes had accumulated in the meantime. Coquelle thought that Mr. Davis had the deed; Mr. Davis thought he had given it to Coquelle with instructions to have it recorded at the courthouse. No one could find it, and in the end, Mr. Litchfield, who lived in Portland, made another quitclaim deed so that the title would clear.[36] The number, variety, and complexity of the real estate transactions Coquelle was involved with over the years provide an excellent catalog of the impact of the Dawes Act on the original allottees and their heirs.

In August 1915, Siletz put on its first "All Indian Fair." All of the automobiles in the area, "besides teams and rigs of all descriptions," ran continuously, bringing hundreds of people from Newport and Toledo. The exhibits were all Indian exhibits: the agricultural, horticultural, and floricultural products were all theirs; the needlework, basket weaving, beadwork, relics, and curios, as well as the work of schoolchildren, were theirs. Games of coho (shinny) and archery, as well as other Indian games were played. There were Feather dances, a minstrel show, and during each evening "the play Hiawatha was staged in the auditorium." According to the newspaper report, *Hiawatha* was "undoubtedly the biggest attraction," and the sale of seats had to be limited. Robert DePoe, the Carlisle-educated son of the Joshua Athabaskan chief Depot Charlie, was now the teacher at the Upper Farm Day School. He was the inspiration and director for the play, using an all-Indian cast, "ages from five to sixty years." The newspaper reported that "to make the play more real and fascinating, real Indian songs and dance were intermingled throughout the play." It was considered a wonderful success.

The play, of course, was taken from Longfellow's book-length poem *The Song of Hiawatha*, the most popular long poem ever published in America. It first came out in 1855, the year before the Indians from southern Oregon were moved to Siletz. It was an instant bestseller, and was to stay in print for the next 145 years and beyond. From the beginning it was subject to parody and ridicule, neither of which diminished its popularity. Virtually everyone could recite passages from it, everyone knew the characters and many of the episodes, and it was the medium through which most people obtained their concept of Indian religion.

In 1916 the fair was repeated, again to great success according to the paper. The *Hiawatha* production was reprised, and again it was a hit. This time, all of the music and dances were from Siletz, choreographed by none other than Chetco Charlie, "the greatest interpreter of the historic dances of the Siletz Tribes," according to the paper. Chetco Charlie was Coquelle Thompson's partner in the Thompson Warm House Dance of 1877–78, and it is quite likely that Coquelle was one of the dancers. Charlie played the part of Paw-Puk-Kee-wiss, who danced at Hiawatha's wedding. Chibiabos, the singer of Indian love songs, was played by Daniel Jordan. According to the newspaper, he was "the best interpreter of religious Indian music." Iagoo, the teller of fanciful tales at Hiawatha's wedding feast, was played by William Brown. The newspaper described him as "the fiery brilliant Indian orator interpreting the Indian stories both interesting and attractive." Nokomis, Hiawatha's grandmother, was played by Marguerite Harney, who had played the same part the year before. But the big surprise of the season was the ingenue who played Minnehaha. "Augusta Smith, a new find," said the paper. Augusta Smith was Coquelle's now sixteen-year-old stepdaughter, and she was stunning.*

Longfellow had been inspired by myths collected by the Michigan superintendent of Indian Affairs, Henry Rowe Schoolcraft (1793–1864), with the help of his Ojibway wife and her mother. Some of the lines and scenes would have resonated clearly with Coquelle. "Then the little Hiawatha / Learned of every bird its language, / Learned their names and all their secrets." As a child Coquelle would imitate the sounds of birds, and late in life he claimed to understand what they were saying.[37] Among Longfellow's descriptions of Hiawatha's friends were some that might have reminded Coquelle of his own friends. Hearing of the gentle Chibiabos, "He the best of all musicians, / He the sweetest of all singers," Coquelle might have thought of his erstwhile brother-in-law Jim David, who sang so well. "When he sang, the village listened; / All the warriors gathered round him, / All the women came to hear him." And the description of Kwasind may have brought memories of Old Hunter going into the beaver houses to put a cord on beaver. "But he reappeared triumphant / And upon his shining shoulders / Brought the beaver, dead and dripping." There was much in the *Song of Hiawatha* that would strike a familiar chord.

The Siletz production of *Hiawatha* was not the first time that the poem had been adapted for the stage with an all-Indian cast. The first time of record was an outdoor opera in 1900 performed as a promotion for the Canadian Pacific Railroad. The first performances were attended by Longfellow's daughters, and a later production ran for decades as a passion play at the Chippewa Garden River Reservation near Sault Sainte Marie, Michigan.[38] In 1908 Joseph K. Dixon

---

* This assessment is based on a photograph of Augusta Smith, in her Minnehaha costume, at the Lincoln County Museum in Newport, Oregon.

attempted his movie version, with an all-Indian cast, during the "second annual Crow Fair" at the Crow Agency, Montana. Financed by Rodman Wanamaker, Dixon shot over 30,000 feet of motion picture film at that time.[39] Dixon's visit to Siletz in 1913 may have been an inspiration to Robert DePoe and others, encouraging them to organize their own all-Indian fair featuring a *Hiawatha* production.*

Whatever the inspiration, the all-Indian performances of *Hiawatha* can be seen as an "astonishing, ironic and ideologically complicated" manifestation of the fusion of white and Indian cultures.[40] At Siletz, it can be seen as a symbol of the extent and direction to which assimilation had reached twenty-two years after final allotment, in severalty, under the Dawes Act of 1887. The twenty-fifth anniversary of the final allotment of the reservation took place on July 26, 1919, marking the end of the original government trust period for the allotted land. One objective of the Dawes Act had been to facilitate assimilation, and the extent to which it actually succeeded has been studied and debated. The lack of consensus on the matter can be attributed to subjective uses of the word "assimilation."

To clarify the issue, we have to bring in another term, "acculturation," referring to a process that may or may not accompany assimilation.[41] Acculturation is the process of adopting superficial cultural traits such as clothing, speech, and etiquette. There seems to be plenty of evidence that Coquelle was acculturated. He was wearing "civilized clothes" almost from the time of his first arrival at Siletz, and numerous photographs show him dressed in appropriate style. He learned to speak and understand English fairly well. He was employed by the agency as a policeman and in other capacities during most of his life. We know something of his lifestyle from his grocery bills at Mrs. Copeland's store. He listed land for sale, and sometimes actually concluded sales and trades. In short, while remaining primarily Indian in outlook and religion, he had taken on most of the cultural trappings of the general population.

The degree to which Coquelle (or anyone else) was "assimilated" at that time is harder to assess. Using the typology of assimilation pro-

---

* There is interest to the present day. A Canadian movie based on *The Song of Hiawatha* and with an all-Indian cast appeared in 1997. Starring: Graham Green (Oneida, played O Kagh); Litefoot (Cherokee, played Hiawatha); Irene Bedard (Inupiat and Cree, played Minnehaha); Russell Means (Sioux, played Mudjekeweis).

posed by Milton Gordon in his influential *Assimilation in American Life* (1964), Peter Salins (1997) came up with four key steps that ethnic groups go through as their assimilation becomes more complete.[42] The first step in Salins's scheme is that the ethnic group and the general population have to accord each other *legitimacy*. Each group has to accede that the other has a right to be there. Congress made its clearest statement of legitimacy of Indians when it passed the Indian Citizenship Act of June 2, 1924, giving all noncitizen Indians full citizenship. But Coquelle asked rhetorically, "How can they make an Indian a citizen, when he was here originally and first?" He then answered his own question. "Intruders," he declared, "have no right to make citizens."[43] Coquelle had denied the legitimacy of the whites.

Salins's second step toward assimilation assumes that the ethnic group has the *competence* to function in American economic and social settings. Here Coquelle seems to have passed the test. He was personally well liked and respected by the whites he associated with. Economically, he worked his own farm; he was employed by the government; he sold and traded land and other commodities. He was clearly competent.

Salins's third step toward assimilation is the exercise of *civic responsibility*. It is certain that Coquelle was a good and respected citizen of the reservation on which he lived, but assimilation into the larger society implies more than that. At a minimum, it implies being a law-abiding citizen respectful of other citizens, and optimally to be active in the political processes. Coquelle was certainly respectful of others; he was law-abiding (except for the liquor laws); he testified in criminal cases and he made numerous sworn depositions on a large variety of legal matters; he worked with the sheriff's office during investigations. Insofar as opportunities presented themselves, he seems to have fulfilled the requirement for civic responsibility.

Salins's fourth, last, and most essential step toward assimilation is that the ethnic group must *identify itself as Americans*, and that identity must be reciprocated by the larger population. World War I occurred, coincidently, at the same time that the twenty-five-year trust period was coming to a close, and those two events decisively instilled within the Indians at Siletz their self-identification as Americans. America entered the war April 6, 1917. By September the first twenty-five men from Lincoln County were selected under the draft to go into the army. One of them was Paul Washington, the first of fifteen Indians from Siletz who went into the service.

On February 8, 1918, Coquelle made a speech about it, either in Jargon or Athabaskan. "The address was interpreted to your correspondent by an Indian woman. It was full of patriotic sentiment," said the article that appeared in the February 15 *Lincoln County Leader.* The occasion of the speech was a "big feather dance" at the home of Billy Metcalf. The dance was in celebration of allotment and the coming end of the trust period. "The dancers had their most brilliant and flashy costumes on and made a good showing," the newspaper article said. "The room was draped with three beautiful American Flags. One was a large silk flag given to the Indians by the Government." The large silk flag was undoubtedly one of the flags that had been presented five years earlier by Joseph K. Dixon of the Wanamaker expedition.

"Before the dance commenced Coquelle Thompson, acting as master of ceremonies, lined up the dancers in front of the flags," said the article. "He made a very impressive and eloquent address in his own language, telling them the flag represented liberty to the Indians as well as whites." The reporter said that Coquelle admonished them to "respect and defend (the flag) to the bitter end." The reason was that "now about fifteen of the Indian boys were in the American army going to a foreign country to fight for Liberty and the Stars and Stripes and if need be to lay down their lives in its defense." It is significant that Coquelle was the chosen master of ceremonies who would give that patriotic speech to the other dancers. In ceremonies at which whites were prominent, and English was used, other, educated Indians would preside and Coquelle would be in the background. But when the Indians were having their own celebration, they chose Coquelle to speak to them in their own language.

"After the conclusion of Mr. Thompson's address the flag was saluted and the dance commenced," the article continued. "Ed Bensell, a chief's son, a war chief also, conducted the old fashioned dance." The writer explained, "This is a religious service and is participated in by the old people. About thirty persons were on the floor dressed up in the best of their costumes. The time is kept by beating of a drum made out of rawhide and a chant or singing by all the dancers." At the conclusion, "a very fine supper was given by the Indians at midnight. John Adams, one of the leaders among the Indi-

Assimilation: End of the Trust Period

ans made a talk by invitation. Mr. Adams has one son in the army and will probably have a second son go."

All of the eligible Indian men at Siletz entered the army soon after the first call in June 1917. Paul Washington went with the first contingent from Lincoln County; his younger brother Andrew would soon follow. A little later Fritz Simmons, who married Coquelle's stepdaughter Augusta, enlisted. Siletz furnished fifteen men, all they had who were single, physically fit, and of military age. They very definitely met Salins's fourth step toward assimilation: they were Indians but they were also Americans. The war proved it.

The war had an unexpectedly profound effect on the Siletz River valley. The lower river was in the so-called fog belt, and the timber had never burned in historic times. As a result there was an exceptionally fine tract of virgin old growth, which was about 70 percent "yellow fir" and 20 percent Sitka spruce, running as much as 125,000 board feet per acre.[44] The newly discovered efficacy of airplanes as a weapon of war made the Sitka spruce a strategic material in great demand. It was known to have one of the highest strength-to-weight ratios of any commercially available wood, and it was needed for the manufacture of a projected 40,000 warplanes. Only about 10 percent of the spruce was of "airplane grade," and about 1,000 board feet were needed for each aircraft (only about 200 board feet actually ended up in the structure of the plane). The government was hoping to cut 10 million board feet of spruce per month to meet the projected demand.[45]

The population of Lincoln County at the outbreak of the war was about 3,000. During 1918, the population more than doubled because 3,000 men arrived to build logging railroads, camps, and the largest spruce sawmill in the world at Toledo. Most of the men were in the newly formed Spruce Division of the U.S. Army. Thus, for a period of about nine months prior to the armistice of November 11, 1918, Lincoln County was very much a part of the war effort and was transformed permanently.

By February 1918, sixty soldiers were stationed on the Siletz school grounds. They prepared to build a "plank and crushed rock road" to Lower Farm so that "motor trucks can convey the riven [split] spruce to Toledo."[46] The rail lines pushed in three directions: south from South Beach toward Yachats, to tap the almost pure stands of spruce south of the Alsea River; north from Newport toward Otter

Rock to tap a pure spruce stand there; and north from Toledo toward Siletz, to tap the mixed stands of fir and spruce on the Siletz River.[47] The huge spruce sawmill was under construction at Toledo, but several smaller mills were already operating near Siltez. The *Lincoln County Leader* said with uncharacteristic understatement, "The prospects for Lincoln County were never so bright as now."[48]

The newspaper reported that for George Washington's birthday in 1918, "the Indians celebrated the day at Metcalf Hall by giving an old fashioned feather dance." It lauded the patriotism of the Indians, and said that extra preparations had been made to please the soldiers in uniform who would be present. "Some of the soldiers were from the east and never saw the dance before and enjoyed it very much," the article said. It paraphrased an Indian speaker as saying, "Big Chief in Washington would be pleased to know the Indians at Siletz stood by the government and were anxious to do something to knock down the kaiser."[49]

The Siletz dancers sometimes took the Feather Dance on the road for special occasions. On June 8, 1918, they probably performed at the most unusual event ever. There was a total eclipse of the sun on that day, with the best observation in Oregon predicted to be at The Dalles, on the central Columbia River. When Elizabeth Jacobs asked Coquelle about eclipses of the moon or sun, Coquelle said, "Indians didn't know about that. But one time I was up at The Dalles. White people had come to see Indian dances. That day about 12 o'clock all at once it was getting dark. People thought the world was getting changed. 'Dance, Dance,' they said. We didn't know about that."[50]

The total eclipse was being observed across the Columbia River, at Goldendale, Washington, by a team of astronomers from Lick Observatory in California. They were hoping to prove or disprove a new theory by a "German scientist," whose name was A. Einstein. "The nubbin of this theory," explained the *Portland Oregonian* on that day, "is that the light from stars beyond the sun is bent by the sun's gravity before it reaches the earth in about the manner that a streetcar rail is bent around a slight curve." The calculations, unfortunately, were inconclusive. The Lick Observatory team had left their best lenses in the Ukraine following the eclipse of August 21, 1914. World War I broke out in Europe that very week, and the team was fortunate to escape with their lives. Their precious lenses were later retrieved, and during the eclipse of September 21, 1922, in western Australia, they at last confirmed Einstein's general theory of relativity.[51]

There were no other total eclipses of the sun that Coquelle could have observed during his lifetime, but there had been three others visible to Indians in the Northwest. The first was visible at Astoria, Oregon, and northeasterly through Washington on July 28, 1860. The second one was on July 29, 1878, best observed in Washington and Idaho. In 1950 Ella E. Clark interviewed Harry Shale, a Quinault Indian from Queets, Washington, who saw that eclipse when he was a small boy. "The old people made all the noise they could," he said. "They got on top of their houses and pounded on the roofs with sticks. They shouted, shot off their guns, and beat on their drums."[52] The third one, mentioned in the last chapter, was on January 1, 1889, and was visible in northern Nevada.

A few days after the eclipse at The Dalles, the Siletz Indian school had an especially large picnic. The 1917–18 school year was its last. From then on the Indian children would attend the public school. Included among the festivities was a pie-eating contest in which Coquelle Thompson, Jr., came in second place.[53] He was thirteen years old.

Celebrations for the Fourth of July, 1918, featured Feather dances from Siletz given for the soldiers camped at Waldport and at Newport.[54] Construction of the logging railroad toward the spruce south of the Alsea River was making good headway with a large crew, and three pile drivers were pushing another railroad from Toledo toward the Siletz River.[55] That railroad would miss the Siletz Agency, but was planned to extend north as far as Euchre Creek, where a crew was surveying for a rail line (which was never built) into Euchre Mountain. It was expected to "open up the entire timber belt of the reservation." "The War effort allowed it," said the *Lincoln County Leader* of August 8, 1918.

Another rail line was planned to cross the Siletz River at Camas Prairie and extend through Coquelle's place. It was to follow Thompson Creek toward its source to tap the timber to the south of Euchre Mountain. The timber on Thompson Creek, however, was too scattered to justify a rail line.[56] On July 28, 1918, Edwin Chalcraft, now the superintendent of the Siletz Agency, appointed an appraiser to cruise the timber on Coquelle's and Emma's allotments and to assess the value. The cruise of Emma's eighty-acre allotment revealed only

467,000 board feet of Douglas fir and a much smaller amount of spruce and hemlock. By comparison, eighty acres of the most heavily timbered lands toward which the railroad was being built would yield about 12 million board feet.[57] The value of the Douglas fir ranged from $1.00 to $1.50 per thousand board feet. All of the timber and piling (and cordwood, which in practice had no monetary value at all) on Emma's eighty acres was appraised at $1223.50.[58] The timber on Coquelle's adjoining allotment was valued at slightly less.

At about the time that Coquelle's timber was cruised and appraised, he moved from his Thompson Creek allotment, where he had lived for at least twenty-five years and probably much longer. He hitched his horses, Bill and Maude, to the wagon, loaded up their household and farming equipment, and moved three miles south, where he leased a part of the Robert Metcalf allotment at the bottom of Government Hill. Agnes worked in the laundry at the Siletz school, and living at the Metcalf allotment was much more convenient for her than walking three miles each way from the home place, which they leased out for $50 per annum. Coquelle, officially a policeman, actually worked at the school as a watchman and disciplinarian, and he was assigned as a teamster to take care of the agency horses.

During those few wartime months at Siletz there was full employment in logging, sawmills, and construction. Logging was most attractive to the Siletz men, and the new steam logging donkeys that were brought in were huge, fast, and dangerous machines. There was a certain kind of freedom while working in the woods, at least compared with the factory-like regimentation of the sawmills. Logging provided an opportunity for young men to prove themselves, because it was demanding and dangerous.

How dangerous it could be is indicated by an article on the first page of the October 11, 1918, *Lincoln County Leader.* "Klamath Billy Killed," said the caption. Klamath Billy was "one of the old-time Indians on the Siletz reservation," the article continued. He was sixty-eight years old. He had been near a logging crew on the lower Siletz River when a log rolled over him and crushed his head, killing him instantly.

All of the economic activity in the county was related to the war effort, and there was no room for dissent. The September 13, 1918, *Lincoln County Leader* had an article that gives a flavor of it. "Two arrested as Pro-German," screamed the headline. An Austrian named Mike

Assimilation: End of the Trust Period

Stabich, working at Miller's logging camp near Siletz, was accused of having "slandered the Red Cross." In the same camp was Pete Ould, a suspected member of the IWW (Industrial Workers of the World), who was alleged to have made "seditious utterances."* Both were arrested by the military police and taken to Portland for arraignment. Lincoln County was under what was effectively martial law.

Even Coquelle had to swear a loyalty oath. The form that was filled out for him revealed that he was employed as a private at Siletz school at a salary of $20 per month ($240 per annum). His year of birth was indicated as 1843, at least five years before his actual birth year. He was listed as 5 feet 6 inches tall and weighing 180 pounds, with two children, age sixteen and six (Coquelle Jr. and George). His stepdaughter Augusta, now eighteen, was not included. Musical ability was listed as "none," ignoring his well-known talent for singing traditional Indian songs. "Besides farming and day labor," read one statement, "I served on the police force at Siletz for several years." That was something of an understatement in view of the fact that by that time he had served for over thirty-five years. The standard oath was administered: "I, Coquelle Thompson, do solemnly swear that I will support and defend the Constitution of the United States against all enemies, foreign and domestic." He signed with his right thumb mark, witnessed by Verne Ross and Alice Chalcraft, the agent's wife.[59]

A week before Klamath Billy was killed, the war had come home to Siletz most dramatically. Paul Washington, the first of the Indian men from Siletz to enter the army, had been killed in action in France. At six o'clock on the morning of September 28, 1918, according to an article in the *Portland Oregonian*, Company G of the 361st Infantry, 91st Division, "was advancing in double time to get into line." An artillery shell exploded alongside the column, instantly killing "Private John Anderson of Ranier, Oregon and Private Paul Washington of Siletz, Oregon." Private Glesen F. Hamlin of Seattle died of his wounds two weeks later; five others who were wounded in the same explosion survived.[60] Paul Washington was one of the 126,000 American military personnel who died during the war, and the manner of his death was probably fairly typical.

---

* The IWW (Industrial Workers of the World) was a radical labor union believed by the government to be in league with the Bolshevik revolution in Russia and was therefore a frequent target of violent repression by the authorities.

As Paul Washington's body was being shipped home from France, his brother Andrew (308th Infantry, 77th Division) died of tuberculosis at the army hospital in Denver, Colorado. The double funeral for the two brothers was the largest ever held at the Siletz cemetery. Three months later Seaman First Class Ralph Spencer died of tuberculosis at the navy hospital in Bremerton, Washington, and was buried at Siletz, his body delivered in the first hearse to be used there. The cemetery was later named in honor of Paul Washington, the first of the Siletz Indian men to die in the war and the only one killed in action.[61]

During the winters of 1917–18 and 1918–19, a new and exceptionally virulent strain of influenza spread worldwide.[62] The "Spanish flu," as it was called, killed more than 550,000 people in the United States during a ten-month period, but for some reason it did not appear at Siletz until mid-December 1918. Two families were quarantined with it at that time, but over Christmas it spread through dances and Christmas parties. "About 150 cases occurred on the reservation among the Indians and whites," the January 24, 1919, *Lincoln County Leader* declared. There were only three or four deaths attributed to the flu, a surprisingly light mortality rate when compared with the apparently high mortality at Siletz during past epidemics of other diseases.*

During the height of the epidemic at Siletz, the dormitory of the school on Government Hill was turned into a hospital, filled with cots bearing the sick. Old Dr. Carter was in charge and Agnes Thompson was his nurse, on her feet day and night, sleeping in her clothes. She cared not only for the patients in the "hospital," but rode horseback to many who were sick at home. None of the patients died who were cared for by Agnes and Dr. Carter. She said in an interview that she used a "big mustard plaster that circled the body," and she soaked the patient's feet in hot water. She was sure that her method healed the patients. If any had died, she feared, "the chain would have been broken and the Indians would have given up the struggle for life."[63]

---

* LCL, 10 January 1919: "only two children" have died "of the effects of the disease." LCL, 24 January 1919: of the 150 cases among the Indians and whites, "the death rate was small, being only about 2 per cent." The burials at the Paul Washington Cemetery on Government Hill reveal only five during the flu seasons of the three years 1918–1920.

The Indian school at Chemawa did not get off so easy. A frontier woman doctor named Mary Canaga Rowland had no sooner been hired as physician at Chemawa when a student from Montana arrived with the Spanish flu and died the next morning. That was the first of the 536 cases that she treated. There were nineteen deaths. She wrote in her memoirs that at first she was afraid of the epidemic, but then decided, "I might as well die of the disease as be scared to death." She said, "Our Protestant instructor at the school did quit and told me when I thought it was safe she would return. The Catholic priest, old Father Goll, never missed a day." There were over one hundred beds filled with the most severe cases, with screens between them. "My head nurse was Mrs. Codding, a Coos Bay Indian who had graduated from Carlisle Indian School in Pennsylvania."[64] Mrs. Codding was the former Daisy Wasson (1874–1963), Coquelle's first cousin once removed, a daughter of Susan Adulsa Wasson of Coos Bay and a granddaughter of Coquelle's paternal aunt Gek-ka (Gishgui).[65]

During October and November 1918, Andrew Cassidy, an attorney for the Indian Service, probated forty-one cases of heirship claims at Siletz.[66] The Indian Service was anxious to get all such claims out of the way prior to granting fee-simple title to the allotments. One of the cases was for the allotment of Coquelle's great-aunt Louisa Pete. Coquelle made a long and detailed deposition to Mr. Cassidy, a partial repetition of his testimony in the same case a year and a half earlier. At the conclusion of the earlier deposition, Coquelle stated, "I just want the Department to decide the case on this testimony as I have no other witnesses. This old woman always lived with me, and always claimed I was her only heir, and there is nobody else claiming. I have already sold some of this land."[67] Probably because there were no other witness, the case was reopened by Cassidy, and Coquelle went through the questioning again. In both depositions, he provided detailed genealogical information concerning his mother and father, including the names of his brother, his mother, and others in the family. Much of that information would not be available except for the existence of this testimony.

At the conclusion of the 1918 deposition, Cassidy asked Coquelle, "Do you claim any interest in this estate?" Answer: "Yes, I think I'm entitled to it all." Q: "Does any other person claim, or has any person other than yourself ever claimed any interest in this estate?" A: "No, sir. No other claimant at all." Q: "Do you write your name?" A: "No. I sign by thumb mark. It is the easiest anyhow." Coquelle sometimes signed with an "x" and sometimes with his thumbprint. He had become quite accustomed to the formalities of providing testimony.

The only case in which Coquelle's interest was in conflict with another's involved the allotments of John Tyee and Abram Mack, which Coquelle stood to inherit through his deceased wife Emma. King Rippin claimed an equally close relationship. William Sheppard was the inheritance examiner in that case, and he appears to have gotten a little testy with Coquelle, asking leading and insinuating questions. Coquelle handled himself quite well.

Mr. Sheppard: "Have you always thought King Rippin was interested in this case?" A: "I always thought so." Q: "Why didn't you mention him in your testimony in Toledo then?" A: "I mentioned his name at Toledo." Q: "So you think he's related the same way you are?" A: "I don't know about that." Q: "You and King Rippin sort of made an agreement in this case, didn't you?" A: "No." ... Q: "You remember you and King Rippin agreeing to sell this land and dividing it even?" A: "No. (Agreement is read to the witness)." Q: "Did you and King Rippin agree to sell this land and divide it?" A: "We never made any agreement." Q: "This agreement is dated here November 13, 1905, don't you remember anything about that at all?" A: "I remember when they made that paper over there, but I didn't understand it that way." Q: "What was your understanding of it?" A: "I understood that we had to go to Toledo court to witness." ... Q: "So you always thought that King Rippin ought to have a share in this estate, did you?" A: "King Rippin can't prove he's the nearest heir."[68]

The case came to an amicable conclusion, however. In the case of the Abram Mack allotment, the inheritance examiners found that Coquelle was the "husband of the subsequently deceased niece of subsequently deceased husband of subsequently deceased grandmother." King Rippin was found to be the "nephew of subsequently deceased husband of subsequently deceased grandmother." They were thus each entitled to one-half of that estate. Emma had inherited the Abram Mack allotment through her uncle John Tyee, who also had an allotment. In the case of the John Tyee allotment, the inheritance examiners found that Coquelle was the "husband of the subsequently deceased daughter (Emma Thompson) of prior deceased sister." King

Rippin was the "son of prior deceased daughter." As a result of those degrees of relationship, they each inherited half. Through a land trade ten years later, King Rippin became sole owner of the John Tyee allotment (where he lived), and Coquelle became sole owner of the Abram Mack allotment (which he intended to keep as a timber investment). It would appear from this and other transactions that Coquelle was perfectly competent to handle his own affairs.

A Competency Commission arrived at Siletz during February 1919. Its purpose was "to determine the number of Indians that are capable of managing their own affairs with a view of issuing patents to their land," according to the February 28, 1919, *Lincoln County Leader*. The writer editorialized, "The Indians and whites have been clamoring for this for a long time and now it will receive the proper attention." At the beginning of the Competency Commission's work there was a big Feather Dance at the Metcalf Hall. "A good crowd was present," said the *Lincoln County Leader*. "This dance was gotten up by the Indians to celebrate the Dawes Act giving the Indians their liberty and also a deed to their land in fee simple after expiration of twenty five years. The time will be up July next. The Indians call this celebration their Fourth of July."[69]

Whatever the attitude of the Indians on other reservations toward the policies of the Dawes Act, at Siletz there appears to have been no opposition. Placing allotments of land in trust, in their individual names, was considered by the adult Indians at Siletz during the 1890s their last, best hope. Through the years of the trust period and heirship cases, it does not appear that attitudes changed at all. At the conclusion of the trust period on July 26, 1919, there was probably a feeling of relief among many that their connection with and partial dependence on the government was over.

Coquelle may have been an exception. He was about seventy years old in 1919, and his relationship with the government had been useful to him throughout his life. He may have seen advantages in maintaining that relationship. In any case, the Competency Commission retained in trust the allotments of the incompetent and the elderly as a matter of policy, and Coquelle, at seventy, was now considered elderly. According to a description of the process reported in the *Lincoln County Leader*, "Each Indian is called to the office and the commission ascertains whether he wants a deed or not; if he wants a deed, the commission will pass upon his ability to manage his own affairs and if they think he is capable he will get a deed whether he wants one or not."[70] If Coquelle had actually wanted fee-simple deeds to his property, he could have shown cause why he wanted them and they would no doubt have been granted, despite his age. It appears that he had no wish to own his property in fee simple, or to lose his status as a ward of the government. For one thing, it would mean having to pay property taxes on the land, and his earlier experience with his son Walker's allotment had taught him to be wary.

On March 15 another Feather Dance was held at Metcalf Hall. This was a memorial dance in honor of the deaths of Paul Washington, killed in action in France, and of his relative, Klamath Billy, killed in a logging accident about the same time. "Mr. and Mrs. Isaac Washington, father and mother of the dead soldier, put the money up for the supper," said the newspaper article. "Not a smile was on the face of any dancer. Not one cheerful look; every thing was as solemn as a funeral. The beat of the drum and the plaintive song of the dancers made a deep impression. This was kept up till midnight when the hour of grief and mourning ceased, then a free supper was served free to all, and it was a dandy feed."[71]

On April 19, 1920, a most remarkable domestic event occurred in the life of Coquelle and Agnes. Agnes was forty-two years old, near the end of her childbearing years, and Coquelle was seventy-one, far past the usual age of new fatherhood. But born to them on that day was a healthy baby daughter. They gave her the unusual name of Sina, in apparent memory of Coquelle's first daughter born forty-eight years earlier, also named Sina.

Coquelle and the rest of his family continued living on a part of the leased Robert Metcalf allotment. He was still a considerable landowner, with his own and Emma's allotments, as well as his inherited interest in the allotments of Abram Mack, John Tyee, and Louisa Pete, amounting in aggregate to about four hundred acres. In 1925 the family consisted of himself and Agnes and the three children: Coquelle Jr., twenty years old, in school at Chemawa; George, twelve years old and living at home; and Sina, now five. Augusta, now twenty-five, was married to Fritz Simmons, son of Hoxie, and living on their own place.

Agnes was described by the agent, Edwin Chalcraft, as being "industrious and is the recognized midwife for this community." Over the years that she practiced midwifery, she delivered most of the babies born to the Indian families and many born to the white families at Siletz. She said in an interview that she was known as "Old Dutch Cleanser," because she was "a great hand to make people clean up!"[72]

Chalcraft described Coquelle as "trustworthy and faithful and has served the agency in the capacity of policeman for many years." Coquelle continued working as a government employee—policeman, watchman, teamster, general handyman—as he had for decades. He farmed a little, putting up enough hay each year to feed the livestock. In a survey done by Superintendent Chalcraft on June 13, 1925, Coquelle had a team of horses, two milk cows, three heifers, one wagon, one plow, one set of harness, and one saddle. At seventy-six years of age, he and his twelve-year-old son, George, had put up "6 tons of hay, one acre of potatoes, and the usual garden truck," according to the survey (which erroneously listed him as eighty-three years of age).

Siletz was changed. After the war, the partially completed "world's largest spruce sawmill" at Toledo, together with the logging railroads and the timber that had been acquired by the government in Lincoln County, was sold by the government to a consortium of timber companies for two million dollars.[73] By 1925 it was fully operational as the Pacific Spruce Corporation, comprising three subsidiaries: C. D. Johnson Lumber Company, which operated the sawmill; Manary Logging Company, which operated the four large logging camps; and the Pacific Spruce Northern Railway Company, which operated the logging railroads. "Camp 12" was built on a hill one mile south of Siletz, connected by rail to Toledo. The rail lines extended into the heavy stands of timber north of Siletz, beyond Lower Farm. Years later, when that timber was exhausted, the rail line was pushed up the Siletz River to Upper Farm where it remained in service, hauling logs to the big mill at Toledo, until the logging train was replaced with logging trucks at the end of 1959.[74] The mill is still operating to this day, as a paper mill, utilizing timber from the lands of the former Siletz/Coast Reservation.

Nineteen twenty-five was the last year that the superintendent maintained an office at Siletz. When Edwin Chalcraft closed the Siletz Agency and moved his family and his office to Chemawa, it ended sixty-nine years of continuous operation. From that time on, Coquelle and the other elderly Indians remaining there (very few of whom could read or write) had the inconvenience of corresponding by mail for their many needs relative to the Bureau of Indian Affairs.

Coquelle received a most unwelcome letter dated July 7, 1927. It was from James H. McGregor, who had recently replaced Edwin Chalcraft as superintendent. "I have been instructed by the Indian Office to drop you from the payroll on account of your advanced age," it began. Mincing no words, it continued bluntly, "The office says the records indicate that you were born in (1863 crossed out) 1843, and they are of the opinion that you are too old to perform the services of a Policeman."

Coquelle filed a claim for retirement compensation. A summary of his services made by the "Indian Office" revealed that "he has served from 1879 to June 30, 1927, almost continuously, and has not been off of the force with exception of a month at a time, on two different occasions." He had served under several different agents as "a Captain of Police, who received his orders from the Agent and in turn transmitted them to his privates." The significance of his long years of service was dismissed summarily. The "Indian Office" found that "he has never belonged to the Indian Scouts. . . . He did no active scouting duty. . . . He has never had to go with a body of men to fight against an enemy. . . . He has no papers, discharges, or medals in his possession that will give information to confirm his claims for compensation." As an afterthought, the report stated, "He remembers of having a paper given to him by Agent Bagley which he has lost."* Bagely had resigned as agent forty-eight years earlier, in 1879.

Predictably, the "Indian Office" turned down his claim for retirement compensation. Coquelle would live another twenty years, his income derived from the very irregular lease or sale of land or timber from his allotments. The Dawes Act had arrived at its logical conclusion.

---

* William Bagley was agent at Siletz from 1876 to 1879.

9

Remembering
Salvage of a Legacy

Coquelle lived to carry his heritage through four generations. Who would now carry on the old traditions, if anyone? Nearing eighty, he had two sons who were coming of age, and a small daughter. The two boys would not inherit tribal titles or prestige—that was gone. They would not inherit tribal wealth in land or other property—the Dawes Act had seen to that. Their wealth, their prestige, their inheritance, would be in their education. Coquelle and Agnes seem to have understood that quite well.*

Upon graduating from Chemawa in June 1927, Coquelle Jr. was accepted as a freshman at Oregon State College at Corvallis. The same year, his brother George graduated from the eighth grade at the Siletz Public School and was ready to begin at Chemawa, if he could get in. It would appear that the family, including Coquelle Sr., was very supportive. On June 24, 1927, Coquelle Jr. wrote a letter to Superintendent James H. McGregor at Chemawa, requesting that his brother George be admitted. The letter reveals a familiarity between Coquelle's family and the superintendent. It read:

---

* It may be that they were in advance of a trend. Lionel Tiger suggests that since the 1990s education has become the most practical and ubiquitous form of dowry or bride price in industrial countries. See Tiger, 138–39.

Dear Sir:

My father asked me to write you concerning my brother, George's entrance at Chemawa this fall. We think it would be good training for him. George is a good scholar and will also abide by the rules. He is 14 years old. He is athletically inclined and it would be fine for him to be out there where he can see more of that stuff.

I saw you as I was coming from work one evening last week.

My folks are all well. Hoping you'll let us know at your earliest convenience.

Respectfully,
Coquelle

Mr. McGregor replied by return mail. "Dear Coquelle," he wrote, "I shall be very glad to accept your brother George this fall, and am inclosing an application blank to be filled out and returned as convenient." As part of the application, old Dr. Carter examined George and stated, "This young man is in perfect health and free from all diseases." The superintendent's certificate, stating why George could not attend the public school at Siletz, said, "Environment not of the best and George is too good a boy to lose."[1]

George was accepted and graduated four years later, on May 26, 1932. The senior class annual, *The Trail*, noted that his interest was in painting, and that his ambition was "to become a master painter."[2] He was a letterman in varsity football and baseball.

Interestingly, the "Pupil's Record," which George signed, indicated the church affiliation of his mother and of himself as "Catholic." His father's church affiliation was left blank. According to his sister, Sina, their mother did not take any of the children to church, and so it is likely that George, like his father, had no church affiliation or preference. On the "Record of Pupil in School," which he did not sign, his church preference was indicated as Protestant, probably the church preference of the person who filled out the form.[3] Church attendance and religious instruction, either Catholic or Protestant, was mandatory at Chemawa.[4]

George attended Chemawa from 1927 to 1932, the years during which his big brother, Coquelle Jr., was attending Oregon State College at Corvallis. And Coquelle Jr. was a *big* brother! He was huge, and a star fullback of the Beaver team. They made much of his Indian heritage in promotions for the games, calling him "Big Chief Thompson." Once, a photographer went home with him to Siletz to make promotional pictures in his father's regalia. The result was a much publicized photograph of Coquelle Jr. standing in a dugout canoe made by Archie Johnson, the last person to make one at Siletz. They were on the Siletz River just a little below town.[5] During that season, on October 27, 1928, the team beat the Washington Huskies at Seattle, 29 to 0. The 1931 yearbook, *The Beaver,* gave a glimpse of "Chief Thompson": "He started playing fullback and earned numerals there, but later was made over into a guard. Wherever punting was needed, Chief came back of the line to do it." Old Coquelle's boys were of good stock.

There are several indications that Coquelle Sr. approved and encouraged his children to gain an education. For the 1929–30 school year, for example, he drew $300 from his trust account to pay for Coquelle Jr.'s college expenses. The following year he drew $200 for the same purpose. Coquelle's income came from the $50 per annum lease of his own allotment, and drawing down the balance of his trust account, which had built up from the sale of land. In 1930 his balance was down to $1,177.26.[6] The United States was entering the depths of its worst economic depression, and there was no market for Coquelle's land or timber. The balance in his trust account would continue to dwindle.

George, like his half-sister Sina of forty years earlier, would not live to take advantage of the education he received. During the summer after graduation he grew thin, developing the symptoms of tuberculosis, and in August he was taken into the hospital at Chemawa where his condition worsened. On January 4, 1933, he and another boy were approved for immediate transfer to the Yakima Sanatorium at Toppenish, Washington.[7] He was, however, too ill to be transferred and died at Chemawa of pulmonary tuberculosis on January 28. He was nineteen years, ten months, and nine days old, the ninth and last of Coquelle's children to predecease him (and the second to die soon after completing the program at Chemawa).[8] George was, as the superintendent had certified four years earlier, "too good a boy to lose," but there was as yet no cure for tuberculosis, still the chief cause of death among the Indians at Siletz.

Nineteen thirty-three seemed to mark another turning point. On March 4, Franklin Delano Roosevelt was sworn in as the thirty-second president of the United States, bringing into office with him a promised "New Deal," including a New Deal for the Indians. His commissioner of Indian Affairs was to be John Collier (1884–1968), an advocate for the preservation of "communities," who had been working ten years for repeal of the Dawes Act and enactment of laws that would permit tribes to become legally incorporated, among other things. Almost immediately upon his appointment, Collier ordered the Solicitor's Office of the Department of the Interior to draw up an omnibus bill that would attain his objectives. The resulting Indian Reorganization Act (Wheeler-Howard Act) of June 18, 1934, gave Republican opponents an opportunity to accuse the Roosevelt administration of imposing an extreme "Communistic experiment" upon the Indians. In fact, it was not "imposed" upon the Indians. The act included an amendment that stipulated that provisions of the law would not be operative within any tribe until that tribe voted on it by secret ballot in elections called by the secretary of the interior.[9] In the end, 181 tribes voted to accept the act; 77 tribes, including the Confederated Tribes of Siletz, voted to reject it.[10]

Coquelle's nephew Jim Buchanan, about eighty-five years old, died near the end of June 1933. He had been living on his allotment on the South Slough of the Siuslaw River, a few miles from Florence. The place was at a railroad siding called Siboco, an acronym for "Siuslaw Boom Company." Logs were loaded from the river onto railcars there, for transportation to sawmills. Frank Drew said it was "a pretty place. 40 acres."[11]

Buchanan made a will dated June 17, 1933, shortly before he died. In it he bequeathed to his nephew, Andrew Charles, "the sum of fifteen dollars, which he owes to me for money he borrowed from me." If there was any money in his trust account in the bank at Roseburg, he bequeathed it to Lillian Severy and Howard Barrett. Coquelle was to get the rest. "I give, devise, and bequeath all the rest and residue of my estate, real personal, and mixed, to Coquille Thompson, my uncle, and in case of his death before I die, then and in that case to his son, Tom Thompson. To any other relatives, if any, I devise and bequeath the sum of One Dollar to each one." The allotment (Roseburg no. 256) consisted of 41.2 acres and was appraised at $1,000. A note in Coquelle's allotment file says, "This land is being deeded to Coquelle Jr. for $1 and love and affection; however, there are claims in the amount of $742.40 against this land which would have to be settled by someone." As in many cases with inherited allotments, it was no sinecure.

As the depression deepened nationally, Coquelle's own economic condition became critical. A letter to the agent at Chemawa, dated June 2, 1933, was written by Coquelle Jr. in his father's name. It concerned, he said, "a loan on the property (80 acres) I own on Sam Creek." The Sam's Creek property was the Abram Mack allotment that Coquelle had obtained title to in the trade with King Rippin. "I asked about getting a loan from the government some time ago, before my money ran out, so that I would have something to go on. I've been waiting ever since and have spoken to Mr. Larsen about it, but he seems to know nothing about it." Coquelle wanted action by July 1, the end of the fiscal year. "If it is impossible to do that I wish you would let me know at once and I will see what I can do otherwise with it. I will have to get some money from it soon because bills are piling up and I've received no money since February."

Two months later Coquelle received this reply: "August 4, 1933. Dear Mr. Thompson: We forwarded your application for reimbursable loan to the Indian Office under date of July 8, 1933, with recommendation that it be approved. . . . As soon as the approved application is returned to this office, we will advise you." Two weeks later, Agnes got into the act in a letter she wrote in Coquelle's name to Superintendent Ryan: "Am writing in regards to the loan I applied for. Have you any returns as to whether I am granted the loan or not. My bills are rapidly piling up and I have no means to offset them. [signed] Coquelle Thompson by Mrs. A. Thompson." The file does not contain documents indicating what, if any, action the "Indian Office" took in this matter, but it is clear that Coquelle was suffering economically along with the rest of the country in 1933.

During the fall of 1933 Siletz hosted another anthropologist, John Peabody Harrington (1884–1961). A compulsive collector of linguistic and ethnographic field notes, Harrington had been with the Smithsonian Institution since 1915, working with so-called last survivors of most of the linguistic families of North America. But this was his first trip to Siletz. Using a kind of triage system, he interviewed "last survivors" he thought to be most in danger of an early death. Coquelle's Upper Coquille Athabaskan language was evidently not of immediate interest to Harrington, or perhaps Harrington considered Coquelle to be in quite good health in 1933. In any case, he was not interviewed at that time but was "saved" for a return trip nine years later.

While at Siletz in 1933, Harrington interviewed Frances Johnson (Takelma), who had worked with Edward Sapir during the summer of 1906. They went on a trip together to southern Oregon to gather place-names, returning to Siletz on November 4.[12] The next day Harrington spoke with Coquelle's first wife, Annetti (Scott), now in her eighties and bedridden. She gave him a few words in her native Applegate, and a few in Takelma, that she had learned from her first husband, Evans Bill, and they discussed the Ghost Dance and other matters.

Annetti was, according to Harrington, the last full-blood Applegate Indian alive in 1933, and the last to speak that language. "Just before I left Mrs. Spencer Scott I paid her $1.00, and asked her again about placenames on the Applegate River. She said *la'kho·ve'* is the name of her father's place." She provided a few more items of information, but was not well enough for an extended interview. Harrington said that Annetti was "a good sized woman, well preserved, but has been in bed for over a month now. Nothing special the matter with her, just old age."[13]

Annetti died two weeks later, on November 19, 1933. Her death certificate was signed in the quite shaky signature of Dr. Carter, who determined the cause of death to be "decline and old age." There was a death notice in the *Portland Oregonian*, November 24, 1933, in which Dr. Carter was quoted as saying, "Mrs. Scott was one of only three Rogue river natives left who wore tattoo, a sign of aristocracy among the aborigines."[14] The three vertical black stripes on her chin, placed there at puberty, were still quite in evidence. Dr. Carter was himself about the same age as Annetti, and died four years later. Annetti's death certificate was one of the very last of the many that old Dr. Carter signed over the years for the Indians at Siletz.

As 1934 began, Coquelle's economic situation had not improved. In January Coquelle Jr., who was working as a teacher at Siletz Public School, received a bill from the Salem Mortuary. "We have a balance of $50 on the funeral of George Thompson your brother. This balance was to be paid by you as the Government would only allow $93.00. As the account is past due we would like to have a payment from (you) at this time, please write and let us know what you will be able to do on this account." Coquelle Jr. sent it on to Superintendent Ryan, at Chemawa, asking that "action be taken at once on it, because of rate of interest charged for over due bills." He signed it "Coquelle Thompson Sr., by C[oquelle]. T[hompson]. Jr."

Sina was now fourteen years old and ready for high school. In an interview in 1999, she revealed some of her memories of home.[15] It was usually windy there, near the river. "We lived on fish, mostly," she said. They would salt some of the fish, some was canned in jars, and they had a smokehouse. They also had a lot of dried fruit, especially apples, "hung up in the rafters on the porch." Besides apples, the orchard also had pears and plums. Her mother, Agnes, took care of the garden. She was a good cook, as Sina remembered. "We had plenty of jam and jelly and all of that." They did their shopping at Bensell's store at Siletz.

During those depression years the problem of getting cash never went away. To help, Agnes took in washing. The house was "just up from the river bank," Sina said, and her mother would carry the clothes down to the river and wash them using a scrub board and a tub. Sina remembered clothes drying in the house in the wintertime, her mother ironing with flatirons heated on the stove, and her dad cutting wood. He was good at cutting kindling and making shavings to start the fire, a task he could perform at his leisure even after cataracts had clouded his vision. Agnes made all of Sina's clothes. "She was always busy. She was always busy doing something."

One source of cash in the late spring was sale of bark from the cascara buckthorn tree *(Rhamnus purshiana)*. Native only to the Pacific Northwest and popularly known as "chittam," it is used in many commercial laxative preparations and had a ready market. In fact, Siletz had been a major source of supply for the bark since at least the turn of the century. In the late spring, buyers would set up shop at Siletz and pay competitive prices for all the bark that came in. The 160 acres of Coquelle and Emma's allotments had a large number of the trees, which grow fairly fast, and so there was something of a perpetual yield available there. Various persons who had leased the property during the 1920s had peeled several thousand pounds of bark, but there was always more. Coquelle could hitch Bill and Maude to the wagon, go up Thompson Creek to a "chittam patch," and come back to Siletz in a few days with a wagonload of chittam, worth (in a typical season) about five to eight cents per pound, dried. A small tree, six inches in diameter, yields about twelve or fifteen pounds. Sina remembers peeling the chittam, drying it, and breaking the dried bark into three- or four-inch pieces for sale. It was not a steady or a reliable source of cash, but it could be a nice supplement in the late spring and early summer when the sap was up.[16]

Coquelle had a couple cows, the team Bill and Maude, and an ancient dog named Shagpo that was always underfoot. The family seldom went to town, meaning Toledo or Newport. They never played cards and they had no radio; their entertainment was limited to visiting with friends. One good friend who came often was Nellie Orton. "Usually they talked Indian all the time and most of the time I didn't know what was going on," Sina said. "I didn't know Indian." Nellie was an expert basketmaker and tried to teach Sina, who like most of the children of her generation, didn't learn.

"But my dad took me everyplace he went," Sina said. "I'd have to know what was going on." When they went to the store, or for a visit, they'd hitch Bill and Maude to the wagon and go. "I was a baby. He babied me, I think, a lot," she said. "All of the children learned to swim." Her brothers, Coquelle Jr. (called Tom) and George, taught her how. Coquelle Sr., a good swimmer even in his old age, sometimes swam with them. Sina said that her dad got along well with the two boys. Sometimes he would cry, and Sina said that it was over the loss of his other children.

Sina would trim Coquelle's handsome, white mustache for him. He would talk to her, telling her of the past, sometimes about his days on the tribal police force. "My dad, he rode horseback when he was a cop," Sina said. "He was a policeman and he was kinda rough all the time, when he took care of those guys. I think he made them behave." She said that he took care of the agency horses, and that he usually wore army clothes. He sometimes had the job of carrying the mail, although that was before Sina's time and she was a bit vague about it. She knew that he had worked as a fishing guide, and he did a lot of salmon fishing, sometimes using nets.

Speaking of her dad, Sina said, "He liked his whiskey. He would carefully measure out his liquor, even after he was old and blind." Sina remembered that he always had it, hidden in her mother's washtub. It was "boughten" whiskey.* He never made his own, but dur-

---

* During Coquelle's lifetime, whiskey was either "boughten," or it was moonshine. "Boughten" whiskey is usually amber and comes in labeled bottles with a tax stamp affixed. Moonshine is usually clear and comes in unlabeled jars or jugs with no tax stamp. On the reservation, both types of whiskey were illicit.

ing Prohibition (1919–33) it would certainly have been illicit moonshine. The children were told that it was medicine. Agnes never said anything about it, and she never drank any of it at all.

Coquelle and Agnes had only two meals per day, a breakfast usually of oatmeal and a supper in the evening. After supper, Coquelle would often go outside and sing in a loud, clear voice. He would "make it echo all around," according to Sina. "He sang Indian songs, would just stand and sing something."[17] Afterward, settled in his chair, he would say to Agnes, "Give me a smoke now." She would take a tailor-made Lucky Strike cigarette out of its package, light it, and hand it to him.[18] He would take one or two long drags, holding the smoke in his lungs awhile, as the men did in the sweathouse during his childhood and youth. That was all, and the smoke was finished. Following that, a carefully measured shot of whiskey would complete Coquelle's nightly ritual.

"Mom, she was a pretty good nurse all around," Sina said. "We had an old doctor, Dr. Carter. She helped him sometimes." But Agnes was best known as a midwife. She would take Sina with her to the house of a woman who was ready to give birth, and of course if the birth was delayed, they might have to stay overnight. "Gee, I remember a lot of times I'd have to go to bed with her and she'd make me stay with them," Sina said.

Coquelle was a very fortunate man indeed, to have as his mate during his old age a much younger nurse such as Agnes. Coquelle, however, "didn't ever seem to be sick," according to Sina. If he was, he might take a small dose of kerosene, which was believed to have medicinal qualities. His general health seems to have held right up to his final few days, in his late nineties. Unhappily, during his last twelve years his eyes were covered with cataracts and he was blind.

Coquelle's blindness began gradually and rapidly worsened. In 1935 he could distinguish only shadows. By 1936 he was declared totally blind. Cataract removal operations were being done in those days, with inconsistent results. Coquelle had been offered hope that he could be given such an operation, but the operation was never authorized or attempted. He remained surprisingly self-reliant, even in his blindness. His son-in-law Fritz Simmons put a rope from the kitchen door to the outhouse so that Coquelle, by following the rope, could go to the toilet by himself. (Sina remembered the old mail-order catalogs that were used as toilet paper.)

With good health, and an alert mind, Coquelle did not let his blindness get him down.

Sina, however, was at an age when she needed sound supervision and secondary schooling. On July 13, 1934, she was given the following recommendation from C. E. Larsen, senior clerk at Chemawa, to enter the school there.

> I recommend the enrollment of Sina Thompson, who is 14 years of age and is five-eighths Indian of the Coquille tribe living on the Siletz Reservation. This child is the only child left at home and is in need of more direct supervision. Her father, Coquelle Thompson, is 93 years of age and is blind.* Her mother, Agnes Thompson, is 59 years of age and has all she can do to take care of her husband.
>
> The main reason this girl should be in school is that she is deserving of better advantages in the way of industrial supervision. She is also greatly in need of supervision as to health.

Chemawa was good for Sina. "I sure liked it," she said. She had a good time and made many friends, including her future husband, Preston Bell. This was a pattern quite common among students at Chemawa at that time, as discovered by Sonciray Bonnell during her interviews with twenty-three alumni during 1996 and 1997. Most of the alumni she interviewed tended to promote the positive and held Chemawa in high regard.[19] Sina lived in Winona Hall, a girl's dormitory named for the legendary mother of Hiawatha.

Before Sina was accepted at Chemawa, the first of a new wave of anthropologists arrived at Siletz. The Indian Reorganization Act of 1934, which sought in part to restore some of the tribal sovereignty that had been lost under the Dawes Act, had stimulated a renewed interest in the study of traditional American Indian cultures. Among the significant projects that resulted from that interest was a Culture Element Survey of native western North America sponsored by the Anthropology Department at the University of California at Berkeley under Alfred L. Kroeber (1876–1960). That project, conducted from

---

* Coquelle was actually about eighty-five years old at that time.

1934 to 1938, was immensely influential and resulted ultimately in twenty-five published studies.*

By 1931, Kroeber had finished his book *Cultural and Natural Areas of Native North America* (published in 1939), in which he presented "an integrated picture of the North American cultural map."[20] He suggested at that time that by counting distinguishable cultural elements, it should be possible to get an "approximately objective measure of cultural intensity." He admitted that no one was ready to finance such an undertaking at that time.

The first of Kroeber's students to arrive at Siletz during this new wave of research was Philip Drucker (1911–82), a doctoral candidate from Berkeley. His specific area of interest was the distribution of cultural traits and their diffusion in Northwest Coast culture, which was the subject of his 1936 Ph.D. dissertation. He worked with Tolowa Indians during the summer of 1933 at Smith River, California, and returned to the field during the summer of 1934 to work at Siletz and Grand Ronde. The primary purpose of his 1934 trip was to gather comparative Oregon Athabaskan data to round out his Tolowa study.

From mid-May until early August 1934, Drucker worked with twenty-seven consultants representing speakers from eight languages, filling over seven hundred notebook pages. This work was not formally a part of Kroeber's Culture Element Survey, but it contributed heavily to it. At Siletz he worked with twelve Indian consultants during a forty-four day period (June 6 to July 20), returning to some of them—including Coquelle Thompson—several times. The work was clearly in the form of a survey, conducted as semi-structured formal interviews organized around a list of some forty cultural elements. In nine sessions with Coquelle Thompson he covered some eighty ethnographic topics.

Drucker drove up the Coast Highway from California, stopping at Coos Bay where he interviewed Ione Baker, one of the last of the Euchre Creek band of the Tututni, collecting eight notebook pages of Tututni words and data on material culture from her. He also talked to Agnes Johnson, daughter of Coquelle's erstwhile paramour, Alice, filling thirty notebook pages from her, and to Annie Miner Peterson.

---

* The following paragraphs draw heavily from Seaburg, *Collecting Culture*, ch. 4, "The Berkeley Connection: Philip Drucker."

He evidently interviewed Annie on parts of two days: Wednesday and Thursday, May 30 and 31, filling forty notebook pages.[21] On Monday morning, June 4, he was at Siletz interviewing Coquelle Thompson.

Drucker worked through the morning with Coquelle, paying him $1.05 for the three hours. He filled eight pages of his field notebook, beginning with the place-names of two locations on the Coquille River and proceeding immediately to certain details of house construction. He moved on quickly to specifics of fish and fishing equipment, hunting and hunting equipment, kinds of foods and cooking techniques, procurement of salt, tanning, clothing, and money. The field note entries appear to be responses to questions, and all but two are in Drucker's voice. One parenthetical entry says that upriver people didn't use mussels and so on. "Don't use much" in quotations indicates Coquelle's actual words. Below it is another entry that describes gathering alkali, scraped up from around swamps, for salt. Men went to get it, "long ways, you know," again indicating Coquelle's actual words. The Upper Coquille words for about twenty items were included. Twice that morning Drucker punctuated an entry with a series of exclamation marks, probably indicating incredulity, and several times he inserted a parenthetical comment followed by a question mark—probably indicating his uncertainty as to meaning or significance. He would come back to Coquelle again and again.

The following morning (June 5) he filled nine and a half pages in a very productive session. He went into much greater detail on house construction, including grass houses and sweathouses. In quotation marks, indicating Coquelle's verbatim words, we find that the support planks of the sweathouse are "just about same as house, but lower," and that the ventilator hole in the side was "about 2 feet wide, had to crawl out." In some cases material not in quotation marks is probably Coquelle's words, but not quite as faithfully transcribed. On the subject of "Doctor," for example, "dream about some kind of bird—dream he's gonna be doctor—he sings at night time. Chief says that "I don't like that, he got to be trained for doctor, got to dance 10 nite." Drucker commented parenthetically, "Apparently person who didn't dance would be suspected of being poisoner, 'have to kill them.'"

The next morning they continued on the subject of "doctors." Coquelle was an accomplished conversationalist and storyteller, and his strength as an ethnographic consultant was in providing extended examples in the form of a story or anecdote, not in responding to specific questions from a checklist with terse answers. By the time of this third session, Drucker had evidently gained confidence in Coquelle's veracity and ability and let him take the lead. Of the eight pages in Drucker's notebook for that session, four appear to be faithful transcriptions of Coquelle's telling of Evans Tom and the doctoring session at Upper Farm described in chapter 6, as well as several other anecdotes connected with doctoring. In the afternoon he interviewed Nellie Lane, also of the Upper Coquille. He copied six notebook pages of information from her, including a one and a half page description of the Ghost Dance. "Coquelle Thompson was sing boss," she said. Drucker evidently had a difficult time communicating with her because at the top of the first page he noted, "inf[ormant] is too damn deaf to hear herself talk."

The morning of June 7 he was back with Coquelle and filled eleven pages with notes, the first half about dances and the second half concerning games and gambling. On June 9 he was back with Coquelle again, filling another eight pages. Beginning with more about doctors and doctoring and ending with short comments on a variety of matters, most of those pages are filled with Drucker's interpretation of Coquelle's statements. Some are in paraphrase, and a few are in direct quotes. The reason some people wanted to become doctors was, Coquelle explained, "want to help people." Drucker added the comment, "makes money too—apparently incidentally." Paraphrasing Coquelle, he wrote, "Man wouldn't want wife, sister be doctor. didn't allow it—(!!!)." On the next line he either quotes or paraphrases Coquelle in what appears to be a direct contradiction. "Man like to marry that kind; bring in money all time." Some of the contradictions would make sense only within the context of Coquelle's longer, narrative approach, but Drucker seldom allowed that.

After taking Sunday off, Drucker was back with Coquelle on Monday morning, June 11, filling seven and a half pages. Most of that session concerned marriage, divorce, slaves, and related issues. Coquelle was allowed to give a few, short narrative examples to illustrate his answers, but for the most part this session was another in which Drucker was filling in the blanks for his survey questions. On June 15 he obtained four pages of notes concerning mortuary customs, mourning, digging graves, and related matters. The grave was dug by a man who was a "kinda relation," but it wasn't dug very deep. "Didn't have shovels in those days," Coquelle said in explanation.

The dead person was in the ground four nights. On the fifth, went to the land of the dead, where he "couldn't ever come back." Drucker punctuated the last statement with three heavy exclamation marks. The discussion then progressed to various dances, and Drucker filled four pages with detailed information about the Warm House Dance. After the Smohalla and the Warm House dances, "Didn't get any more new dance till Shakers came in," he quoted Coquelle as saying.*

The next day Drucker was back with Coquelle again. It was during this session that he obtained significant biographical and genealogical information about Coquelle and his ancestors, and the names and locations of some of the settlement sites on the Upper Coquille River. Coquelle said that the Tututni sometimes married "second cousins," but that his own people "wouldn't allow it." In attempting to fill in his checklist of cultural traits, Drucker seems to have asked hypothetical questions that were sometimes hard to answer. Occasionally Coquelle would have to think it over. If, for example, a man was married to his wife's sister, would his sons inherit her if the man died? Drucker noted that Coquelle "didn't think at first" that it could happen. "Then thot that if there weren't any other close male kin, she might be." Coquelle finally settled the matter by stating, "They just do that way very once in while." It is doubtful that he had ever heard of such a thing.

Drucker took off the next day, a Sunday. He didn't get back to Coquelle for over a month while he interviewed others, most notably Abe Logan (Rogue River). On July 18 Coquelle and Drucker had their final session together. This one was probably quite pleasant for Coquelle, because it was all about hunting and fishing. There were seven pages filled with information about hunting dogs, fishnets, tools, and miscellaneous related subjects. Who can guess what emotions the nearly blind Coquelle might have experienced as he recalled those activities that he had once so greatly loved? As usual, Drucker didn't permit Coquelle to stray into the narrative, but kept him strictly giving specific answers to specific questions, thus depriving himself of the richest and most valuable memories that Coquelle had to offer. Fortunately, other interviewers would come who were more attuned to Coquelle's style and knowledge.

---

* The Indian Shakers, a messianic cult originating in Washington in 1881, first arrived at Siletz in 1926. See Amoss (1990) and Barnett (1957).

Drucker had worked three hours on each of nine days with Coquelle, or twenty-seven hours. He paid thirty-five cents per hour, and thus Coquelle received a total of $9.45.* According to his daughter Sina, Coquelle was always talking about the people who came to interview him. "He kind of liked them. I think they kinda liked him, maybe," she said.[22] That was probably true.

Drucker's monograph, *The Tolowa and Their Southwest Oregon Kin*, was published by the University of California Press in 1937, and was his only published use of the 1934 interviews. He noted in the preface, "The culture of these people exists in memory only."[23] Drucker made his research available to Homer G. Barnett, another graduate student from Berkeley. Barnett was working on a part of Kroeber's Culture Element Survey while Drucker was at Siletz, and they may have been there at the same time.** In any case, Barnett incorporated part of Drucker's data into his own Oregon coast culture element distribution monograph (1937).[24] Thus the 1934 fieldwork at Siletz was used at least twice.

Ironically, the culture element distribution studies were something of a disappointment for Kroeber, whose brainchild they were. He is said to have made very little actual use of them. The trait-list format was too confining for most field-workers and their Indian consultants alike, and the material was often unsuitable for tabular listing and direct comparison, which had been its original purpose. As a result, the richest material in many of the reports is contained in the extensive footnotes and appendices.[25] Coquelle was likely not the only one to have felt frustrated by this form of inquiry.

During that busy summer of 1934 Siletz had yet another anthropologist from the University of California. This one was different. Cora Du Bois (1903–91) had received her Ph.D. under Alfred Kroeber and Robert H. Lowie two years earlier, her dissertation being a "dull and tedious library job," according to her own description of it. She was now finishing up a two-year postdoctoral project of salvage anthropology, compiling material relative to the Ghost Dance of 1870.

---

* The first page of Drucker's Notebook #2 contains a note "Coq Tom" June 4, 5, 6, 7, 9, 11, and 15 at $1.05 each. The June 16 and July 18 sessions are not indicated, but it is clear that his interviews were normally each of three hours' duration, for which he paid $1.05.
**See Barnett 1983 for an account of his methodology.

Her approach was topical, and she sought her data from among the remnants of the northern California tribes. "No preliminary problem was set," she said in her preface. The objective was merely to trace the introduction and course of the 1870 Ghost Dance in northern California. Her title at Berkeley was "research associate."

She undertook the project at the suggestion of Alfred Kroeber, whose advice on the conduct of ethnographic fieldwork she had asked prior to her first expedition among the Wintu several years earlier. He told her only "to take pencil and paper." With that useful though superfluous advice, Cora Du Bois was to become a highly respected field researcher whose 1944 publication, *The People of Alor*, was a landmark in ethnography. During her fieldwork on the 1870 Ghost Dance her methods were comparatively unsophisticated and resembled oral history more than ethnography. Her analysis of the data, and the formulation of her conclusions, however, reveal an exceptionally sharp and disciplined mind. She considered her fieldwork "the determining polish of professionalism in Anthropology."[26]

By the time she got to Siletz during the summer of 1934, she had already interviewed approximately 125 elderly Indians in California and several on the Klamath Indian Reservation of Oregon. Those interviews had been conducted intermittently over the previous eighteen months. She had mapped out in unprecedented detail the diffusion of the complicated series of interacting cults that had developed after the initial stimulus of the 1870 Ghost Dance of the Paviotso Paiute in northwestern Nevada. It became obvious that study of the interactions with Oregon groups at Siletz, Grand Ronde, and the Oregon coast was essential to understanding the phenomenon as a whole. A grant-in-aid from the Social Science Research Council permitted her to conduct her 1934 research in western Oregon. Traveling alone in a "dilapidated car," she stayed at roadside cabins, on a minimal living and travel allowance. "I never really left my own culture," she said, "except by an act of imagination."[27]

She obtained her data "largely in biographical form." Almost none of it was autobiographical, even from among actual participants of the movement, such as Coquelle. She found a "deep-rooted fear of the risk incurred" in speaking freely about one's own dream experiences, "although," she said, "one may gossip freely about those of others."[28] Much of her data contains fascinating "gossip about others."

She found four recurring obstacles in gathering her materials. First was the reticence of her informants in speaking autobiographically: they wouldn't talk much about themselves. This was true of Coquelle as well as the others. The second obstacle was the severely limited number of possible participants of the Ghost Dance: a witness to events near the beginnings of the movement would have to be seventy or eighty years old in 1934. In that regard Coquelle, with his excellent memory, was a perfect consultant. Her third obstacle was the "contempt in which earlier cult frenzy and credulity is held," particularly pronounced in certain groups. Even Coquelle called some of the practices "crazy." The fourth obstacle was inherent in the topical approach: Du Bois was frustrated by the necessarily superficial contact that she had with each local group.[29]

Coquelle Thompson was her principal informant on the Ghost Dance of 1870 in western Oregon.* Of him, she gave the following assessment: "Coquille Thompson. Lower Coquille; born at Myrtle Point; taken to Siletz as an infant. Ca. 84. English fair. Clear mind, willing, well informed, accurate. Does not need questioning. Circumstantial and detailed data. Blind."[30] Her guess as to his age was very close. In 1934 he was actually between eighty-four and eighty-six years old, and in very good physical shape. He was, of course, Upper Coquille, not Lower, and he was actually a child, not an infant, when he arrived at Siletz. Other than that, Du Bois's characterization of him appears quite perceptive.

Du Bois noted that the material on the Ghost Dance in Oregon was "exceedingly fragmentary." Based on the clues she had obtained through her interviews in northern California, however, she was able to frame direct questions and thus unscramble a puzzle that otherwise could probably not have been solved. The clearest and most detailed account that she obtained was from Coquelle, "a thoroughly trustworthy informant." Coquelle's account began, "About one year before Bogus Tom [Shasta] came, some Grand Ronde Indians went down to California and learned about the dead coming back. They said the grass would be about 16 inches high when the dead arrived.

---

* Du Bois (1939), "Western Oregon" chapter (pp. 25–37) included 871 lines of direct quotes from her informants. 502 lines (58 percent) are from Coquelle Thompson. None of the other eleven informants have more than 7 percent of the total.

On the way back they told Sixes George [Tututni], who was living at Lower Farm on Siletz Reservation. That started them . . . dreaming and getting excited."

In a footnote Du Bois said that Coquelle "used the characteristic gesture to indicate the height of the grass." She knew from her previous interviews that "everywhere in northernmost California" the advent of the dead was expected in late spring or early summer. All of Coquelle's verifiable statements matched perfectly. "No informant who lived on Grand Ronde Reservation during this period was able to give so detailed account" as Coquelle.[31]

In Du Bois's published report, *The 1870 Ghost Dance*, the chapter on western Oregon has a section on the Earth Lodge Cult, which as Du Bois notes, was called the Warm House Dance in Oregon. "The introduction of the Earth Lodge cult was so ably related by one informant that his account is given in full," she said. Opening his narrative in the finest style of the raconteur, Coquelle began, "I was a grown man when the Warm House Dance was brought from California by Bogus Tom, Peter, and Mollie. They belonged to the Shasta tribe." Then follows a 1,500-word account that holds the reader's interest to the very end.[32] Working with Cora Du Bois, Coquelle was in his element. She let him take the lead and relate his account in his own accomplished style. Her job was to write it all down.

Her field notes of the Ghost Dance research project have not been found, and so it is not possible to deconstruct the published narratives in light of the originals. She does explain in her preface that "certain liberties" were taken with informants' statements. "Less comprehensible colloquialisms" were rendered into standard English; "in the interest of brevity and clarity" repetitions were eliminated, and "circumlocutions" were sometimes replaced with a single word; statements were sometimes rearranged in "more or less systematic order."[33] In reading the rather voluminous material she derived from Coquelle, it is possible to detect places in which she took such "liberties." The style and content of the narratives, however, seem to be very much Coquelle's own style and content. The voice of Cora Du Bois herself is a separate voice, placed in a different type font or in footnotes.

The section of the study that provides greatest insight into Coquelle's participation is "Thompson's Warm House Dance." Du Bois provided a separate subheading for each of the four dance centers (Waldport, Florence, Gardiner, and Empire), and each begins with a general statement by Coquelle. She said, "It should be noted that Coquille Thompson was somewhat reticent about his activities and tried to disclaim responsibility for the movement, whereas other informants uniformly recognized him as leader and instigator of the dance." Coquelle said, for example, "I wouldn't preach because I wasn't sure whether it was true." In a footnote, Du Bois says, "From other informants it would appear that Coquille Thompson did a great deal of the preaching."[34]

One of Coquelle's more interesting contributions to the study was his secondhand description of an event at Jacksonville (in southern Oregon) in connection with the "Big Head Cult." George Harney and John Adams were sent by the agent at Siletz to investigate the dance, and Coquelle no doubt obtained his description of the event directly from them. Again, Du Bois compliments Coquelle on his descriptive powers. "A circumstantial and detailed account of this conference was secured from an excellent informant on Siletz Reservation. His statements are quoted almost in full." There follows a 600-word account by Coquelle, concluding with a paraphrase of John Adams's speech to the Shasta following the dance. "He said that the Siletz Indians were trying to become civilized and become law-abiding citizens. He tried to calm the Shasta. He said they didn't want to stop the dance. He said they didn't want to buy those Big Heads."[35] Evidently a main incentive of the Shasta in introducing the cult to Oregon was to sell the large feathered headdresses that went with the dance!

Du Bois considers the Ghost Dance of 1870 and its successor movements to be of dual significance. "On the one hand," she says, "it is allied with a cultural category of universal if sporadic distribution." It is, she points out, an example of the recurrent pattern of messianic or revivalistic movements that sometimes arise among traditional cultures as a reaction to "the crushing impact of European culture." "On the other hand," she continues, "it is bound up in its specific aspects with the struggle of northern California and Oregon Indians to integrate their cultural life in the unavoidable demands of European invasion." She finds that the "modern cults of the Pacific Coast . . . not only symbolize but also represent in part the whole struggle between two divergent social systems."[36] She sees the Ghost Dance of 1870 and its successor cults to be transitional factors, intermediate between the traditional culture and the marginal Christian sects that later became popular among the same Indians. She believes that the Ghost Dance movement made possible the introduction and acceptance of the Indian Shakers, various Pentecostal churches, and the Four-Square Church, each of which shares much of the Ghost Dance's revivalist psychology.

Not least of the significance of her work with the Ghost Dance is that it provides a classic, historically substantiated, and finely detailed example of the actual process of diffusion, a major concept of anthropology. Du Bois suggests that the concept of the diffusion of cultural traits had long been a tool of historical reconstructions, but that until the process was more clearly understood, "it seems premature to use it as a tool in cases where history fails us."

In this case, she finds that at least five factors contributed to the surprisingly rapid and widespread diffusion of the Ghost Dance. First, was intertribal marriage. Depot Charlie, for example, was married to a Tolowa woman whose sister lived at Smith River, California. That gave him a connection that facilitated his proselytizing efforts in bringing the Warm House Dance to California. The second factor was language. At Siletz, both English and Jargon were used as the lingua franca. When Coquelle brought his Warm House Dance down the Oregon coast to Coos Bay, all the preaching was in Jargon "so it could be understood," he said. The reservations themselves were the third factor. In the cases of Siletz and Grand Ronde, the reservations brought together tribal groups that in the precontact era may not have known of each other's existence. The reservations also split some tribal groups, as for example those with members on both sides of the Oregon-California border. Bogus Tom was Shasta from California; he had relatives at Siletz who were Shasta from Oregon. The same type of split occurred with the Tolowa, who remained in California, and their relatives the Chetco of Oregon, who were on the Siletz Reservation. The fourth factor was transportation. Most of the travel between groups was by horseback, and the horse was an introduced means of transportation. Fifth, Du Bois mentions the Indian labor in agriculture. The hop fields in central California and in the Willamette Valley brought members of many divergent groups together and provided a ripe environment for proselytizing. It was during a hop harvest near Corvallis that Coquelle attended his first Warm House Dance.

Coquelle contributed significantly to the outcome of the study of the Ghost Dance of 1870, and it must have been a satisfying experience for him. With Cora Du Bois, he was able to display his remarkable observations, memory, and storytelling techniques. In contrast with the restrictive question-and-answer sessions he was experiencing with Philip Drucker at about the same time, the sessions with Du Bois were probably quite refreshing. It is to her credit that the material was published in an expansive form that gave prominence to the actual words of her 140 informants from throughout northern California and western Oregon.

An interesting tribute to Cora Du Bois and her informants is found in the journal of the poet-monk Thomas Merton. He was a constant and omnivorous reader, and on November 7, 1967, he had been reading *The 1870 Ghost Dance*. "I have been working on the Ghost Dance canto of Lograire. Goes like a charm!" he wrote. "Everything is there in Cora Du Bois, a mimeograph report from Berkeley. Beautiful, haunting, sad stuff. All you have to do is quote the Indians' own words!"[37] Quoting the Indian's own words is exactly what he did in writing the "Ghost Dance" canto of his book-length poem *The Geography of Lograire*. And that is exactly what Cora Du Bois had done. Some of that beautiful, haunting, sad stuff was Coquelle Thompson's own words.

After Cora Du Bois and Philip Drucker left Siletz and went back to Berkeley at the end of the summer, attention at Siletz focused on the upcoming referendum to decide whether to accept or reject the Wheeler-Howard (Indian Reorganization) Act of June 18, 1934. The Wheeler-Howard Act was the first law ever passed by Congress that gave individual tribes the option of accepting or rejecting it. The issue at Siletz boiled down to whether or not the distribution of land that emerged as a result of the Dawes Act would stand, or whether the Confederated Tribes wanted to open up the possibility of a new redistribution.

A number of meetings aimed at making the issues fairly clear preceded the referendum called by the Department of the Interior in 1935. Much was at stake for Collier and the Roosevelt administration, and so rules for the elections were made to favor accepting the new law. Thus, under the rules of the 1935 vote, nonvoters were counted as "yes" votes. Anyone who was indifferent to the issue, or for any other reason did not wish to vote, could stay home and would count as a "yes" vote. "No" votes had to be made either in person or by absentee ballot.

The vote was 123 "NO" (against the Wheeler-Howard Act), and only 54 "YES." Another 55 eligible voters did not vote and their "votes" counted as "YES." Even counting them, the measure still failed 109 to 123, the official tally.* Historian E. A. Schwartz has suggested that the outcome of the vote was "a manifestation of the acculturation of allotment."[38]

There were at the time 7,046 acres of land remaining in trust at Siletz. There were only ten allotments held for living persons (of whom Coquelle was one), totaling 828 acres; there were 92 allotments held in trust for deceased allottees (of which Coquelle held trust patents on three), totaling 6,218 acres. There were therefore 102 allotments remaining in trust out of the original 551 allotments to living members in 1894.[39] The remaining 449 allotments had been patented in fee simple, and most of them had been sold by the allottees or their heirs.

The vote rejecting the Wheeler-Howard Act at Siletz is not difficult to interpret if it is assumed that people tend to vote their self-interest. Individuals such as Coquelle, who held trust patents to allotted land (including inherited land), would probably not have gained if the land were redistributed again. In fact, they stood to lose. Some individuals (or their heirs) who had sold their inherited trust lands might see possible self-enrichment in another redistribution, and might vote yes. Obviously, the vast majority of those who voted saw an advantage in maintaining the status quo rather than opening another can of worms with a new law.**

The probate of Coquelle's inheritance of the allotment of his nephew Jim Buchanan occurred after passage of the Wheeler-Howard

---

* Schwartz 1997, 243

	nonvote	yes	no	total
total	55	54	123	232
official tally:		109	123	232
resident		25	110	135
nonresident		29	13	42

** Generalities fail, because each reservation was a separate case, each with its own reasons for accepting or rejecting the Wheeler-Howard Act. At nearby Grand Ronde, it passed by a narrow margin due to a majority of absentee ballots voting "yes."

Act, but before the Confederated Tribes of Siletz voted to reject it. That left the inheritance examiner in an uncertain position (but for us, an interesting one). He needed to find the tribal relationship of Coquelle with Jim Buchanan because he interpreted the act as prohibiting transfer of trust land from one tribe to another. The examiner found that Jim Buchanan was "of the Coos Tribe," while Coquelle Thompson was "of the Coquelle Tribe." In a letter dated October 16, 1934, he stated, "So this inquiry simply is whether Buchanan and Thompson belonged to the same tribe and the answer to this [is] important in view of the provisions of the Wheeler-Howard Act."[40] Of course, Coquelle's mother was Coos; his father was Upper Coquille. All marriages of either the Coos or the Coquille during his parents' time were exogamous; the wives came from other tribes, or at least from other villages. The Wheeler-Howard Act had not taken such a possibility into consideration! Coquelle was granted the trust patent.

10

The Last Decade
Jacobs, Marr, and Harrington

The referendum on the Wheeler-Howard Act was barely over when Coquelle was honored by the visit of yet another interviewer, also a woman, and the same age as Cora Du Bois. From all we know about Coquelle, he enjoyed the company of women, and one suspects that even at eighty-five and blind he was still appreciative. It has been suggested that the effect on a child of growing up with several loving "mothers" in a polygamous household may be quite positive, and may carry through life with easy, natural relations with strong women.* Whether true or not in a general sense, it was apparently true in the case of Coquelle.

The woman was Elizabeth Derr Jacobs (1903–83), wife of the University of Washington anthropologist Melville Jacobs. Born in Montana, raised in Idaho, and educated at the University of Washington in Seattle, she was a product of the West. Her B.A. degree was "based on a major course of studies in English literature and drama," according to her own description of it. She graduated in 1930 and mar-

---

* This was most recently suggested in Anthony Sampson's authorized biography of Nelson Mandela of South Africa, who was also raised in a polygamous household (*Mandela* [New York: Knopf, 1999]).

ried "Mel," as he was known, in January 1931. She spent two post-baccalaureate years at the University of Washington completing premed courses, after which she spent one year at the University of Minnesota Medical School. Her goal was to become a psychiatrist, but she left after the first year (1933) "for financial and emotional reasons."

During November and December 1933, the Jacobs were at Garibaldi (Tillamook County), Oregon. Melville was recording extensive vocabulary and grammatical material in Tillamook from Mrs. Ellen Center, with a $200 grant-in-aid provided through his former professor Franz Boas. While there, Melville became acquainted with Mrs. Clara Pearson, who, he discovered, could provide "ethnographic and folkloristic data" relative to the Nehalem Tillamook. "I persuaded Mrs. Jacobs to do the work," Melville wrote in 1959. Elizabeth said in a 1975 interview, "I didn't think I would be interested or do well but he got me to try. And I loved it."* This was her first ethnographic fieldwork.

In September 1934, she returned to Tillamook County for two weeks during which she recorded Mrs. Pearson's extensive repertoire of myth and folktales in English. Her training in anthropological and linguistic matters came from her husband (and from Mrs. Pearson). "He told me what to ask at first," she said in her 1975 interview. "What to start out with, things that wouldn't—that wouldn't be bothersome to a Native who didn't know me, like house types and canoe types and stuff [like] that...." She said that the process at the beginning was "*very* difficult for me."

Her consultant, Clara Pearson, was evidently a patient and understanding person who, Elizabeth said, "taught me." After the preliminaries concerning material culture, in which Elizabeth had little interest, "we could begin to talk about the material in which I was interested." Her interests were in the psychological aspects of culture as revealed, for example, in religion and in the expressive culture of oral traditions. Clara Pearson's myth and tale texts, edited by Elizabeth and Melville Jacobs, were eventually published in 1959 (reprinted 1990) as *Nehalem Tillamook Tales*. The ethnographic notes remain in manuscript form.**

---

* Elizabeth Jacobs's interviews mentioned in the following paragraphs all refer to the 1975 interview by William R. Seaburg.
** Currently being edited by Seaburg for publication by Oregon State University Press.

Melville Jacobs was a strict adherent of the "Americanist text tradition" in collecting myths and tales.* That tradition went back to the 1870s with the work of Albert S. Gatschet and J. Owen Dorsey, and was fully subscribed to by Franz Boas, who instilled it in his students (including Jacobs). The foundation of that tradition was the phonetic recording of texts in the native language with a close translation into English. The ideology behind it assumed that such texts were communal products and thus representative of the culture, and that they existed independently of the ethnographer and the storyteller. The process of transcribing them was thought to fix them as unchanging objects of study, similar to the objects in a museum collection. Texts recorded in native languages were considered more valuable than those recorded in English because they provided documentation of the language, and of the storytelling style in that language.

English style and the expressive content of the dominant white culture supposedly contaminated texts recorded in English. Such texts were considered to be useful primarily as models of cultural breakdown and acculturation. There were times, however, when texts had to be collected in English if they were to be collected at all. The anthropologist sometimes lacked the training or skill in phonetic transcription, or the informant might not be able to dictate in the native language, or both. Or, as in the case of Coquelle, the informant might not be temperamentally suited to giving slow, stop-and-go dictation.

During the summer and fall of 1935, Melville and Elizabeth Jacobs were again in the field in Oregon. Writing to Boas from Siletz on October 28, Mel described the work that Elizabeth was doing: "My wife is obtaining some Upper Coquille folktales in English here, and she is also securing some Chetco texts and miscellaneous grammatical data in various southwest Oregon Nadéné dialects. Her phonetics is not yet perfect, but she already seems to have an excellent preliminary picture of the morphology."

Her Chetco informant was Billy Metcalf, son of Robert Metcalf, part of whose allotment Coquelle had been leasing. She recorded about sixteen folktales from him, in phonetic transcription and English translation. She also obtained a few pages of Galice Creek linguistic forms from Hoxie Simmons and Nettie West, as well as a small

---

* The following pages draw heavily from chapter 5, "Elizabeth D. Jacobs and the Americanist Text Tradition," in Seaburg 1994a.

amount of Upper Umpqua from John Warren and two others. The bulk of her time at Siletz during 1935, however, was spent obtaining Upper Coquille ethnography and folklore, in English, from Coquelle Thompson.

In her first work with Coquelle, she evidently asked him for lexical and grammatical forms in the Upper Coquille language, which she recorded on unbound sheets of paper. After a few days, she asked him for a folktale text in the Upper Coquelle language. Twice Coquelle began a text dictation, but both times he finished telling the story in English. Elizabeth just could not record the material fast enough for him. When he started a story, he needed to go right on through to the end, without the many interruptions that Elizabeth must have imposed on him as she struggled with the phonetic transcription. He simply did not have the patience for the slow and tedious dictation needed for Elizabeth's transcription in his native language. She said that he was quite impatient and would not sit and be silent. In any case, all of the rest of her several hundred pages of Upper Coquille folklore was recorded in English with only an occasional Athabaskan term. Writing in pencil, abbreviating a word here and there, she was able to keep up with Coquelle's dictation in English in a nearly verbatim transcript.

Elizabeth was in her element, and so was Coquelle. Her interest was in oral traditions; Coquelle's forte was in storytelling. To get what she wanted, she needed only to follow Coquelle's lead, and she dutifully copied whatever he told her. For example, at one point Coquelle briefly discussed the Dream Dance. Perhaps in response to a question, he said that dreaming of a ghost didn't bring anyone power. This discussion of ghosts evidently reminded him of a story, which Elizabeth wrote down and eventually titled "Ghosts Dance in Empty House." This text was followed immediately by Coquelle's personal experience story about his own encounter with ghosts, which was followed, again apparently without a break, by his version of the Orpheus tale. This tale was titled by Elizabeth as "A Man Followed his Wife to the Land of the Dead." Nearly all of Coquelle's seventy-five myth and folklore texts recorded by Elizabeth Jacobs relate to the immediate ethnographic topics under discussion.

Both Elizabeth and her husband, Mel, used this "nondirective" method. They would ask their informant to "tell what he wished to tell." She said that she told Coquelle "to tell me what he remembered that was important to his people." The objective of such an approach was to discover and document the native point of view with as little distortion as possible from the bias of the anthropologist. Elizabeth explained that it "was our way of letting the informant run the show and showing our respect. It was their culture, not something we were supposed to dig out. They were telling us how they lived and how they felt."

It is evident from her notebooks that Elizabeth sometimes initiated topics with questions designed to elicit specific information. She had quite a list of those questions, all eventually lined through, indicating that she and Coquelle were finished with the subject. Only occasionally did she ask for a particularly well known tale type. Unlike Philip Drucker, whose Oregon field notebook pages contain doodles, sketches of people's faces, and sometimes unflattering remarks about his consultants, Elizabeth seldom wrote a comment about the fieldwork itself. She told William Seaburg that she saw herself as "an amanuensis," a faithful recorder of everything Coquelle wanted to tell her. Her notes are overwhelmingly straight transcriptions of Coquelle's responses to questions or of his longer self-initiated narratives, which she tried to copy verbatim. She sometimes paraphrased a sentence, or replaced one of his words with one of her own, but that was the exception, not the rule.

Her preservation of Coquelle's nonstandard grammar, pronunciation, and lexical choice is evidence that she was usually striving toward word-for-word transcriptions. We have a fair idea of Coquelle's actual speech pattern in English from a few sound recordings in which he uses English phrases and sentences. The style within those sound recordings is consistent with Elizabeth's notebook recordings. She would copy, "But nobody come in house," very probably Coquelle's exact words. His contractions such as "doin'," or "'cause" were characteristic, and she copied them faithfully. Probably most significant was his unique phrasing and choice of words in sentences such as "every since White people came in," or "He just get girl once in while, get her knocked up." Through most of Elizabeth's notebooks we get the distinct impression that we are reading the words as Coquelle spoke them.

She saw a problem, however, in eventual publication of Coquelle's words. This was *oral* literature, but she wanted the texts to be accorded the same respect given to *written* literature. During the year or two following her interviews with Coquelle, she edited the folklore collection for possible publication, and in her first draft she almost completely rewrote Coquelle's narratives, putting them into standard, literate English. Her husband Mel told her that she had done too much rewriting and suggested that she edit the texts again, maintaining a closer fidelity to the notebook transcriptions. She did so, but even in that final edit, she changed much of Coquelle's grammar and phrasing. In her 1975 interview she explained herself. She said that she didn't want the worth of the stories to be prejudged by readers' negative responses to nonstandard English. The sound recordings of Coquelle's voice are sometimes beautifully poetic and evocative, but they do not translate well onto paper for the general reader. "It's like Tonto," said one person upon reading the words of the verbatim transcript.*

Elizabeth Jacobs was not the first person to wrestle with the problem of how to present Native American verbal art to the literate world. William M. Clements, in his excellent book *Native American Verbal Art,* pointed out that while many nineteenth-century writers recognized literary tendencies in such art, they believed that it lacked what was needed to be truly literate in a European or American sense.[1] Thus, attempts were made to convert it into "full-fledged literature" by sometimes imposing regular meter upon it, and by extending the metaphors, characterization, and scene description far beyond what was in the original. Scatological and overtly sexual or otherwise "objectionable" scenes were usually either changed or eliminated. Henry Rowe Schoolcraft had done all of those things prior to publication of his important collection of Ojibwa myths and folktales, the source for Longfellow's *Song of Hiawatha.*

Elizabeth Jacobs found herself imposing some of those kinds of changes upon Coquelle's narratives. In the text of the folktale "Panther and Deer Woman," for example, she made several. She could not refrain from changing Coquelle's short, Anglo-Saxon word (and his even shorter Upper Coquille Athabaskan word) to "defecate" and "feces." For emphasis or confirmation she would sometimes interject "indeed" into a sentence that would almost certainly not have contained that adjective in Coquelle's original. Words such as "epithet," "protested," and "daren't" appear in jarring contrast to Coquelle's obviously rural Oregon vocabulary. While some of her impositions

---

* Tonto was the "faithful Indian companion" of the Lone Ranger, the title character of an immensely popular radio, film, comic book, and television series that began in 1932. Tonto spoke in a stereotyped, nonstandard English.

into the text tend to weaken the impact of Coquelle's narrative, they are easy to spot and a critical reading reveals the clear voice of the master storyteller underneath.

Coquelle, as we know, also had an extensive repertoire of songs. During four days in December 1935, Mel and Elizabeth recorded approximately sixty of them on twenty-one RCA Victor pregrooved home-recording discs. There were a variety of song types: nineteen Ghost Dance songs; thirteen myth songs; twelve dream-power songs; seven gambling songs; three songs from a make-doctor dance; two doctoring songs; two lullabies; a love song, and a prehunting sweathouse song.² It was an impressive repertoire, ably performed by an expert.

Most of the songs are fully documented as to type, with the words in Upper Coquille Athabaskan and English translation, along with other pertinent information. The sound quality is not as good as recordings Melville Jacobs made during the summers of 1933 and 1934 with Annie Miner Peterson of Coos Bay, but it is good enough to demonstrate that Coquelle was a fine singer, whose voice even in his late eighties remained strong and sure. Some of the songs, particularly the Ghost Dance songs, reveal an almost contemporary, jazz-like quality, with which the singer was fully engaged. Some of the folktale songs are in the voice of animals, and it is a delight to hear old Coquelle imitating Beaver or one of the other myth-characters.* It is a pity there were no recordings of his bird imitations, a skill in which he had taken pride from childhood.

In listening to the recordings it is clear that Elizabeth Jacobs and Coquelle had a fine rapport. There is sometimes laughter even after the recording needle is on the record. Coquelle might ask, "All right?" before he began to sing, and given the go-ahead by Elizabeth, there is no hesitation. He is not shy. He goes about it like a professional recording artist.

Mel and Elizabeth recorded him telling one folktale in the Upper Coquille Athabaskan, the "Pitch Ogress" myth. The recording is of fairly good quality and clearly demonstrates Coquelle's range of expression.** He told his stories in short bursts of speech, punc-

---

* His beaver imitation is most clearly heard on RCA pregrooved disc #14721a, song #3, MJC.
** The Pitch Ogress myth is on RCA pregrooved disc #14712, MJC.

tuated by dramatic pauses. One can imagine the blind old man sitting before the recording microphone and telling the story as he would have told it two or three generations earlier to an audience of young people hanging on his every word. Now there was no audience except this young white couple, who probably understood only a few of the words. But they were interested, and it was Coquelle's opportunity to tell the story one more time.

In William Seaburg's 1975 interview with her, Elizabeth talked about her work with Coquelle. She thought that he knew so much about his culture because, as the son of a chief, "he had to know everything." "He was the carrier" of the culture, she said. The avaricious nature of that culture came as something of a shock to her, however. She was surprised at the extent to which they had to pay for everything, including wives or the public killing of a shaman, and that they kept slaves. Everything had its price, which was in diametric opposition to her own strong socialist ideals. So strong were those ideals that she had joined the Communist party in Seattle that very year (1935).[3] "From each according to his abilities, to each according to his needs," was the slogan on which she stood. She had, in her idealism, imagined tribal society to be a kind of pure communism. Coquelle shook that utopian dream to its foundation!

Coquelle clearly enjoyed the interviews. "He liked to talk about the old days," Elizabeth said. In places where one of the characters in a myth or tale had performed an antic that particularly tickled him, he would stop and laugh to himself. Elizabeth would note "laughter" in her transcription. Occasionally he would make an ironic or humorous remark aside from the narrative. For example, he was telling the tale of the man who followed his wife to the land of the dead. In it he described the person who, when a dead person arrived at the edge of the abyss, would holler for the canoe to take the dead person across. "That's his business," Coquelle said. He then added by way of aside, "Government pay him, I guess."[4]

Coquelle probably enjoyed the hunting stories best. In the tale of "Panther and Deer Woman," he laughed as he has Wildcat say that he "killed three big deer but they took them away from me." The incongruity of Wildcat passively allowing "two men" to take his deer away from him struck Coquelle as funny. Later in the story, after a long period of famine during which no one killed a deer, he said, "They starve, grub all gone." But Coyote, Coquelle pointed out, "he worse one to starve pretty quick!" Here he laughed at the image of the self-indulgent Coyote, probably the first one to complain. Later, Wildcat dreams that he can find the deer if someone taps him "all over your belly." Coyote, instead of tapping, "hit him hard, with his fist." Coquelle laughed as he said, "Coyote always done wrong, he tricky man!" Twice he laughed at Coyote's attempt to "holler" for the deer. "Coyote want to holler, no, they won't let him. He in way!" And Coyote didn't want dried meat. "Fresh meat for me!" and again Coquelle laughed. He had no doubt known men who were not unlike Coyote.

Elizabeth thought that Coquelle considered the interests of women to be less significant than those of men, that he "suffered from not being able to imagine what a woman would want to know." Of course to him, the son of a chief, women's interests *were* less significant. She also said that he showed embarrassment at or a certain reticence about telling stories to her that showed women in a derogatory light. However, her notes are replete with remarks from Coquelle that were quite open and candid in respect to possibly embarrassing sexual matters. For example, he once told Elizabeth, "I've seen women dry humming birds and June bugs in a bottle." He said that he asked, "what's that for?" The woman laughed and replied, "Oh, you don't want to know that!" Coquelle thought it was funny. "One old lady was said to have 'man-medicine.' I didn't believe it. Maybe its chicken shit, I told her."[5] He quite openly maintained an irreverent, ribald humor, and there is little evidence in Elizabeth's field notes of embarrassment or reticence on his part.

But Coquelle himself appeared shocked at some of Elizabeth's questions. For example, in the course of her elicitation questioning she asked about sibling incest. Coquelle repeated the question indignantly: "If a man lives with his sister, like wife?" There was perhaps a pause, then he demanded, "Is there no law for white people about that? Indians wouldn't stand for it for one minute." With finality, he declared, "They have to get out if they don't want to be killed."[6]

Coquelle was between eighty-five and eighty-seven years old. For a number of years there had been mistaken birth years of 1836 and 1838 on some of his records. That would have made him about one hundred, and he delighted in passing himself off as being of that age. In an interview, Elizabeth told Seaburg, "He *said* he was a hundred." Of course, she knew better but let it go at that.[7]

He was witty, affable, healthy, and acutely bright, but he was blind. "He sees shadows—sees best in the dark," Elizabeth wrote in her notebook. "Awfully sensitive to light."[8] Ironically, one of the very few drawings she had made in her notebook is a drawing of a tarweed paddle, which looks somewhat like a tennis racket. She placed alongside the drawing the notation, "Coquelle accepted this drawing."[9] It would be interesting to know just how the blind Coquelle did that! She also noted that "Mr. Thompson never heard it called tarweed." He always called it "Indian oats." The wealth of information in Elizabeth Jacobs's field notebooks is a treasure that remained virtually unread and unknown for sixty years or more.

The Jacobs had no sooner returned to their academic life in Seattle when Coquelle and Agnes were again concentrating on monetary matters. By the end of 1935, the market for timber was picking up slightly from its low point in 1931. Perhaps they could finally realize something from sale of the timber on Coquelle's and Emma's allotments. In November 1935, a letter from the forester at the Indian Affairs office in Spokane indicated that the "papers all appear to be in order with the exception that there is no written appraisal." The appraisal made in 1918 estimated a total volume of Douglas fir on the two allotments at a little under 900,000 board feet. The volume had probably more than doubled during the ensuing eighteen years, and so by the time the timber was finally cut in 1936, there was probably around two million board feet.* The Depression value (per thousand board feet) however, was estimated to be about half the inflated World War I "wartime prices." At $1 per thousand, Coquelle might have realized as much as $2,000 on the timber sale.

The reply from Charles E. Larsen, senior clerk at Chemawa, included the 1918 appraisal. It ended with the following comment: "As stated above these tracts of land have very little timber and the only reason this sale is recommended is because of the need of the allottee who is ninety-four years of age, blind, and in need of clothing and bedding."

---

* The increase would depend largely on the age of the timber in 1918 (which is unknown). But this estimate of eighteen years' growth of the Douglas fir is based on the increase of the hemlock in the same stand: 204,000 in 1918; one million in 1948 when it was finally sold.

At about the time the timber sale was progressing, Coquelle Jr. wrote a letter in his father's name asking the superintendent at Chemawa to serve notice on a Mr. Helmar, who was living on Coquelle's allotment. The letter said in part, "I have a chance to rent the place to a very reliable person and I wish Mr. Helmar to move off because he pays no rent. Please send a lease so that I can have it filled out and get things fixed up. This will help me out financially also. Mr. Helmar is not under a contract to me or anyone—it has been a free gratis condition."[10] The allotment usually leased for $75 per annum, when a lessee could be found. The economic situation was such that not even the absentee ownership of tax-free land could provide reliable income.

By this time Agnes was taking care of Coquelle almost full-time. He had been declared totally blind, and had applied for blind assistance from the county. The timber sale of 1936 brought some relief, paying their current debts, but in 1937 they were dealt a serious blow. The details are sketchy, but some time during those wintry first weeks of February, their house burned down with all of their possessions. They lost their clothing, their bedding, and all of their household and personal items (including Coquelle's Indian regalia that he had used for so many years doing the Feather Dance).

There was a vacant "cottage" on Government Hill, one of several cottages built the previous summer for "aged and indigent" Indians. They were in a row, and Coquelle and Agnes moved into the one that was vacant at the time, second on the right. Martha Case lived in the cabin on one end; Lucy Dick lived on the other end. The cabin had only one small room, about ten by twelve feet, and a kitchen with some shelves for a pantry. It was unfurnished.

After they moved, there ensued a series of poignant and revealing letters between Agnes and the superintendent at Chemawa. The first letter from Superintendent Paul T. Jackson, dated February 19, 1937, began, "We were indeed sorry to learn that your house burned down." He enclosed $25 from Coquelle's Individual Indian Money (IIA) account, "to help you take care of your immediate needs." He pointed out, however, that to continue to live in the cottage, they would need written authority from him, through the Tribal Council. This was evidently obtained through the help of Agnes's daughter, Augusta, who was now Mrs. Frederic Simmons. On the 24th Jackson sent Agnes and Coquelle a purchase order for beds and bedding. He declared that "it is all that we can possibly do to assist you at this time."

Agnes returned the purchase order unused, along with an itemized list that more nearly met their actual needs, and requested a new purchase order. She said, "The Red Cross has been very effective in helping us, and we appreciate it very kindly. They gave us a mattress and blankets and a few other articles. Different people here have gave things such as pillows, and slips, dish towel, and so forth." Writing the letter in Coquelle's name, she listed their furniture needs. She said, "It is also necessary that we have two stoves, some chairs, an easy chair for myself, since the remaining days of my life will be spent mostly sitting. Also I wish to get myself a couch or day bed so that I might use it to sleep on. Therefore I wish you will mail me a check from my I.I.M. account for $150, as soon as possible." The balance in the account was $174.69.

On March 4 Agnes received an answer which would surely have infuriated her. "After carefully studying your request for an advance of $150 to purchase a stove and other household necessities I have found that Section 4 of the Individual Indian Money regulations, issued by the Washington Office on November 6, 1930, does not allow the Superintendent to draw checks in favor of an Indian in excess of $50 per month." Enclosed was a check for $50, which left a balance in the account of $124.69. Coquelle's allotment file contains receipts for twenty-nine small household items purchased at McKay's Hardware Store in Toledo for a total of $20.97, and $20 at J.C. Penney Company for clothing and blankets.

They soon had an airtight wood heater and a bed for the living room and a wood cook stove for the kitchen. Out the back door of the kitchen was the outhouse. A rope connected the edge of the porch to the outhouse so that Coquelle could go to the toilet by himself.[11]

Agnes applied to the Lincoln County Relief Office for blind assistance for Coquelle. She pointed out that he "had all examinations and was pronounced totally blind." The annual Indian Family Survey, made out in September 1938, indicated that he had received no relief assistance up to that time. It contains some other interesting data. He had no cash on hand in the bank, and was living on about $120 per year. He owned 240 acres of land, in trust, valued at $6,100. He owned a "good house—place rented," and he had "1 good cookstove" valued at $10, and two beds valued at $20. He had no livestock and the main family diet was "meat, vegetables, fruit." The agent deemed the family "adeqately [sic] housed and clothed," housekeeping was deemed "sanitary," and there had been some efforts toward "home beautification." Under "health," it was noted that "Mr. Thompson is partially blind but in good health considering his age." Under remarks is the statement, "The Thompsons have a good house that is rented on their own land. Some timber was logged from his place, but she said that she did not know the value."

Judging from the correspondence in Coquelle's allotment file for this late period in his life, it appears that Agnes and Coquelle Jr. were actively and competently taking care of Coquelle's affairs. On September 26, 1938, Coquelle Jr. asked Superintendent Wooldridge for authority to sell the Abram Mack allotment on Sam's Creek. "I gained this piece of land by trade and due to the fact that I need assistance which I never could gain through waiting I am offering it for sale," Coquelle Jr. wrote in his father's name. "I have had the surrounding acreage priced and will take $1600 for this piece of land. I have a man who wishes to buy it for cash." Wooldridge was apparently a new superintendent unacquainted with Coquelle, and so Coquelle Jr. took the opportunity to provide a little background information. "I am blind, but with a possibility of restoration of sight by proper medical attention by a specialist. I have given 47 years of my life to the Government service and have never realized as much a dollar for past work which I so faithfully had done." Wooldridge replied that he would take the matter up with the "Washington Office." The land was not sold, but later he received more than $1,600 for the timber.

While waiting for land or timber sales to bring in some needed cash, Coquelle actually began receiving $30 per month for blind assistance from the Lincoln County Public Welfare Office. Even so, the following letter written by Agnes in Coquelle's name reveals some of the frustration of working with a government bureaucracy. She scolded the new superintendent for being unresponsive to their needs.

> Siletz, Oregon
> February 24, 1939
> Dear Sir: Please send me the amount of money that I asked for $150. I am surprised that I am not in trust of my own money after all these years. When I make a request, I

am no doubt in need of it. You do not know the condition here evidently. Do you know how I am living? I suppose you think I squander it away, well you may at any time investigate my record and see my character status. I am in need of this money so please send it at once.
Truly yours,
Coquelle Thompson Sr.
by Mrs. A. Thompson (wife)

Coquelle's two children and his stepdaughter were apparently doing all right during those years. Sina was progressing well with her studies at Chemawa, and during her summer vacations from school she worked for the wealthy Currier family at their lodge on Tenmile Lake (Lakeside), Coos County, Oregon.[12] Augusta was married to Fritz Simmons, son of Hoxie, and had five children. Coquelle Jr. was married to Elma Chapman of Siletz, a fellow tribal member who had been a student with him at Chemawa. He obtained a position there as boys' adviser in 1938, and it was there that their first son, George Thompson, was born in January. In 1940 another son was born, also at Chemawa, and he was given the name of Coquelle Thompson III.

Coquelle Sr. was at last a grandparent, and from all accounts he loved it. He wouldn't allow anyone to discipline the grandchildren at all. In an interview, Elma remembered that if she tried to stop them from some mischief, Coquelle would interfere saying, "Let 'em mind, let 'em mind." Even a slight verbal correction of the children on the part of Agnes, Augusta, or Elma would bring a repetition: "Let 'em mind. Let 'em mind."[13] Perhaps because the lives of so many of his own children had been fragile and fleeting, he could not tolerate interference with the freedom of the children around him.

The demand for lumber had picked up in response to the war in Europe, generating interest on the part of the Tribal Council in finding a buyer for the tribal timber—timber that stood on the five sections of land retained for the tribe at the time of allotment in 1894. Such a buyer was found, but there was a major problem in determining exactly who of the descendants of the original tribal members would share in the distribution of the proceeds. Word filtered down to Coos Bay that perhaps descendants living there might be eligible, even some who had never been enrolled at Siletz. The chief of the Coquille people at Coos Bay at that time was Frederick Sandberg.

He and his wife Ocea, along with Wally and Ann Anderson, went to Siletz to attend a meeting on the subject.

As Ann remembered it, the meeting was chaired by Coquelle Jr. She doesn't remember any particulars about it, but the expected picnic, or potluck, did not take place. Coquelle Jr. graciously invited the Coos Bay contingent to his house for lunch. Ann remembered Mrs. Elma Thompson (1919–2001), "a beautiful lady" who served them the finest local delicacies, among them the most highly prized of all, smoked eels. Poor Ann and Wally found that they could not eat the eels, having been raised at Coos Bay, too far removed from the traditions that had been maintained on the reservation. Ann thought that the Thompsons might have been offended.[14]

By 1941 there was a developing market for small tracts of "second-growth" timber, tracts of eighty acres or so. Frequently a small sawmill would be brought in, and the timber would be cut into lumber on the site. Lumber or railroad ties cut from such a sawmill would bring eight to twelve dollars per thousand board feet; the cost of the timber would be one to two dollars per thousand. It appeared to many potential entrepreneurs that a profit could be made, and during the 1940s and 1950s the "gyppo" sawmills, as they were called, proliferated.

Such enterprises were within the reach of almost any mechanical genius with a keen business sense and an overwhelming drive to succeed, and who could find an agreeable owner of a suitable stand of timber! The credit to build the sawmill was secured through using the timber as collateral, usually obtained through a timber contract between the owner and the potential sawmill operator. Thus it was possible to get into the sawmill business with virtually no capital, providing the suitable supply of timber could be found.

Coquelle Jr. thought he had found exactly the stand of timber he needed to get into the business. Ironically, the timber was on the allotment of his father's first love, Annetti, deceased. His letter to the new superintendent, Ralph Fredenberg, began, "Dear Sir. For some past months I have been interested in helping to get a second-growth mill into the Siletz country, especially on some Indian timber." He had engaged a timber cruiser to estimate the volume, and found there to be 800,000 board feet on the allotment. "I wish to make application for the purchase of all the timber on the Annetta Brown Scott allotment for $1.00 per thousand feet stumpage. I believe this is a good price for this timber, because of its distance from the market." He asked that the request be expedited "because the dry season is becoming shorter all the time, and it takes time to move a whole mill into a new setting."[15] This appears to be the first entry of Coquelle Jr. into the timber business, which occupied him off and on during most of the rest of his life.

Annetti's husband, Spencer Scott, had inherited her allotment. He, like Coquelle and the few others of the older generation who were still living, needed cash and Scott was depending on the timber sale. "Dear Mr. Fontelle," began a letter apparently written for Scott by someone else to the office of the Siletz/Grand Ronde Agency in Salem. "Will write a few lines for some information in regard about the Sawmill that was to be built up on my place.... As you know, all the land that I've got is not earning me any living. Something's got to be done. Others down here & elsewhere are getting their pensions. And why should I be deprived of my old age pension? I have been trying to get a pension for ever so long but it seems to be all in vain." He had asked others to help him, including a Mr. Marr. "Mr. Marr was at my place some time ago to interview me," he wrote. "I told Mr. Marr for him to go to Salem office to look (at) my record. Mr. Marr said that he would go and see your people."[16]

John P. (Jack) Marr had arrived alone at Siletz from Eureka, California, in a red 1935 Ford convertible on the morning of Sunday, March 16, 1941. He was an eighteen-year-old student, the youngest son of John Peabody Harrington's Santa Ana, California, neighbor Blanche Marr. Jack started working with Harrington as a research assistant in 1934, when he was thirteen, "running the battery driven sound recorders at 25 cents per day." In 1939 he accompanied Harrington to Arizona and New Mexico, helping with the sound recording on the Hopi and Navajo reservations. As soon as the boy got his driver's license, Harrington had him seeking out elderly Indians in the backwoods of northern California to make phonograph records of their songs and speech.[17]

Harrington had been temporarily forced by his superiors to remain in Washington, D.C., during the summer of 1941 to prepare a technical paper for publication. Meanwhile, elderly Indians, the last speakers of languages, were dying and Harrington would not be available to record their last words. So as not to waste a minute, Jack Marr was in the field as Harrington's surrogate with a 150-pound "portable"

Fairchild recording phonograph, prepared to record songs and stories on eighteen-inch aluminum disks. The phonograph ran from a six-volt automobile battery.

Harrington would have preferred to be in the "field" interviewing Indians all the time, but to keep his job he had to occasionally prepare something for publication. He hated it, but over his thirty-nine years with the Smithsonian he managed to publish more than one hundred scholarly and technical papers while collecting over one million pages of field notes from Indians speaking ninety different languages from throughout the Western hemisphere. It is a record never approached by any other anthropologist in the world. However, he was terrified that some of the Indians he had slated for interview would die before he got to them.

One of the Indians Harrington had slated for interview was Coquelle Thompson. Harrington called him "Kokel" in his letters, and had probably been apprised of his significance during his visit with Melville and Elizabeth Jacobs in Seattle during December 1939. In a letter to Marr on March 11, 1941, he instructed him to "go from Eureka directly to Siletz." He told him to "work first with Hoxie [Simmons]," and "get from him his fifty coyote songs, and all his stories, everything in the Galice language." "Also," he added, "do a lot of recording from Kokel Thompson, he is a hundred years old, knows songs and dawn of the world galore and lives on the corner in the same block as Hoxie."*

During his first day Marr found no one at home, except Hoxie Simmon's wife, "Lizzie". He was puzzled about Coquelle Thompson. "This Kokel Thompson here is not 100 years old," he said. "He is about 35 years old. I also talked to his wife, she is very young." Of course, he had talked to Coquelle Jr. and his wife, Elma. The next day he worked with Spencer Scott until noon. "Spencer Scott doesn't know very much," he said. But in the afternoon, working with Hoxie Simmons, he hit pay dirt. "Hoxie is one of the most valuable Indians I have seen. He knows lots of songs and stories. He also loves to sing and talk!"

---

* *Dawn of the World: Myths and Weird Tales Told by the Mewan Indians of California*, by C. Hart Merriam, 1910 (reprint, 1993). Apparently, when Marr's consultants couldn't produce narrative texts in their native languages, Marr was instructed by Harrington to read stories from Merriam's book and have the consultants translate the stories back into their own languages. A singularly unorthodox field procedure!

The daily letters and telegrams between John Marr and John Peabody Harrington are almost surreal. Harrington expressed dire fear that Coquelle would be dead. "He is awfully old," he said in his letter of March 18. "Commonly said to be 100 but most likely 110. The people at Siletz all call him Kookwehl. Just record him to a finish, he is likely to die soon." On the 22nd he commented, "There is no place like Siletz for extinct languages. Hope you work every person there dry." On the 24th Harrington wrote, "If old Kokel Thompson is still alive, get down on your knees and thank God and go to him the first day that Hoxie can't work or goes to a funeral or something, for Kokel might take sick and die any day. Get all he knows before he dies." Two days later he wrote, "Am afraid old Kokel Thompson will die when we are even this near to using him."

Their letters were crossing in the mail. Marr had already located Coquelle. On the 23rd he reported, "I worked old Kokel all day yesterday (Sunday)." On the 24th he was ecstatic. "Am having the best of luck," he said. "Have worked old Kokel until he was breathless. I can still do another good days work with him though. Have been getting some good songs and stories from old Kokel." Harrington's letter of the 27th, after he learned that Marr had contacted Coquelle said, "I am delighted. Just think that you worked with old Kokel Sunday. It is oh what a privilege." After a discussion of the car battery, he continued, "What you are doing with old Kokel is something for the ages; you are robbing the cemetery. You are getting Indian stuff from the REMOTE past." Two days later, he told Marr, "Do get another lick at old Kokel."

The young and impressionable Jack Marr was very much caught up in the excitement of it. On April 4 he said, "I had another talk with him tonight and in the morning I am going to do more recording with him.... I agree with you that old Kokel is really the chance of a lifetime. After he is gone there will be no more. I know that a chance like this with old Kokel will never be gotten by anyone so I am going to get everything possible from him." His long letter of April 6 is worth quoting in full, as it describes his relationship quite well.

> Have been keeping the turntable whirling with old Kokel at the mike. You will also be glad to know that Kokel has remembered still many many stories and songs and valuable stories they are too! I have had translated in English all of his stories—do you realize that you could merely play

the English part of the recordings and write such as [illegible] had done. I have discovered that old Kokel has a hole in his nose too. I had him tell all about it. He was a chief's son—he tells me that he was more than once bothered by ghosts. He also says, if ever you see a ghost coming to just step to the side and the ghost will go right on by. He says that he knows just what every little bird says when it chirps outside his windows. "They can talk," he says—"They were once people." Kokel is very old and a chance with him is like pennies from Heaven. I am taking every advantage. I have learned a lot from Kokel—I have listened carefully to everything he has said, making note in a little book. Today is Sunday, and since he and his wife do not eat any lunch (only two meals a day—breakfast—supper) I worked with him right on through stopping only long enough to go and get the live battery and leave the dead one to be recharged. He told me of the tribe of long ago who instead of burying their dead, would put them in a canoe and shove it out into the lake. Alsea did this—they did not believe in burying under ground. I know that you are really and truly going to be pleased with what I have accomplished with old Kokel these last few days. Will send you the list of recordings tomorrow night. Every day learn something new about recording and every day I am growing more and more intent on this. I only wish you were here to hear these grand stories come out of Kokel's mouth and strange as it seems, good and clear. The recordings are perfect! Jack.

There were, however, continual problems with the recording phonograph. It frequently broke down, and twice Marr had to take it to Portland for repair, a round trip of 265 miles. He had five spare batteries, but he had to make one or more daily trips to a service station to exchange for a charged one. "Both my pants and my jacket are all falling apart," he wrote ten days after arriving. "The acid from the batteries has eaten them and I'm afraid I will have to buy a pair of pants next time I get into a town or someplace." Harrington was so ecstatic at learning that Marr was recording Coquelle that he magnanimously stated, "I am going to give you a suit. They are much cheaper in the east than on the coast. But for the present you'd better get a pair of pants. And remember, that's on me." His next admonition was quite in character: "BUT DON'T WEAR THEM," he ordered. "That acid will cut them to pieces too. What in the hell do you care even if your skin shows around old Siletz. Wear the new pants when you're NOT handling batteries." A few days later Marr replied, "I had pants washed and acid stopped. Won't buy pants now. It would just be another expense and I can get along without them. You're right I don't care what kind of old clothes I wear."

The eighteen-year-old Jack Marr made thirty-four eighteen-inch aluminum recording disks of Coquelle's songs and stories. His problems with the recording phonograph, however, did not bode well. "Bad news. The recorder has gone haywire, just won't work at all," he wrote a few days after arriving. A few days later he wrote, "Have had the recorder fixed again. This time I had them check everything." Two weeks later he wrote, "Two of the tubes are burned out. I cannot make any recording." Of the original quality of the recordings, we have only his word. As of today, none of them are usable. Coquelle recorded much of his repertoire of songs and stories in Athabaskan and in English, but only Marr heard them.* We can probably be sure that the ninety-two-year-old blind Coquelle derived at least a modicum of pleasure from doing it. It was his last full performance.

During June through November 1942, John Peabody Harrington was himself in western Oregon, and he made several trips to Siletz. Coquelle was still alive and well and in command of his faculties, and Harrington spent parts of several days with him and Agnes. This was Harrington's last field trip before World War II put a stop to nonwar-related activities, and this was Coquelle's last stint as an anthropological informant. These two legends, Harrington and Coquelle, had finally met. Harrington, the most dedicated of all salvage ethnographers, and Coquelle Thompson, one of the oldest and most experienced informants Harrington would ever meet, together symbolized

---

* The following year Jack Marr was with Harrington in the Aleutian Islands when the Japanese attacked Pearl Harbor. Marr enlisted and spent the entire war in Europe. Following the war, he studied law and engineering and worked most of his life as an engineer in Alaska and the Far East. He retired in 1989, never having returned to the study of anthropology. The Smithsonian Institution has over three hundred items, mostly sound recordings, cataloged under his name. All of them were gathered by the time he was eighteen years old.

the very end of that period of American anthropology, the period of salvaging the memories of the oldest of the old. After Harrington's 1942 visit to the Oregon coast, those days were over.

Seventy-five of Coquelle's myths and tales had been gathered in English by Elizabeth Jacobs; about forty-six had been recorded by phonograph in Upper Coquille Athabaskan and in English by Jack Marr; Harrington copied down about thirty-five, in English. Because most of Harrington's texts had also been recorded by Jacobs, there was excellent data for a comparative study. The most interesting point of comparison was that of voice: whose voice dominated, Coquelle's or the anthropologist? And, how might one separate the voice of the anthropologist from the voice of the narrator?*

The reader can easily detect the anthropologist's voice in the use of the longer words, in certain choices of sentence construction, and in generally "better English." Examples of Harrington's voice: "we were *scrutinized* and the woman took in that we were wearing camas;" "the corpses they placed together *preparatory* to carrying them home." "Scrutinized" and "preparatory" are very decidedly *not* Coquelle's words. Coquelle's voice, on the other hand, is often apparent in the use of words and phrases that are also found frequently in the transcriptions by Elizabeth Jacobs: "Those that caught hold of him were not *stout* enough," and "He was *a good hand* to run on the ocean." There were typical kinds of similes used in both the Jacobs and the Harrington texts: "The two old father and mother *chewed up human bones like carrots*." As part of his storytelling style, Coquelle would often give precise numbers, time, and measurement. For example, "Then that man packed in deer meat *at about 10 o'clock*," or "You will run by here where I am, only *four feet* ahead of her." Coquelle also used dialogue quite extensively, and in those cases where Harrington recorded dialogue, he was probably faithfully recording Coquelle's actual words.

Harrington's collection is an important addition to the record for several reasons. First, he recorded a few texts that Jacobs did not get. Second, his texts are useful for sorting out the voice of storyteller versus anthropologists. Third, some of his texts show changes to a story that had previously been told to Elizabeth Jacobs, reflecting differences as the story was told on different occasions. Fourth, after a story

---

* The following two paragraphs draw heavily on Seaburg 1994b.

was told, Harrington sometimes asked for clarification or more details, providing Coquelle's own interpretation. Jacobs rarely obtained this added perspective. Unlike Elizabeth Jacobs and Philip Drucker, Harrington listened to and took notes on things that Agnes told him. He was interested in the history and genealogy of his subjects, and if Agnes (or anyone else) could add something, he included it.

No detail was too small for him, and among his special interests were native words (usually nouns) and place-names. He discovered from Coquelle, for example, that the "native Siletz name of where the Siletz Catholic Church stands" was *nách'is-shíla*. "Very important," he wrote. "Volunteered as one of Thompson's rarest pieces of information."[18] If Harrington could become excited about an arcane piece of information such as that, he could wax even more ecstatic when Hoxie Simmons volunteered that the Galice Creek name for winter was "khaii" *(kai)*. "This is the first language I have found which has 'kh' in the word for winter," Harrington noted.[19] His reputation for remembering such apparent trivia from among the four hundred languages he had studied was a source of great amazement and amusement among his contemporaries. M. W. Stirling, his former boss at the Smithsonian, wrote at the conclusion of his obituary, "Anecdotes concerning his bizarre career would fill a large volume."

After Harrington departed, Coquelle was not visited by another anthropologist. By that time, about $2,000 for the sale of timber from the Abram Mack allotment had been placed in his Individual Indian Account. Because he was receiving blind assistance from the county, however, there was justifiable concern that if the County Welfare Office discovered the existence of the account they would either take the money or drop him from blind assistance. Agnes understood the problem perfectly, as revealed in a letter to the superintendent on December 29, 1942. Written in Coquelle's name in Agnes's very legible handwriting, it began, "Dear Mr. Wooldridge, Recently I sold some timber from the Allotment of Abram Mack, on Sam's Creek." She explained that they had sold the timber from their two allotments "and have used all funds to the best of my ability to take care of my family and myself." She explained that Coquelle had gone blind "6 years ago" and "after about four years of constant application and many examinations, I was given assistance to the blind." The problem was clearly stated by Agnes. "If the State or Mr. Maw at Toledo finds out that I have money to my credit in your office, they will drop me at once and cut off my allowance—I know—because they have did this very thing to many people here. Now, I am better off on state assistance because they can do a hundred times more for me than $2,000, especially with eye trouble, which is a costly cure."

Agnes requested, in Coquelle's name, that the $2,100 in the account be distributed as follows: $1,000 to Coquelle Jr., $500 to Sina, and $500 (or the balance) to remain with Agnes and Coquelle. Surprisingly, the superintendent agreed and obtained authorization for the distribution. "These two children have always contributed continually to the support, comfort and welfare of their parents and undoubtedly deserve such consideration," he said in his letter to his boss on March 17, 1943.

It was October before the State Welfare Office began inquiring into Coquelle's timber assets, by which time his account had built back up to $1,622.50 from more timber income. "We are particularly interested in knowing whether it is possible for Mr. Thompson to realize any cash from the sale of this property or any cash income from the sale of the timber on it," Mr. Maw asked. All the timber on all his allotments had by now been sold, however, and the Jim Buchanan allotment of forty-one acres, which he inherited, did not have marketable timber on it. "We have no other record of any income for Mr. Thompson other than the sum mentioned above," the superintendent informed the Welfare Office.

By that time, of course, the country was fully engaged in World War II. In Harrington's letters to Jack Marr during early 1941, he sometimes expressed his dread of it. "The next will be a mass attack on England with men dying like flies," he wrote on January 31. And before the end of the year we were in that "total war." The hop fields in the Willamette Valley closed, but there was unlimited employment in the shipyards in Portland, and Camp 12 was putting on more men, increasing log production. Coquelle told Harrington that his daughter-in-law's youngest brother, Fritzie Chapman, eighteen years old, was working at Camp 12.[20]

"At least 18 volunteers joined the military from Siletz; one of them a woman," according to a booklet published by the Confederated Tribes of Siletz.[21] The woman was Sina Thompson, Coquelle's daughter. Sina had graduated from Chemawa in 1940 and worked for a while as a matron at the school. At twenty-three and at loose ends, she wished to do something significant with her life and so she enlisted in the Women's Army Corps. Before she departed, she left her electric radio with her parents, who couldn't play it because there was no electricity at the housing for aged and indigent Indians at Siletz.

She was one of the "few hundred Indian women" from among the 150,000 women who served in uniform during World War II. The Women's Auxiliary Army Corps, created in May 1941, was converted to the Regular Army in July 1943.[22] Sina enlisted the following month, on August 16, and was assigned to the Air Corps. Following basic training she was sent to Elveden Hall, England, where she served as a communications operator at Third Bomber Division Headquarters (Eighth Air Force) until the end of the war. Elveden Hall is in Suffolk, East Anglia, where most of the Eighth Air Force bomber bases were located. As a measure of the activity going on there at that time, 20,000 flyers from those bases were killed and 9,300 were wounded during the course of the air war over Europe. An additional 26,000 were shot down and became prisoners of war.* As a communications operator during the height of that activity, Sina certainly experienced stress.

Coquelle was by now in his late nineties. The once large, full-bodied man was slowly shrinking into a mere shadow of his former self. His health, his mind, and his wit remained, but photographs reveal that he just got smaller and smaller. He retained his impish, even childlike, love of the practical joke. His grandson George remembered Coquelle pretending that he couldn't put on his jacket, playfully attempting to put his legs through the sleeves. Agnes would ignore him as long as she could, but eventually would come over and untangle him and put the jacket on correctly for him. Coquelle would laugh as though it had been a great joke. Sometimes at the table he would begin tapping his cup with a spoon, keeping it up irritatingly until Agnes would finally lose patience and gently remove it from his hand, as one would from a small child. Coquelle had attained Shakespeare's "last age of all, . . . second childishness."

Coquelle wanted to attend to his own final arrangements while he was still living. He and Agnes had talked about getting a tombstone for their son George, who had died in 1932. They planned to get one that they too could use, at a cost of about $150. The funeral arrangements, they thought, might be about $250. In June, Agnes

---

* "U.S. Eighth Air Force: The Wings of War," *National Geographic* 185 (March 1994):90–113.

wrote a request in Coquelle's name that those amounts be set aside from their Individual Indian Account. She also asked for $50 to wire the house for electricity, $75 for a radio, and $62.50 for "five cords of wood for winter." They might as well spend what was left, and live in comfort. In August the social worker from the county, Mary Joaquin, followed up on the request, as no action had been taken. Concerning the tombstone, she said, "Coquelle talks about it all the time." They didn't want to draw the money out for the burial, but wanted it set aside for that purpose. Concerning the radio, Mrs. Joaquin explained that the Thompsons had the radio belonging to their daughter Sina, but couldn't use it because "they didn't have the electricity to operate it." Besides, she continued, "Sina was being released from the WAC's now, and planned to take her radio with her when she established her new home." Mrs. Joaquin explained the Social Security law to Agnes, "that anyone who had resources at their disposal was not eligible to assistance from the Social Security Office."

The war ended suddenly on August 14, 1945, one week after the second of two atomic bombs was dropped on Japan. There was almost instant demobilization, and Sina was among the troops who returned immediately to the states from Europe. She was discharged at Camp Beale, near Marysville, California, on September 12, just ten days after the final surrender ceremonies. Already, while on furlough in Salem, she had married Preston Bell, an Assiniboine Indian from Fort Belknap Reservation, Montana. They had been students together at Chemawa, and he, too, had been in the army. As she went forward to receive her honorable discharge from the WAC, she was "the first woman to bring her husband with her," according to a notice in the *Lincoln County Leader*.[23] The objective of almost all the young people at the end of World War II was to get married, start a family, and get on with their lives. Sina lost no time in getting started.

The passenger train, then as now, departed Marysville in the evening, arriving in Albany, Oregon, the next afternoon. Connections were made there for Toledo, and then by a local shuttle bus to Siletz. When Sina arrived at her parents' home, it was as though time had stood still during those hectic war years. They were still living in the tiny cottage on Government Hill, and Agnes was still taking in washing, boiling water in a big kettle hung over a fire in the backyard. She had hoped to have the inside of the little cottage painted, so that it would be "nice and bright" when Sina came home, but in that she was disappointed.[24] It was the same as when Sina had left, and her radio had not been played while she was gone.

Not quite four months after Sina returned home, her father at last went into his final illness. His eight-year-old grandson George Thompson was there at the end. "The whole family was there," he said in an interview. "The doctor was there too. He could have done something to make him hold out a little longer but grandma said, 'let him go. It's his time.'"[25] It was January 4, 1946.

What a very long time it had been. During his century he had seen the end of the Indian wars of 1855 and 1856 and lived on to the invention of the radio and the atomic bomb. He was buried at the Indian cemetery on Government Hill, next to his Tututni wife, Emma, and several of his deceased children. Near him is Old Hunter and Coquelle Jim, and countless others whose graves have no markers. Coquelle Thompson is in good company.

Afterword

Coquelle's gravestone shows him as dying at 106 years old. His death certificate has him born January 20, 1839, but he was almost certainly born ten years later. He wouldn't have minded the error at all; in fact he liked being considered a centenarian and even encouraged it. That was only the first confusion about Coquelle. The second was confusion with the name of his son, Coquelle Jr. (called "Tom" by everybody who knew him). Tom's second son, Coquelle III (called "Snooks" by everybody who knew him), was the third generation of that name. As the years passed, legends grew up around each of them, and in the midst of a discussion someone would frequently be heard to ask, "How many Coquelle Thompsons were there, anyhow?"

Coquelle (Tom) Thompson, Jr. (1905–74), was probably better known in Lincoln County than his father. He was, as described in previous chapters, a star fullback with the Oregon State Beavers, where his reputation was established. He graduated with a B.S. in vocational education in 1932 and married Elma Chapman of Siletz. They had two boys, George and Coquelle III, both born at Chemawa. Until 1938 he was a teacher at the Siletz High School; then from 1938 until 1946 he was the boys' adviser at Chemawa Indian School. During those years as a teacher and adviser he frequently worked as a logger, sometimes the owner/operator of his own gyppo logging company. In 1946 he left the field of education altogether and logged fulltime, and in 1956 became a partner in a dealership for logging equipment at Philomoth, a town about ten miles west of Corvallis. He was back to logging again from 1961 until 1973. At that time he was appointed tribal judge at the Warm Springs Indian Reservation, where he died the following year at the age of sixty-nine.

His youngest son, Coquelle Thompson III (1940–1964), went into the U.S. Marine Corps in 1958. After completing his enlistment he went to work as a logger for the M & W Logging Company at Waldport, Oregon. He was married and had three small children when he was killed in an automobile accident on June 29, 1964. He is buried at the Paul Washington Cemetery on Government Hill at Siletz.

Coquelle Jr.'s oldest son, George (b. 1938), was, like his father, a football star with the Oregon State Beavers. Taken out of play due to a football injury, he lost his sports scholarship and became a logger. Returning later to the university, he graduated with a degree in secondary education and worked for the Siletz School District until, like his father, he discovered that the low pay and lack of excitement was not his calling. By 1976 he left the field of education for good and has worked as a logger ever since, never regretting the change. He has a daughter and two sons, all living in Lincoln County.

Coquelle Sr.'s daughter Sina (1920–2002) moved to the Fort Belknap Indian Reservation, Montana, with her husband, Preston Bell, shortly after their marriage at the end of World War II. They lived for many years on their 1,300-acre ranch at Lodgepole, Montana, where they raised horses and Sina worked for the Indian Health Service at Fort Belknap. She had six children, twenty-one grandchildren, and nineteen great-grandchildren at the time of this writing.

After Coquelle Sr. died, Agnes (1878–1965) remained at Siletz for several years, where she was known as the "Florence Nightingale of Siletz."[1] She nursed Spencer Scott and others in their final days before moving to Montana to be with her daughter, Sina. Agnes died in Montana on February 21, 1965, at the age of eighty-six and is buried at the Paul Washington Cemetery at Siletz. Her daughter Augusta Smith Simmons (1900–1976) had seven children and many grandchildren and great-grandchildren.

Coquelle Sr.'s estate at the time he died was appraised at $6,000. He had a full interest in his own allotment (S-456), appraised at

$2,000; a full inherited interest in Emma Thompson's allotment (S-457), appraised at $2,000; a full inherited interest in the Abram Mack allotment (S-338), appraised at $1,000; and a full inherited interest in the James Buchanan allotment (R-256), appraised at $1,000. There were three heirs: his widow, Agnes, and their two living children, Coquelle Jr. and Sina.

Neither Agnes, Coquelle Jr., nor Sina wanted to keep any of the land. In 1948 they applied for fee-simple patents so that they could sell it. In the case of Emma's allotment, the old growth Douglas fir had been logged in 1936, but the hemlock had no market at that time and was not cut. By 1948 a stand of over one million board feet of "poor quality" hemlock, valued at about $3 per thousand, had grown up on the cutover land—which gave the land and timber a newly appraised value of $4,000.

In her application for the fee-simple patent, Agnes stated, "The land is useless to any of us and has been idle since 1917. Good prices are paid for lands now, and I believe we can do very well if a patent is given us." Sina said in her application, "I am married to a man from Montana and I will probably not return to Oregon to live. . . . The land is practically useless to anyone in our family because it is too far away from the work that my brother follows and too far for my mother, who is now quite old." Coquelle Jr., who gave his occupation as "logging," stated, "Our family does not live on or near these lands, and we do not have any intention of ever moving on them."[2]

The changes in timber prices over the ensuing years were profound. During practically all of Coquelle's lifetime the "stumpage" price of standing Douglas fir timber hovered around one dollar per thousand board feet. During World War II it rose to around $2.50 per thousand, and after wage and price controls were lifted at the end of the war, it jumped to about $12. By 1957 stumpage prices had doubled, to $25. Ten years later the price was $100 per thousand, and at a peak in 1994 it was as high as $1,000 per thousand board feet, quickly declining to around $700. Those phenomenal increases were the result of changes in the structure of international corporate power and could not possibly have been foreseen by anyone at Siletz.

In Oregon, the new era was launched in December 1951, when the Georgia Pacific Corporation purchased the C. D. Johnson Lumber Company of Toledo for $16,800,000. The purchase included the mill, railroad, Camp 12, and "nearly a billion feet of standing timber, some of it the finest old growth fir on earth," according to the *Newport News*, December 13, 1951. Two years later Georgia Pacific purchased the Boeing tract of timber.[3] This was a watershed event in the economy of the Pacific Northwest, and in the history of the timber industry; it was a harbinger of the future, marking the new era of "internationalization of trade and investment policy."[4] The days were numbered for closely held, family-owned sawmill and timber companies such as those created by C. D. Johnson and William Boeing. Modern centers of finance and corporate power shift their capital regionally within nations, and internationally beyond the influence of any given nation. The Georgia Pacific Corporation exemplified that process as it went on to purchase other closely held, undercapitalized timber companies at home and abroad.

The philosophy of laissez-faire capitalism, which was so prevalent during the early 1950s, also manifested itself in many areas of social policy. It included a widespread belief that government should be less intrusive, and in any case should not be involved with Indian tribes. The strident anticommunism of the era colored attitudes toward tribal organization, which was touted by certain politicians as being "un-American." As a result there was strong support in Congress to terminate the federal government's supervision of the smaller and more thoroughly assimilated tribes. Governor Douglas McKay of Oregon appointed Coquelle Thompson, Jr., to a committee to study the problem and make recommendations.[5] In 1955, all of the tribal entities in western Oregon, including the Confederated Tribes of Siletz, were terminated in keeping with that shifting political trend, and there was very little opposition.

The reason for a lack of opposition to, or interest in, the subject of termination at Siletz was summed up by Hardy Simmons, a grandson of Agnes Thompson, in a statement to the Senate Subcommittee on Indian Affairs. He said, "I was in the 8th Air Force in World War II. I returned to Siletz and worked as a logger after the war. I was young and not much interested in Termination. I didn't go up to the meetings. A lot of people couldn't see the purpose of those meetings. I don't think there was more than a handful of people who knew what Termination was."[6] The first meeting on termination held by the Department of the Interior at Siletz was on Sunday, November 1, 1953. The report on that meeting states, "Due to continued good weather for logging and harvesting there were only 30 adult members present, mostly women." The second, and final, meeting was held on November 22, at which the group "favored enactment."[7]

Tribal vice-chairman Robert Rilatos described the economic situation at the time of termination. "Basic employment for the Siletz Indian people at the time of termination was the lumber industry, primarily logging. During World War II and the Korean conflict, jobs were plentiful for the Indians. It was a tradition of our men prior to that era as well." In contrast with the situation a few years later, Rilatos said, "At one time, there were sixty sawmills in Lincoln County and numerous outside companies transported logs to other areas. The majority of our people, the bread winners and some of our Indian women, were associated in some manner with the lumber industry. The Siletz Indian men were recognized as the best loggers ever known. I started logging at age fourteen and worked as a logger for 19 years."[8]

At the time that federal supervision of the Confederated Tribes of Siletz was terminated, there were 929 enrolled members, descendants of the 551 individual Indians who received allotments in 1894.[9] As a tribe, they still owned 2,561 acres of the 3,200 acres of timberland that had been reserved for them from the time of allotment. They were given the choice of forming a tribal corporation and placing title to the property in the name of the corporation, of naming a trustee and placing title with the trustee, or of requesting the government to sell the property and distribute the proceeds to the members. The 2,561 acres of Siletz tribal timberland was sold for $726,935. The proceeds were distributed to enrolled tribal members in two installments: $250 per person in December 1954, and a final payment of $542.50 per person in August 1956.[10]

There were also seventy-seven inherited allotments, aggregating 5,390 acres, all held in trust for individuals.[11] The Termination Act specified that trust restrictions would be removed from all of those allotments within two years, or prior to August 13, 1956. Most were sold at the request of the owners, and the proceeds distributed to them. A few of the owners requested fee-simple title, which they received, but some took no action. Those who took no action received fee-simple titles without restrictions at the end of the two-year period, after which the land was subject to property taxes.[12] The 39.23 acres of tribal land on Government Hill was deeded in trust to the city of Siletz.[13] The cemetery was subsequently deeded to a cemetery district formed for the purpose. The Confederated Tribes of Siletz ceased to exist as far as the federal government was concerned.

The number of Indians, nationwide, who were affected by termination was actually quite small. Francis Paul Prucha estimates that it was about 3 percent of the total Indian population, and about the same percentage of land area.[14] Political trends swing, left and right, and by the early 1970s there was strong momentum nationally to restore federal supervision to some of the terminated tribes. The first to receive restoration was the Menominee of Wisconsin in 1973. The second tribe to be restored was the Confederated Tribes of Siletz, on November 18, 1977 (Public Law 95-195). After long debate, the city of Siletz deeded the 39.23 acres on Government Hill back to the tribe, which in 1980 received 3,666 acres of timberland from the federal government, to be held in trust. In 1995 they opened a successful gambling casino in Lincoln City under the Indian Gaming Regulatory Act of 1988. The net revenue from the casino is rumored to be in the millions, and is increasing yearly. The tribe is self-governing, and compacts directly with the Department of the Interior.

The years during which there was no tribal organization at Siletz created a loss of continuity and considerable confusion as to who should and should not be enrolled upon restoration. As noted in the BIA "Report on Termination," October 3, 1957, "These groups of Indians are not tribes in the usual sense of the word." The report recognized that the groups were "made up of individuals with membership stemming from an original allotment or by descent of allottee rather than by tribal affiliation."[15] The Siletz Restoration Act of 1977 specified that membership would be restricted to those who were on the tribal rolls as published by the Federal Register on July 12, 1956. Deceased members were to be stricken from the roll, and any individuals who were entitled to be on that roll but were not on it were to be added. In addition, "The name of any descendants of an enrollee shall be added to the roll provided such descendant possess at least one-fourth Siletz Indian blood."[16]

The fact of intermarriage and its consequent reduction of "blood quanta" in the children of such marriages, had been a matter of interest as early as 1908, when Franz Boas spoke to the American Association for the Advancement of Science at Baltimore, Maryland. He said that as soon as social barriers to marriage are removed, intermixture is "exceedingly rapid." He did the calculations and found that "if the choice of mates is left entirely to accident," in the fourth generation there will be "less than one person in ten thousand of pure descent." That, according to Boas, is the result if the two populations are of equal size. If the ratio were nine to one, "there will be among the more numerous part of the population only eighteen in one thousand in the fourth generation that will be of pure blood."[17] The implications of reduction in blood quanta were obvious to the Siletz Tribal Council, and in 1978 they reduced the required blood quanta for tribal membership from one-quarter to one-eighth. In 1995 it was again reduced, this time to one-sixteenth.*

Meanwhile, in Coos County, the Confederated Tribes of Coos, Lower Umpqua, and Siuslaw Indians was restored to federal recognition in 1984 (Public Law 98-481). In 1989, the Coquille Indian Tribe was restored (Public Law 101-42). The Coquille Tribe was one of the last of all the small tribes to receive its federal recognition during this new wave of tribal restorations. Neither of the two newly restored tribal entities at Coos Bay required a specified blood quanta for tribal membership; merely showing descent, however remote, was sufficient. Thus all of Coquelle's distant relatives, descendants of his various maternal and paternal aunts and uncles, and great-aunts and great-uncles, are enrolled in one or another of the three federally recognized tribal entities on the Oregon coast. It might be said that Coquelle's legacy has been salvaged.

---

* Lisa Norton, Enrollment Specialist, personal communication with author, 17 July 2000.

Appendix 1

Upper Coquille Athabaskan Culture

Much of our knowledge of Upper Coquille Athabaskan culture is based on the work of Elizabeth Jacobs, Philip Drucker, and Cora Du Bois.[1] Each of these investigators relied heavily—in Jacobs's case exclusively—on the observations and opinions of one consultant, Coquelle Thompson, the subject of this biography. Only Drucker worked briefly with one other Upper Coquille consultant, Nellie Lane. Any description of a culture group that is based largely on one consultant is necessarily flawed. While much of the information that Thompson provided is consonant with the general cultural patterns reported from other groups in the southwest Oregon–northwest California region, some is not. Do such differences represent cultural difference or the misrememberings of an elderly man? Clearly, Thompson knew best the cultures of the peoples living during the Siletz Reservation period. Perhaps the greatest difficulty in utilizing materials provided by him lies in separating observations about pre-reservation experiences from those about post-reservation experiences. Nevertheless, without the extensive ethnographic notes anthropologists recorded from this extraordinary man, we would know very little about either pre- or post-reservation Upper Coquille Athabaskan culture.

Language

The Upper Coquille language was formerly spoken in southwestern Oregon. It belongs to the Pacific branch of the widely distributed Athabaskan language family and is related to Athabaskan languages spoken in Canada and Alaska and in the American Southwest.

Culture

Subsistence and Division of Labor

As throughout the Northwest Coast culture area, there was a general gendered division of labor: women dug roots such as camas and wild carrots, collected berries and harvested acorns and other wild plant foods; they gathered firewood, carried water, processed foods for winter storage, and cooked meals; they made baskets and mats and looked after small children. Men hunted deer and elk. Elk were hunted with specially trained dogs. Men also fished for Chinook and Coho salmon, trout, and lamprey; they tanned hides, made nets, canoes, planks for houses, and prepared and tended areas for growing tobacco.[2]

Structures and Transportation

Residences, too, were gender distinct. The men and boys of a village slept together in semisubterranean earth-covered sweathouses. Larger villages might have two or more sweathouses. Here the men sweat, then swam in a nearby stream, told stories, instructed the young boys, and ritually prepared themselves for a long life and good luck in gambling and in other of life's uncertain endeavors. Women, infants, and young children lived and slept in plank winter houses, which served as a center for food preservation and storage, preparation, and consumption and as a general work area for men and women. The plank winter house consisted of "rectangular gabled structures over a shallow pit, with roof and walls of cedar planks. The space between the double front wall was, as usual, used as a woodshed. The outer doorway was closed by a sliding door.... Houses of grass thatch were used at summer fishing camps."[3]

Two types of canoe were employed, the Yurok-Tolowa-Rogue River "blunt-ended dugout" and a "double-pointed dugout" made either by the Upper Coquilles themselves or traded from the Coosans.[4]

Social Organization

Upper Coquille social stratification seems more flexible than among the more northerly Northwest Coast groups. Each Upper Coquille village had a headman or chief and his immediate family, "the well-to-do, the poor, and a small number of captured or purchased slaves" and their offspring.[5] The responsibilities of a headman included organizing work teams, negotiating with strangers, conducting "slave and punitive" raids on other villages, arbitrating village disputes, levying fines for various social infractions, and generally overseeing "the lives of everyone in his community."[6]

The position of headman was inherited through the father's line, "subject to village consensus on the wealth reserves and personality of the heir." Wealth was the key to a headman lineage: it allowed him to have more than one wife and to purchase slaves who worked for him. Indeed, the "hallmark of a chief seems to have been that he was involved in all financial transactions as the donor of treasure, as an arbitrator, and as the recipient in a division of any acquired wealth."[7]

Wealth items included dentalium shells, flints, and redheaded woodpecker scalps. Different sizes of dentalia were named; the larger the shell, the more valuable it was. Shells were also strung in strands of ten and valued according to the length of the strand.[8] A persistent theme in Upper Coquille oral traditions is the acquisition of wealth-giving powers (e.g., the ability to be successful in gambling), either through ritual preparation or by means of a wealth-encounter experience.

Life Cycle

A baby's birth was attended by "a midwife or female shaman. The midwife took the baby, cut the [umbilical] cord with an heirloom flint knife, and washed the baby using a deer tail and warm water. The afterbirth was put into a split sapling.... A man pierced the nasal septum and each ear in three places when the baby was a week old."[9]

Babies received a nickname after five days and a "good name" at ten years of age. This latter name had belonged to a "paternal relative of the same sex" who had been deceased for at least a year. A boy's first kill was distributed to each household in the village. Similarly, a girl distributed to everyone the first acorns and berries she had gathered."[10]

There were no puberty rites for adolescent boys. In contrast, "at puberty a girl was secluded . . . 10 days on her bed platform. She wore her finery, used moss menstrual pads, a shell scratcher attached to her wrist to avoid touching her hair and skin, and ate only dry food for a year afterward. She swam early and late each day. Her father could not gamble, hunt, or fish at this time."[11]

Marriage was an arrangement between families that encouraged alliances and that served to preserve or enhance their prestige and make claims to offspring. Although marriage was not primarily an economic transaction, "to be respectable a woman had to be purchased in marriage." If their mother had not been paid for, children were considered illegitimate. Marriages were arranged by the parents of the bride and groom. "If the parents, the chief, and a man 'who knew dentalia' approved, the bride with her family and chief went to the groom's village after five days, gave half the bride price to the groom's father, and held a feast with acorn soup. The bride gave her mother-in-law a fine buckskin dress decorated with shell beads. The bride slept in the home and the groom in the sweathouse. Both sets of parents exchanged gifts and foods. The male members of the families of the groom and bride exchanged their weapons and clothes. The next night the bride and groom slept together in a corner bed platform of the house on a bearskin." Marriage alternatives included the levirate, where a woman married her deceased husband's brother; the sororate, where a widower married his deceased wife's sister; and "a rich couple purchasing a husband to live with their daughter in her own home village."[12]

Women had a lower status in Upper Coquille culture, as evidenced by the bride price in marriage transactions and "females' confinement to rather narrowly domestic" activities until after menopause.[13]

An Upper Coquille man confessed his wrongdoings to his wife or son before dying. As a result of his confession, if he didn't die right away, his family was obliged to make a settlement payment. When a person died, a nonrelative washed the face; women tended women, men tended men. Before the corpse was lowered into the grave, an old man "who knows how" (a formulist?) would quietly talk to the dead person's ear. After he talked, the corpse was lowered and raised five times, then put in the ground. A man's treasures were buried with him. The deceased's soul remained in the grave for five days before it crossed the ocean.[14]

Shamans

Perhaps the second most powerful individual in Upper Coquille society, after the headman, was the shaman or Indian doctor. Although both men and women could become shamans, women could doctor only after menopause, as was true for female shamans throughout the Northwest Coast. Many Upper Coquille shamans were women. "The object of their medical treatment was the removal of a 'pain': a tiny living object sharply pointed at both ends and holding in its midsection the blood it had sucked from the patient."[15] Shamans were paid for their services.

Spirit powers came to individuals in dreams, and a shaman's powers included "Eel, Big Snake, Dog, Knife, Bullet, Otter, or birds (Hawk, Flicker, Hummingbird). Coyote was the best power and Grizzly Bear the most dangerous. A person might have shamanistic powers for years before they finally made him ill."[16] The only cure for this spiritual illness was the public acknowledgment of his or her powers in an initiation ceremony known as the Make-Doctor Dance.

Other people who were "gifted with specific shamanistic abilities" by their spirit powers included those with the ability to cure dog and rattlesnake bites, to "talk to medicines and herbs for remedies and love-charming", to cure war wounds, and to call forth South Wind. Other spiritual specialists included those with "the power of the spoken word or spell, sometimes called a formulist," or a "ritualist." One important function of a ritualist was to conduct the cleansing rite of gravediggers and those who had handled the corpse in preparation for burial. Spell power normally was inherited but could also be purchased.[17]

Gaming and Ceremonials

Women—most likely men as well—played a popular stick-and-ball game known as shinny. Women also played a game using four long split sticks that were shot like dice. People also enjoyed footraces and a throwing game involving a javelin-like pole.[18] The most prestigious game was the stick (guessing) game, played by men only. Upper Coquille oral traditions suggest that considerable time and care went into ritual preparation for luck in these stick game gambling contests, which could continue for several days.

The number five and its multiples were the dominant pattern or ritual numbers for the Upper Coquille, as for other groups in the southwest Oregon–northwest California area. Aboriginal rites included the ritual eating of the first five or ten chinook salmon and a Lamprey Dance celebrating the catching of the first lampreys. After the killing of a bear "a feast had to be given. All the meat was cooked at once, and had to be eaten then and there. It must never be dried. The skull was not saved, however, and the hide was dressed for use as a robe, etc."[19] Rituals also included feasts and gift giving at the birth of a child, the child's naming, a boy's first animal kill, a girl's puberty, war, and death as well as in "celebration of the Make-Doctor Dance for new shamans."[20]

When a man or woman dreamed something repeatedly (e.g., of dead people), he or she had to sing what had been dreamed "in front of all the people" in what was referred to as a Dream Dance. "If the song is good enough, the people dance with it for five nights." If one tried to conceal the fact of one's dreaming, one would get sick and a shaman would be called in to find out what was wrong. The shaman "told the sick man he was hiding a song and he had better give a dance the next night. After the dance, the sick man felt better. Dreamers of songs had no curing power."[21] Anyone could hold a Dream Dance. Every month or so there might be one.[22]

Although Dream Dances apparently predated reservation times, they seem to have been used "as a vehicle not only for the Ghost Dance doctrine but also for its subsequent outgrowths," such as the Feather Dance.[23]

Warfare

Wars between neighboring groups were precipitated by feuds, the avenging of wrongful deaths by shamans, the need to settle uncompensated injuries, and murder. "The usual tactics, ambushes, and surprise attacks on sweathouses were customary."[24] Warriors performed a war dance when they returned home, and people remained vigilant against a possible counterattack. To settle the fighting, each group hired negotiators—often from villages not involved in the dispute—five "good speakers" to meet with both sides and mediate a settlement. "If the claimants were not satisfied with the settlement, one of them kicked the fire to signal the start of a fight between the sides. They fought until the arbitrators stopped it and negotiated the amount of treasure each side had to supply."[25]

Appendix 2

Upper Coquille Athabaskan Villages

Among the various researchers who recorded place-name data on the Upper Coquille Athabaskans, there is some disagreement regarding the transcriptions, etymologies, and especially the geographic locations of many of the village sites. To assist future scholars we include in this appendix all of the Upper Coquille Athabaskan names identified as village sites in both the published and unpublished literature with which we are familiar.[1] Numbers placed before sites listed here correspond to numbers placed before site names on the accompanying map. For each name we include our normalized transcription, sometimes a brief discussion of the problems of reconciling discrepancies in the available data, the phonetic transcription of each researcher, and a verbatim transcription of whatever information the researchers provided regarding the site, and

(1) hweshdan

From the location he gives, Harrington apparently has mistaken *hweshdan* for *lhanhashdan* (see below).

Dorsey (1890, 232)
"[Qwēc´dûnnĕ] #3. [no location, description, or etymology provided by Dorsey]"[2]

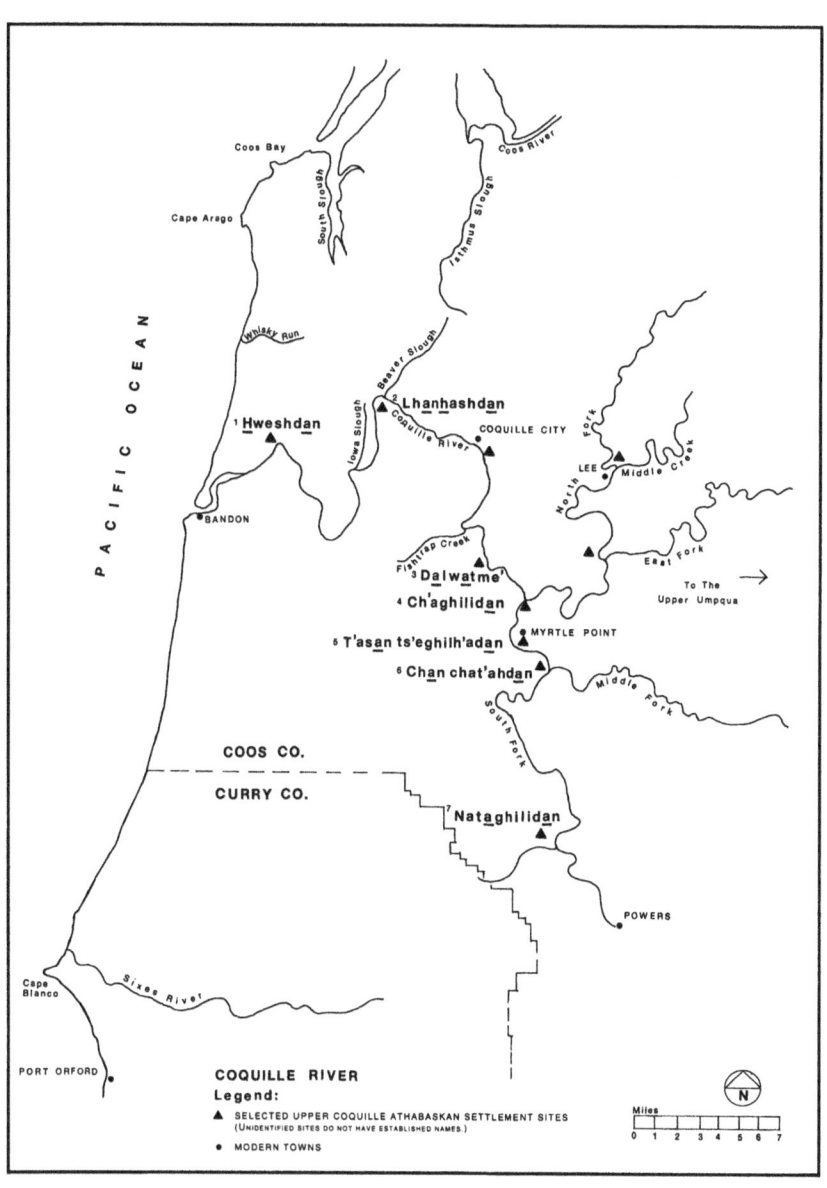

Drucker (1934, 2:118)[3]
   [hwɛctun]'s weren't relations—they went there to buy women."

Drucker (1934, 2:140)
   "Below [ʟunhɔstun] was [hwɛctun]"

Drucker (1937, 279)
   "[hwɛctun] Farthest downriver. Perhaps partly Kusan."

Jacobs (1935 unpublished field notes)[4]
   "[x̣wé·cdən] Up the [Coquille] river 5 or 6 miles from the ocean, at the "big bend" in the river, (about ½ way between towns of Riverton & Bandon), was a Coquille village called [x̣wé·cdən]. 'They spoke Coq. just like us. Bensil Orton's mother was a [x̣wé·cdən] woman. His father was Chasta q̓wista—they talked same like us. Our language just the same only kind of slow sounding when we say it.'
   at big bend near ocean—their last chief died a long time ago"

Harrington (26, 0184)[5]
   "[x̣wæ̂·ʃdɑn] kw., Dorsey's 3. 2 or 3 m. from Coq. City. A man if trouble wd go there in 20 mins. & be ready for war.
   Rhg. Ω is on the n side[6]
   Tyee David (n. his Ind name) was the chief of Ω).
   Thomp rhg. Kw. [x̣wæ̂·ʃdɑn], a big town with lots of people, they call the people [x̣wæ̂·ʃdɑnnɪ].
   On the n side of the Coq. R.—there were few villages on the s. side."

(2) Ih<u>a</u>n<u>h</u>ashd<u>a</u>n

Dorsey (1890, 232)
   "[Tqlûn-qas´dûnnĕ´] #1. Above the Mûllŭk and below where Coquille City now stands."

Drucker field notes (1934, 2:10)
   "[ʟunhɔstun] (30 mile (?) upriver, about site of town of Coquille)."

Drucker field notes (1934, 2:118)
   "[ʟunhɔstun] yak/sŭn — main xusʀɛ [chief] at [ʟunhɔstun]"

Upper Coquille Athabaskan Villages

Drucker (1937, 279)
    "[Lunhɔctun] Said to have been founded by man and three sons, with families, from Upper Umpqua; 'they moved because of a quarrel.' Informant was great-grandson of one of the brothers, dating founding about 1800."

Jacobs (1935 unpublished notes)
    "[tɬənxácdən] Ca. 3 miles below Coquille City on the modern maps was a large Coquille permanent village called [tɬənxácdən]. 'Just the land there, I guess.'"

Harrington (26:0181)
    "[ɬɑnxɑ·ʃdɑn] no. etym. ca. 3 m. below Coq. City on same side. No etym. Also vs. [ɬánxá·sdɑnnæ:] [. . .]
    The Indian chief of that place was yák'ṣɑn.
    There were lots of people living there.
    Thomp. rhg: knows [ɬɑnxɑ·ʃdɑn] instantly as the Tyee yáksɑn
    A village, on the *n*. side of the Coq. R.

(3) da̲lwa̲tme'

This is possibly the name of the "largest fishing village" noted in pioneer accounts as being at the "place now occupied by the Arago creamery" (Dodge, 129). The pioneers named the nearby creek "Fishtrap Creek." We are grateful to Reg Pullen for calling our attention to this site, which he spelled TUL-WAT-ME-TUN.

Dorsey (1890, 232)
    "[Dûl-wût´-me] or [Dûl´-wût-me´ dûnně´] #8. People on the open prairie."

Harrington (26:0196)
    "[dɑlwát'mæ'] Kw & at once [dɑlwát'mæ'], an open place, a natural clearing. [. . .] [dálwát'mǽ·-ddɑnnæ']—people. Thomp takes this to be the name of an Ind town and guesses the open place to be on the n. side of the Coq. R. and maybe 5 m above Coq. City."

(4) ch'aghilida̲n "place where water flows apart"

This is site of the 1855 treaty, called Chac-re-le-a-ton. Drucker says it was the "largest town," and it could be at the forks of the North Fork and the main river, a little north of Myrtle Point. Harrington (26:182) describes it as probably the site at Fishtrap Creek, but (26:185), "big ra. of the Coq. Forks" would not be Fishtrap Creek, but more likely at the confluence of the North Fork.[7] In another citation (26:201) Harrington talks of a big creek from the south, "about as big as the Coq River itself," "where the trail to the Rogue River goes up that way." Only the South Fork answers to that description. In (26:202) Harrington makes it more certain that he is talking about the South Fork. In both (26:201 and 202) his informant, Coquelle Thompson, apparently uses the term *ch'aghilidan* as the name for the South Fork itself, not the name for a village site. The mouth of the South Fork was often historically considered to be at the confluence of the North Fork, not at the confluence of the Middle Fork as is shown on modern maps. This helps explain some of the confusion over a location for the site. The term seems to have been used sometimes as the name of the South Fork of the river; sometimes as a large village site, probably at about the confluence of the North Fork and the main river. In the census of July 10, 1854, by Indian Agent J. L. Parrish, it is the term used to name the Upper Coquille Athabaskan tribe. In the 1855 treaty it is used for that part of the tribe over which Coquelle Thompson's father, Washington Tom, was chief. Hence the confusion. Elizabeth Jacobs's field notes mistakenly place it twenty miles up the North Fork, "at a town called Lee." Here she probably has two mistakes: she is probably confusing *ch'aghilidan* (which Thompson uses when referring to the South Fork of the river) with the site of *nataghilidan*, which is some miles up the South Fork. And she is confusing the North Fork for the South Fork, a mistake she also makes when she describes *nataghilidan*.

Dorsey (1890, 232)
    "[Çltc'a-rxi´–li-i´dûnnĕ´] #4. People away from the Forks, the *Choc-re-le-a-tan* of Parrish's list (1854) and *Chak-re-le-a-ton* of Kautz (1855)."

Drucker (1937, 279)
    "Parrish's list gives "Choc-re-le-a-ton" (Dorsey, Cltc'a-rxi-li-í-tunné, 'People away from the Forks'), indicating it as largest town. At forks of Coquille."

Jacobs (1935 unpublished field notes)
    "[tc'aɣíli(t)dəni], [tc'aɣíliDəni] The North Fork of the Coquille

Upper Coquille Athabaskan Villages

[river] divided at approx. a town called 'Lee.' Right at that forking was formerly a Coquille village known as [tc'aγíli(t)dəni] or [tc'aγíliDəni]."

Harrington (26:0182)
"[tʃ'a·ɾɪ·llɪ·ddɑnnæ:] A (ra) on the s side of Coq River, 7 m or so upr. of Coq City. On rhg gives: [tʃ'a·ɾɾɪ·llɪ·ddɑn-dɑnnæ'] [tʃ'á·ɾɾɪ·llɪ·ddɑn], forks"

Harrington (26:0185)
[tʃ'ɑ·ɾɾɪ·llí·ddɑnn dɑnnæ'] People of the big (ra) of the Coq R Forks."

Harrington (26:0201)
"[tʃ'a·ɾɾí·llɪ·ddɑn] is the name of a big creek, about as big as the Coquille R. itself, which comes into the Coquille R. from the s. (since the trail from Coq. R. to Rogue R. goes up that way). When I ask Thomp how far [nátt'aɾɾí·llɪ·ddɑn] is up the Ω [tʃ'a·ɾɾí·llɪ·ddɑn] creek from the Coq. R., he says it is about 40 miles up! The mouth of Ω is about 6 or maybe 10 m. downriver from 'our place.' The Tidewater does not reach 'our place' but it reaches the mouth of Ω."

Harrington (26:0202)
"On rhg. says the plcn. is [ná·tt'aɾɾí·llɪ·ddɑn], derived from [ná·tt'aɾɾí·llɪ], dam.
This dam was pretty near at the head of Coq. River. This dam (cald [ná·t'aɾɾí·llɪ·ddɑn) is in the fork of Coq. R. called [tʃ'ɑ·ɾɾí·llɪddɑn], & pretty well up that fork. A trail goes up this fork & after passing the dam goes over a divide into Rogue River. There was a ra. on both sides of the dam. My pat grm belonged to that ra."

(5) t'asan ts'eghilh'adan "myrtle-point place"

Jacobs (1935 unpublished field notes)
[t'ásin sεγíɬ'adən] Myrtle Point was called [t'ásin sεγíɬ'adən]. [t'ásin] 'myrtle nuts', [sεγíɬ'adən] 'to point ?' (I guess, says Coq.)"

Harrington (26:0323)
[t'a·ssɑn- ts'æ·ɾɾɪɬ-'a·ddɑn] I rem. that the Inds. called Myrtle Point [t'a·ssɑn- ts'æ·ɾɾɪɬ-'a·ddɑn] mg. myrtlewood trees close to

the (Coq.) River. Thomp. kind-of thinks Myrtle Point is a flat or a kind-of a level place on the n side of the Coq R—Thomp has never been there."

(6) cha̱nchat'ahda̱n

Harrington (26:190 and 193) describes what is probably a settlement site at the forks of the Middle Fork and the South Fork. The first pioneer account (Dodge 1898, 127–28) tells of descending from the Umpqua trail at that place. Jacobs places the site three or four miles up the North Fork. This may reflect a consistent error on her part, in mixing the South Fork with the North Fork, but in fact there was (and is) a route to the Umpqua via the East Fork of the North Fork. It was, for example, the route taken by McLeod on his departure from the Coquille River in 1827. Colonel Silas Casey's punitive expedition of November 1851 engaged in a skirmish at the Middle Fork/South Fork site, leaving a confirmed five (and a reported fifteen) Indian dead. *Cha̱nchat'ahda̱n* was said by Coquille Thompson (Harrington 26:188, 190, and 193) to be his father's village, yet Thompson never mentioned the Casey incident in any of his narratives to any of his many interviewers. There are ambiguities here.

Dorsey (1890, 232)
"[tcûn – tcaˊ-tă-aˊdûnnĕˊ] #7. People by the large fallen tree"

Jacobs (1935 unpublished field notes)
"[tcə́ntc'at'a·dən] above there [i.e., tc'aɣíli(t)dəni] on the N. Fork 3 or 4 miles was a fishing village, permanently occupied by many Coquille families known as [tcə́ntc'at'a·dən] 'timber place.'"

Harrington (26:0189)
"[tʃ'án – t'á·t'a:ddɑn] home village of Thomp."

Harrington (26:0190)
[tʃ'án t'á·t'a:ddɑn] My father was chief at [tʃ'án t'á·t'a:ddɑn], a village at the head of the Coq. River where the road from Ump R came in."

Harrington (26:0188)
"[tʃ'án tʃ'á·t'ahdɑn] (Thomp's father's village). Ca. 10 or 20 houses, & many canoes on both sides."

Harrington (26:0193)
"[tʃ'ɑntʃ'â·tt'ɑhdɑn] The trail from Ump. descends to this place. They cd look up the hill & see people from Ump descending the trail."

(7) nataghilidan "waterfall-place"

The only major contradiction in descriptions of this site is in Jacobs "N.F.," which should be "S.F."

Dorsey (1890, 232)
"[Ná-ta-rxi'li-i'dûnnĕ'] #12. People at the big dam (in the river)."

Drucker (1937, 279)
"[natgʀilitun] (Bend there.) Three sweat houses."

Jacobs (1935 unpublished field notes)
"[natiɣílidən] Way up the N.F. of the river at the big dam was a village known as [natiɣílidən], "falls" Nellie Lane was from [natiɣílidən]."

Harrington (26:0201)
[ná·tt'ɑrrí·llı·ddɑn] [tʃ'a·rrí·llı·ddɑn] is the name of a big creek, about as big as the Coquille R. itself, which comes into the Coquille R. from the s. (since the trail from Coq. R. to Rogue R. goes up that way). When I ask Thomp how far [ná·tt'ɑrrí·llı·ddɑn] is up the Ω creek from the Coq. R., he says it is about 40 miles up! The mouth of W is about 6 or maybe 10 m. downriver from 'our place.' The Tidewater does not reach "our place" but it reaches the mouth of Ω."

Harrington (26:0202)
"[ná·tt'ɑrrí·llı·ddɑn] On rhg. says the plcn. is [ná·tt'ɑrrí·llı·ddɑn] derived from [ná·tt'ɑrí·llı], dam
This dam was pretty near at the head of Coq. River. This dam (cald [ná·t'ɑrrí·llı·ddɑn] is in the fork of Coq. R. called [tʃ'a·rrí·llı·ddɑn], & pretty well up that fork. A trail goes up this fork & after passing the dam goes over a divide into Rogue River. There was a ra. on both sides of the dam. My pat grm belonged to that ra."

stɔneRuLtuL

Drucker (1937, 279)
"[stɔneRuLtuL] suburb of natgRiltun, across river"

lhts'a̱sme' "in the sand"

We have no clues as to the location of this site.

Dorsey (1890, 232)
"[Çlts'ûs-me´dûnnĕ´] #31. People at or on the sand; subsequently removed to Flores Creek (on the coast, between Coquille River and Sixes Creek)."

Harrington (26:0231)
"[ɬts'ás̱-mæ'] At any sandy place in the Coq. River, possibly up by Riverton or Beaver Slu, he agrees. Has heard of Beaver Slu & its portage. Rhg. Call the people that belong there [ɬts'ás̱-mæ̂·ddɑnnæ']
On rhg. He says definitely that Ω is on the n side of the Coq R 2 or 3 m below [tʃ'ɑrrílı·ddɑn]."

se - ha̱scha̱nda̱n

Harrington says this site is "straight opp. [tʃ'ɑntʃ'á·t'ahdɑn]"; unfortunately, we are not able to locate [tʃ'ɑntʃ'á·t'ahdɑn] with any degree of certainty.

Dorsey (1890, 232)
"[Se-qûc´-tûndûnnĕ´] #6. People at the big rocks (se, rock?)."

Drucker field notes (1934, 2:118)
[seṭhɔstcuntun]

Drucker field notes (1934, 2:123)
[sɛhɔstcuntun]

Drucker (1937, 279)
[not listed in Drucker]

Jacobs (1935 unpublished field notes)
[sɛx̣éctcəndən]

Upper Coquille Athabaskan Villages

Harrington (26:0188)
"[θǽ·x̠x̠ástʃʻɑn-dɑnnæː] mg. big rocks people. On n side of Coq. R. straight opp. [tʃʻántʃʻá·tʻahdɑn] ca. 10 or 20 houses, & many canoes on both sides. (Thom's father's village)
On rhg. says big rocks stood"

Appendix 3

A Guide to the Normalized Spelling of Indian Words

The anthropologists who transcribed Upper Coquille Athabaskan words used a wide range of phonetic orthographies. We have created a "normalized" spelling to represent our broad phonetic interpretation of these various transcriptions wherever we had enough information to do so. When we did not have enough linguistic information to normalize an Indian word, we have reproduced it exactly as it appears in the published manuscript or source. Our normalized spelling of Indian words is italicized. Below is a chart of our normalized symbols, followed by their equivalent phonetic symbols, and, when possible, a sample word illustrating approximately how these sounds would be pronounced.

Normalized Symbol	Phonetic Symbol	Words Illustrating Approximate Pronunciation
a	[a]	the "o" in English *lot*
a̱	[ʌ], [ə]	the "u" in English *but*; the "a" in English *sofa*
ch	[č']	the "ch" in English *church*
ch'	[č']	no equivalent in English; similar to the "ch" of English *church* but with an

Guide to the Normalized Spelling of Indian Words

		explosive release, indicated by the apostrophe
d	[t]	no equivalent in English; similar to the "t" in English *stop*
dj	[č]	no equivalent in English; similar to the "ch" of English *church* but without the aspirated release
e	[ɛ], [æ^]	the "e" of English *met*
g	[k]	no equivalent in English; similar to the "k" in English *skull*
gh	[γ]	no equivalent in English; similar to the "*h*," below, but with voiced pronunciation
h	[h]	the "h" in English *hill*
ḥ	[x], [x̣]	no equivalent in English; similar to the "ch" in German *Ich*, the "ch" in German *Ach*
ḥw	[xʷ], [x̣ʷ]	no equivalent in English; the same sounds as [x] and [x̣], above, but with the lips rounded
i	[i]	the "ee" in English *beet*
k	[kʻ]	the "k" of English *keep*
k'	[k']	no equivalent in English; similar to the "k" of English *keep* but with an explosive release, indicated by the apostrophe
l	[l]	the "l" of English *leave*
lh	[ɬ]	no equivalent in English; similar to the Welsh pronunciation of "ll" in *Lloyd*
m	[m]	the "m" of English *met*
n	[n]	the "n" of English *net*
s	[s]	the "s" of English *set*
sh	[š]	the "sh" of English *sheep*
t	[tʻ]	the "t" of English *team*
t'	[t']	no equivalent in English; similar to the "t" of English *team* but with an explosive release, indicated by the apostrophe

tlh'	[ƛ']	no equivalent in English; a combination of the "t" and the "lh," above, but with an explosive release, indicated by the apostrophe
ts'	[c']	no equivalent in English; similar to the "ts" in English *cats* but with an explosive release, indicated by the apostrophe
u	[u]	the "oo" of English *boot*
w	[w]	the "w" of English *wet*
y	[j]	the "y" of English *yet*
'	[ʔ]	a brief glottal stop or pause, represented by "-" in English *uh-oh*

Notes

Introduction

1. JPH, 30:12.
2. JPH, 30:43; Jacobs 1937.
3. Kelly 1998, 44.
4. Denzin, 7.
5. Cf. Denzin; Kirshenblatt-Gimblett; Blackman; Malcolm.
6. Nagourney, 92.
7. Denzin, 20.
8. Hodge and Kress, 230.
9. Doty, 11.
10. Nagourney, 93.
11. Malcolm, 89.
12. Seaburg 1994a.
13. Youst 1997

Chapter 1

Note on sources: The authors relied most heavily on two primary sources for the history and ethnology of the precontact Upper Coquille River: the field notes of Elizabeth Derr Jacobs in her interviews with Coquelle Thompson during the summer of 1935 (EDJ/WRS), and the "Journal of a hunting

Expedition . . ." of Alexander McLeod (1826). Other primary sources that were useful include the field notes of John Peabody Harrington (JPH) and the notebooks of Philip Drucker (PD). Secondary sources that were useful included Pullen 1995 and Hall 1995.

1. Seaburg 1994a, 198.
2. PD, 2:10.
3. Pullen, interview 1999c.
4. Ibid.
5. Hall 1995, 40.
6. Pullen, interview 1999c.
7. EDJ/WRS, 1:1.
8. EDJ/WRS, 2:175; PD, 2:119.
9. Drucker 1937, 279; Hall 1995, 38.
10. Jacobs, interview.
11. JPH/1943.
12. McLeod, 182 n. 2.
13. PD, 2:19, 23.
14. JPH, 26:232.
15. Pullen, interview 1999c; Pullen 1995.
16. Ibid.
17. PD, 2:119.
18. T. C. Elliott, 37–38.
19. McLeod, 175 n. 1.
20. Schlesser, 37.
21. PD, 2:118.
22. EDJ/WRS, 6:192.
23. McLeod, 189.
24. McLeod, 193.
25. PD, 2:119.
26. McLeod, 193.
27. McLeod, 196.
28. JPH, 26:190.
29. PD, 2:123.
30. McLeod, 197.
31. McLeod, 195.
32. McLeod, 208.
33. McLeod, 202.
34. McLeod, 208.
35. McLeod, 210.
36. PD, 2:40.
37. McLeod, 210.
38. EDJ/WRS, 1:46.

39. JPH, 26:192.
40. Seaburg 1994a, 200.
41. PD, 2:41.
42. NA/ACF, allotment S-379, Coquelle Thompson testimony, 15 March 1917.
43. JPH, 24:46.
44. PD, 2:118.
45. EDJ/WRS, 1:26–27.
46. EDJ/WRS, 1:47–48.
47. JPH, 27:616.
48. Dodge, 129.
49. Hall 1991, 70.
50. EDJ/WRS, 4:61–64.
51. Dodge, 131.
52. Pullen 1995, 264–66.
53. Ibid.; LaLande and Pullen.
54. EDJ/WRS, 5:142.
55. EDJ/WRS, 5:142–43.
56. Boyd, 139.
57. Dodge, 109.
58. Hall 1995, 40.
59. Walling, 127.
60. Walling, 133.
61. Walling, 143.
62. Walling, 148.
63. O'Donnell, 12–39.
64. Walling, 149.

Chapter 2

Note on sources: Primary sources that proved most useful for the immediate postcontact and Rogue River War period of Upper Coquille River history and ethnology are Elizabeth Derr Jacobs's field notes of her interviews with Coquelle Thompson during 1935 (EDJ/WRS) and pioneer narratives (reprinted in Dodge 1969). Secondary sources that proved most useful include Beckham (1971), Schwartz (1997), and Douthit (1992–99).

1. JPH, 26:190.
2. EDJ/WRS, 1:46–48.
3. Ibid.
4. NA/ACF, allotment S-379, Coquelle Thompson deposition, 14 October 1918.
5. JPH, 26:349–50.

6. Seaburg 1994a, 203.
7. Jacobs 1939, 77.
8. JPH, 27:624.
9. Dodge, 27; Beckham 1971, 62–63.
10. Robert Carlton Clark, 25.
11. NA/DC, Casey to Col. Hooker, 24 October 1851.
12. NA/DC, Casey to Col. Hooker, 24 November 1851.
13. Ibid.
14. Ibid.
15. Ibid.
16. Ibid.
17. Seaburg 1994a, 203.
18. EDJ/WRS, 4:118.
19. JPH, 27:211.
20. Seaburg 1994a, 204.
21. JPH, 27:211.
22. Seaburg 1994a, 204.
23. EDJ/WRS, 3:151–52.
24. EDJ/WRS, 3:68.
25. Dodge, 126–27.
26. Dodge, 128.
27. Dodge, 127.
28. Dodge, 127–28.
29. Dodge, 128.
30. Pullen, interview 1999b.
31. Dodge, 129.
32. Jacobs 1939, 32.
33. EDJ/WRS, 4:10–14.
34. Douthit 1999b, 417.
35. Work, 77, 102.
36. Douthit 1999b, 417.
37. Jacobs 1939, 101.
38. JPH, 22:1130.
39. JPH, 26:90–91.
40. Seaburg 1994a, 200
41. JPH, 26:191.
42. Wooldridge, 275–76; Dodge, 291–306.
43. EDJ/WRS, 4:126–27.
44. EDJ/WRS, 5:130.
45. EDJ/WRS, 2:139–43.
46. Dodge, 184.
47. Dodge, 105.

48. Seaburg 1994a, 206–207.
49. Dodge, 329.
50. Schwartz 1997, 83.
51. Ibid., 90.
52. Douthit 1994, 503–507.
53. EDJ/WRS, 5:125–26.
54. Dodge, 98.
55. Ibid.
56. EDJ/WRS, 5:126–31.
57. Beckham 1971, 171.
58. EDJ/WRS, 5:131.
59. Beckham 1971, 173; Douthit 1999b, 414–20.
60. EDJ/WRS, 5:131.

Chapter 3

Note on sources: Primary sources relative to the removal of the Indians by sea from Port Orford to Siletz in 1856 include Coquelle Thompson's narrative recorded by Elizabeth Derr Jacobs in 1935 (EDJ/WRS), his narrative recorded by John Peabody Harrington in 1942 (JPH), and the diary and uncataloged documents of Joel Palmer in the Oregon Historical Society manuscripts collection (MSS 114 and 114-2). Secondary sources include Victor (1894) and Dodge (1969).

1. OHS, MSS 114, Palmer diary, 20 June 1856.
2. *Lewis & Dryden's Marine History*, 35 n. 7.
3. OHS, MSS 114, Palmer diary, 20 June 1856.
4. Ibid., 21 June.
5. EDJ/WRS, 5:131–32.
6. JPH, 27:574.
7. Palmer to Manypenny, 3 July 1856, in Senate letter 1893, serial 3144 (cited in Schwartz 1997, 146 n. 56).
8. Heyl, 97.
9. Ibid.
10. *Lewis & Dryden's Marine History*, 35 n. 7, and 57.
11. JPH, 27:574.
12. Ibid.
13. OHS, MSS 114, Palmer diary, 22 June 1856.
14. *Lewis & Dryden's Marine History*, 57.
15. OHS, MSS 114-2, Palmer letter, 23 June 1856.
16. Seaburg 1994a, 208.
17. JPH, 27:574.
18. Ibid.

19. Schwartz, 149.
20. *Lewis & Dryden's Marine History*, 50; Dodge, 101.
21. Dodge, 101.
22. *Lewis & Dryden's Marine History*, 63.
23. Seaburg 1994a, 211.
24. Dodge, 101.
25. O'Donnell, 266.
26. Beckham 1977, 143.
27. JPH, 27:575.
28. JPH, 24:235, 316.
29. Schwartz 1997, 128; O'Donnell, 279.
30. NADP, D41, Palmer to Commissioner, 20 September 1856, OIA, *Letters Received..., 1824–1880*, NA microcopy 234, roll 609.
31. Seaburg 1994a, 209–10.
32. Dodge, 365–67.
33. EDJ/WRS, 5:135.
34. Ibid.
35. Ibid., 5:136.
36. NADP, D46, Hedges to Commissioner, 7 November 1856, OIA, *Letters Received..., 1824–1880*, NA microcopy 234, roll 609.
37. EDJ/WRS, 5:136.
38. EDJ/WRS, 1:29.
39. EDJ/WRS, 3:50.
40. JPH/1943.
41. JPH, 20:648.
42. EDJ/WRS, 1:29.
43. NADP, D46, Hedges to Commissioner.
44. NADP, D49, Metcalfe to Hedges, 12 December 1856, *Letters Received..., 1824–1880*, NA microcopy 234, roll 610.
45. EDJ/WRS, 5:163.
46. NADP, D47, Hedges to Manypenny, OIA, *Letters Received..., 1824–1880*, NA microcopy 234, roll 609.
47. EDJ/WRS, 5:136.
48. JPH, 27:624.
49. NADP, D51, Roberts to Commissioner, 17 August 1857, OIA, *Letters Received..., 1824–1880*, NA microcopy 234, roll 611.
50. EDJ/WRS, 3:172–74.
51. Seaburg 1994a, 210.
52. Bell, interview.
53. Seaburg 1994a, 210.
54. NADP, D64, Mott to Commissioner, 11 February 1859, OIA, *Letters Received..., 1824–1880*, NA microcopy 234, roll 611.

55. EDJ/WRS, 1:188.
56. NA/ACF, allotment S-379, testimony of Coquelle Thompson, 14 October 1918.
57. EDJ/WRS, 6:184.
58. EDJ/WRS, typescript, "The Old Hunter."
59. JPH, 27:624.
60. Victor, 416.

Chapter 4

Note on sources: The best primary sources for the first years of the Coast Reservation at Siletz are Coquelle Thompson's narrative to Elizabeth Derr Jacobs (EDJ/WRS); the annual reports of the agents; Oregon Historical Society archives, MSS 442, Siletz Indian Reservation documents; and Bensell (1959). The most useful secondary source was Schwartz (1997).

1. NADP, D69, Rector to Dole, 16 May 1862, OIA, *Letters Received...*, *1824–1880*, NA microcopy 234, roll 613.
2. NADP, D67, Browne to Commissioner, 12 November 1861, OIA, *Letters Received...*, *1824–1880*, NA microcopy 234, roll 612; Schwartz 1997, 170.
3. Bensell, 123.
4. *Oregonian*, letter, "C to Editor," 22 January 1879.
5. EDJ/WRS, 2:162.
6. EDJ/WRS, 4:110.
7. Schwartz 1991, 174.
8. Bensell, 171.
9. Bensell, 130.
10. Nelson, 12–13.
11. EDJ/WRS, 2:73–74; 4:90.
12. PD, 2:90.
13. Bensell, 135.
14. NADP, D73, "Report of the speeches made by the Chiefs," 24–26 May 1862, NA microcopy 234, roll 613.
15. Bensell, 124.
16. Ibid., 125.
17. NADP, D73, "Report of the speeches made by the Chiefs," 24–26 May 1862, NA microcopy 234, roll 613.
18. See, e.g., MJC, sound recordings 14710, 14711a, 14714, and 14721.
19. EDJ/WRS, 4:79.
20. EDJ/WRS, 5:171.
21. Seaburg 1994a, 216.
22. JPH, 28:347.
23. NA/ACF, allotment S-531, testimony of Lucy Watts Smith, 24 February 1923.

24. JPH, 28:347.
25. JPH, 28:337; Gilsan, *Journal of Army Life*, 348–50, in Beckham 1971, 189.
26. Schwartz 1997, 146–47.
27. CDB, "tatooing," np.
28. Seaburg 1994a, 216–17.
29. EDJ/WRS, 5:161.
30. EDJ/WRS, 4:108.
31. EDJ/WRS, 1:53.
32. EDJ/WRS, 1:69.
33. Kentta, personal communications.
34. Bensell, 194.
35. JPH, 26:104.
36. NADP, D83, Palmer to Meacham, 15 July 1871, OIA, *Records of the Oregon Superintendency of Indian Affairs*, NA microcopy 2, roll 27.
37. Bell, interview.
38. JPH, 23:807.
39. NADP, D54, Swan to Commissioner, 28 August 1882, *Report of the Secretary of the Interior*, vol. 2, 1882, 199–202; NADP, D60, Wadsworth to Commissioner, 13 August 1883, *Report of the Secretary of the Interior*, vol. 2, 187–90.
40. JPH, 27:599.
41. EDJ/WRS, 3:66.
42. Ketcham.
43. O'Donnell, 291.
44. O'Donnell, 292.
45. NADP, D83, Palmer to Meacham; *Oregonian*, 17 July 1871.
46. OHS, MSS 555, Palmer to Raymond, 10 August 1871; O'Donnell, 291 n. 12.
47. OHS, MSS 114, Palmer diary, 1872.
48. Schwartz 1997, 188–89.
49. EDJ/WRS, 3:165.
50. EDJ/WRS, 2:31.
51. PD, 2:34.
52. EDJ/WRS, typescript, "A doctoring session at Siletz."
53. EDJ/WRS, 2:31. The following story is from the typescript, "A doctoring session at Siletz."
54. EDJ/WRS, 4:115.
55. EDJ/WRS, 4:124.
56. EDJ/WRS, 4:124–25.
57. Douthit 1994, 479.
58. PD, 2:98–99.
59. PD, 2:100.

60. PD, 2:104.
61. PD, 2:101.
62. PD, 2:100.
63. Johnson, 36.
64. EDJ/WRS, typescript, "They Killed One Doctor."
65. NA/ACF, allotment S-379, testimony of Coquelle Thompson, 14 October 1918.
66. EDJ/WRS, 3:64.
67. PD, 2:121.
68. JPH, 27:615.

Chapter 5

Note on sources: The best primary sources are Coquelle Thompson's own narratives of the Ghost Dance. The most complete is Du Bois (1939). The others are Elizabeth Derr Jacobs (EDJ/WRS), Drucker (PD), and John Peabody Harrington (JPH). Also useful is Jacobs (1939). Beckham, Toepel, and Minor (1984) is a useful secondary source.

1. Du Bois 1939, 5; Jorgensen, 660–62.
2. Du Bois 1939, 9.
3. Ibid., 37.
4. Jacobs 1939, 63–64; Du Bois 1939, 37; Youst 1997, 74–76.
5. Du Bois 1939, 25.
6. Ibid.
7. Ibid., 26.
8. Ibid., 27.
9. Ibid.; PD 2:114.
10. Ibid.; JPH, 27:621.
11. PD, 2:114.
12. Du Bois 1939, 27.
13. Jacobs 1945, 72.
14. Du Bois 1939, 27.
15. Ibid.
16. PD, 2:114–15; EDJ/WRS, 4:83.
17. NADP, D83, Palmer to Meacham.
18. Schwartz 1997, 188–89.
19. Youst 1997, 95–96.
20. NADP, D94, "Petition of the chiefs and Head men," 12 February 1878, OIA, *Letters Received . . ., 1824–1880,* NA microcopy 234, roll 625.
21. EDJ/WRS, 5:165–67.
22. Du Bois 1939, 27–28.
23. EDJ/WRS, 5:173.

24. Du Bois 1939, v.
25. EDJ/WRS, 3:45.
26. Ibid.
27. Du Bois 1939, 28.
28. Spier 1927, 44.
29. Du Bois 1939, 29.
30. JPH, 28:454.
31. JPH, 28:338.
32. Du Bois 1939, 29.
33. Du Bois 1939, 32.
34. EDJ/WRS, 2:105.
35. EDJ/WRS, 3:57.
36. Du Bois 1939, 28.
37. Jacobs 1939, 63–64; Youst 1997, 75.
38. Du Bois 1939, 32–33.
39. Frachtenberg 1913, 1922.
40. Du Bois 1939, 33.
41. Ibid.
42. Beckam, Toepel, and Minor, 1984, 99.
43. Ibid.
44. Du Bois 1939, 33.
45. CIT, Egbert to H. G. Wilson (Roseburg superintendent), 3 February 1912.
46. Ibid.
47. Van Kirk, 50–51.
48. Hall 1991, 77–82.
49. JPH, 26:135.
50. JPH, 27:575.
51. EDJ/WRS, 2:95.
52. EDJ/WRS, 5:138.
53. Du Bois 1939, 34–35.
54. JPH, 23:944.
55. Du Bois 1939, 35.

Chapter 6

Note on sources: Elizabeth Derr Jacobs interview (EDJ/WRS) and allotment files at the National Archives and Records Administration, Pacific Alaska Region, Seattle, are the most valuable primary sources for this period of Siletz history. For the J. Owen Dorsey visit, see his letters and reports to the BAE director, National Anthropological Archives, Smithsonian Institution;

for the Franz Boas visit, see his diary (1969). The best secondary source for the Boas visit is Cole (1999).
1. EDJ/WRS, 4:99.
2. EDJ/WRS, 5:160–61.
3. EDJ/WRS, 3:48.
4. EDJ/WRS, 4:106.
5. OHS, MSS 114-2, Palmer to Secretary of Indian Affairs, Washington, D.C., 23 November 1872.
6. Summers, 32, 104, 107.
7. OHS, MSS 442-2, Seghers to Secretary of the Interior, 25 July 1883.
8. JPH, 27:623.
9. Bell, interview.
10. Glenda Kaufman Kantor, "Alcohol and Spouse Abuse: Ethnic Differences," in *Alcoholism and Violence*, ed. Marc Galanter, vol. 13 of *Recent Developments in Alcoholism* (New York: Plenum Press, 1997), 57–79.
11. OHS, MSS 442-2, Palmer letter, 26 December 1871.
12. Ibid., 23 November 1972.
13. NADP, D101, Boswell to Editor, *Corvallis Gazette*, 10 January 1879, OIA, *Letters Received . . ., 1824–1881*, NA microcopy 234, roll 627.
14. NADP, D54, Swan to Commissioner.
15. NADP, D60, Wadsworth to Commissioner.
16. L. H. Morgan, viii.
17. JOD, letter, 20 August 1884.
18. JOD, Powell to Dorsey, 6 August 1884.
19. Hewitt.
20. JOD, Dorsey to Powell, 20 August 1884.
21. JOD, Dorsey to Director, 1 October 1884.
22. JPH, 27:600, 619; NA/PNW, Siletz annual Indian Census Rolls, 1885–1938.
23. Seaburg 1994a, 69.
24. Ibid., 71.
25. Ibid., 91.
26. JOD, report, 1884, "A Visit to the *Siletz* Agency [Tillamook Co., Oregon] by Rev. J. Owen Dorsey."
27. JOD, Dorsey to Director, 17 October 1884.
28. Powell, 121.
29. Powell, vi, vii.
30. JOD, Dorsey to Director, 20 August 1884.
31. JPH, 27:602.
32. Ibid.
33. JPH, 27:601–602.

34. EDJ/WRS, 2:42.
35. EDJ/WRS, typescript, "A hunt Coquelle Thompson, Sr., was part of."
36. Scott, 236.
37. Bonnell, 37–38.
38. NA/PNW, Chemawa School Records.
39. NADP, D55, Wadsworth to Commissioner, 20 August 1884, *Report of the Secretary of the Interior*, vol. 2, 189–91.
40. Bonnell, 35.
41. Bonnell, 39.
42. Bonnell, ii.
43. EDJ/WRS, 6:194–95.
44. LCL, 7 October 1897, has a description of the Devils Lake area before it was settled.
45. JPH, 27:615.
46. NA/ACF, allotments S-291 and S-382, Martha Johnson Wood deposition, 23 October 1925.
47. NA/ACF, allotment S-457, Coquelle Thompson testimony, 13 October 1915.
48. NA/ACF, allotment S-457, John Adams testimony, 13 October 1915.
49. EDJ/WRS, 2:42.
50. McKeehan, 100.
51. JPH, 27:615.
52. Boas 1969, 116.
53. Ibid.
54. Ibid., 117.
55. Cole, 147.
56. Tax.
57. Hall 1995, 42–43.
58. EDJ/WRS, 2:153.
59. Ward 1987, 10–13.
60. Munnick and Beckham, Register II, B-33.
61. Bensell, 140n
62. Seaburg 1994a, 226–27.

Chapter 7

Note on sources: For a general overview of the effects of the Dawes Act, the authors used McDonnell (1991); for an overview relative to the Siletz Reservation, Schwartz (1997) was very helpful. The weekly *Lincoln County Leader* from 1893 until the end of the trust period at Siletz in 1919 contains frequent articles relative to allotments and inherited lands. The individual allotment files at the National Archives and Records Administration, Pacific Alaska

Region, Seattle, were indispensable for gauging the impact of the Dawes Act upon an individual family.

1. Schwartz 1997, 219–21.
2. McDonnell, 8.
3. JPH, 26:82.
4. CIT documents, esp. "Statement of Facts on Appeal of Descendants of Agnes (Aggie) Johnson," BIA, Portland Office, 3 May 1955.
5. Schwartz 1997, 219–21.
6. Wyatt, np.
7. NA/ACF, allotment S-456, Coquelle Thompson.
8. EDJ/WRS, 5:179.
9. YP, 19 January, 25 May, 31 August, 2 and 23 November, 1901, contains a running commentary on the distribution of the fund.
10. NA/ACF, allotment S-456, Coquelle Thompson.
11. Prucha 1975, 186–89 (52d Cong., 2d sess., H. Exec. Doc. 1, serial 3088, 28–31).
12. Hittman, 63–105.
13. Du Bois 1939, 34.
14. LCL, 8 September 1899.
15. Bernstein, 3.
16. YP, 17 August 1901.
17. EDJ/WRS, 3:172.
18. Ibid.
19. Schwartz 1997, 224–25.
20. EDJ/WRS, 4:103. Also see Du Bois 1939, 35, for a discussion of Coquelle Jim by Coquelle Thompson.
21. NA/ACF, allotment files S-467, James Thompson, and S-468, Anna Thompson.
22. Quoted in Schwartz 1997, 222.
23. U.S. Stats. 28 (25 July 1895), 326, and U.S. Stats. 31 (17 May 1900), 179, quoted in Puter, 470.
24. Robbins 1988, 124–27.
25. LCL, 13 July 1900.
26. See esp. Puter, who wrote his exposé, *Looters of the Public Domain*, while himself serving time for land fraud.
27. A. W. Morgan, 2–3.
28. Ibid., 45.
29. Ibid.
30. Schwartz 1997, 251.
31. A. W. Morgan, 7–9.
32. Ibid. 17.
33. Ibid. 7–9.

34. Ibid.
35. McDonnell, 55.
36. NA/ACF, allotment S-548, Walker Thompson.
37. Seaburg 1994a, 221–22 (NA/PNW, "Records of Employees at the Siletz Agency and the Siletz Training School").
38. JPH, 27:520, 527.
39. CTS documents, Lincoln County Marriages, book 1. The wedding was December 21, 1902.
40. EDJ/WRS, 5:178–79
41. Oregon State Archives, Death Certificate 389, Lincoln County.
42. Schwartz 1997, 225.
43. These two adjoining properties are described as W ½ of the NW ¼ of section 33, T9S R9W; and S ½ of NE ¼ of section 32, T9S R9W.
44. NA/ACF, allotment S-460, Mary Tyee, and allotment S-337, Jacob Mack.
45. EDJ/WRS, 5:179.
46. LCL, 1 April 1904.
47. Interviews with June Austin, Frank Simmons, Dolly Fisher, George Thompson, and Alma Chapman Thompson all confirmed that Coquelle was tolerant of and loving toward children.
48. JPH, 27:263.
49. LCL, 17 June 1904.
50. PD, 5:39; EDJ/WRS, 6:195.
51. Frank Simmons and Dolly Fisher, interview.
52. LCL, 15 November 1945, 4.
53. NA/ACF, allotment S-457, Emma Thompson, application for a patent in fee by Agnes Thompson, 7 May 1948.
54. LCL, 15 November 1945, 4.
55. YP, 24 May 1902; LCL, 1 April 1904; census, marriage, and death records.
56. LCL, 4 December 1903, from the *Sunday Oregonian*.
57. See Seaburg 1992 for an analysis of this incident.
58. JPH, 26:137, 161.
59. NA/ACF, allotment S-379, Louisa Pete, testimony of Coquelle Thompson.
60. EDJ/WRS, 1:89.
61. EDJ/WRS, 4:105.
62. EDJ/WRS, 5:182.

Chapter 8

Note on sources: Our best sources for Siletz during this period were in the weekly *Lincoln County Leader*. A partial set of the microfilm series was available at the Toledo Public Library, and a full set was available at the University of Oregon Library. Those newspaper accounts, coupled with the individual allotment files at the National Archives and Records Administration, Pacific Alaska Region, Seattle, provided the authors with rare insights into the end of the trust period at Siletz. Helpful in placing the Siletz experience into a national perspective were parts of Clements (1996), Britten (1997), and Gidley (1998) (see bibliography).

1. JPH, 27:615.
2. Youst 1995, 213; Frachtenberg 1913, 1920.
3. Frachtenberg 1920, 5.
4. Du Bois 1939, 27.
5. LCL, 5 August 1904.
6. LCL, 31 July 1906.
7. Thompson, interview, 2000.
8. LCL, 15 November 1945.
9. Reprinted in LCL, 15 September 1916.
10. See Tollefson, 43, regarding a similar event at Puget Sound.
11. EDJ/WRS, 4:123.
12. LCL, 20 January 1905.
13. LCL, 24 June 1904.
14. Kasner, 29.
15. See Gogol (1984) and Kasner (1976) for discussions.
16. Lane, interview.
17. NA/PNW, box 29 (copies of letters sent by Siletz agents 1908–13).
18. McDonnell, 4.
19. LCL, 7 February 1913.
20. JPH, 27:589.
21. Frachtenberg 1913, 1.
22. Frachtenberg 1913 is the collection of myth texts, in Hanis Coos with English translation; Frachtenberg 1922 is an illustrative sketch for a full grammar of the Hanis Coos language.
23. LCL, 22 August 1913.
24. Britten, 32–34, 48–49.
25. LCL, 22 August 1913.
26. LCL, 3 October 1913.
27. NA/ACF, allotment S-458, Walker Thompson.
28. Prucha 1975, 185 (U.S. Statutes at Large, 26:794–96).
29. CIT, "Statement of Facts on Appeal of Descendants of Agnes (Aggie) Johnson," with attachments.
30. LCL, 1 May 1914.
31. LCL, 10 December 1915.
32. LCL, 3 December 1914.
33. Lincoln County Clerk, land titles, Coquelle Thompson.

34. NA/ACF, allotment S-331, Abram Lincoln.
35. NA/ACF, allotment S-456, Coquelle Thompson.
36. NA/ACF, allotment S-458, Walker Thompson.
37. JPH/JM
38. Lockard.
39. Britten, 32; William Hammon Mathers Museum, University of Indiana, Web site, www.indiana.edu/~mathers.
40. Lockard.
41. Salins, 56.
42. Gordon, 70–71; Salins, 49–50.
43. JPH, 27:530.
44. Johnson, 32.
45. Hyman, 177.
46. LCL, 22 February 1918.
47. Lloyd Palmer, 29–58.
48. LCL, 22 February 1918.
49. LCL, 1 March 1918.
50. EDJ/WRS, 4:104.
51. Osterbrock, Gustafson, and Unruh, 164–67.
52. Clark, 100.
53. LCL, 21 June 1918.
54. LCL, 12 July 1918.
55. LCL, 12 April 1918.
56. Lloyd Palmer, 104.
57. Johnson, 21, 32.
58. NA/ACF, allotment S-457, Emma Thompson.
59. OHS, MSS 442, 1 July 1919.
60. LCL, 2 May 1919; *Oregonian*, 28 April 1919.
61. Parry, 107, 121, 123–24.
62. Crosby, 203–207.
63. LCL, 15 November 1945, p. 4.
64. Rowland, 179–82.
65. CIT, letter, 6 August 1956; Hall 1991, 80, 101.
66. LCL, 20 December 1918.
67. NA/ACF, allotment S-379, Louisa Pete.
68. NA/ACF, allotment S-459, John Tyee.
69. LCL, 14 February 1919.
70. LCL, 7 March 1919.
71. LCL, 21 March 1919.
72. LCL, 15 November 1945, 4.
73. Johnson, 13.
74. Lloyd Palmer, 112.

Chapter 9

Note on sources: In this chapter we relied heavily on interviews with Coquelle's descendants, and with the individual allotment files at the National Archives and Records Administration, Pacific Alaska Region, Seattle. For insights into Philip Drucker's field methods at Siletz, we used his field notes (PD). For insights into Cora Du Bois field methods at Siletz, we used her 1939 monograph, *The 1870 Ghost Dance*.

1. NA/PNW, Chemawa Indian School records.
2. CIT, Chemawa yearbooks donated by William Sandberg.
3. NA/PNW, Chemawa Indian School records, record group no. 75.
4. Bonnell, 52.
5. Thompson, interview, 1999.
6. NA/ACF, file S-456, Coquelle Thompson.
7. NA/PNW, Chemawa Indian School records.
8. JPH, 27:615. In 1942 Coquelle said, "Nine of my children have died, from my 4 wives (or livings together)." His only children to survive with progeny were Coquelle Jr. (1905–74) and Sina (1920–2002).
9. Bernstein, 4–10.
10. Schwartz 1997, 243.
11. JPH, 23:501.
12. Mills, I:78–79.
13. JPH, 28:337, 347.
14. NA/ACF, allotment S-30, Annetta Brown Scott.
15. Bell, interview.
16. Ross, 66; Frank Simmons and Dolly Fisher, interview; Bell, interview; LCL, 25 March 1904.
17. Bell, interview.
18. Frank Simmons and Dolly Fisher, interview.
19. Bonnell, ii, 7–9.
20. Wolf, 39–40.
21. Seaburg 1994a, 92, 93. See Youst (1997) for a biography of Peterson with full accounts of her work as a linguistic and ethnological informant.
22. Bell, interview.
23. Drucker 1937, 221.
24. Seaburg 1994a, 86. See also Barnett 1983.
25. Beal, 458.
26. Seymour, 73–74.
27. Seymour, 74.
28. Du Bois 1939, v.
29. Ibid.
30. Ibid., 141.

31. Ibid., 25.
32. Ibid., 26–30.
33. Ibid., v–vi.
34. Ibid., 32.
35. Ibid., 126.
36. Ibid., v.
37. Merton 1999, 10.
38. Schwartz 1997, 244.
39. Ibid., 243.
40. CIT, letter, James T. Rahaly, Yakima Indian Agency, to Mr. Charles E. Larson, Salem Indian School, Chemawa, Oregon, 16 October 1934.

Chapter 10

Note on sources: For details of Coquelle's last years, we relied heavily on interviews with family members and the individual allotment files at the National Archives and Records Administration, Pacific Alaska Region, Seattle. For insights into Elizabeth Jabobs's field techniques, Seaburg's 1975 interviews with her were indispensable. The Marr–Harrington letters at the Smithsonian (JPH/JM), and personal communication with Jack Marr in 1999 provided a vivid portrayal of the relationship between those two men and the techniques used by Marr as Harrington's "field assistant." For Harrington himself, there are several fine published sketches of his career; among the most accessible are Hinton (195–210) and Laird.

1. Clements, 101.
2. Seaburg 1982, 68–72.
3. Seaburg and Amoss, 13–14.
4. EDJ/WRS, 2:65.
5. EDJ/WRS, 4:79.
6. EDJ/WRS, 3:63.
7. Jacobs, interview.
8. EDJ/WRS, 6:185.
9. Ibid., 2:116.
10. NA/ACF, allotment S-456, Coquelle Thompson.
11. Thompson, interview, 1999.
12. Bell, interview.
13. Thompson, interview, 1999.
14. Anderson, interview.
15. NA/ACF, allotment S-30, Annettie Brown Scott, letter, 21 July 1941.
16. Ibid., letter, 30 July 1941.
17. Marr, letter to William Seaburg, 12 July 2000.

18. JPH, 26:67.
19. JPH, 28:54.
20. JPH, 27:586.
21. Kasner, 32.
22. Bellafaire, 1–28.
23. LCL, 3 January 1946.
24. LCL, 15 November 1945, 4.
25. Thompson, interview, 2000.

Afterword

1. LCL, 15 November 1945, 4.
2. NA/ACF, allotment S-457, Emma Thompson.
3. Lloyd Palmer, 108–109.
4. Robbins 1988, 166–67.
5. LCL, 14 February 1952, 1.
6. Siletz, 140.
7. Siletz, 324.
8. Siletz, 143.
9. Siletz, 208–17.
10. Siletz, 340.
11. Siletz, 268.
12. Siletz, 242–43.
13. Zucker, Hummel, and Hogfoss 112.
14. Prucha 1985, 71.
15. Siletz, 353–54.
16. Siletz, 8.
17. Boas 1989, 327–28.

Appendix 1

1. EDJ/WRS; Drucker 1937; Du Bois 1939.
2. Miller and Seaburg 1990, 580–82.
3. Drucker 1937, 279.
4. Ibid., 279–80.
5. Jacobs ca. 1959, 16.
6. Ibid., 17.
7. Miller and Seaburg 1990, 583.
8. Drucker 1937, 280, 273.
9. Miller and Seaburg 1990, 584.
10. Ibid.
11. Ibid., 384–85.
12. Ibid., 585.

13. Jacobs ca. 1959, 16–17.
14. EDJ/WRS.
15. Miller and Seaburg 1990, 583.
16. Ibid., 584.
17. Ibid.
18. EDJ/WRS.
19. Drucker 1937, 281.
20. Miller and Seaburg 1990, 585.
21. Du Bois 1939, 34–35.
22. EDJ/WRS.
23. Du Bois 1939, 34.
24. Drucker 1937, 274.
25. Miller and Seaburg 1990, 586.

Appendix 2

1. We have included names for only those villages that have been given a geographical location in the literature. For example, we have excluded many of the village names listed in Dorsey (1890, 232) because he does not provide a possible location for the site.

2. We have substituted a "d/D" for Dorsey's upside-down "t/T" symbol.

3. Drucker's field notebooks are located in the National Anthropological Archives, Smithsonian Institution, Washington, D.C.

4. From notes in the possession of William R. Seaburg.

5. Harrington's notes are from the microfilm edition of *The Papers of John Peabody Harrington in the Smithsonian Institution, 1907–1957.*

6. Harrington's Greek capital omega (Ω) is a cross-reference symbol, here meaning the name under discussion.

7. Harrington's abbreviation, "ra.," means rancheria.

Bibliography

Interviews

Anderson, Ann and Wally (Coquille tribal elders). 1999. Interview by Lionel Youst. Bandon, Oreg., 2 July.

Austin, June (step-granddaughter of Coquelle Thompson, Sr.). 1999. Telephone interview by Lionel Youst. 12 July.

Bell, Sina Thompson (daughter of Coquelle Thompson, Sr.). 1999. Interview by William R. Seaburg. Fort Belknap Indian Reservation, Mont., 31 July and 1 and 2 August.

Fisher, Dan (oldtime Siletz resident). 2000. Telephone interview by Lionel Youst. 21 March.

Jacobs, Elizabeth Derr (interviewer of Coquelle Thompson, Sr.). 1975. Interview by William R. Seaburg. Tape recordings. Seattle, Wash., 23 March and 30 June.

Kentta, Robert H (Cultural Resources Director, Confederated Tribes of Siletz Indians), and Frank Simmons (step-grandson of Coquelle Thompson, Sr.). 1999. Interview by William R. Seaburg and Lionel Youst. Siletz Tribal Cultural Center, 3 June.

Lane, Maude (acquaintance of Coquelle Thompson). 1999. Interview by William R. Seaburg, Lionel Youst, and Robert Kentta. Siletz, Oreg., 3 June.

Pullen, Reg (archaeologist). 1999a. Telephone interview by Lionel Youst. 21 June.
———. 1999b. Interview by Lionel Youst. Coquille Tribal Hall, North Bend, Oreg., 26 June.
———. 1999c. Interview by William R. Seaburg and Lionel Youst. Prosper, Oreg., 7 September.
Simmons, Frank, and Dolly Fisher (step-grandchildren of Coquelle Thompson, Sr.). 1999. Interview by Lionel Youst. Siletz Tribal Cultural Center, Siletz, Oreg., 24 June.
Thompson, George (grandson of Coquelle Thompson, Sr.). 1999. Interview by Lionel Youst. Siletz, Oreg., 11 November.
———. 2000. Interview by William R. Seaburg and Lionel Youst. Siletz, Oreg., 14 January.

Other Sources

Amoss, Pamela T. 1990. "The Indian Shaker Church." In *Northwest Coast*, edited by Wayne Suttles, 633–39. Vol. 7 of *Handbook of North American Indians*. Washington, D.C.: Smithsonian Institution.
Applegate, Shannon. 1988. *Skookum: An Oregon Pioneer Family's History and Lore*. New York: Beech Tree Books.
Barnett, Homer G. 1957. *Indian Shakers: A Messianic Cult of the Pacific Northwest*. Carbondale: Southern Illinois University Press.
———. 1983. "Learning about Culture: Reconstruction, Participation, Administration, 1934–1954." In *Observers Observed: Essays on Ethnographic Fieldwork*, edited by George W. Stocking, Jr., 157–74. Vol. 1 of *History of Anthropology*. Madison: University of Wisconsin Press.
Basso, Keith H. 1996. *Wisdom Sits in Places: Landscape and Language among the Western Apache*. Albuquerque: University of New Mexico Press.
Baun, Carolyn M., and Richard Lewis, eds. 1991. *The First Oregonians: An Illustrated Collection of Essays on Traditional Lifeways, Federal-Indian Relations, and the State's Native People Today*. Portland: Oregon Council for the Humanities.
Beal, Ralph. 1968. "Kroeber, Alfred L." In *International Encyclopedia of the Social Sciences*, edited by David L. Sills, vol. 8, 454–63. New York: Macmillan.
Bean, Lowell John, ed. 1992. *California Indian Shamanism*. Menlo Park, Calif.: Ballena Press.
Beckham, Stephen Dow. [1971] 1996. *Requiem for a People: The Rogue Indians and the Frontiersmen*. Reprint, Corvallis: Oregon State University Press.
———. 1977. *The Indians of Western Oregon: This Land Was Theirs*. Coos Bay, Oreg.: Arago Books.

Beckham, Stephen Dow, Kathryn Anne Toepel, and Rick Minor. 1984. *Native American Religious Practices and Uses in Western Oregon.* University of Oregon Anthropological Papers, no. 31. Eugene: Department of Anthropology, University of Oregon.
Bellafaire, Judith A. [1990?]. "The Women's Army Corps: A Commemoration of World War II Service." U.S. Army Center of Military History Publication 72-15.
Bensell, Royal A. 1959. *All Quiet on the Yamhill: The Civil War in Oregon: The Journal of Corporal Royal A. Bensell,* edited by Gunther Barth. Eugene: University of Oregon Books.
Bernstein, Alison R. 1991. *American Indians and World War II.* Norman: University of Oklahoma Press.
Blackman, Margaret B. 1991. "The Individual and Beyond: Reflections of the Life History Process." *Anthropology and Humanism Quarterly* 16, no. 2:56–62.
Boas, Franz. 1969. *The Ethnography of Franz Boas.* Edited by Ronald P. Rohner. Chicago: University of Chicago Press.
———. [1974] 1989. *A Franz Boas Reader: The Shaping of American Anthropology, 1883–1911.* Edited by George W. Stocking, Jr. Reprint, Chicago: University of Chicago Press.
Bonnell, Sonciray. 1997. *Chemawa Indian Boarding School: The First One Hundred Years, 1880–1980.* Master's thesis, Dartmouth College. Disertation.com.
Boyd, Robert T. 1990. "Demographic History, 1774–1874." In *Northwest Coast,* edited by Wayne Suttles, 135–48. Vol. 7 of *Handbook of North American Indians.* Washington, D.C.: Smithsonian Institution.
Britten, Thomas A. 1997. *American Indians in World War I: At Home and at War.* Albuquerque: University of New Mexico Press.
Caldwell, Earl. 1995. "Nay-Dosh Celebrates World Renewal." *News from Indian Country: Ethnic News Watch* 9, no. 23 (15 December):4b.
Cawley, Fr. Martinus. 1996. *Father Crockett of Grand Ronde.* Lafayette, Oreg.: Guadalupe Translations.
———. 1997. *The Singing Priest of Siletz, Father Raymond of Ocean Lake.* Lafayette, Oreg.: Guadalupe Translations.
Clark, Ella E. 1953. "Indian Story-telling of Old in the Pacific Northwest." *OHQ* 54 (June):100.
Clark, Robert Carlton. 1935. "Military History of Oregon, 1849–59." *OHQ* 36 (March):14–59.
Clements, William M. 1996. *Native American Verbal Arts: Texts and Contexts.* Tucson: University of Arizona Press.
Cole, Douglas. 1999. *Franz Boas: The Early Years, 1858–1906.* Seattle: University of Washington Press.

Collins, Cary C. 1997. "Through the Lens of Assimilation: Edwin L. Chalcraft and Chemawa Indian School." *OHQ* 98 (winter):390–425.
Crosby, Alfred W., Jr. 1976. *Epidemic and Peace, 1918*. Westport, Conn.: Greenwood Press.
Curtis, Edward S. 1924. *Hupa, Yurok, Karok, Wiyot, Tolowa, Tututni, Shasta, Achōmawi, Klamath*. Vol. 13 of *The North American Indian*. Norwood, Conn.: Plimpton Press.
Denzin, Norman K. 1989. *Interpretive Biography*. Newbury Park, Calif.: Sage.
Dodge, Orville, ed. [1898] 1969. *Pioneer History of Coos and Curry Counties, Or.: Heroic Deeds and Thrilling Adventures of the Early Settlers*. Bandon, Oreg.: Coos-Curry Pioneer and Historical Association.
Dorsey, J. Owen. 1890. "The Gentile System of the Siletz Tribes." *Journal of American Folklore* 3:227–37.
Doty, Mark. 2000. "On the Serengeti: Rewriting a Life." In *Tales from the Couch: Writers on Therapy*, edited by Jason Shinder, 1–17. New York: Morrow.
Douthit, Nathan. 1992. "The Hudson's Bay Company and the Indians of Southern Oregon." *OHQ* 93 (spring):25–64.
———. 1994. "Joseph Lane and the Rogue River Indians: Personal Relations across a Cultural Divide." *OHQ* 95 (winter):472–515.
———. 1999a. *Guide to Oregon's South Coast History*. Corvallis: Oregon State University Press.
———. 1999b. "Between Indian and White Worlds on the Oregon-California Border, 1851–1857: Benjamin Wright and Enos." *OHQ* 100 (winter): 402–33.
———. Forthcoming. *Uncertain Encounters: Indians and Whites at Peace and War in Southern Oregon, 1820s–1860s*. Corvallis: Oregon State University Press.
Drucker, Philip. 1937. *The Tolowa and their Southwest Oregon Kin*. University of California Publications in American Archaeology and Ethnology, vol. 36, no. 4, 221–300. Berkeley: University of California Press.
Du Bois, Cora. 1937. *The Feather Cult of the Middle Columbia*. Menasha, Wis.: George Banta.
———. 1939. *The 1870 Ghost Dance*. Anthropological Records, 3:1. Berkeley: University of California Press.
———. [1944] 1960. *The People of Alor: A Social-Psychological Study of an East Indian Island*. Reprint, Cambridge: Harvard University Press.
Elliott, Michael A. 1998. "Ethnology, Reform, and the Problem of the Real: James Mooney's Ghost-Dance Religion." *American Quarterly* 50 (June):201–33.
Elliott, T. C. 1929. "Oregon Coast as Seen by Vancouver in 1792." *OHQ* 30 (March–December):35–42.
Engle, Bruce Linn. 1961. "Oregon Coast Indian Reserve: Establishment and Reduction, 1855–1875." Bachelor's thesis, Reed College, Portland, Oreg.

Frachtenberg, Leo J. 1913. *Coos Texts*. New York: Columbia University Press.

———. 1914. *Lower Umpqua Texts and Notes on the Kusan Dialects*. New York: Columbia University Press.

———. 1920. *Alsea Texts and Myths*. Bureau of American Ethnology Bulletin 67. Washington, D.C.: Government Printing Office.

———. [1914] 1922. *Coos: An Illustrative Sketch*. Extract from *Handbook of American Indian Languages*, part 2, edited by Franz Boas, Bureau of American Ethnology Bulletin 40, 295–429. Reprint, Washington, D.C.: Government Printing Office.

"Frachtenberg, Leo Joachim." 1962. *Who Was Who in America: Vol. I, 1897–1942*. Chicago: Marquis.

Gidley, Mick. 1998. *Edward S. Curtis and the North American Indian, Incorporated*. Cambridge: Cambridge University Press.

Gill, John. [1909] 1960. *Gill's Dictionary of the Chinook Jargon*. Portland, Oreg.

Goddard, Ann. 2000. "Dancing at Siletz." Early draft of unpublished article, personal communication with author.

Gogol, John M. 1984. "Traditional Arts of the Indians of Western Oregon." *American Indian Basketry* 4, no. 14:2.

Gordon, Milton Myron. 1964. *Assimilation in American Life: The Role of Race, Religion, and National Origin*. New York: Oxford University Press.

Gray, Dennis J. 1987. *The Takelma and Their Athapascan Neighbors: A New Ethnographic Synthesis for the Upper Rogue River Area of Southwestern Oregon*. University of Oregon Anthropological Papers, no. 37. Eugene: Department of Anthropology, University of Oregon.

Hall, Roberta L. [1984] 1991. *The Coquille Indians: Yesterday, Today and Tomorrow*. Reprint, Corvallis, Oreg.: Words and Pictures Unlimited.

———, ed. 1995. *People of the Coquille Estuary: Native Use of Resources on the Oregon Coast: An Investigation of Cultural and Environmental Change in the Bandon Area Employing Archaeology, Ethnology, Human Biology and Geology*. With chapters by Don Alan Hall, Lee W. Lindsay, Jr., Sylvia Lindsay, and Betty L. Vogel. Corvallis, Oreg.: Words and Pictures Unlimited.

Harger, Jane M. 1972. "The History of the Siletz Reservation, 1856–1877." Master's thesis, University of Oregon.

Hartwick, L. M., and W. H. Tuller. 1890. *Oceana County: Pioneers and Business Men of To-Day*. Pentwater, Mich.: Pentwater News Steam Plant.

Hays, Marjorie H., ed. [1976] 1991. *The Land That Kept Its Promise: A History of South Lincoln County*. Reprint, Newport, Oreg.: Lincoln County Historical Society.

Hewitt, J. N. B. 1895. "James Owen Dorsey" (obituary). *American Anthropologist* 8 (April):180–83.

Heyl, Erik. 1953. *Early American Steamers*. Buffalo, N.Y.

Hinsley, Curtis M., Jr. 1981. *Savages and Scientists: The Smithsonian Institution and the Development of American Anthropology, 1846–1910*. Washington, D.C.: Smithsonian Institution Press.
Hinton, Leanne. 1994. *Flutes of Fire: Essays on California Indian Languages*. Berkeley, Calif.: Heyday Books.
Hittman, Michael. 1997. *Wovoka and the Ghost Dance*. Lincoln: University of Nebraska Press.
Hodge, Robert, and Gunther Kress. 1988. *Social Semiotics*. Ithaca, N.Y.: Cornell University Press.
Hoop, Oscar Winslow. 1929. "History of Fort Hoskins, 1856–65." *OHQ* 30 (December):346–61.
Hyman, Harold M. 1963. *Soldiers and Spruce: Origins of the Loyal Legion of Loggers and Lumbermen*. Los Angeles: Institute of Industrial Relations, University of California.
Jackson, Virginia. 1998. "Longfellow's Tradition; or, Picture-writing a Nation." *Modern Language Quarterly* 59, no. 4 (December):471–96.
Jacobs, Melville. 1937. "Historic Perspectives in Indian Languages of Oregon and Washington." *Pacific Northwest Quarterly* 28:55–74.
———. 1939. *Coos Narrative and Ethnologic Texts*. Seattle: University of Washington Publications in Anthropology, vol. 8, no. 1.
———. 1940. *Coos Myth Texts*. Seattle: University of Washington Publications in Anthropology, vol. 8, no. 2.
———. 1945. *Kalapuya Texts*. Seattle: University of Washington Publications in Anthropology, vol. 11.
———. 1959. *The Content and Style of an Oral Literature: Clackamas Chinook Myths and Tales*. Chicago: University of Chicago Press.
———. [ca. 1959]. Unpublished manuscript on Northwest States Indian folklore. In Melville Jacobs Collection, University of Washington Libraries, Seattle.
———. 1962. "The Fate of Indian Oral Literatures in Oregon." *Northwest Review* 5, no. 3:90–99.
James, Carolyn. 1984. "A Field Linguist Who Lived His Life for His Subjects." *Smithsonian Magazine* 15 (April):153–66.
Johnson, Bolling Arthur, ed. [1924] 1995? *Pacific Spruce Corporation and Subsidiaries: C. D. Johnson Lumber Company, Manary Logging Company, Pacific Spruce Northern Railway Co*. Reprint, Newport, Oreg.: Lincoln County Historical Society.
Jorgensen, Joseph G. 1986. "Ghost Dance, Bear Dance, and Sun Dance." In *Great Basin*, edited by Warren L. D'Azevedo, 660–72. Vol. 11 of *Handbook of North American Indians*. Washington, D.C.: Smithsonian Institution.
Kasner, Leone Letson. 1976. *Siletz: Survival for an Artifact*. Dallas, Oreg.: Confederated Tribes of Siletz.

Kelly, Robin D. G. 1998. "Check the Technique: Black Urban Culture and the Predicament of Social Science." In *In Near Ruins: Cultural Theory at the End of the Century*, edited by Nicholas B. Dirks, 39–66. Minneapolis: University of Minnesota Press.

Kent, William Eugene. 1973. "The Siletz Indian Reservation 1855–1900." Master's thesis, Portland State University.

Kentta, Robert. 2000. "A Siletz History." *Siletz Tribal Newspaper* (serial, six parts).

Ketcham, William H. 1910. "Bureau of Catholic Missions." In *The Catholic Encyclopedia*. Online edition: www.newadvent.org/cathen/.

Kirshenblatt-Gimblett, Barbara. 1989. "Authoring Lives." *Journal of Folklore Research* 26, no. 2:123–49.

Krech, Shepard, III, and Barbara A. Hail, eds. 1999. *Collecting Native America, 1870–1960*. Washington, D.C.: Smithsonian Institution.

Laird, Carobeth. 1975. *Encounter with an Angry God: Recollections of My Life with John Peabody Harrington*. Banning, Calif.: Malki Museum Press.

LaLande, Jeff, and Reg Pullen. 1999. "Burning for a 'Fine and Beautiful Open Country': Native Uses of Fire in Southwestern Oregon." In *Indians, Fire, and the Land in the Pacific Northwest*, edited by Robert Boyd, 255–76. Corvallis: Oregon State University Press.

La Mere, Rev. Cletus Edward. 1996. *Father Felix Bucher, S.D.S. Missionary and Mystic of Grand Ronde, Oregon*. Lafayette, Oreg.: Guadalupe Translations.

Leavelle, Tracy Neal. 1998. "We Will Make It Our Own Place: Agriculture and Adaptation at the Grand Ronde Reservation, 1856–1887." *American Indian Quarterly* 22 (fall):433–55.

Lewis & Dryden's Marine History of the Pacific Northwest. [1895] 1967. Edited by E. W. Wright. Reprint, Seattle: Superior Publishing Co.

Limerick, Patricia Nelson. 1987. *The Legacy of Conquest: The Unbroken Past of the American West*. New York: Norton.

Lockard, Joe (Joseph Franklin). 1997. "Translating Hiawatha, Translating Indian-ness." In "'Writing Race' in Nineteenth-Century America." Ph.D. diss., University of California, Berkeley.

———. 2000. "The Universal Hiawatha." *American Indian Quarterly* 24 (winter):110–25.

Longfellow, Henry Wadsworth. [1855] 1993. *The Song of Hiawatha*. Reprint, London: Everyman.

Malcolm, Janet. 1993. "The Silent Woman." *New Yorker*, 23 and 30 August, 84–159.

Marr, John P. n.d. "Harrington, In Haste." Manuscript in author's possession.

Maud, Ralph. 2000. *Transmission Difficulties: Franz Boas and Tsimshian Mythology*. Vancouver, B.C.: Talonbooks.

McArthur, Lewis A. 1982. *Oregon Geographic Names*. 5th ed. Portland, Oreg.: Western Imprints.
McDonnell, Janet A. 1991. *The Dispossession of the American Indian, 1887–1934*. Bloomington: Indiana University Press.
McKeehan, Patrick Michael. 1981. "The History of Chemawa Indian School." Ph.D. diss., University of Washington.
McLeod, Alexander Roderic. [1826] 1961. "Journal of a hunting Expedition to the Southward of the Umpqua under the command of A. R. McLeod, C. T. September 1826." In *Peter Skene Ogden's Snake Country Journal, 1826–27*, edited by K. G. Davies, 175–219. London: The Hudson's Bay Record Society.
Merriam, C. Hart. [1910] 1993. *The Dawn of the World: Myths and Weird Tales Told by the Mewan Indians of California*. Cleveland: Arthur H. Clark; reprint, Lincoln: University of Nebraska Press.
Merton, Thomas. 1968. *The Geography of Lograire*. New York: New Directions.
———. 1999. *The Other Side of the Mountain (1967–1968)*. Vol. 7 of *The Journals of Thomas Merton*, edited by Patrick Kart. San Francisco: HarperCollins.
Miller, Jay, and William R. Seaburg. 1990. "Athapaskans of Southwestern Oregon." In *Northwest Coast*, edited by Wayne Suttles, 580–88. Vol. 7 of *Handbook of North American Indians*. Washington: Smithsonian Institution.
Mills, Elaine L., ed. 1981. *The Papers of John Peabody Harrington in the Smithsonian Institution, 1907–1957*. New York: Kraus International Publications.
Mooney, James. [1896] 1965. *The Ghost Dance Religion and the Sioux Outbreak of 1890*. Reprint, Chicago: University of Chicago Press.
———. 1910, 1912. "American Indians," and "Siletz Indians." In *The Catholic Encyclopedia*. Online edition: www.newadvent.org/cathen/.
Morgan, A. W. 1959. *Fifty Years in Siletz Timber*. McMinnville, Oreg.: Author.
Morgan, Lewis Henry. [1877] 1971. *Ancient Society*. Reprint, New York: New York Labor News.
Munnick, Harriet Duncan, and Stephen Dow Beckham, eds. 1987. *Catholic Church Records of the Pacific Northwest: Grand Ronde Register I (1860–1885) and Grand Ronde Register II (1886–1898)*. Portland, Oreg.: Binford & Mort.
Nagourney, Peter. 1978. "The Basic Assumptions of Literary Biography." *Biography* 1, no. 2:86–104.
Nelson, Earl M., ed. 1951. *Pioneer History of North Lincoln County, Oregon*. McMinnville, Oreg.: North Lincoln Pioneer and Historical Association.
O'Donnell, Terrence. 1991. *An Arrow in the Earth: General Joel Palmer and the Indians of Oregon*. Portland: Oregon Historical Society Press.
O'Hara, Edwin V. 1911. "Oregon." In *The Catholic Encyclopedia*. Online edition: www.newadvent.org/cathen/.

Osterbrock, Donald E., John R. Gustafson, and W. J. Shiloh Unruh. 1988. "In the Shadow of the Moon, 1889–1930." In *Eye on the Sky: Lick Observatory's First Century*, by Osterbrock, Gustafson, and Unruh, 149–72. Berkeley: University of California Press.

Osterreich, Shelly Anne. 1991. *The American Indian Ghost Dance, 1870 and 1890: An Annotated Bibliography*. New York: Greenwood Press.

Palmer, Lloyd M. 1982. *Steam Towards the Sunset: The Railroads of Lincoln County*. Waldport, Oreg.: Lincoln County Historical Society.

Parry, Evelyn, comp. 1979. *At Rest in Lincoln County*. Waldport, Oreg.: Lincoln County Historical Society.

Pilling, James C. *Bibliography of the Athapascan Languages*. Bureau of American Ethnology Bulletin 14. Washington, D.C.: Government Printing Office.

Powell, J. W. [1891] 1966. *Indian Linguistic Families of America North of Mexico*. Reprint, Lincoln: University of Nebraska Press.

Prucha, Francis Paul, ed. 1975. *Documents of United States Indian Policy*. Lincoln: University of Nebraska Press.

———. 1985. *The Indians in American Society*. Berkeley: University of California Press.

Pullen, Reg. 1990. "Stone Sculptures in Southwestern Oregon: Mythological and Ceremonial Associations." In *Living with the Land: The Indians of Southwest Oregon: The Proceedings of the 1989 Symposium on the Prehistory of Southwest Oregon*, edited by Nan Hannon and Richard K. Olmo, 120–25. Medford: Southern Oregon Historical Society.

———. 1995. *Overview of the Environment of Native Inhabitants of Southwestern Oregon, Late Prehistoric Era*. Grants Pass, Oreg.: USDA Forest Service.

Puter, S. A. D., with Horace Stevens. [1908] 1972. "The Story of Siletz." In *Looters of the Public Domain*, 469–82. Reprint, New York: Arno Press.

Robbins, William G. 1986. "The Indian Question in Western Oregon: The Making of a Colonial People." In *Experiences in a Promised Land*, edited by Thomas G. Edwards and Carlos A. Schwantes, 51–67. Seattle: University of Washington Press.

———. 1988. *Hard Times in Paradise: Coos Bay, Oregon, 1850–1986*. Seattle: University of Washington Press.

———. 1997. *Landscapes of Promise: The Oregon Story 1800–1940*. Seattle: University of Washington Press.

Ross, Charles R. 1978. *Trees to Know in Oregon*. Extension Bulletin 697. Corvallis: Oregon State University.

Rowland, Mary Canaga, M.D. 1994. "Physician at Chemawa." In *As Long as Life: The Memoirs of a Frontier Woman Doctor*, 176–94. New York: Ballantine Books.

Sackett, Lee. 1973. "The Siletz Indian Shaker Church." *Pacific Northwest Quarterly* 64 (July):120–26.
Salins, Peter D. 1997. *Assimilation, American Style*. New York: Basic Books.
Schlesser, Norman Dennis. 1973. *Fort Umpqua: Bastion of Empire*. Oakland, Oreg.: Oakland Printing Co.
Schwartz, E. A. 1991. "Sick Hearts: Indian Removal on the Oregon Coast, 1975–1881." *OHQ* 92 (fall):229–64.
———. 1997. *The Rogue River Indian War and Its Aftermath, 1850–1980*. Norman: University of Oklahoma Press.
Scott, Leslie M. 1915. "The Yaquina Railroad: The Tale of a Great Fiasco." *OHQ* 16 (March–December):228–45.
Seaburg, William R. 1982. *Guide to Pacific Northwest Native American Materials in the Melville Jacobs Collection and in Other Archival Collections in the University of Washington Libraries*. Seattle: University of Washington Libraries.
———. 1992. "An Alsea Personal Narrative and Its Historical Context." *Western Folklore* 51:269–86.
———. 1994a. "Collecting Culture: The Practice and Ideology of Salvage Ethnography in Western Oregon, 1877–1942." Ph.D. diss., University of Washington.
———. 1994b. "A Comparison of J. P. Harrington's and E. D. Jacobs' Text Collections from Coquelle Thompson, Sr." Prepared for the 3rd Working Conference on the Papers of John P. Harrington, 5–7 August, at Mission San Juan Capistrano, California.
———. 1997. "Expressive Style in an Upper Coquille Athabaskan Folktale Collection Recorded in English." *Northwest Folklore* 12:23–34.
Seaburg, William R., and Pamela T. Amoss, eds. 2000. *Badger and Coyote Were Neighbors: Melville Jacobs on Northwest Indian Myths and Tales*. Corvallis: Oregon State University Press.
Seaburg, William R., and Jay Miller. 1990. "Tillamook." In *Northwest Coast*, edited by Wayne Suttles, 560–67. Vol. 7 of *Handbook of North American Indians*. Washington: Smithsonian Institution.
Seymour, Susan. 1989. "Cora Du Bois." In *Women Anthropologists: Selected Biographies*, edited by Ute Gacs et al., 72–79. Urbana: University of Illinois Press.
Siletz Restoration Act. 1976. U.S. Senate Subcommittee on Indian Affairs of the Committee on Interior and Insular Affairs. *Hearings on S-2801*, 94th Cong., 2d Sess.
Spaid, Stanley S. 1954. "The Later Life and Activities of General Joel Palmer." *OHQ* 5 (March–December):311–32.
Spier, Leslie. 1927. *The Ghost Dance of 1870 among the Klamath of Oregon*. Seattle: University of Washington Publications in Anthropology, vol. 2, no. 2.

———. 1935. *The Prophet Dance of the Northwest and Its Derivatives: The Source of the Ghost Dance.* Menasha, Wis.: George Banta.
Summers, Robert. W. [1897] 1994. *Indian Journal of Rev. R. W. Summers: First Episcopal Priest of Seattle (1871–73) and of McMinnville (1873–81)*, edited by Martinus Cawley. Lafayette, Oreg.: Guadalupe Translations.
Tax, Sol. 1998. "Boas, Franz." *Encyclopaedia Britannica CD.* Standard edition.
Thompson, Laurence D. 1978. "Melville Jacobs 1902–1971" (obituary). *American Anthropologist* 80:640–49.
Tiger, Lionel. 1999. *The Decline of Males.* New York: Golden Books.
Tollefson, Kenneth. 1994. "The Snoqualmie Indians as Hop Pickers." *Columbia* 39 (winter):40–44.
Tomlan, Michael A. 1992. *Tinged With Gold: Hop Culture in the United States.* Athens, Ga.: University of Georgia Press.
Vander, Judith. 1997. *Shoshone Ghost Dance Religion: Poetry Songs and Great Basin Context.* Chicago: University of Illinois Press.
Van Kirk, Sylvia. 1980. *Many Tender Ties: Women in Fur-Trade Society, 1670–1870.* Norman: University of Oklahoma Press.
Victor, Frances Fuller. 1894. *The Early Indian Wars of Oregon, Compiled from the Archives and Other Original Sources, with Muster Rolls.* Salem: State Printer.
Walling, A. G. 1884. *History of Southern Oregon, Comprising Jackson, Josephine, Douglas, Curry and Coos Counties, Compiled from the Most Authentic Sources.* Portland, Oreg.: A. G. Walling.
Walsh, Frank K. 1970. *Indian Battles of the Lower Rogue.* Eugene, Oreg.: Te-cum-tom Enterprises.
Ward, Beverly H. 1986. *White Moccasins.* Myrtle Point, Oreg.: Myrtle Point Printing.
———. 1987. *Early Days on the Siletz.* Myrtle Point, Oreg.: Myrtle Point Printing.
Wolf, Eric B. 1981. "Alfred L. Kroeber." In *Totems and Teachers: Perspectives on the History of Anthropology*, edited by Sydel Silverman, 39–40. New York: Columbia University Press.
Wooldridge, Alice H., ed. 1971. *Pioneers and Incidents of the Upper Coquille Valley.* Myrtle Creek, Oreg.: The Mail Printers.
Work, John. [1833] 1945. *Fur Brigade to the Bonaventura: John Work's California Expedition 1832–1833 for the Hudson's Bay Company*, edited by Alice Bay Maloney. San Francisco: California Historical Society.
Wyatt, Steve M. 1999. "Mother Copeland: A Woman Ahead of Her Time." *The Bayfront* (Newport, Oregon), 9, no. 7 (August).
Youst, Lionel. 1992. *Above the Falls: An Oral and Folk History of Upper Glenn Creek, Coos County, Oregon.* Coos Bay, Oreg.: South Coast Printing.

———. 1995. "The Anthropologists Themselves." In *South Slough Adventures: Life on a Southern Oregon Estuary*, edited by Melody Caldera, 211–30. Coos Bay, Oreg.: Friends of South Slough.

———. 1997. *She's Tricky Like Coyote: Annie Miner Peterson, an Oregon Coast Indian Woman*. Norman: University of Oklahoma Press.

Zucker, Jeff, Kay Hummel, and Bob Hogfoss. 1983. *Oregon Indians: Culture, History & Current Affairs*. Portland: Oregon Historical Society Press.

Index

Adams, John, 95, 166, 187, 192–93, 223
Agency Farm (Siletz Reservation), 56
Ah-ches-see (Euchre band chief), 60, 69
Albert, John (Alsea), 186
All Indian Fair (Siletz), 188–89
Alsea Indians, 74, 94
Alsea Subagency, 65, 89, 94, 102, 104, 152
Anderson, Ann, 242
Anderson, Wally, 242
Annetti (Annetta, Annet, Nettie) (wife), 71–73, 76, 87, 88, 92, 93, 99, 100, 101, 103 & n, 125–27, 139, 210, 242; birthplace, 71; employment, 144, 176; marriage to Evans Bill, 72 & n; marriage to Spencer Scott, 76, 176
Annie, Sixes, 86
Applegate (Athabaskans), 42, 71 & n
Athabaskan Indians: migration of, xv–xvi; Pacific Coast, xvi
Austin, June (step-granddaughter), xxii

Bagley, William, 204 & n
Baker, Ione (Euchre), 215

Baldwin, Harry, 39–40
Ball, Major Ebenezar Burgess, 38
Barnett, Homer G., 219 & n
Beads-in-Her-Hair (Hanis Coos) (mother), 14, 20–21, 45, 61
Beaver, hunting for, 14–15; trapping for, 9–12
Beaver Slough, 10, 11
Beck, Bill, 138–39
Beckham, Stephen Dow, xxi–xxii
Bell, Preston (son-in-law), 214, 252, 255
Bell, Sina Thompson (daughter): xxii, 70, 76, 128, 141, 219; in Army Air Corps (WAC), xviii, 250–51; birth, 202; death, 255; graduation from Chemawa, 250; marriage to Preston Bell, 252; memories of home life, 211–13; schooling at Chemawa, 214, 241
Bensell, Arthur, 180
Bensell, Ed, 192
Bensell, Corporal Royal A., 66–67, 69, 75
Big Head Cult, 223
Bill, Evans, 72 & n, 210

Billy, Klamath, 196, 202
Black-Mark-on-Wrist (half-brother), 80
Blood payment, 34
Boas, Franz: 175, 180, 229, 230, 259–60; fieldwork at Siletz, 144–46
Bob, Louisa, 158
Bonnell, Sonciray, 140, 214
Boswell, Dr. John, 131
Bride price, 13 & n, 72. *See also* Upper Coquille Athabaskan, marriage customs
Brush, Gilbert, 22, 25
Buchanan, James (Jim) (nephew), 81, 102–103, 176, 181; allotment, 208–209, 226–27, 250, 256; mother, 81–82
Buford, T. Jay, 141, 157
Bureau of American Ethnology, 132
Bureau of Indian Affairs, 94

California Gold Rush, 38
California-laurel. *See* Oregon myrtle
Calumet (schooner), 57
Camas Prairie (Siletz Valley), 54, 56, 59, 64, 80, 137
Cape Arago, Oreg., 46
Cape Blanco, Oreg., 8, 44, 46
Carter, Dr. Franklin, 146, 154–55, 198, 206, 210, 213
Cascara bark (chittam), 211–12
Case, Martha, 238
Casey, Lieutenant Colonel Silas, 22–26, 28
Catholic missionaries, 18, 77–78
Center, Ellen (Tillamook), 229
Ch'adúghilh (Chief Washington Tom name), 13, 29
Ch'aghilidan (Upper Coquille village), 5, 12, 22–23, 35, 36, 38
Chalcraft, Edwin L., 178, 185–86, 195, 202–203
Chanchat'ahdan (Upper Coquille village), 5, 11, 24, 25, 27, 28, 35
Chapman, Fritzie, 250
Charlie, Chetco, 49, 95, 101–105, 107, 188
Charlie, Coquelle (uncle), 49, 56, 72, 87, 88, 93, 99, 132

Charlie, Depot (Tututni), 49, 90, 172, 188, 224
Charlie, Klamath, 99, 100
Ch'ashéne (kind of Indian doctor), 158
Chash yadílyi (Coquelle Thompson name), 21, 42
Chatham (ship), 8
Chemawa Indian Boarding School, xviii, 125, 139–41, 178, 203; influenza, 199; tuberculosis at, 143
Chetco (Athabaskans), 42, 74
Chief John (Applegate), 40, 71
Chief Washington. *See* Tom, Chief Washington
Chimley (Indian lookout on *Columbia*), 48
Chimá·t'u' (greeter at Warm House Dance), 92–93, 99
Chinook Jargon, xvii, 22, 34, 50, 71, 93, 102, 106, 224
Chittam. *See* Cascara bark
Choc-re-le-a-tan. *See Ch'aghilidan*
Church, William, 51
Civil War, 65–68
Clements, William M., 233
Coast Range, xv–xvi, 3, 6, 16, 35–36, 51, 56
Coast Reservation: xviii, 50, 52, 57, 58, 61, 94; changes brought by the Civil War, 65–70; gambling on, 66–67; games played on, 66; Indian doctors, 79–80; land reduction of, 94, 125; population decline on, 95; slavery on, 68; tribal police and court, 91; white interest in, 74. *See also* Siletz Reservation
Collier, John, 208, 225
Collins, George, 148, 149
Columbia (steamship), 22, 43–50, 71
Columbia River, 47
Columbia University, 175, 180
Competency Commission, 201
Confederated Tribes of Coos, Lower Umpqua, and Siuslaw Indians, 260
Confederated Tribes of Siletz, xxi, 208; gambling casino, 259; membership criteria, 260; restoration, 259–60; termination, 257–59

Index 315

Cooley, D. H., 74
Coos Bay, Oreg.: 28; anthropologists at, 215–16, 234; Corporal Bensell visits, 66–67, 69; and Coos Bay Commercial Company, 28, 31; and Coquelle's mother, 13–14; Hudson's Bay Company at, 9–13; logging camp, 163; and mixed marriages, 130–31; and Siletz allotments, 152, 184–85; and South Slough Miluk, 32; and Thompson Warm House Dance, 104–107; tribal entities at, 260; visiting Indians from, 172–73
Coos Bay Commercial Company, 28, 31, 35
Coos Indians, 12, 16, 20, 21, 65, 94, 102
Coos River, compared with Siletz, 56
Copeland, Mrs. Clarinda G., 152–54, 159, 168, 169, 174; basketry collection, 178; Indian trader, 178
Copeland, Private Josiah, 75
Coquille City, Oreg., 5 & n, 11
"Coquille Guards, The," 39–40
Coquille Indian Tribe, xxi, 260
Coquille River: and California Gold Rush, 19, 30; and census of 1854, 35; compared with Siletz, 56; and Coos Bay Commercial Company, 28–29; description and first inhabitants, 3–8; drainage area, 3; early settlement, 3–4; Hudson's Bay Company at, 9–13; mouth of, 16, 22, 31–32; murder of "Venable and Burton," 32–33; and Nasomah massacre, 31–32; and population change, 18; and Rogue River War, 39–40; and Lt. Col. Silas Casey, 22–26; tsunami, 4
Coquille River, Upper: Athabaskan culture sketch of, 261–67; Athabaskan villages on, 268–77; Coquelle's childhood on, 26–27; few outside visitors, 17; and Dr. Alec (shaman), 82–83; and forest fire, 15–16; and Joel Palmer treaty, 36–38; and removal of Indians, 41–42; and T'Vault party, 21–22

Coquille River Forks: 5, 8, 11, 24, 32; Middle Fork, 12, 21; North Fork, 5, 12–13, 21, 23–24; South Fork, 24, 38
Coquille River valley: xvii; Athabaskan-speaking settlements, 4–6, 10–13; drainage of, 3, 11; fish runs, 7; rainfall, 6; settlements of, 3–5, 10–13; vegetation, 7
Corvallis, Oreg., 74, 75
Cow Creek (Athabaskans), 42
Coyote (myth character), 73–74
Croquet, Father Adrian, 77, 127–28, 143, 147
Cultural pattern number, 6, 21, 63, 266
Culture Element Survey, 214–19
Curly (Euchre), 141–42

Dall, Captain William, 44–48
Dalwatme'dan (Arago), 29
David, Jim (Upper Coquille), 56, 87, 95–97, 167
Dawes Severalty Act, 94, 150–52, 154–55, 158, 165, 179, 184, 188, 201, 204, 208, 214; and assimilation, 190
Dayton, Oreg., 49, 50, 51
Dead Indian Act, 159–60, 165, 179
Dentalium, 13, 30, 41, 87
Denzin, Norman, xix
Depot, Robert, 188, 190
Depot Slough, Oreg., 75
Devils Lake (Lincoln Co.), 151, 165
Dick, Lucy, 238
Dick, Mary, 186
Dick, Chief Umpqua (Siuslaw), 103
Diffusion, 224
Discovery (ship), 8
Diseases: ague, 157–58; consumption, 157; influenza (grippe), 157, 198–99; malaria, 18, 31, 157; measles, 18, 59; smallpox, 18, 54, 59, 127, 157; tuberculosis, 143, 198, 207
Dixon, Dr. Joseph K., 181–83, 189–90, 192
Dixon, Roland B., 175 & n
Dr. Alec, 56, 80, 82–86, 95
Doctor (Alsea) Johnson (Tillamook), 136–37, 141
Dogs, trained to hunt elk, 20–21

Dorsey, J. Owen, 6, 230; fieldwork at Siletz Reservation, 132–36
Doty, Mark, xx
Douglas, David, 7, 9
Douthit, Nathan, xxi, 11n, 29n, 39n, 107n
Dream Dance, 90, 97, 101, 106–107, 155–56, 159, 231, 266
Drew, Frank, 90, 102, 103, 104, 107, 208
Drucker, Philip, xvi, 6; fieldwork at Siletz Reservation, 215–19, 225, 232, 249
Du Bois, Cora, xvi, xxii; fieldwork at Siletz Reservation, 219–25

Earth Lodge Dance (Cult). *See* Warm House Dance
Eels, 27–28, 169–70
Egbert, Knott C., 104, 179, 183
Elk City, Oreg., 75, 87
Elkton, Oreg., 14
Empire, Oreg., 14, 31, 105, 106, 223
Enos (Ignace) (French Canadian Métis), 30, 40, 53–54
Euchre (Tututni band), 62
Euchre Creek (Curry Co., Oreg.), 62
Euchre Creek (Siletz Valley), 59
Euchre Mountain, Oreg., 62, 63
Evanoff, Lottie, 32, 52, 103, 106
Evans, Ned, 163
Everette, Willis E., 133

Feather Dance, 155–56, 179–80, 182, 188, 192, 194, 195, 201, 202, 266. *See also* Dream Dance
Felix, Robert (Tututni), 143
Fire, Indian's customary use of, 16–17
Fisher, Dolly (step-granddaughter), xxii
Fish Lake Valley, Nev., 89
Florence, Oreg., 102, 223
Fort Belknap Indian Reservation, Mont., 141, 252, 255
Fort Hoskins, 66, 69
Fort Umpqua, 14, 104
Fort Vancouver, 18; Indian Tariff, 12
Frachtenberg, Leo J., 180–83

Fredenberg, Ralph, 242
French Canadian Métis, 30, 31, 40, 76–77
French Prairie, 30, 77
Fuller, Louis (Tillamook), 90

Galice (Athabaskans), 42
Gambling, 66–67. *See also* Upper Coquille Athabaskan, gaming
Gardiner, Oreg., 104, 223
Gatschet, Albert S., 230
Geisel, Mrs. Christina, 53
Gek-ka (Gishgui) (paternal aunt), 199
General Allotment Act. *See* Dawes Severalty Act
General Jackson. *See* Jackson (*Yáksan*), Chief
Gentile system, 125 & n
George, Sixes (Tututni), 85, 90, 222
George Washington. *See* Tom, Chief Washington
Ghost Dance of 1870, xvi–xvii, xxii, 89–93, 97 & n, 155, 219–25. *See also* Warm House Dance
Ghost Dance of 1890, 155
Gilman, Lieutenant (Casey expedition), 24
Giscuae (father's aunt), 105
Glas-eh (Tututni), 142
Good talkers (intermediaries), 85, 267
Grand Ronde, 51; Reservation, 55, 76–77, 226n
Grant, President Ulysses S., 77
Grant, U. S. (Alsea), 166–67, 172
Gravelford, Oreg., 12
Groslouis brothers (Métis), 30–31, 40
Groslouis, Charles, Sr. (Métis), 31

Hall, Roberta, 145
Hanis Coos language, 102, 175–76, 181
Harney, George, 95, 223
Harrington, John Peabody, xv–xvi, xviii, 6, 243–45, 250; fieldwork at Siletz Reservation, 209–10, 247–49
Harris, William, 28–29
Hashe (chief, rich man), 14
Hashe-gali (Chief Washington Tom name), 13

Index

Hedges, Absalom, 52, 55, 57, 58
Hewitt, J. N. B., 133
Hiawatha, Song of, 188–90, 233
Hill, J. J., 39
Hodge, Robert, xx
Hodgkiss, Charles, 105
Hoffman, Abraham, 35, 39
Hoffman, Jemima, 35
Hollis, Tom (Coos), 176
Homestead Act, 161, 162 & n
Hoosier (side-wheeler), 50
Hops, 132, 134, 176–78, 183, 224, 250
Howard, Joseph, 129
Howard, Victoria, xviii
Hudson, John, xviii
Hudson's Bay Company, 9, 12, 14, 18–19, 77
Hunter, Polly, 174. *See also* Old Hunter
Hweshdạn (Upper Coquille village), 4, 5, 8, 13, 20, 29

Indian doctors, 34, 35, 79–86, 146–47, 155, 157, 158. *See also* Upper Coquille Athabaskan, shamans
Indian money. *See* Dentalium
Indian oats. *See* Tarweed
Indian Reorganization Act, 208, 214, 225–27, 228
Indian Shakers, 218 & n, 224
Indian women, employed to pack cargo, 76
Industrial Workers of the World (IWW), 197 & n
Insanity, 98–100
Isthmus Slough (Coos Bay), 10

Jackson, Alsea, 95
Jackson, Daloose (Coos chief), 14, 32, 105, 106, 107
Jackson, Dick, 84–86
Jackson, Jim, 86
Jackson, Paul T., 238
Jackson, Tom (Alsea), 164, 169–70
Jackson, Tyee. *See* Jackson (*Yáksạn*), Chief
Jackson, William (Alsea), 102
Jackson (*Yáksạn*), Chief, 23, 29, 40, 56, 60, 61, 63, 83, 86, 95

Jacksonville, Oreg., 21, 28, 38, 223
Jacobs, Elizabeth Derr, xv–xviii, xxii, 6; fieldwork at Siletz Reservation, 230–37, 248, 249; fieldwork with Tillamook, 228–29
Jacobs, Melville, xv–xvii, 21, 29–30, 228–31, 233, 234
Jacobs Research Fund, xxii
James, Dandy (Tututni), 142
Jeanne Clark (sternwheeler), 49
Jefferson, President Thomas, 9
Jennings, Berryman, 57
Jerden, Dan, 127
Jim, Coquelle (first cousin), 159, 253
Jim, Grisco, 100–101
Jim, Nina, 159
John, Hyas (Tillamook), 145
Johnny, Smith River (Tolowa), 143
Johnson, Agnes (Aggie), 184–85, 215
Johnson, Alice (paramour): 104–105, 184–85, 215; children, 152; marriage to "Sailor" Mack McDonald, 152
Johnson, President Andrew, 74
Johnson, Archie, xvii, 175, 207
Johnson, Ben, 138
Johnson, Coquille, 84
Johnson, Frances (Takelma), 100, 210
Johnson, Ida, 184
Johnson, Jacob, Jr., 160
Johnson, Martha (sister-in-law), 142, 167, 173
John Work expedition, 31
Joshua (Tututni band), 64

K'ạmá (split-stick clapper), 92, 98, 101, 102
K'ạmashdạni (Miluk village), 33
"King David" (Chief from *Hweshdạn*), 29
Kiowinds, George, 158
Klamath Reservation, Oreg., 88n, 89, 100, 220
Kress, Gunther, xx
Kroeber, Alfred L., 214–15, 219, 220

Laderoute, Xavier Seguin, 11
La'kho·ve' (Applegate Creek village), 71, 210

LaLande, Jeff, 17
Lane, Chief (Lower Coquille Miluk), 105–106
Lane, Maude, xxii, 179
Lane, Minnie, 179
Lane, Nellie (Upper Coquille), 5–6, 83–84, 217
Lane, Scott, 163
Lann, Jerry, 44
Latenosa (brother), 20, 45, 61
Lee, Reverend Jason, 18
Lee, John, 140
Lewis and Clark expedition, 9
L̲h̲a̲n̲h̲a̲s̲h̲d̲a̲n̲ (Upper Coquille village), 5, 10–11, 23, 29
Lháyu·shi (Upper Coquille man), 87–88
Lincoln, Abraham (Abram), 68, 186
Lincoln County Historical Society, 178n
Lip-ma-shell (Santiam chief), 128
Logan, Abe, 101, 167, 172, 218
Loggers: at Gardiner, 104; Indians as, 163, 196, 250, 254–55, 257–58; and IWW, 196–97. *See also* Sawmills; Timber at Siletz
Longfellow, Henry W., 188–89
Lower Coquille Miluk Indians, 23–25, 42, 74, 105
Lower Farm (Siletz Reservation), 55, 56, 62, 75, 78, 94, 101, 126, 132, 134, 137, 185, 203
Lower Umpqua Indians, 65, 94, 102
Lowie, Robert H., 219
Ludson, Major (Alsea), 164
Lupton, James, 38
Luse, H. H., 105

McDonald, Agnes. *See* Johnson, Agnes
McDonald, Claudia, 180–81
McDonald, Frank, 152, 184–85
McDonald, Ida, 152
McDonald, "Sailor" Mack, 152, 184–85
McGregor, James H., 204, 205–206
Mack, Abram, 158, 168; allotment, 200–201, 249
Mack, Jacob, 168–169
McKay, Governor Douglas, 257
Mackenzie, Alexander, 9

McKoin, John J., 172
McLeod, Alexander Roderick, 9–13, 17–18, 21, 28, 31
McMinnville, Oreg., 127
MacNamarra, "Big Mac," 31
McVey, "Little Mac," 31
Make-Doctor Dance, 80, 265, 266
Malaria. *See* Diseases
M̲a̲l̲h nát'a. *See* Dream Dance
Malhúsh (Columbia River), 47–48
Manchester, D. W., 154
Manypenny, George, 48
Marr, John P. (Jack), xvi, 250; fieldwork at Siletz Reservation, 243–47, 248
Martin, Albert, 167, 171, 172
Martin, Isaac (Coos), 104
Martin, Jesse (Coos), 104
Meacham, Alfred B., 79, 130
Measles. *See* Diseases
Medicine Rock (Siletz River), 136–37, 141
Megginson, George, 70, 75
Men-in-the-middle. *See* Good talkers
Merriam, C. Hart, 244n
Merton, Thomas, 107 & n, 225
Metcalf, Billy, 192, 230
Metcalf, Lucy, 72
Metcalf, Robert, 95, 172, 187, 196, 202, 230
Metcalfe, Robert, 57–59, 61, 64–65
Methodist Episcopal Church, 59, 78
Methodist missionaries, 18
Miller, Jay, xxii, 13n, 71n
Miluk Coos: 5, 8, 23–25, 32, 42. See also Lower Coquille Miluk Indians
Miscegenation, 130
Morgan, A. W. (Jack), 162–64
Morgan, Lewis Henry, 133
Mormons, 89n
Mott, C. H., 60–61
"Moving people", 9 & n
Myrtle Point, Oreg., 3–4, 40
Myrtle tree. *See* Oregon myrtle

Nasomah (Miluk village), 32, 36
Nay-Dosh World Renewal Dance, 156n
Nataghilid̲a̲n̲ (Upper Coquille village), 5, 83

Index

Newberry, Agnes. *See* Thompson, Agnes Newberry
Newberry, Mary, 170
Newcomb, David, 65
Ni-Lae-Tun (Miluk village), 22
Nindanano (Dirt Eater), 71
North Bend, Oreg., 105
Northwest Fur Company, 9

Oats, 70, 153
Old Fred (Corvallis Kalapuya chief), 68
Old Jack (Shasta), 99
Old John (Chasta Costa doctor), 167
Old Hunter (uncle): 87, 95, 138, 174–75, 253; death, 174; hunting beaver, 14–15; story of great forest fire, 15–16; story of shooting elk, 62–63
Old Taylor (Coos), 107
Oregon, admitted to the Union, 65
Oregon City, Oreg., 49, 50
Oregon Country, emigration to, 18
Oregon Donation Claims Act, 29, 35
Oregon Land Frauds, 162
Oregon myrtle, 7, 12
Oregon Pacific Railroad, 144
Oregon State College, xviii, 205–207, 254, 255
Orton, Nellie, xvii, 212
Oysterville, Oreg., 69, 144

Pacific Spruce Corporation, 203
Palmer, Ephraim, 54
Palmer, Joel, 18, 35–39, 70, 130, 151; agent at Siletz, 76, 78–79, 90, 91, 94, 127, 130–31; removal of Indians to Coast Reservation, 44–56, 60, 61
Parrish, Josiah L., 18, 35
Pattern (ritual) number. *See* Cultural pattern number
Paul Washington Cemetery (Siletz Reservation), 87n, 148, 159, 168, 174, 198n
Pearson, Clara, xviii, 229
Pepperwood. *See* Oregon myrtle
Perit, J. W., 74
Pete, Louisa (great-aunt), 158, 173; allotment, 199, 202

Peterson, Annie Miner (Coos), xviii, xxii–xxiii, 21, 90, 102, 215–16, 234
Pierce, President Franklin, 35
Polly, Alsea, 166
Portland, Oreg., 48–49
Port Orford, Oreg.: Indian Agent at, 31, 40; and makeshift reservation, 41, 42; naming of, 8; removal of Indians, 43–46, 49, 52, 58, 71; and Rogue River War, 41; and Lt. Col. Silas Casey expedition, 22; and steamship *Columbia*, 43–44; and trial of Enos, 53–54
Powell, John Wesley, 133–36
Protestant missionaries, 77–78
Prucha, Francis Paul, 259
Pullen, Reg, 3, 12, 17, 22n

Qw'ánnán'-tlh'û·mhe' (Prairie-huckleberry Prairie), 151

Railroads: from Corvallis to Yaquina Bay, 139; and timber, 195–96, 208. *See also* Oregon Pacific Railroad
Randolph, Oreg., 34, 38
Rector, William H., 69
Reynolds, Major, 71
Rheumatism, Indian cure for, 82
Rilatos, Robert, 258
Riley, Michael, 53
Rippin, King, 200–201
Roberts, William, 59
Rodman Wanamaker Expedition of Citizenship to the American Indian, 181–83, 192
Rogue River, Upper: Annetti's birthplace, 71; and Rogue River War, 38–39
Rogue River War, xvii, xxi, 32, 38–41, 52, 53
Rooney, Stewart, 160
Roosevelt, President Franklin D., 207–208, 225
Rose, Bill, 105
Ryan, James T., 209

St. Clair, Harry Hull, II, 175–76
Salmon River, Oreg., 51–54, 84

Saltchuck Indians, 22, 34, 74
Salvage anthropology, 179. *See also* Thompson, Coquelle, work with anthropologists
Sandberg, Frederick, 241–42
Sandberg, Ocea, 242
Sapir, Edward, 210
Sa-tusk-ka, 142
Savage Creek (Curry Co., Oreg.), 62
Savage Creek (Siletz Valley), 62
Sawmills: at Coos Bay, 46, 105; at Grand Ronde, 67–68; gyppo, 242–43; and Indian workers, 105, 131–32; in Lincoln County, 258; at Siletz Reservation, 49, 67, 75, 131–32, 161; Sutter's Mill, 19; at Toledo, 194, 203. *See also* Loggers, Timber at Siletz
Schoolcraft, Henry Rowe, 189, 233
Schwartz, E. A., xxi, 95n, 226
Scott, Annetta Brown. *See* Annetti
Scott, Spencer, 76, 100, 176, 243, 244, 255
Seaburg, William R., xxii, 13n, 71n, 146n, 215n, 229n, 230n, 232, 235, 236, 248n
Second Oregon Volunteer Infantry, 156
Seghers, Archbishop Charles J., 128
Se-ma-chus-cha. *See* Beads-in-Her-Hair
Sercombe, Laurel, 97n
Shamans. *See* Indian doctors
Shasta Indians, 42, 90
Shinny, 66
Siletz, Oreg., 56, 186
Siletz Agency, 53, 79, 186; closing of, 203
Siletz Bay, Oreg., 57
Siletz Dramatic Club, 180
Siletz Indians (Salish), 54, 136, 145
Siletz Indian school, 195
Siletz Reservation, xvii, xxi, 78–79, 125; alcohol, 129, 172; allotments on, 150–52, 158, 169; domestic disputes, 129; Indian police force, 128–29, 131; languages spoken on, 133; medicine men outlawed, 155; opening of unallotted land, 160–61; population, 157; and World War I, 191–97

Siletz Valley, 55, 56, 70
Simmons, Augusta. *See* Smith, Augusta
Simmons, Frank (step-grandson), xxii
Simmons, Frederic (Fritz) (son-in-law), 193, 202, 213, 238, 241, 244
Simmons, Hardy, 257
Simmons, Hoxie (Galice), xviii, 100, 163, 230, 241, 244, 249
Simpson, Asa, 164
Simpson, Benjamin, 67, 76, 79
Simpson Lumber Company, 164
Siuslaw Indians, 102
Sixes (Tututni band), 22, 64, 84–86
Sixes George, 69, 70
Smallpox. *See* Diseases
Smith, Agnes. *See* Thompson, Agnes Newberry
Smith, Arthur, 171
Smith, Augusta (step-daughter), 171, 189, 193, 238, 244, 255
Smith, Louis (Lower Umpqua), 171, 181
Smith, Marie (step-daughter), 171, 176
Smith, William (Alsea), 102
Smith River, Calif., 90
Smithsonian Institution, 247n
Solomon, Coquelle (Solomon, Old Solomon)(uncle), 5–6, 87, 102, 134
Spier, Leslie, 100
Stirling, M. W., 249
Stoneman, Lieutenant George (Casey expedition), 24
Strong, Bill, 126–27
Sugarloaf Mountain, Oreg., 27, 32
Summers, Richard W., 127–28
Sutter's Mill. *See* Sawmills
Swan, Edmund A., 128–29, 131
Sykes, Joshua B., 65

Table Rock Reservation, 38
Takelma Indians, 39, 42
Tarweed, 8, 17, 30, 237
T'asan Ts'eghilh'adan (Myrtle Point), 3, 4, 5, 29
Tattoos, 72, 210
Thomas, Enos. *See* Enos
Thompson, Agnes Newberry (wife), xviii, 167, 169–74; children with

Index

Louis Smith, 171; death, 255; marriage to Coquelle, 169; marriage to Louis Smith, 171; midwife, 177, 202–203, 213; mother, 170; nurse, 198, 213; schooling, 170–71
Thompson, Anna, 159
Thompson, Blanche (daughter), 176
Thompson, Coquelle: absentee landowner, 183–84; acculturation of, 190; allotments, 150–51, 195–96, 227, 237; Applegate co-wife, 72; assimilation of, 190–92; birth, xvii; birthplace, xvii; blindness, 213, 221, 237–40; death, 253; employment, xviii, 76, 91, 128–29, 134, 137, 166, 196, 203, 212; estate worth, 255–56; father, 11, 13; grandmother's encounter with bear, 27; house at Thompson Creek, 168; marriage to Agnes, 169; marriage to Annetti, 71–72; marriage to Emma, 143; mother, 14; names, 21; pronunciation of name, xvi; separation from Annetti, 142; shopping habits, 153–54; siblings, 20; songs, 71, 234, 247; story of Bill Strong's wife's suicide, 126–27; story of bout with pneumonia, 146–47; story of death of Dr. Alec, 82–86; story of encounter with ghosts, 148–49; story of Evans Tom's doctoring session, 80–82; Warm House Dance involvement, 99–107; work with anthropologists, xvi–xviii, 132–36, 216–19, 221–25, 230–37, 243–49; Upper Umpqua grandfather, 3–4, 6, 8, 10
Thompson, Coquelle, Jr. (Tom) (son), 141, 238, 242, 244, 254, 257; advisor at Chemawa, 254; birth, 173; graduation from Chemawa, 205; logger, 254–55; student at Oregon State College, 205–207, 254; teacher at Siletz Public School, 210, 254; tribal judge, 255
Thompson, Coquelle, III (Snooks) (grandson), 254, 255
Thompson, Elma Chapman (daughter-in-law), xxii, 242, 244, 254

Thompson, Emma (wife), 142; allotment, 150 & n, 168–69, 187, 195–96, 237, 256; death, 168; father, 142; marriages, 142–43; mother, 142
Thompson, Eva, 73
Thompson, George Earl (son), birth, 181; death, 207, 210, 251; graduated from Chemawa, 206; student at Chemawa, 205–207
Thompson, George Louis (grandson), xxii, 58n, 251, 253, 255
Thompson, Jacob Walker (son), allotment of, 142, 150 & n, 165–66, 187; birth, 147; death, 148, 160
Thompson, James (first cousin), 159
Thompson, Lulu (daughter), 176
Thompson, Paul (son): birth, 143; death, 148
Thompson, Sina (I) (daughter), 73, 88, 93, 125, 127; attends Chemawa Indian Boarding School, 139–40, 142, 143; death, 144, 148
Thompson, Sina (II). *See* Bell, Sina Thompson
Thompson, Washington (son): birth, 147–48; death, 159
Thompson Creeks (Lincoln Co.), 151
Thompson Warm House Dance. *See* Warm House Dance
Tichenor, Cyrus (Tututni), 90
Tichenor, Captain William, 58
Tillamook language, 56, 145, 229
Timber at Siletz: Coquelle Thompson and, 151, 250, 256–57; descriptions of, 85, 160, 162; and Georgia Pacific Company, 256–57; and plank roads, 185; and railroad construction, 195–96, 208; speculation in, 161, 164–65; tribal sale of, 241; values of, 152, 237 & n, 256–57; and World War I, 193–94. *See also* Loggers, Sawmills
Tobacco, cultivation and use of, 17
Toledo, Oreg., 75, 144, 180, 193, 194, 203
Tolowa (Athabaskans), 42, 90, 156 & n
Tom, Bogus (Shasta), 91–93, 103, 221, 224

Tom, Chief Washington (father), 11–14, 20, 22–23, 25–26, 32, 35–37, 39, 40, 45, 52, 56, 59–62, 72, 82–83, 86, 87, 95; Indian names, 13, 29; slaves, 68; wives, 20
Tom, Evans, 80–82
Transvestite doctor, at Grand Ronde, 77
Tronson, Bob, 163
Tuberculosis. *See* Diseases
Tututni: 42, 53, 63, 85; Athabaskan settlements, 8; language, 135. *See also* Euchre; Joshua; Sixes
T'Vault, William, 21–23, 25
Tyee, John, 158, 168, 200–202
Tyee, Mary, 158, 168–69
Ty-gon-ee-shee (Port Orford chief), 60

University of California, Berkeley, xvi, 214–15, 219
University of Washington, xv, 228–29
Upper Coquille Athabaskan: xvii–xviii, 42; burial customs, 87, 264–65; ceremonials, 266; chief (headman), 14; discipline of children, 26; division of labor, 262; dreams, 83–84; eclipse of sun or moon, 194; fidelity in marriage, 126–27; formulist (ritualist), 265; gaming, 265–66; kinship terms, 20; language, xvii, 262; life cycle, 263–65; marriage customs, 13 & n, 72, 264; naming, 264; puberty rites, 264; shamans, 34, 265; social organization, 263; storytelling, 26, 73; structures, 262; subsistence, 262; sweathouse, 26–27, 55, 67, 73; transportation, 263; warfare, 266–67; wealth, 29–30, 101, 263; weaning practices, 26; women's sleeping quarters, 26
Upper Farm (Siletz Reservation), 56, 72, 94, 103, 138, 173, 180, 185
Upper Umpqua: Indians, 3–5, 28; rainfall of territory, 6; territory, 3, 6; vegetation, 8
Upper Umpqua River, 7

Vancouver, Captain George, 8–9
"Venable and Burton," 33
Villard, Henry, 176, 180
Wadsworth, F. M., 129, 132, 139, 153
Waldport, Oreg., 102, 223
Walker, Courtney, 51
Walker River Reservation (Nevada), 155
Wanamaker, Rodman, 190. *See also* Rodman Wanamaker Expedition of Citizenship to the American Indian
Warm House Dance, xvii, 91–93, 97–107, 155–56, 188, 222; dance house, 92, 103; music, 92, 97–98. *See also* Ghost Dance of 1870
Warren, John (Upper Umpqua), 231
Washington, Paul, 192, 193; death, 197–98, 202
Wasson, Daisy, 199
Wasson, George, 105
Watson, Chief John (Alsea), 102, 103n
West, Nettie, 230
Wéste (Upper Coquille storyteller), 56, 73
Whatcom Museum of History and Art, xxii
Wheeler-Howard Act. *See* Indian Reorganization Act
Whiskey Run, Oreg., 31, 38
Wilkinson, Lieutenant Melville, 140
Willamette Falls, Oreg., 49, 50
Willamette Valley, Oreg., 18, 74, 132, 134, 176–78, 183, 224, 250
William (Chetco chief), 69
Williams, Emma, 158
Wilson, President Woodrow, 179, 182, 186
Wodziwob (Northern Paiute), 89, 155
Woodward, H. H., 39
Wooldridge, Earl, 240, 249
Wovoka (Northern Paiute), 155
Wright, Benjamin, 40
Wright, Lieutenant (Casey expedition), 23–24

Yachats, Oreg., 52, 65, 90, 102, 152
Yamhill River, Oreg., 50, 51
Yaquina Bay, Oreg., 55, 61, 69, 74–75
Yaquina Indians, 74
Youst, Lionel, xxii–xxiii, 163n
Yú·gi Mountain. *See* Euchre Mountain, Oreg.

www.ingramcontent.com/pod-product-compliance
Lightning Source LLC
Chambersburg PA
CBHW022102150426
43195CB00008B/233